HELPING SKILLS FOR COUNSELORS

FUNDAMENTAL COUNSELING SKILLS AND PRINCIPLES

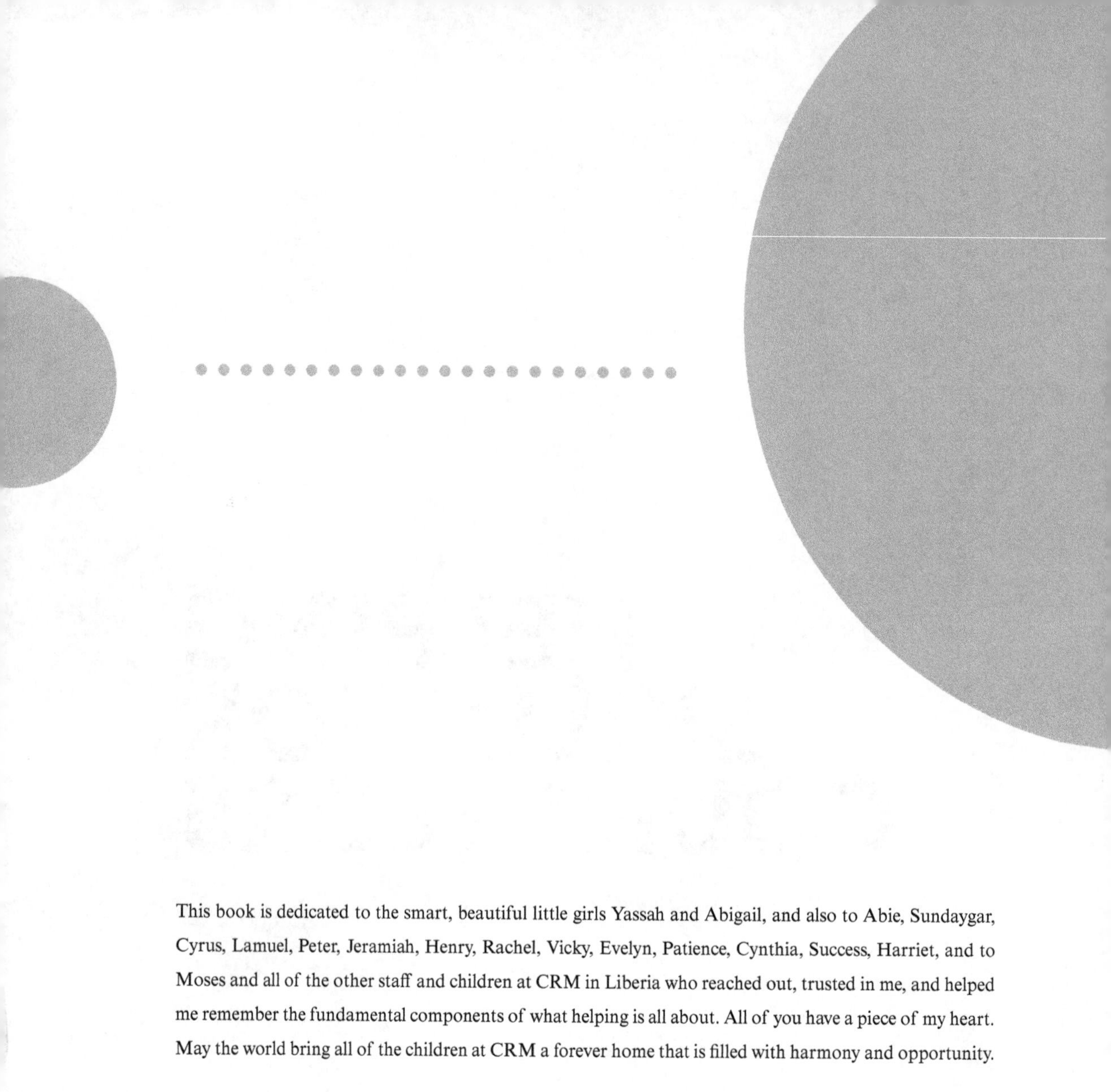

This book is dedicated to the smart, beautiful little girls Yassah and Abigail, and also to Abie, Sundaygar, Cyrus, Lamuel, Peter, Jeramiah, Henry, Rachel, Vicky, Evelyn, Patience, Cynthia, Success, Harriet, and to Moses and all of the other staff and children at CRM in Liberia who reached out, trusted in me, and helped me remember the fundamental components of what helping is all about. All of you have a piece of my heart. May the world bring all of the children at CRM a forever home that is filled with harmony and opportunity.

HELPING SKILLS FOR COUNSELORS

FUNDAMENTAL COUNSELING SKILLS AND PRINCIPLES

Anne Geroski
University of Vermont

Bassim Hamadeh, CEO and Publisher
Leah Sheets, Project Editor
Laureen Gleason, Production Editor
Jess Estrella, Senior Graphic Designer
Alexa Lucido, Senior Licensing Specialist
Jennifer Redding, Interior Designer
Natalie Piccotti, Senior Marketing Manager
Kassie Graves, Vice President of Editorial
Jamie Giganti, Director of Academic Publishing

Printed in the United States of America

ISBN: 978-1-5165-1443-4 (pbk) / 978-1-5165-1444-1 (br)

BRIEF CONTENTS

DETAILED CONTENTS

PREFACE

My children generously like to tell me that I am not old. But there is no glossing over the fact that I have been in the field of counseling for a very long time!

When I was first in graduate school in the late 1980s, there were few if any states with mental health counselor licensure. Now all 50 states and Washington, D.C., have counseling licensure laws. I was schooled in Rogerian practice, which was the movement in counselor education at the time. The profession still holds dear the humanistic principles that Rogers aptly named *client-centered* practice, and these premises are now bolstered by research showing, for example, the therapeutic value of a strong client–counselor relationship for facilitating change. Despite this commitment to humanistic practice, the counseling profession never veered too far from the gospel of psychodynamic thought. Still today, I see this grounding in psychodynamic thought—an implicit truth that still fertilizes the field of practice. Its roots can be seen from the academy right down to the trenches. I remember, too, when Aaron Beck's original book of cognitive behavioral therapy (CBT) was newly minted. Back then we eagerly engaged in the study of these novel ways of working with clients. Now CBT is a staple of therapeutic practice. CBT has also worked its way into colloquial understandings about therapy, and I see that even our local medical school teaches its students the value of CBT as a credible therapeutic treatment for some mental health challenges!

More recently, new developments in neurobiology have been translated into understandings that have worked their way into the vernacular of the counseling profession. These have provided important insights into ways in which in early life events and experiences of stress and trauma can adversely affect everyday functioning. They also have encouraged new approaches to therapy that no longer permit us to see the body as separate from the mind. Meditation was jettisoned to the fringes of "professional" practice when I was first trained as a counselor, but now I see many clinicians scampering to be trained in mindfulness practice. The concept of externalization has traveled from Australia and New Zealand to work its way into the therapeutic lexicon here in the United States and abroad. Importantly, after decades of advocacy and professional risk taking on the part of many, multiculturalism and diversity awareness are finally seen as mainstream. Counselors are now being held accountable for understanding the ways in which power and privilege are not just enacted in the everyday lives of people in marginalized social locations but also to ensure that they do not surface in their therapeutic relationships.

Clearly, much has changed in the profession over the past 30 years. But, one thing that has stayed constant is a foundational set of basic counseling skills used to carry out the important work of helping. These skills—sometimes referred to as micro-skills—are the tools that clinicians use to conduct assessments, build therapeutic relationships, and carry out interventions across the multitude of therapeutic modalities. They are used in individual counseling, group work, advocacy, and even crisis response. They are the *how* of the implementation of various counseling approaches—the essential tools in the trade of counseling. Clinicians really cannot get by without them. It is these skills that are the focus of this text. This book is aimed at orienting new students to the skills needed to practice mental health counseling or therapy.

To have a decades-old set of skills that is fundamental to the practice of counseling is not to diminish the importance of creativity and embracing the many important changes in the field. I confess that an inspiration for writing this text was to have an opportunity to present these skills in a larger landscape of contemporary ideologies. As will be obvious when you read this text, I am particularly interested in ideologies that privilege those things that the client brings into therapy and that promote agency. This is part of what makes this text unique. But at the end of the day, I hope to inspire a blending of old with new and to promote a vision of counseling that moves away from boxes of disparate modalities to an approach that is grounded in professional skills and philosophies that enable a variety of therapeutic approaches.

The first section of this text focuses on a broad introduction to the practice of professional helping. Chapter 1 begins by exploring the scope of practice and professional roles in clinical mental health counseling. Here I discuss common helping terms and establish common language that is used throughout the text. We then move into a brief synopsis of the literature on key variables known to be effective in promoting change. These variables are relevant across multiple counseling modalities and important to our focus on counseling skills. We end Chapter 1 with a review of essential components of the helping contract. In Chapter 2 important concepts related to working with a wide variety of clients—across cultures and identities—is discussed. These ideas are framed in the premise that the experience of clients must be understood in a context of power and privilege. The point articulated here and carried into discussions throughout this text is that clinicians must be intentional in addressing these realities in their work with clients, understanding that inequities and systems of power are the root causes of the challenges that many people face. Also, the reminder here and also a thread throughout the text is that clinicians must use care not to reenact these inequities in therapeutic relationships. Positioning theory is introduced in this chapter as a frame for understanding these interpersonal dynamics.

Chapter 3 follows with a discussion about helping ethics. This discussion is largely focused on underlying moral principles that cut across the codes of ethics in many mental health helping disciplines. In this chapter, key legal mandates and ethical positions that are relevant to all helpers in mental health are highlighted. Chapter 4 follows. This short chapter offers an introduction to concepts in neurobiology that are relevant to the practice of clinical helping. While not typically included in most skills texts, I felt it important to include this information, as it gives insights into the personalization issues and bias discussed in the chapters that follow. This introduction also helps us better understand some of the skills and practices used by counselors that are outlined in the second section of this book. The final chapter in this section is devoted to discussion about the ways in which the personal experiences of counselors can be altered by and also influence the work of helping. Understanding the occupational hazards of helping, including personalization, vicarious traumatization, compassion fatigue, and burnout, is the starting place for preventing them from contaminating our work as helpers.

The second part of the book begins with descriptions of the key counseling skills that have been used by clinicians for decades. I have tried to concretize them as much as possible, forcing them into discrete categories for the sake of instruction. We start with Chapter 6, which invites examination of the nuances in welcoming, listening, and expressing empathy. We then move into the basics of reflections, paraphrases, and questions in Chapter 7. A range of additive skills, designed to bring more depth to therapeutic conversations, are described in Chapter 8. All of these skills are discussed with a focus on promoting client agency and working from the premise of client as expert. This focus does not diminish the counselor's ability to see patterns and provide insights; it just reminds us to endeavor to understand the experiences of the client and to respect and work with the perspectives and insights that clients bring to therapy.

Although assessment and intervention planning typically begins at the start of therapeutic helping conversations, we address these skills in Chapter 9. This is because the ability to conduct an assessment and outline therapy goals and interventions is prerequisite upon the foundational helping skills discussed in Chapters 6, 7, and 8. Chapter 10 outlines a number of change strategies that are used by a variety of clinicians, despite their particular theoretical orientations. These include motivating change, deconstructing conversations, psychoeducation, problem solving, advocacy, and the use of affect regulation and mindfulness strategies. Of course, counselors will need more training and supervised practice for implementation of these strategies—this is also true for the skills reviewed earlier in this section of this text. The purpose here is to describe these skills and strategies in a way that invites counselors in training to begin using them in their learning settings.

Chapter 11 offers a brief introduction to group work. This is important because many practitioners—particularly school counselors—find themselves conducting a large part of their work in group venues. This chapter builds on the skills outlined in previous chapters but offers a set of additional skills for leading therapy, counseling, psychoeducation, and task groups. Again, this chapter is intended to offer an overview that will require additional training and practice. Finally, the text closes with a review of the skills and practices that every counselor hopes he or she will not need: crisis management skills. In Chapter 12 we review the nature and needs of clients who face natural or human-made disasters or crises as well as those who are in crises of potential harm to self or others. This discussion includes harm assessment guidelines and suggestions for responding to aggression. Having information and practice in these areas early on helps clinicians work from a solid footing in times when these skills are needed.

Counseling skills are not only the territory of mental health counselors, of course. My aim has been to try to make this information and my writing accessible to clinicians across a variety of professional mental health disciplines. This has been no small challenge. The field of mental health is in constant change, and the specific disciplines within the field each have their own changing lens for thinking about, talking about, and carrying out their work. Yet the skills outlined in this text are used widely across the various mental health–related helping disciplines. My hope is that my discussions about these skills serve to promote, at least in some small way, practice across these disciplines that is both multidisciplinary and collaborative.

Those of us who educate counselors and clinicians have a grave responsibility to impart a wide scope of important information and skills, and to facilitate training to the best of our ability so as to enable practitioner competence. But, at the end of the day, it is up to the clinician in the trenches to use these skills and information wisely. No tools are helpful if they are not used with intentionality. It is intentionality that renders each of these skills effective, powerful, and beneficial.

ACKNOWLEDGMENTS

I believe that "new" ideas are never truly novel—they are always formed from existing knowledge and shared minds working together. Thus, the result of one's labor is always to be shared by the many who are busy at work behind the scenes. It is in this spirit that I offer appreciations to the many who contributed to the making of this textbook.

First, I offer a heartfelt thank-you to four mentors who contributed to this book in hugely formative and perhaps unknowing ways: John Winslade, Kathie Crocket, Lorraine Smith, and Wally McKenzie. All of you patiently, generously, and unceremoniously offered me a new landscape of ideas that forever changed my relationship with counseling theory and practice. I hope you will see that the torch you passed to me is alive and well within the pages of this text. I am still moved by the wisdom and kindness each of you offered me all those years ago. Thank you. I also thank Dorothy Breen, Diana Hulse-Killacky, Ted Coladarci, and my dear friend, Kurt Kraus, for your knowledge, wisdom, challenge, support, and friendship. You all fertilized the ground under my feet in different yet hugely meaningful ways. Even after all these years have passed, you are still here in this book with me. And, of course, a huge appreciation goes to Kassie Graves, editor extraordinaire at Cognella. Kassie, your wisdom, guidance, flexibility, encouragement, and generosity of spirit are all of the things I needed to make this book reach fruition. I am in awe of how you work endlessly in such a demanding profession and yet always find a way to offer warmth that crosses the terrains of deserts, mountains, and oceans to reach me in my wanderings. The world of publishing is a better place because of your presence.

And big thanks also go out to these colleagues who offered helpful comments on earlier versions of this text: Kevin A. Curtin, Alfred University; Rebecca M. Dedmond, The George Washington University; Crystal L. George-Moses, Long Island University; Jeffery Haynes, Bethune Cookman

University; Mark L. Kilwein, Clarion University of Pennsylvania; Suzanne T. Mallery, La Sierra University; Cheryl Maykel, Rivier University; and Cynthia L. Trumbo, Lone Star College System, Houston, Texas. Thanks, too, go to Lauri Scherer for the careful copyediting of this text, and to production editor Laureen Gleason at Cognella.

This book would never have met deadline without the generous support from the dean's office at the University of Vermont. Thank you, Dean Thomas, Associate Deans Bishop and Shepherd, and my dear colleague, Dr. Jane Okech. With your collective support, I was able to bring in friend and fellow Peace Corps Response-Liberia colleague, Kristen Grauer-Gray, who meticulously reviewed every citation within the pages of this text, tracked down every missing doi, and corrected every last error in the reference list. Kristen, you are truly amazing. Thank you for your help in the countdown at the end—you saved me!

And thanks, too, go to my family who helped this book emerge. First, a huge thank-you to my partner, Kevin, who cooked rice and beans for dinner when I could not be dragged away from the computer, cheered me on in the moments of frustration, and, importantly, coaxed me to put things down from time to time so that we could play and explore the world during this writing journey. A warm thank-you also goes to our four children, Monica, Curtis, Yuol, and Griffin, and also to Lisa and Adam. Thank you, guys, for checking in on me regularly so that I did not fall into the abyss of writing, thank you for chipping in to help in areas neglected at home, and thank you for dragging me away from this project when I needed a break. You pulled out all the stops for me while I was writing this text—the shared quiet evenings at home, family meals, vacations, hot tub soaks, road trips, runs, ManU games on TV, and all of the WhatsApp calls and texts to check in on me. Thanks. All of you are an inspiration to me in ways that you will never know. Finally, my acknowledgments would not be complete without mention of Mama Cat and her litters of kitties in Monrovia, who frolicked in my house as I labored away on this text, and Michi and Lila in Vermont, who also pleasantly distracted and cuddled with me when I worked on this project.

There are, of course, many others who contributed to this book in unknowing but not insignificant ways. These others are the authors of the texts that raised me in the profession of counseling, the students and clients who graciously invited me into their lives, the staff and colleagues in the various places I have worked and volunteered, and, especially, my Peace Corps and CRM families in Liberia, who reminded me of the fundamental importance of just being there for others. The spirit of kindness kindles the powers that heal. It is my hope that everyone who has these healing powers will use them to make this world a little bit more fair, a little bit safer, and a little bit kinder for all.

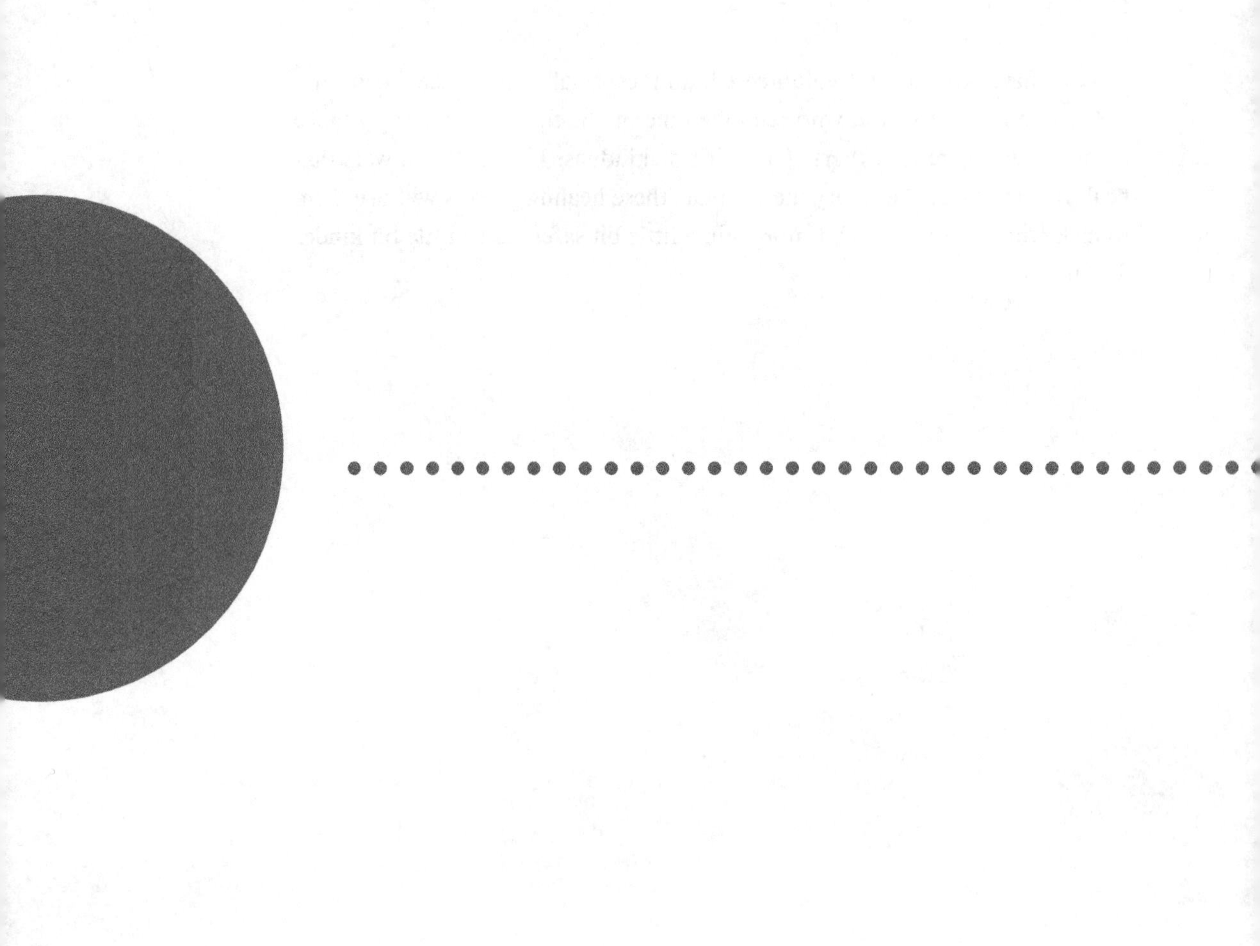

SECTION I

FOUNDATIONAL CONCEPTS FOR ESTABLISHING THERAPEUTIC RELATIONSHIPS

CHAPTER

Therapeutic Helping and Helping Relationships

Chapter Outline

INTRODUCTION

I start this chapter with many questions—questions that I sometimes hear from my students, family, friends, and acquaintances: What is counseling? Psychotherapy? Therapy? Advocacy? What are "therapeutic relationships"? What is a counselor? A social worker? A psychologist? A psychiatrist? Why would one see a social worker, for example, rather than a psychiatrist? How about a mental health counselor? How is a school counselor different from a mental health counselor? What is the difference between a clinical social worker and a "regular" social worker?

These are great questions!

In an attempt to clarify some of this, we begin this chapter with some very general definitions and descriptions of the various disciplines within the field of mental health. We will also navigate through some of the terms and concepts used in professional helping and review of some of the general factors known to promote change in therapy. The chapter concludes with a discussion about the helping contract, which is the concrete foundation for what we do as mental health clinicians.

HELPING PROFESSIONS

Helping roles come in all shapes and sizes, and it is sometimes difficult to distinguish between the various professionals who do this important work—this is especially difficult for people with no training in mental health and those who are seeking mental health services. Professional identity shapes the kind of training that one receives, the orientation to the important work of counseling, and even has political and financial implications for both the practitioner and the client. The truth is, however, that there is quite a bit of overlap in the thinking and practice across the various mental health professional disciplines, and the standard of care in the field across disciplines is for *collaborative* and *multidisciplinary* practice.

The risk I take here in describing these various professional disciplines is that some may be offended by the oversimplification of their professional qualifications, affiliations, and scope of work. This is not my intent. Each discipline has its own history, its own nuanced orientation, and its own set of training and practice standards and affiliations. I highly encourage readers to spend time investigating the "small print" of the various professional disciplines for a better understanding of how each one is unique. But also keep in mind that there is extensive variation *within* each of these professional disciplines. The work of social workers varies considerably, depending on the role they serve within an agency and the ways in which they were trained. Clinical mental health counselors practice in a variety of contexts and with different populations. The work of school counselors varies across school level and district. The same is true for psychologists, psychiatrists, and other mental health practitioners. What unites all of these helpers, though, is a

Photo 1.1

desire and commitment to helping others as well as an adherence to a basic set of concepts and skills that can be applied to the broadest scope of mental health practice styles and situations. This book is designed to introduce you to these ideas and skills.

CLINICAL MENTAL HEALTH PROFESSIONALS

Clinical mental health professionals is an overarching term for professionals who work in a wide variety of roles providing therapeutic services to individuals and groups of people grappling with a variety of social, personal, and/or interpersonal challenges. For example, they help people cope with difficulties posed by addictions, trauma, mental illness, experiences of stress, relational difficulties, adjustment, and social, emotional, and behavioral challenges. The type of services offered by these professionals may include "talk therapy," psychopharmacological (medication) therapy, the therapeutic use of creative arts or play media, psychoeducation, and/or advocacy. They work in a variety of settings, including residential homes, hospitals, clinics, institutions, community agencies, universities, schools, and small private practice offices. What sets clinical mental health professionals apart from those who do not engage in *clinical* practice is that they typically have advanced-level training (master's or doctoral degrees) that includes extensive supervised clinical practice experience, and they must be licensed to practice in their state of residence and area of practice. Here we will briefly review the disciplines of clinical mental health counseling, clinical social work, psychiatry, psychiatric nursing, psychology, rehabilitation counseling, school counseling, and school social work.

Clinical mental health counselors and **clinical social workers** are nonmedical mental health service providers. Typically trained at the master's level, these professionals must complete a supervised clinical internship as a part of their training, and they are state-licensed professionals. Neither are trained or licensed to prescribe psychopharmacological medication; however, they often work in close contact with medical doctors or psychiatrists if such medication is needed. So, knowledge about psychopharmacology is sometimes a part of their training. Clinical mental health counselors and clinical social workers both work in a large variety of settings, including inpatient psychiatric facilities, partial hospitalization programs, private practice, community mental health agencies, and schools, offering assessment, diagnosis, intervention, and, sometimes, prevention services. The foundation of training for clinical mental health counselors focuses on human development, wellness, and prevention (American Mental Health Counselors Association [AMHCA], n.d.). The profession of social worker comes from a long history of providing social welfare services to individuals on the fringes of society and advocating on behalf of underserved populations (National Association of Social Workers [NASW], n.d.b). Although both disciplines hold strong affiliations to their respective professional orientations, they may appear indistinguishable in everyday practice.

Psychiatrists are trained as medical doctors with a specialty in working with individuals who grapple with mental health, emotional, and behavioral challenges (American Psychiatric Association, n.d.). Psychiatrists receive at least 4 years of post–medical school residency training in diagnosis and use a variety of interventions, including psychotherapy, psychopharmacological medications, and, in some cases, electroconvulsive therapy (American Psychiatric Association, n.d.). Psychiatrists are state licensed and may work in hospital, institutional, agency or private practice settings. Also with a background in medicine, **psychiatric nurse practitioners** (also sometimes referred to as psychiatric mental health nurses) are also trained to provide mental health diagnostic and treatment services, including the prescription of medication (American Psychiatric Nurses Association, n.d.). Psychiatric mental health nursing is a specialty within the nursing profession and is licensed at the state level. Advanced-level psychiatric mental health nurses may hold master's- or doctoral-level degrees. They often work with patients in medical or psychiatric facilities or hospitals.

Clinical psychologists provide clinical services to people who have mental health and related challenges. They are also trained to diagnose and assess mental health functioning and well-being, and many psychologists administer and interpret a variety of cognitive, vocational, neuropsychological, intelligence, and personality assessments (American Psychological Association, n.d.). Psychologists work in a variety of settings, including inpatient medical and mental health facilities; community mental health, public health, and social service agencies; school districts; and private practice. Those who work in mental health or educational settings—clinical psychologists, school psychologists, cognitive psychologists, and forensic psychologists, for example—are typically trained at the PhD level with a supervised clinical internship as a part of their training. Although not too common, psychologists trained at the master's level may also be licensed to provide clinical services in some states. Unlike psychiatrists and psychiatric nurse practitioners, psychologists are not trained in the practice of medicine, so the scope of their practice, typically, is in the area of clinical nonmedical mental health. However, in a very small number of states across the United States, some psychologists are licensed to prescribe psychopharmacological medication to clients when working under the supervision of a medical doctor. There are a number of other areas of specialization in the field of psychology that are focused on nonclinical practice. These include developmental, experimental, community, educational, and industrial psychology.

OTHER MENTAL HEALTH PROFESSIONALS

Rehabilitation counselors work with individuals who have disabilities to overcome barriers or to manage the personal, social, or psychological effects of their disabilities on employment or independent living (Bureau of Labor Statistics, 2015). In some settings, these practitioners may not be considered "clinical" helpers as their focus is often more on advocacy and case management. Typically, rehabilitation counselors require a master's-level degree training with a supervised internship experience. They may work in hospitals, senior centers, community rehabilitation centers, or service organizations, and some rehabilitation counselors are employed by insurance companies or government agencies, working with the administrative aspects of service provision. Others may work in legal offices or private practice, providing legal services or advocacy to individuals with disabilities. Some but not all states license the practice of rehabilitation counselors.

School counselors work with students in schools to foster academic achievement, personal/social development, and career development (American School Counselor Association [ASCA], n.d.). The focus of their work is in supporting students for success in the school environment, and they do not typically offer long-term therapeutic intervention. For this reason, they are sometimes not considered "clinical" service providers. School counselors often work with individual students, conduct counseling groups, and offer psychoeducational services in classrooms, and they act as consultants to other teachers and administrators in the school as well as to parents who need advice or support. Most school counselors hold a master's degree that includes an internship experience and are licensed or certified through state boards of education.

School social workers similarly work in school settings with students to address social and emotional or psychological issues that interfere with learning (NASW, n.d.a). In many cases their work is very similar to that of school counselors, although they may be considered "clinical" providers in some schools, and they may even use third-party payment billing systems, which typically requires that they are "clinically" trained. In some schools, however, school social workers do not provide "clinical" services and instead work more closely with community agencies and families and in the area of case management. School social workers may hold a bachelor's or master's degree in social work, and their training includes supervised fieldwork. Credentialing is also typically governed through state educational credentialing bodies.

NONCLINICAL HELPERS

Nonclinical helpers work in a variety of positions and have a range of job titles within the field of mental health. They often provide some level of supervised therapeutic services to individuals who have behavioral, emotional, social, or mental health challenges, and they are often hired in the roles of behavioral interventionist, case manager, advocate, program administrator, or (nonclinical) counselor. What sets these helpers apart from those discussed above is that they have typically not received an advanced level of clinical mental health training, and while some hold a master's-level degree, most are bachelor's-level trained, often in liberal arts, human services, social work, or a variety of other disciplines.

HELPING TERMS

COUNSELING, PSYCHOTHERAPY, AND THERAPY

The terms *counseling* and *psychotherapy* tend to be used interchangeably across many mental health practice settings, with the exception of schools. These terms generally refer to the clinical practice of helping others with personal, social, or psychological issues or concerns. The term *therapy* is just a shorted version of the word *psychotherapy*. In school settings, many resist the use of the term *therapy* to describe the services offered by school counselors or social workers, preferring instead the term *counseling*. In this context, counseling may connote providing guidance or offering advice rather than addressing mental health issues. *Helping* is a more general term that is also sometimes used in reference to counseling and therapy, but typically this term connotes assistance that is offered by a non-clinically trained professional and may not refer to work specifically associated with mental health concerns. *Scope of practice* refers to the particular area in which a clinician is working. Some clinicians, for example, work with families, others solely with children. Some have expertise in the area of substance abuse, others with issues related to sexual abuse, with inmates in prison, or with people who are suicidal or otherwise in crisis. An individual's professional scope of practice has to do with the types of client issues he is trained and prepared to address in therapy.

ADVOCACY

In the mix of all of these mental health related practices, we also sometimes hear the term *advocacy*. Although *advocacy* is more commonly used in reference to services provided by nonclinical helping professionals, it is also viewed as an integral component of the work of clinical mental health counselors and social workers. Here we will talk briefly about what advocacy means, foreshadowing the more extensive discussions about advocacy in later chapters.

The effects of everyday experiences such as classism, racism, sexism, etc., and the effort required to navigate social institutions that are colored by subtle and not-so-subtle forms of bias and discrimination are an everyday challenge for many. In fact, for many people who identify in marginalized social locations, these adverse experiences are at the very root of the difficulties and challenges they face—the challenges that are sometimes labeled "mental health issues." When people are challenged by the effects of social forces such as prejudice and discrimination, therapeutic helping interventions should focus on those external sources of the problems rather than on the individual. Advocacy, then, refers to actions taken by professional helpers to address unjust social and/or institutional practices and the challenges and barriers they cause in people's lives. In mental health circles, advocacy is defined as acting with or on behalf of others at an individual, community, and/or societal levels so as to affect change (Funk, Minoletti, Drew, Taylor, & Saraceno, 2006; Lewis, Lewis, Daniels, & D'Andrea, 1998). The implicit goal of most advocacy efforts is to increase peoples' sense of personal power or agency. Again, we will return to these discussions throughout this text.

A WORD ABOUT THE TERMINOLOGY USED IN THIS TEXT

In an attempt to make the language in this text less cumbersome and less repetitive, and also to honor the differences in terminology used across the various mental health–related disciplines and the literature referenced in this text, I will use most of these terms interchangeably: *clinician*, *therapist*, *counselor*, *mental health practitioner*, and *clinical practitioner*. I interchange these terms in an attempt to respect and represent the work of a broad scope of trained mental health practitioners who do the important work of counseling, psychotherapy, and helping. My intent is inclusivity.

Also, you will notice that in most chapters in this book, I use the term *clients* in reference to the recipients of therapeutic services. This is because my own professional training and orientation compels me to identify those receiving mental health services differently from those who receive medical services. I recognize, however, that some clinical helpers us the term *patients* rather than *clients*. In discussions about clients in school settings, I use the term *students*, and in Chapter 11, where basic principles of group work are discussed, I switch into the terminology of *group members*.

You will also see my references to *helping*, *helping relationships*, *therapeutic relationships*, *clinical helping*, *counseling*, *therapy*, *clinical helping relationships*, and *counseling relationships* used throughout this text. These terms, which all speak to the work of helping in the field of mental health, are used interchangeably here for the similar purpose of avoiding cumbersome and repetitive language. Please understand that when used in this text, these terms are intended to reference clinical work conducted by those who have received advanced-level training to provide some form of mental health services.

While I and many mental health professionals have no qualms with using these terms interchangeably (e.g., see Sommers-Flanagan & Sommers-Flanagan, 2004), it is important to point out that many mental health professionals do. Some argue that significant philosophical differences exist between generic helping, counseling, and psychotherapy and that these differences reflect divergent practices in the field. Some suggest, for example, that counseling refers to a problem-solving and time-limited approach to helping, whereas psychotherapy is likened to the longer term psychodynamic or psychoanalytic approaches to helping. Others disagree, pointing to solution-focused brief therapy as an example of a time-limited therapeutic intervention that is considered to be therapy. Still others suggest that *counseling* refers to interventions conducted by nonclinical counselors (think here of a residential camp "counselor"). Some school counselors, as mentioned, refrain from using the term *therapy* for philosophical or political reasons. They disagree with the idea that counselors should be offering mental health services in schools, or they worry that school administrators or parents would be uncomfortable with the term *therapy* being used in a school setting.

These divergent perspectives, I believe, occur because the field of mental health is in constant evolution and change. Some of the professional affiliations or specific disciplines within mental health are older than others, which may give a sense of proprietary ownership of some helping terms and practices. Also, some disciplines have stronger lobby capabilities than others, which can make their specific professional affiliation more visible and thus associated with the terms that they favor. The truth is, most professional organizations and the members that they represent have a strong sense of history and pride in what they do as well as in what makes them unique. These are infused in the ways in which they talk about themselves and their work. Professional titles denote identity.

Words are powerful, and they are important. So, I find myself in a dilemma of how to embrace the diversity of perspectives in the field so that everyone feels included, but also not wanting to burden the reader with a repeated and cumbersome list of terms. I understand that some may not always agree with me regarding the interchangeability of these terms and that my attempt of inclusivity may not be appreciated by all. Most mental health professionals, regardless of specific discipline, however, work from a shared repertoire of basic helping skills, even if their practice orientations and settings differ. And the instruction of basic helping skills is, of course, the primary focus of this book. The philosophical overlay that you receive in your particular mental health discipline and the training that delivers this orientation are the important ingredients that will shape how you will use the skills and concepts discussed in this text. I leave it to you, the reader, to adjust your reading of these terms and concepts according to the nomenclature that suits you and your particular professional affiliation. Thank you in advance for your flexibility.

THE PRACTICE OF THERAPY

There is an infinite array of ideas proffered by mental health practitioners over decades and across oceans that have shaped the practice that we now call therapy. In general, these clinical practice trends are influenced by social and political movements, research findings, popular ideas, practice setting constraints, and consumer demand, and they shape the ways in which clinicians understand clients, conceptualize problems, and go about the work of therapy. We pause here briefly to talk about two important ways in which clinicians think about their work. The first is called theoretical orientation and the second, clinical modality.

Theoretical orientation, as used in this text, refers to the ways in which clinicians understand how people develop, grow, and change. These ideas are based on psychodynamic, ethological, humanistic, behavioral/learning, contemporary, social, and developmental theories. Each has its own explanation of how people develop and many also offer ideas about what can go wrong, leading to problems that bring people into therapy. The theoretical orientation of a clinician is critically important because the ways in which one thinks about growth and how one conceptualizes the etiology of problems influences how one thinks about intervention and change.

Clinical modality refers to theory-based ideas (sometimes supported by empirical research studies) that direct clinical decision making and therapeutic intervention. Other terms used for clinical modality include *therapeutic modality*, *intervention strategies*, *treatment strategies*, *psychological theories*, and *counseling strategies*. Wikipedia ("List of Psychotherapies," n.d.) recently listed 154 types of modalities used in therapeutic practice, although, admittedly, this is not a professional reference site and there are some approaches on the list that are unconventional, are questionably ethical, and lack adequate data regarding their efficacy. But, the point is that there are many different ways to approach therapy. Some examples of clinical modalities that are used by contemporary therapists include client-centered therapy, cognitive behavioral therapy, internal family systems, narrative practice, and motivational interviewing. The National Institute of Mental Health ([NIMH], n.d.) reminds us that there is no "one-size-fits-all" approach to psychotherapy; therapy should be matched to the needs of each and every client. Across various practice settings, across the various professional disciplines, and across most theoretical orientations and clinical modalities, however, is a set of skills that is almost universally used by all clinical mental health clinicians. And those skills are the focus of this text and will be outlined in more detail in the second part of this text.

FACTORS THAT LEAD TO CHANGE

While some people who face challenges are able to get better, grow, or change even without the benefit of therapy (Bohart & Tallman, 2010), we also know that clinical therapeutic intervention, very generally, does help many clients in positive ways (American Psychological Association, 2005; Lambert, 2013; NIMH, n.d.; Wampold, 2010). As mentioned, the range of potential clinical intervention strategies is quite large—the number is so large, in fact, that many researches recommend focusing on *common factors* or fundamental underlying mechanisms for promoting change, rather than specific techniques or therapeutic modalities (Chatoor & Kurpnick, 2001; Hubble, Duncan, Miller, & Wampold, 2010; Tschacher, Haken, & Kyselo, 2015). Some therapeutic factors that affect success in therapy are unique to each individual client—for example, temperament, motivation and readiness to change, developmental factors and experiences, coping style, baseline functioning level, strengths, and social conditions such as personal and social resources and socioeconomic status (Beutler, Alomohamed, Moleiro, & Romanelli, 2002; Hubble et al., 2010). Success in therapy is also associated with variables related to the specific issue or presenting concern brought to therapy. These include, for example, level of impairment and chronicity and complexity of the problem (Beutler et al., 2002). And finally, successful therapy also depends on who the clinician is and what the clinician does—these are discussed in more detail here. We begin with clinician competence, and then move to a few words about intentionality, empathy, therapeutic alliance, the instillation of hope, and promoting agency. These variables are outlined in Table 1.1.

Table 1.1: Factors That Lead to Change

COMPETENCE	INTENTIONALITY	EMPATHY	ALLIANCE	HOPE	AGENCY
Knowledge	Goal-directed interventions	Warm, non-threatening acceptance	Attunement	Client hope	Respect for client decisions
Confidence	Goal consensus	Nonjudgmental presence	Unconditional positive regard	Clinician hope and optimism	Unconditional positive regard
Flexible and versatile	Adherence to method	Understanding the client's feelings	Ethic of care	Success expectations	Choice
Communication and counseling skills	Common factors	Connection			
Ethical and responsible behavior		Centered on the interests of the client			
Professionalism					
Cultural competence					

COMPETENCE

Chatoor and Kurpnick (2001) point out that therapist competence is an important variable in producing successful therapeutic outcomes. The concept of professional competence, most generally, refers to an ability to perform the required task (Beauchamp & Childress, 2013). But, identifying a particular standard of competence required for success in therapy is difficult because competence is contextual—it varies by task and particular profession (Beauchamp & Childress, 2013). However, we do know that clinicians must be **knowledgeable** to be effective (Hubble et al., 2010). In this context, being knowledgeable refers to having information about the population one is working with, the challenges that are being addressed, and current information regarding evidence-based practice. As will be discussed in Chapter 3, being knowledgeable in the area of one's practice, keeping informed of new developments in the field, and not working in an area that is outside of one's expertise or training are ethical mandates for clinical helpers.

When clinicians are knowledgeable about their work, they exude a sense of **confidence**, and this sense of confidence instills a sense of hope that the work will be successful. As we will discuss later, it turns out that an expectation of success can have a strong influence on the helping outcome. Having said this, however, Wampold (2010) warns that sometimes when therapy is not successful, clinicians tend to respond by continuing to deliver the same type of help, sometimes with more vehemence, rather than turning to a different approach. And so, while clinicians must be knowledgeable, capable, and confident, they also must be **flexible and versatile**. When things are not going as planned or when a particular approach is not working, a clinician should review the goal and the intervention plan and consider using a different approach.

Of course, clinical knowledge is not helpful and an air of confidence could be hazardous if the clinician lacks basic **communication and counseling skills**. All of us have probably known teachers who are brilliant in their subject area but unable to articulate that information to their students. Many of us have read articles with important information that is laid out in such a way that it is incomprehensible. Research shows that almost 80% of the people who need therapy do not seek it because they do not have confidence that it will help (Hubble et al., 2010). This reminds us that clinicians must be knowledgeable and must also be able to communicate what they know.

In addition to being knowledgeable and having strong communication and counseling skills, clinical competence also has to do with engaging in **ethical and responsible behavior**. While specific codes of ethics vary some across the various mental health professional disciplines, most of these codes are based on the set of moral principles discussed in Chapter 3. These principles and professional codes of ethics offer guidelines for clinical decision making when situations become murky, and they offer some assurance to clients that clinicians will be working in their best interests. Along these lines, helper competence also has to do with engaging in **professional behavior**—acting professional. Being professional encompasses a wide scope of actions, from maintaining the commitments regarding the provision of services to being respectful to one's clients—we will discuss this in more detail below.

Cultural competence is another component of professional competence that is critical for professional and ethical clinical practice. Clear definitions of what, exactly, it means to be culturally competent remain somewhat elusive. Arredondo et al. (1996), however, assert that for clinicians, it must include having an awareness of one's own attitudes and beliefs; racial or cultural heritage; and about one's beliefs, values, lifestyle, and worldview. It also includes working to understand the attitudes, beliefs, heritage, values, lifestyles, and worldviews of one's clients and engaging in culturally appropriate interventions that are aligned with the specific beliefs, values, and needs of the client. Tomlinson-Clarke (2013) adds that having the understanding that the complex dynamics of culture and cultural practices are rooted in a sociopolitical context and having the ability to confront biased attitudes and practices is critical to clinician competence. Understanding how the social context of power and privilege affects how clients who identify in various social locations are treated by others in their communities and the larger society, and how these circumstances affect mental health as well as mental health therapy, will be discussed more in Chapter 2.

INTENTIONALITY

Intentionality refers to the ways in which one's actions are thoughtful and purposeful. The point made by Hubble et al. (2010) that a lack of structure and focus in therapy is associated with negative clinical outcomes is a good starting point of our discussion about intentionality. Intentionality begins with being sure that counseling is **directed toward some type of goal** or accomplishment. It refers to working in a careful and thoughtful manner toward the desired outcome of the helping contract. We speak more about the helping contract later in this chapter and about the drafting of counseling goals and intervention plans in Chapter 9.

Goal-directed interventions are important, and Norcross (2010) points out that when the client and clinician are in agreement about the goals for helping, positive clinical outcomes are even more likely to result. This may be because **goal consensus** strengthens the therapeutic alliance (Gaston, 1990; Norcross, 2010), which we know affects clinical outcomes. It makes intuitive sense that the process of discussing and agreeing about the intended focus and goals of counseling is important (Anderson, Lunnen, & Ogles, 2010; Norcross, 2010)—therapy is not something we do *to* clients, it is something we do *with* them. Goal consensus assures that our work is centered on something the client is motivated to work on. So, working with intentionality means working toward goals that are identified by the client and the clinician working together.

Another aspect of intentionality has to do with theoretical conceptualization and counseling modalities. Chatoor and Kurpnick (2001) suggest that therapist **adherence to a specific treatment method** is also associated with positive clinical outcomes. In a seemingly contradictory statement, Wampold (2010) points out, however, that it is not one particular modality or method that is associated with clinical success. In fact, after decades of research attempting to discern what modalities are most effective for addressing different mental health problems, there is no consensus about what works best with whom and in response to what particular problem (Hubble et al., 2010). In the words of these authors: "The data are unequivocal: All treatment approaches have won, and all deserve prizes" (Hubble et al., 2010, p. 33). "Bluntly put," they say, "the existence of specific psychological treatments for specific disorders is a myth" (Hubble et al., 2010, p. 28). So, when Chatoor and Kurpnick (2001) assert that adherence to a specific treatment modality is important, the emphasis is on intentionality rather than a particular therapeutic approach. When clinicians do what they have carefully thought out and intend to do, they are more likely to be successful.

Given the lack of clear evidence that one counseling modality is more effective than another, many researchers point to the importance of **common factors**, mentioned earlier, that cut across different therapeutic techniques and modalities as the key to clinical success (for more on this, see Chatoor & Kurpnick, 2001; Hubble et al., 2010; Wampold, 2010). These common factors, they suggest, may be the "essential ingredients" and the "foundation" (Chatoor & Kurpnick, 2001, p. 24) upon which all interventions should be constructed. The point here is that clinicians must be intentional in allowing these factors to guide their therapeutic work.

EMPATHY

The term *empathy* comes from the German concept of *einfuhlung*, which means "feeling into" (Frankel, 2009; Neumann et al., 2009). We use it in the clinical therapeutic context to describe the ways in which a clinician is able to recognize and understand the emotions and experiences of a client. It is the "ability to understand and respond to the unique affective experiences of another person" (Lamm, Batson, & Decety, 2007, p. 42); it is about connection (Brown, 2013). When we attempt to truly understand the client's experiences, we are then able to make a connection.

According to Carl Rogers (1975), empathy "means entering the private perceptual world of the other and becoming thoroughly at home in it" (p. 4). Further, Rogers (1975) famously referred to empathy as an ability to "perceive the internal frame of reference of another with accuracy and with the emotional components and meanings which pertain thereto … *as if* one were the person, *but without ever losing the 'as if'* condition" (p. 3). Reiterating this point, Baron-Cohen (2011) says that empathy can occur when "we suspend our single-minded focus of attention, and instead adopt a double-minded focus of attention" (p. 11). It requires "some monitoring mechanisms that keep track of the origins (self vs. other) of the experienced feelings" (Lamm et al., 2007, p. 42). Empathy happens, then, when we are able to engage into the perspective of the other and simultaneously be aware of ourselves and our own thoughts, emotions, experiences, and reactions.

When we attempt to enter into the world of our clients, we can never fully understand their experiences and we can never fully know what they are thinking and feeling. This means that we must be careful when we make assumptions about our clients, and we must also not lose ourselves in their stories, emotions, and experiences. So, empathy requires us as clinicians to have good self-awareness (Wiseman, 1996), to be able to regulate our own emotional states (Neumann et al., 2009), and to be careful with our assumptions.

The remainder of Baron-Cohen's (2011) definition of empathy is this: "Empathy is our ability to identify what someone else is thinking or feeling, and to respond to their thoughts and feelings with an appropriate emotion" (p. 12). This leads us to the second important component of empathy: It isn't enough to just feel empathic toward our client. Empathy doesn't happen unless the client feels our empathy (Frankel, 2009; Wiseman, 1996; Wynn & Bergvik, 2010). Empathy requires that the clinician be able to identify the experience (feelings and thoughts) of the other person and also to communicate that understanding to the client. We know from research on empathy that clinicians typically are inadequate judges of empathy—that is, they are often not able to accurately determine if their clients experience them as empathic (Norcross, 2010). The primary way to determine if the clinician truly is empathic is to ask the client (Frankel, 2009; Norcross, 2010). So, adding this important component to our definition of empathy is Frankel's (2009) point that empathy is a three-part process that includes (a) an initial expression or communication from the client (an empathic opportunity); (b) the empathic response that is felt and understood by the clinician and then communicated back to the client; and (c) the full-circle feedback loop, in which the client lets the clinician know (verbally or nonverbally) that she felt the empathy expressed by the clinician.

Even though most of us can sense when someone is being empathic, it is extremely difficult to pinpoint what, exactly, empathy looks like as a concrete behavior. And, of course, everyone feels empathy differently. But, having some sense of what empathy looks like as a concrete behavior can be helpful. So, as I describe what empathy might look like in a therapeutic helping relationship, please recognize that empathy is far more than these limited descriptors.

First, empathy has to do with creating a **warm, nonthreatening,** and **accepting** atmosphere in therapy (Rogers, 1951) that allows for a **nonjudgmental engagement** with the client (Rogers, 1975). It also means being able to **understand the helpee's feelings** in all of their complexities (Rogers, 1975; Wiseman, 1996), and being able to sense "meanings of which he/she [the client] is scarcely aware" (Rogers, 1975, p. 4). Empathy has to do with forging a **connection** with the client (Brown, 2013) and being **focused on the interests of the other** (Baron-Cohen, 2011). This means that we must stay connected with our clients, even when we feel disappointed about their choices or frustrated with their lack of progress. It requires us to remain present and nonreactive, even when we feel challenged. And finally, having empathy means that we must be able to withhold judgment and condemnation, in spite of our own personal values and life decisions. Empathy requires us to be centered on the needs of our clients and to be engaged in a therapeutic relationship with them, even when that is difficult to do.

At this point you may be asking yourself why empathy is important. It is important because research shows that empathy is a critical factor in what makes therapy work (Norcross, 2010; Wiseman, 1996). In fact, Norcross (2010) found that empathy accounts for one third of change that is associated with therapy. It makes people feel heard, valued, acknowledged, and respected (Baron-Cohen, 2011). While Brown (2010) emphasized that connection (empathy) gives meaning to people's lives, Norcross (2010) proposed that empathy fosters a "corrective emotional experience" (p. 119) for a client. A corrective emotional experience refers to the reexposure to an emotional situation that was challenging in the past under more current favorable circumstances (Fried, 2002). The idea behind this concept of a corrective emotional experience is that in reliving problematic events from the past within a current context of a therapeutic relationship, clients are able to develop new ways of engaging in interpersonal relationships, try out new patterns of thinking and behaving, and develop insight.

THERAPEUTIC ALLIANCE

According to Hubble et al. (2010), of all of the therapeutic factors involved in clinical work, creating a strong therapeutic relationship is the most crucial. In fact, the establishment of a therapeutic alliance is more conducive to positive therapeutic outcomes than any one specific therapeutic treatment modality (Chatoor & Kurpnick, 2001; Lambert, 2013). Effective therapeutic relationships are formed when the clinician demonstrates understanding, acceptance, kindness, warmth, and compassion and is able to provide a safe space where the client feels supported and heard (Bohart & Tallman, 2010; Lambert, 2013; Norcross, 2010). In such a space, the client is able to take risks, explore the unknown, and try out new feelings, thoughts, and behaviors.

One important component of a therapeutic relationship has to do with being highly attuned to the client—his experiences and needs. **Attunement** refers to the ability to accurately read one's cognitive, emotional, physiological, and behavioral cues and to respond accordingly (Blaustein & Kinniburgh, 2010). Another component of the therapeutic relationship that is critical has to do with the Rogerian concept of **unconditional positive regard** (Rogers, 1951). This refers to offering "warm acceptance of the client's experience without conditions" (Norcross, 2010, p. 123). Finally, Eliot (2013) reminds us that clients "want more from clinicians than 'reasons' and 'evidence,' or exercise of competence; they want connection, communication, and caring, or evidence of compassion" (p. 629). The therapeutic relationships must be rooted

Photo 1.2

in **trust and caring** (Barnett & Johnson, 2015). In line with this, Noddings (2002) coined the concept of an *ethic of care,* identifying it as a fundamental component of helping relationships.

INSTILLATION OF HOPE

Hope is optimism—having an expectation of positive outcomes, despite challenges. Psychiatrist Viktor Frankl (1963) deemed hope to be essential for life and for the continued existence of humanity. One must have hope, he said, to survive. Similarly, in the world of clinical mental health, positive psychologists identify hope to be a critical ingredient for therapeutic change (Larsen & Stege, 2010). Hope is "the reason patients keep doing whatever their treatment entails, however arduous" (Eliot, 2013, p. 630). As it turns out, when a client believes that she will be able to live her life in ways that are in line with her hopes and expectations, successful therapeutic change is more likely to result (Bohart & Tallman, 2010). This means that when a **client has hope**, she is likely act in ways that will realize her expectations.

Similarly, **counselor hope and optimism** is important. A cornerstone of Carl Roger's (1951) client-centered therapy is the idea that the therapist should be steadfast in his belief in the client's capacity to grow and change. That is, a clinician must have hope and expectation that change is possible. And indeed, research has shown that clinician hope and positive expectations are conducive to positive outcomes in therapy (Hubble et al., 2010). It is not just believing in the client's potential to be successful that promotes success; a clinician's **expectations about using a particular counseling modality** is also important. Clinicians' expectations that the particular modality they are using in therapy (one's allegiance to method), regardless of what specific approach is being used, is associated with clinical success (Hubble et al., 2010). This is because, these authors suggest, a clinician's hopes and expectations around the work they are doing arouse the client's confidence that, indeed, the approach will be effective. Thus, clients, too, become hopeful, and that hope turns into success.

PROMOTING AGENCY

Rogers (1961) emphasized the importance of fostering client freedom as a part of creating a therapeutic relationship that embodies unconditional positive self-regard and acceptance. In fact, he asserted that fostering freedom is a critical way in which therapists promote self-actualization. In therapy, Rogers (1961) pointed out, "some of the most compelling subjective experiences are those in which the client feels within himself the power of naked choice" (p. 192). A client should be free, he continues,

> to become himself or to hide behind a façade; to move forward or to retrogress; to behave in ways that are destructive of self and others, or in ways that are enhancing; quite literally free to live or die, in both the physiological and psychological meaning of those terms. (Rogers, 1961, p. 192)

For Rogers (1951), the self-actualizing tendency—to move in the direction of maturation, in the direction of taking responsibility for one's life, and in the direction of self-government, self-regulation, and autonomy—is based on freedom of choice. The tools for promoting self-regulation, he proposed, are to create a therapeutic relationship and environment that is based on **respect** and **unconditional positive regard.**

These notions about freedom are not just historical ideas from a bygone era in therapy. They are inherent to many contemporary strength-based, solution-focused, feminist, and narrative therapies as well. For example, Sommers-Flanagan and Sommers-Flanagan (2004) remind us that the belief that women should be fully engaged in economic, social, and political decision making is a core foundation of feminist theory underlying a wide scope of feminist therapeutic practices. Narrative therapy and other constructionist theories, these authors also point out, are also rooted in the importance of promoting client agency. Gestalt theory is based on enabling clients' awareness so as to increase self-direction (Yontef & Jacobs, 2008). All of these therapies promote the idea that when individuals are empowered to see what they are capable of, they will move in the direction of growth and change.

THE HELPING CONTRACT

Therapy is a unique experience. And within therapy, the therapist–client relationship is like no other. This therapeutic relationship requires a kind of empathic connection that is at once similar to and at the same time very different from the kinds of relationships we have with friends and loved ones. One of the central ways in which the therapeutic relationship is different from other relationships is that it is a *contractual relationship*. It is a contractual relationship wherein one comes to the table in need of services and the other is in the role of providing those services.

Clinicians need to be clear that no matter how much they like, care about, are hopeful about, have unconditional positive regard for, and are invested in the success of their clients, they are in a contractual relationship. In fact, many clinicians use the term *client* in reference to the recipient of their services, as it emphasizes the idea that the recipient of therapeutic services is a consumer. It connotes the idea that a client is someone who is an agent in the negotiation of services, and it emphasizes the point that the clinician is working for the client. *Therapy*, then, is a contracted and collaborative process in which all parties are informed about what will happen, when, and by whom. The *helping contract* is the articulation of this exchange of services.

While it makes some of us uncomfortable to think of and describe the therapeutic relationship in terminology that is more often associated with business or industry, doing so speaks to important components of the therapeutic process. The helping contract helps ensure that the clinician is providing

Photo 1.3

services that the client has asked for and has agreed to, and that these services are ones that the clinician is capable of providing. A helping contract begins with an explicit informed consent discussion and includes a number of other implicit professional behaviors. These components of the helping contract are reviewed below and are summarized in Table 1.2 at the end of this discussion.

INFORMED CONSENT

Providing information to clients about the parameters of the therapeutic relationship—what the client can expect from therapy—is referred to as the informed consent process (Wheeler & Bertram, 2012). It is helpful to think of informed consent as the explicit part of the helping contract that articulates the commitment made to a client and what the therapist will be accountable for. Informed consent conversations and documents typically include an articulation of the services that the therapist is trained and prepared to deliver;

therapist credentials; counseling modalities that may be used in therapy; expectations regarding client engagement in therapy; information related to any risks associated with therapy; an articulation of confidentiality polices, including exceptions to confidentiality and policies related to duty to warn and supervision practices; and information related to ethics, complaints, and policies related to records, fees, and insurance reimbursement (Wheeler & Bertram, 2012). The onus of responsibility to engage a client in an informed consent process, as well as the responsibility to see to it that those conditions are maintained throughout therapy, sits squarely with the clinician. Since providing informed consent is an ethical obligation for clinicians, we will talk more about this in Chapter 3.

PROFESSIONAL BEHAVIORS

The helping contract, as mentioned, is a contractual agreement regarding the professional delivery of services. At the risk of sounding pedantic and, perhaps, condescending, it would be a glaring omission here if we were to gloss over discussion about concrete therapist behaviors that communicate professionalism.

Professionalism in therapy, very generally, includes being clear about the services you are prepared to offer and not offering services for which you are not trained, being fair and consistent in compensation arrangements (i.e., payment for services), being careful and respectful in all communications and actions, and overall, adhering to ethical practice guidelines. More concretely, it also includes being on time for meetings, maintaining confidentiality, being fully present during the time together, and attending to paperwork, phone calls, and any other situations that require follow-through.

Of course, there is a range of acceptable clinician behaviors that vary according to work setting, community, client population, and cultural norms. All clinicians should be aware of and abide by the norms that are appropriate for their particular situation. For example, in most settings, the importance of being on time for appointments is critical—it is a matter of respect. However, there are good reasons for why a clinician may, on occasion, be running late for an appointment. Emergencies do happen, and the ways in which they unfold and how they might affect subsequent clients and appointments is sometimes unpredictable. At the very least, a waiting client needs to know what to expect in terms of his own scheduled appointment. Similarly, while most all clinicians are expected to complete paperwork related to assessment, diagnosis, intervention planning, and case notes, as will be discussed in Chapter 9, the specifics of how these are completed and the expectations around completion vary extensively across practice settings.

Phone calls, as mentioned, are another important issue related to professionalism. It is disrespectful in most settings to accept phone calls when providing clinical services—answering calls when in session with a client can communicate to a client that something or someone else is more important than she is. If a clinician is on call and might need to respond to an emergency call during a counseling session, clients should be informed of this possibility in advance. However, therapists should obviously not be taking personal phone calls during therapy sessions. Offering one's personal phone number to clients is also an important concern. In many settings, this is inappropriate because it poses undue burden to clinicians by cutting into their own personal lives, and some clinicians have concerns that it inappropriately fosters dependency. Yet, many clinicians do this to facilitate scheduling or because it is part of the therapeutic practice being used. Many agencies provide clinicians with on-call phones for these purposes, thus avoiding the situation where clients have their therapists' personal phone numbers. In any case, arrangements around emergency contact numbers and processes are important to discuss during the informed consent process. Cancellation policies are also negotiated during the informed consent process. Obviously, it can be problematic for clients when the clinician cancels a therapy appointment. Yet clinicians are human, and there will always be situations that require the rescheduling of appointments.

Clinicians should also be thoughtful of other behaviors that may be interpreted by some clients as unprofessional or confusing. The practice of eating or drinking while providing therapy to a client, for example, is worth mentioning. While this may be considered inappropriate in some practice settings, drinking a cup of tea with a client is an important ritual and is completely appropriate in many therapy offices. Appropriate dress is another component of professionalism, and this, too, varies according to setting and culture. Office decor and where therapy takes place are also important to think about. Except in unique situations, therapy should not happen in personal settings. Having said this, some clinicians have offices in their homes, others work in the homes of their clients, and still others in nontraditional settings—wilderness therapy comes to mind here. So, there is much variation in where therapists work. However, most of us would be hard-pressed to identify a situation in which it is appropriate for a clinical therapist to make plans with their clients to go shopping or meet in a coffee shop to talk about what is happening in their personal lives. If this is a practice that makes therapeutic sense in the clinical work, then it should be in alignment with the client's goals and intervention plans and thoroughly discussed in the informed consent process.

Finally, it is important to add that being professional also means that clinicians are responsible for attending to their own mental health and personalization issues. Clinical work is extremely taxing, and when counselors are not functioning at their full capacity level, it is easy for them to become triggered by client issues, lose their ability to be objective, become confused about boundaries, or lose their ability to be fully present with their clients. We will discuss these issues in more detail in Chapter 5, when we address practitioner self-awareness and self-management. The point here is that the practice of mental health counseling is a professional practice, and all clinicians need to be thoughtful about how their behavior communicates a high level of professionalism.

NONMUTUALITY

Nonmutuality is a concept that describes the directionality of the therapeutic relationship. In the practice of therapy, the focus of the work, the specific conversations that happen, and all of the decision making that occur within the therapeutic relationship must be based on the interests and needs of the client and outlined in the helping contract. Nonmutuality means avoiding a focus on the clinician's personal history and avoiding discussion about aspects of the clinician's personal life that are tangential or irrelevant to the helping contract; it also refers to a caution around the more subtle ways in which a therapist may elicit praise or affirmation from a client that is self-serving to the therapist's own needs rather than about the client or therapy. The point here is that clinicians have the responsibility to assure that the therapy is about their client, not about themselves.

BOUNDARIES

When emphasizing the needs of the client in the helping contract, it would be naive to say that clinicians do not have any needs and never derive benefit from their work. Helpers do get something out of helping—financial compensation, a certain degree of prestige, and, perhaps, moral satisfaction related to a sense of contributing to the welfare of others. Honestly, if therapists did not receive any benefit at all from their work, they would likely not continue to be therapists.

Arguably, one of the most rewarding aspects of working with others in a clinical setting is the return that clinicians get on the investment in the therapeutic relationship. Shouldn't we admit—perhaps cautiously—that liking this work includes liking our clients and the emotional connection we have with them? We share their joys, we feel their frustrations, and we champion their causes. It might even be true that those of us who are good at this work are good because of the investment we have in our clients, with all of its inherent challenges. This is, perhaps, part of the informal compensation that we receive from our work. Too, as we have already noted, caring about our clients helps them succeed. Yet, the caution we feel in saying this is that it puts us dangerously close to the boundary around nonmutuality that we have just discussed. And this caution is important.

This occupation of trafficking in human relationships is a nuanced business. For example, when we like our clients so much, our liking can influence our clinical work in ways that we do not always anticipate. What if, for example, the guitar we lend our client from our own personal collection is never returned? What happens when we like our client so much that we are tempted to overlook the sure signs of physical abuse we see on the arms of his child? Or when we are reluctant to report a "dirty" urine screen to a probation officer, knowing that doing so may cause the client we like so much to go back to jail? How many of us would be reluctant to offer difficult feedback to a favorite student who sits in our office for counsel? A professional position with appropriate boundaries means that we like our client enough to be committed to what is best for her or for the welfare of others in her life, even if that compels us to be uncomfortable. We need to remember that the commitment we make to our clients is to help them attain their goals; it is, of course, not a mutual relationship that serves our own social and emotional needs.

And here we should also talk about the need to be liked. Many of us would jump quickly to say that we don't *need* to be liked. But as Alder argued in his theory of individual psychology, humans are born social, and healthy development requires *social interest*—a sense of being part of and contributing to one's social community (Mosak & Maniacci, 2008; Prochaska & Norcross, 2007). People often act in ways that will give them access to that social community, and one important way that we do this is to become likable. Therapists are not immune from wanting to be liked by others.

Wanting to be liked by others is by no means a bad thing. We can probably all agree that lending money to a friend, for example, is usually a nice thing to do. And, when we lend someone money, it will probably cause that person to like us. We also know that people feel good when we acknowledge them, and their response to such acknowledgments can make us feel liked. But, when we are in a position of *needing* to be liked by our clients, the focus in therapy shifts from the client back to us. It can easily underlie our inability to confront an important issue, to provide needed feedback, or to take action that makes others uncomfortable. We may say that we don't want to "hurt" our client, but what we may mean is that we need him to "like" us. And this shift is usually so subtle we are not aware of its existence.

Liking and being liked are nice, but they should never get in the way of the work that needs to get done in therapy. The investment that we have in our clinical work comes with restrictions, and these restrictions are the boundaries we need to set in our therapeutic relationships. They include prohibitions against forming personal friendships with our clients, intimacy, and physical contact. It is the duty of the clinician to manage the therapeutic relationship so that it is always focused on the best interests of the client and the conditions set forth in the helping contract—not to fulfill the needs of the clinician.

Another murky issue in therapy has to do with the extent to which counselors should be honest and truthful to their clients. This issue may emerge when clients are curious about who the counselor is or what she does outside of therapy. For example, clients sometimes ask questions about who we live with, what politician we will vote for, or if we have ever struggled with the issue they are struggling with. These questions may be subtle, so subtle sometimes that we are drawn into them before we even realize it. And they ask us to respond honestly, when our truthful opinion is not always therapeutically helpful. It is easy to be tempted to jump at these opportunities to reassure our clients that we really do have the expertise to help them, that we truly understand them and what they are grappling with, or that we are human beings outside of the therapy office. However, doing so can easily shift in the conversations from the client to the therapist, and it may have other potential consequences as well. For example, might the client who asked about your substance use then tell others, thus tarnishing your reputation in the community? How might others respond to this if your work setting is with youth or in a school? Or, might this client start to minimize her own use because she thinks that clearly you had similar problems and got over them? All of these situations are very complicated, and they are even more hazardous when the counselor has a strong need to be liked by others.

Of course, when clients ask us these questions, they are probably not doing so from maleficence. These questions sometimes are an artifact of the awkward nature of a nonmutual therapeutic relationship. Clients may be curious about us, they may be uncomfortable being the center of our attention, they may feel vulnerable and want assurance that they are not weird or somehow damaged, and many want to know about their therapist before trusting him with their deep dark secrets. Kottman (2002) suggests responding to clients' questions by first determining the intent of the question and then responding appropriately to that intent. Although her work is in the area of play therapy with youth, this recommendation seems broadly appropriate—when we understand the meaning and intent of the questions we are asked, we are better able to determine a therapeutically appropriate response.

A final important point in this conversation about the boundaries of the therapeutic relationship has to do with the extent to which the client and counselor are invested in the therapeutic work. Clients sometimes come to therapy discouraged, unconvinced about the seriousness of the problem, doubting their ability to change, and with few intentions around fully engaging in therapy or making any changes in their lives. For therapy to be effective, clients must be invested in the therapeutic process. Some clinicians respond to a client's questionable investment by encouraging, cheering, working harder, and becoming overly invested in the client's success. If the counselor is more invested in the therapeutic process than the client is, however, success will be hard to accomplish. Clinicians must maintain their therapeutic boundaries so that they are not more invested in the process than their clients are, and so that they are not doing all of the work of therapy for their clients. Here the point is that clinicians need to have boundaries around their own level of investment in the welfare of the client so that they are fully with him but not taking over the therapeutic process and its outcomes.

CONFIDENTIALITY

Confidentiality is the final component of the helping contract that we will mention here. Confidentiality refers to maintaining and protecting the privacy of the client and the helping contract. The ethical responsibility to maintain confidentiality refers to verbal, written, and all third-party communications regarding the clinical relationship and work with the client. This means not sharing information about a client and your work together unless you have the explicit (and typically written) consent of the client. It also means not acknowledging that you are in a clinical relationship with the client to others outside of your setting—this even extends to refraining from greeting the client in public unless you are approached by her first. The issue of maintaining client privacy is about trust and protection. It is so important, in fact, that there are a host of ethical and legal requirements around the protection of client confidentiality in clinical medical, mental health, and educational settings. These will be discussed in more detail in Chapter 3.

Table 1.2: The Helping Contract

Informed consent: The explicit part of the helping contract that articulates the commitment made to a client and what the therapist will be accountable for.

Professionalism: Maintaining the implicit commitments of the helping contract in a way that is consistent with professional competence and accepted norms of professional behavior within the context of the practice setting and community.

Nonmutuality: Insuring that the focus of therapy is always centered on the interests and needs of the client, not on the needs of the therapist.

Boundaries: The limits set by the clinician to assure that the therapeutic services are focused on the needs of the client and the agreements made in the helping contract and pose no undue burden on client or therapist.

Confidentiality: Clinician and agency actions that respect and protect client privacy.

CHAPTER SUMMARY

The work of clinical mental health professionals is encompassed in the terms *counseling*, *psychotherapy*, and *advocacy*, and these terms are often used interchangeably in the field. What sets the work of clinical helpers apart from nonclinical and medical helpers is the focus on and extensive training in the area of mental health and the specifics of the helping contracts they set with their clients. Research has revealed a number of factors that are associated with effectiveness in therapy. These include competence, intentionality, empathy, therapeutic alliance, the installation of hope, and promoting agency. The explicit parameters of the helping relationship are outlined in the informed consent process. Other unique features of the therapeutic contract include professionalism, nonmutuality, boundaries, and confidentiality. Many of the concepts reviewed in this chapter will be discussed in more detail in subsequent chapters in this book.

REFLECTION QUESTIONS

1. When might it be reasonable for a clinical therapist to move from the role of counselor and into the role of advocate? Was there a time in your life that a helper intervened with you or on your behalf in the role of advocate? Was that helpful (and if so, how) or not?

2. Empathy is identified as a necessary although not solely sufficient ingredient of change. Why is empathy important? Was there a time in your life when you needed to feel the empathy of a helper, but it was not there/it was not expressed appropriately? What was that experience like for you?

3. The research suggests that a wide variety of therapeutic modalities (i.e., the counseling orientation used in therapy) can be effective. What, then, determines what a therapist should use at a given time/with a particular client?

CHAPTER

Counselor Positioning and Cultural Competence

Chapter Outline

INTRODUCTION

An important premise of this chapter is that identity is a fluid construct that develops in social and cultural contexts. This is an idea that stands in contrast to some of the more long-standing, conventional, and colloquial notions of identity that describe it as a stable internal personality trait. We will also explore how systems of power and privilege influence social context and the ways in which individuals come to be known to self and others—how these factors influence identity development, as well as everyday experiences in the world.

We then move into an exploration of the concept of clinical cultural competence. Cultural competence is not easily defined, but we will refer to the literature that attempts to concretize it in terms of knowledge, attitudes, and skills that can help clinicians navigate some of the cultural and social nuances in therapeutic encounters. Positioning theory is introduced as a model for understanding how social norms structure the ways in which people interact with each other and how we think about identity. It offers a theoretical frame for helping clients navigate through some of the power dynamics that cause them difficulties in their lives. Positioning theory is also helpful to clinicians as they navigate through the complex influences of social location dynamics in their clinical therapeutic relationships.

SOCIAL AND CULTURAL FACTORS IN DEVELOPMENT

Communities, towns, states, and regions across the United States are vastly different from one another. Even within these communities, neighbors, families, and friends have different life experiences, ways of thinking, and divergent values and belief systems. Intuitively, we can comprehend how different experiences of gender, religion, spirituality, race, class, and even geography shape people's everyday experiences at home and in their community. For example, consider how identifying as Muslim, Christian, or Jewish shapes the values, beliefs, and rituals of everyday life for individuals in these specific communities. Also, we know that life in cities is vastly different from life in rural America. Finally, it is easy for some to forget that growing up with wealth offers more privilege, particularly with regard to material and educational options, than growing up in poverty. Social and cultural context influence our everyday experiences in the world; inarguably, social and cultural experiences also influence development. However, Sue and Sue (2003) point out that many traditional theories of human development, and more specifically, models of identity development, offer little in terms of explaining how development is influenced by cultural and social experiences. As a result, Sue and Sue (2003) conclude that theories of human development are at risk of offering biased, class-bound, culture-bound, and gender-bound conclusions about identity.

Sue and Sue (2003) present a tripartite framework that maps the complicated mix of universal, individual, and group influences on personal identity development (see Figure 2.1). *Universal* characteristics are those that are common to all humans. These are the things that make one person similar to another. In this category are biological and physical attributes—we all have vital body organs to maintain life, for example. Also, the ability to be self-aware and the ability to use language symbols for communication are included in this category. The idea is that all humans are similar in that they share these and some other universal characteristics. *Individual* characteristics are those features that make us unique. These include one's specific biological and genetic makeup, family and personal attributes, experiences that are not shared with others, and the unique ways in which one experiences a particular event, regardless of how that event is experienced by others. For example, a third-born child in a family has a different family experience than the first-born. Even identical twins have unique characteristics and experiences in the world. Sue and Sue (2003) argue that all of our experiences in family and community, as well as our unique biological and genetic structures, exert an influence on identity development. *Group* level experiences refer to the ways in which the beliefs, values, and practices of one's particular social or cultural group shape the identities of those within that group. For example, my father's parents immigrated to the United States when they were young adults, so he is considered a first-generation American. His cultural group affiliation

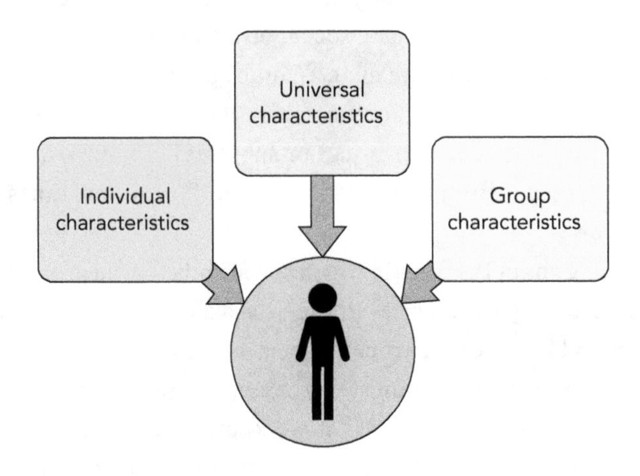

Figure 2.1 *Tripartite Framework*

as a child was Polish American. My father spoke Polish at home when he was growing up and still, some 90 years later, he has an affinity for polish sausage and *Chruściki,* the traditional sweet, crisp pastry made out of fried dough and sprinkled with powdered sugar. These are outward manifestations or artifacts of an identity that continues to have a significant place in my dad's perceptions of self and the world around him. As we will see shortly, social group affiliation is a powerful shaping influence on identity development.

Understanding how context, including social and cultural influences, gives meaning to people's behaviors and relationships is critical for understanding others, particularly when working across cultures. Some writers use the term *worldview* to talk about the ways in which individuals in various social groups interpret their experiences in the world and interact with others (Diller, 2007; Ivey, Ivey, & Zalaquett, 2010). The concept of worldview includes the attitudes, values, opinions, concepts, morals, and decision-making processes that are constructed from our racial, ethnic, gender, and other social group experiences (Davis, 2015; Sue & Sue, 2003). Most of these are passed down through generations. Worldview is the lens and the mediator for how we understand the world around us, as well as how we choose to behave (Sue & Sue, 2003).

Others use the metaphor of stories and narratives to describe the ways in which individuals develop understandings of self and others in the world. For example, Freedman and Combs (1996) assert that "people make sense of their lives through the narratives they construct in relation to the cultural narratives" (p. 32). That is, the dominant narratives within one's family, community, culture, and one's immediate social setting articulate normative ways of thinking and behaving. Freedman and Combs point out, however, that the values and ideas within dominant culture narratives are not always consistent with the beliefs and values of individuals or subgroups within a given society. The imposition of ideas from one culture onto another is sometimes referred to as *colonization*.

While thinking about the ways in which social and cultural group identities shape peoples everyday experiences in life, it is also important to remember that not all individuals within particular social or cultural group act or think the same. For this reason, we must be careful to not make assumptions about others' worldview based on what we know or think we know about their cultural or social group. Monk, Winslade, and Sinclair (2008) suggest that when defining a particular cultural group, a boundary is created that distinguishes between those within that group and those who do not fit in that group. Those who do not easily fit within a particular group—those who straddle the border between different identities—are in a position of what Monk et al. (2008) refer to as "border identities" (p. 33). In fact, most of us hold membership in multiple and overlapping social groups—this is an idea that is typically referred to as identity *intersectionality*. For example, while my father still holds values and beliefs and still at times engages in social practices that are reflective of his Polish American identity, he also moved from a position of being the poor son of extremely poor immigrant parents who did not speak the language of their new country to a well-educated, white-collar professional (thanks to the generous support of the post–World War II GI bill). This move into the upper middle class offered him access to another and very different social identity. Roccas and Brewer (2002) point out that some people hold simultaneous membership in multiple social groups and that social group identity may vary for individuals during different periods of their life or under various situations. For example, now that my father is 94 years old and long since retired from his career as an architect, he appears to be returning to his cultural practices of long ago. He now often craves the comforts of Polish cuisine, frequently speaks about his childhood growing up in New York City during the Great Depression, and seems more comfortable among the eastern European immigrants than the upper middle class retirees in his local community.

Intersectionality is complex, but it becomes even more so, Roccas and Brewer (2002) point out, when one holds membership in various social identity groups that have little overlap. These authors use the term *social identity complexity* to speak about the ways in which people navigate membership in various social or cultural groups. As an example of social identity complexity, let us consider a woman who is a corporate executive. Identifying as a woman and a corporate executive means that she holds identity claims in two very different social groups. Speaking to this complexity, consider that women occupy only about 6% of all CEO positions in the top Fortune 1000 firms (Helfat, Harris, & Wolfson, 2006). This means that while women corporate executives enjoy relatively high-paying and, perhaps, more prestigious jobs than many other working women, this position of privilege also sets them apart from other women. And, at the same time, they are not like their male corporate executive counterparts. Women in corporate America can expect to experience overt discrimination, sexual harassment, and, on the whole, earn less money than their male peers in comparable jobs and with the same level of education (Bell, McLaughlin, & Sequeira, 2002). They are also likely to experience unique health problems associated with their leadership positions (Nelson & Burke, 2000). A key variable in the complexity around navigating multiple and discordant social identities is the existence of overt and subtle power hierarchies that give unique meaning to the experiences of those within various social groups. "Understanding the structure of multiple social identities is important because representations of one's ingroups have effects not only on the self-concept but also on the nature of relationships between self and others" (Roccas & Brewer, 2002, p. 88). Not surprisingly, Roccas and Brewer claim that individuals who identify in a number of divergent social locations are likely to assume a more visible affiliation with the group that holds the highest status in a particular situation.

SOCIAL DISCOURSES AND IDENTITY DEVELOPMENT

Markers of social group identity—such as where one grows up and one's culture, ethnicity, religion, gender, age, sexual orientation, ability status, gender identity, and socioeconomic status—influence the ways in which individuals are perceived and treated by others (Pieterse, Lee, Ritmeester, & Collins, 2013; Sue & Sue, 2003). And, how we are viewed by others, it turns out, also influences how we come to view ourselves. As Monk et al. (2008) remind us, "It's not enough to just celebrate the rainbow of colors of diversity without taking seriously the ways in which cultural divisions lead to differential opportunities in life" (p. 49). Social location affects more than just self-perception; it influences who we become.

Foucault (1972) used the term *discourse* in reference to structuring ideas within a particular culture or social context. Discourses are the taken-for-granted assumptions about ourselves and others in the world; the meanings that sit behind our everyday understandings of our world (Winslade & Geroski, 2008). Van Langenhove and Harré's (1994) concept of *cultural stereotype,* which refers to "generalized expectations about how others are motivated, behave, feel, etc." (p. 360), is one way of explaining the concept of discourse. For example, "welfare mom" is a discourse that stories single mothers who struggle to make ends meet with low-paying jobs as being somehow deficit, lazy, and a burden to society. Many of us would like to deny that this discourse still holds social currency, but current political discussions on how we as a nation spend money confirm that poverty discourses such as this one are alive and well among us. We can also see that contemporary discourses about gender are clearly on display with the profusion of color-coded infant diapers, clothes, and child paraphernalia in department stores across America. They invite us to associate gender with traditional symbols of what it is like to be a boy or a girl, and many would argue that these symbols are codes for how girls and boys should dress and behave.

Discourses tend to have a norming influence on social behavior. As a result, they often go unquestioned. Why does it matter that diapers for girls are pink? It matters because pink represents a set of ideas about little girls and women that do not embody the total of women's experiences or desires in the world. Some women ascribe to pink, and others just don't. Discourses influence the interpretations that we make about events in our lives as well as descriptions of self—what narrative therapists call *identity claims* (Freedman & Combs, 1996). Prettiness, for example, is colloquially defined by popular ideas or discourses about beauty—and we use these ideas to make judgments about the beauty of self and others. We also can identify discourses about what it means to have a mental illness, about being gay, or about being an immigrant. Individuals who hold membership in these particular groups are affected by the social discourses that are typically associated with these identity claims, and all of them come with values regarding what society considers to be right, wrong, weird, strange, good, and bad. These ideas, in turn, structure the ways that individuals in these various groups not only see themselves, but also how they are perceived and treated by others. For example, many who experience mental illness see themselves as damaged, and this is reflected in our society that has struggled with the legacy of inhuman institutionalization and funding for their care. People who identify as gay have struggled long and hard to come out from under the grips of socially accepted definitions of what constitutes normal intimate relationships, including marriage.

> It would be nice if all the social groups to which people belonged were equally valued in our communities. ... A moment's reflection

on life in the United States at the moment, however, is enough to see that this situation does not exist. (Monk et al., 2008, p. 141)

The point is that discourses are not neutral; they are formulated in complex and unequal societies where some groups are privileged over others (Drewery, 2005). For example, Bertrand and Mullainthan (2004) found that with identical résumés, White job applicants are twice as likely as applicants of color to receive a callback for a job interview. Roth (2011) reported that in 2007 the median income of Black families was 61% of that of White families, and that young Black college graduates earn on average 11% less than their White counterparts. Shin, Smith, Welch, and Ezeofor (2016) reported that even practicing counselors and psychologists may engage in systemic racial practices in the ways in which they respond to potential client's requests for services. All of these experiences are not due to an individual client's cultural identity or worldview; they are due to the ways in which people of color are viewed and treated by others. They are a reflection of social location discourses and related inequities in our society. We will get back to these ideas shortly when we talk about micro-aggressions and sociocultural trauma (below).

CLINICIAN CULTURAL COMPETENCE

As we make sense of the ways in which discourses influence how we see ourselves and how we are treated by others, we need to take into account Sue and Sue's (2003) point that clinician multicultural competence must go beyond a discussion about sameness and difference. Cultural competence—and here we use this term most broadly to include race, ethnicity, age, ability status, sexual orientation, gender identity, religion, language, and socioeconomic status—must also acknowledge and address the influence of existing systems of power and privilege that benefit individuals from various social locations unequally (Andersen & Collins, 2004; Pieterse et al., 2013). As multiculturally competent clinicians, we need to be curious not only about how culture shapes development but also how discourses associated with various cultural and social group affiliations influence the everyday lives and experiences of our clients. Not only is this a good idea, the professional codes of ethics for counselors and social workers *require* us to engage in culturally competent practice (for example, see standards A.2.c., B.1.a., E.5.b., E.8., F.2.b., F.7.c. in the 2014 ACA Code of Ethics [American Counseling Association, 2014] and standards 1.05, 6.04, and the ethical principle of challenging social injustice in the National Association of Social Workers [NASW] Code of Ethics [NASW, 2008]).

TERMS

Racial classifications are typically used for US census data, research (Winker, 2004), and in public health conversations around determinants of health, health disparities, risk status, and access to resources—all of which are associated with race (Collins, 2004; Hahn & Stroup, 1994; Mays, Ponce, Washington, & Cochran, 2003). Understanding clients' racial, ethnic, and cultural identities can also help clinicians better know their clients and should factor into decisions regarding appropriate clinical practice (Cardemil & Battle, 2003; Pope-Davis & Liu, 1998; Sue & Sue, 2003). Having a clear sense of what is meant by race, ethnicity, and other social location identity categories is important in any discussion about service delivery and cultural competence, yet defining these terms is fairly complex. As it turns out, there is surprisingly little consensus regarding the exact definitions of these terms (Cardemil & Battle, 2003; Collins, 2004; Mays et al., 2003). In the words of Winker (2004), "race and ethnicity are constantly evolving concepts, deceptively easy to measure and used ubiquitously in the biomedical literature, yet slippery to pinpoint as definitive individual characteristics" (p. 1612). They are largely social constructs (Andersen & Collins, 2004; Monk et al., 2008; Waters, 2004) that are associated with historic and present systems of stratification and related social and institutional practices of discrimination (Andersen & Collins, 2004). Saying that these terms are social constructs does not in any way diminish the fact that racial, ethnic, and other identities are real and very important in people's lives. It just means that the definitions of these terms are not associated with distinguishable biological or genetic characteristics and that they are defined differently in different contexts.

Historically, the term ***race*** has referred to physical or assumed biological characteristics that were believed to be genetic in origin (Cardemil & Battle, 2003; Monk et al., 2008). However, there really are no genetic markers that define various racial groups, and there is a large amount of genetic diversity within individuals in groups that are classified by race (Winker, 2004). This, then, defies the idea that race is a fixed category (Andersen & Collins, 2004) and underscores the point that race is typically decided in fairly arbitrary ways.

Pope-Davis and Liu (1998) identify three commonly used and overlapping definitions of race that range from distinguishing race by common physical attributes such as skin color, to including the sociopolitical context of race in its definition recognizing that this includes domination and subjugation, and thirdly, using a cultural context that includes shared values, customs, and traditions in classifications of race. These ideas are in line with the words of Monk et al. (2008), who say, "Everyone thinks she knows what race means. Yet it remains a problematic concept" (p. 82). They also point out that race is a term that is associated with colonization. For these reasons, many authors (e.g., Freedman & Combs, 1996; Pope-Davis & Liu, 1998; Winker, 2004) suggest that individuals should self-designate their racial affiliation rather than have it defined for them by someone else.

Ethnicity typically refers to a shared common ancestry, language, use of cultural symbols, and in some cases, nationality, tribal affiliation, and religion among a group of people (American Psychological Association, 2008; Cardemil & Battle, 2003; Monk et al., 2008). For example, the foods that are commonly eaten, the music that is created and enjoyed, the customs or rituals displayed by members of various groups, as well as group image and a sense of identity based on shared values, beliefs, language, and history are typically considered one's ethnicity. Ethnicity is usually transmitted from one generation to another (Pope-Davis & Liu, 1998), although ethnic identities may also change across generations (Waters, 2004). Monk et al. (2008) also point out that belonging to a particular ethnic group should be based more on individual choice rather than institutional assignation.

Just as race and ethnicity are somewhat elusive concepts, **culture**, too, does not have a clear definition (Prochaska & Norcross, 2007). The American Psychological Association (2008) defines *culture* as a set of attributes—ideas, beliefs, and a system of meaning—that are created by and shared among members of a particular group. Culture, then, typically refers to the values, norms, and lifestyles of a particular social group that are transmitted generationally, largely through language and nationality, and culture gives meaning to people's experiences and behaviors (Hogan-Garcia, 1999; Monk et al., 2008; Sue & Sue, 2003). While there is ongoing debate about whether age, gender, socioeconomic status, sexual orientation, gender identity, and individuals who congregate around common spiritual or religious beliefs constitute distinct cultural groups (Collins & Arthur, 2010a), we do know that the experiences of people who identify within these categories shape how they understand and act in the world and how they are viewed by others (Sue & Sue, 2003). As Lee comments, culture "is an intensely personal phenomenon. … Culture as a construct can only really be comprehended by listening to personal narratives and trying to understand how people make meaning for their lives" (as cited in Monk et al., 2008, p. 28). This underscores Monk and colleagues' (2008) point that culture may be best described as a system of interpreting life, rather than a fixed set of practices and beliefs.

The term ***diversity*** is used both professionally and colloquially in a number of ways. Sometimes it refers to a collective of people in various racial and cultural groups. Tomlinson-Clarke (2013) suggests, for example, that *diversity* refers to "personal identity and individual differences" (p. 1). Other times it refers to people who identify in nondominant or minority racial groups. As an example, a teacher might comment that his classroom is very diverse. By that he means that it includes students from a variety of racial and cultural groups. In both of these referents, diversity is intended to convey that nondominant or racial minorities groups are accounted for. For others, diversity is defined in comparison to multiculturalism. Here, instead of focusing solely on race or ethnicity, it extends to other identity categories such as age, gender identity, sexual orientation, ability status, religion, and so forth as well (Arredondo et al., 1996). Used in a different context, we see *diversity* also used to identify social initiatives that are aimed at identifying or celebrating racial, class, and gender differences (Andersen & Collins, 2004). For example, a teacher might be in charge of leading a "diversity awareness" program in his school.

Social location is a term that attempts to capture the idea that one's social, racial, or ethnic group affiliation is part of a larger structure of social stratification (Kubiak, 2005; Pearlin, 1989). This term, like *diversity*, is inclusive of a variety of social and cultural identities. The term *social location* reminds us that identity is situated in contexts of power, privilege, and inequalities that exert subtle and overt influences on the perceptions and experiences of those in various social or cultural groups (Monk et al., 2008; Prochaska & Norcross, 2007). This is especially true, these authors remind us, for those who identify in nondominant or marginalized groups. For example, as mentioned earlier, race is associated with bias and discrimination that affects everything from job outlook and educational attainment to access to mental health services and experiences in everyday encounters with others, including clinical helping relationships. Sadly, privilege and bias associated with race is learned at a very early age (Van Ausdale & Feagin, 2001).

MICRO-AGGRESSIONS

The concept of ***micro-aggression*** is another important term in this discussion. Micro-aggressions are defined by Sue et al. (2007), as the "brief and commonplace daily verbal, behavioral, or environmental indignities, whether intentional or unintentional, that communicate hostile, derogatory, or negative racial slights and insults toward people of color" (p. 271). They are often expressed by individuals who are situated in dominant or privileged social groups (Sue, 2010; Smith, Geroski, & Tyler, 2014). Three types of micro-aggressions identified by Sue et al. (2007) include *micro-assaults*, which refer to intentional and explicit racial denigrations; *micro-insults*, which are more subtle racial putdowns that are likely to be unintentional; and *micro-invalidations*, which include the denying the lived experiences, thoughts, and feelings of people of color.

Micro-aggressions are often subtle—so subtle, in fact, that recipients are sometimes confused about whether they actually happened, or they may be so nuanced that they are difficult to understand (Smith et al., 2014). Part of this confusion is because they are typically expressed more passively than more overt forms of racism (Smith et al., 2014). Also, because micro-aggressions are part of a conditioning process of bias and prejudice that has widely permeated our culture to the point of being normalized (Sue et al., 2007), they often go unquestioned. This is why many well-meaning people, including clinicians, can commit micro-aggressions without even being aware of it.

In their study of racial micro-aggressions in therapy, Hook et al. (2016) found that the most common racial micro-aggressions reported by clients were micro-invalidations—denial of clients' experiences of bias or of being victim to stereotypes, and the avoidance (on the part of the therapist) of talking about cultural issues at all. These authors point out that counselor bias and racism expressed passively through micro-aggressions may be one reason for high premature therapy dropout rates among racial and ethnic minority clients. Not surprisingly, Hook et al. (2016) also report that micro-aggressions are associated with clients' perceptions that their counselors are not competent, with poor therapeutic alliance, with low levels of client psychological well-being, and with negative outcomes in therapy. Clients can easily become mistrustful and reluctant to engage in helping relationships when they perceive that their therapist is insensitive to their unique cultural and personal experiences (Day-Vines et al., 2007; Sue & Sue, 2008). These perceptions may be in response to something that the clinician has said or done, they may be because the therapist avoids talking about social location or any issues related to social location, or because something about the messaging from the clinician leaves clients anticipating that they will be misunderstood. And, of course, all of these result in yet another experience of marginalization for the client.

So, as clinicians, we must be vigilant about not replicating these experiences of marginalization in our therapeutic relationships. More concretely to this end, Hook et al. (2016) recommend that therapists learn about micro-aggressions, particularly those that are most likely to occur in therapy. They also suggest that clinicians initiate conversations about race (as well as other social location identities), explore how their social location may affect the counseling relationship, and conduct a thorough audit of their own biases and assumptions based on culture (and race, class, etc.). These important self-exploration initiatives lead to what these authors call "cultural humility" (Hook et al., 2016, p. 271), which is the ability to assume an other-oriented position in regard to the cultural identity. Cultural humility includes not only being sensitive to and respectful of the cultural identity of the client, but also being able to acknowledge one's own limitations and address relationship ruptures that result from these limitations.

SOCIOCULTURAL TRAUMA

Experiences of chronic stress and trauma, as will be discussed more in Chapter 4, can have adverse effects on one's emotional, cognitive, interpersonal functioning, and overall well-being (Baron-Cohen, 2011; Blaustein & Kinniburgh, 2010; Cook et al., 2005; Johnson, 2005; Mertin, 2014; Perry & Szalavitz, 2006; Rathus & Miller, 2015; Siegel, 2012). Fully understanding these effects of chronic stress and trauma, Hardy (2013) uses the terms ***racial trauma*** to talk about the ways in which one's experiences of micro-aggressions, institutional bias, and other overt or covert forms of racial and cultural oppression can also evoke trauma symptoms. That is, when individuals repeatedly experience marginalization, they are likely to develop trauma symptoms. Racial trauma,

Hardy (2013) points out, is a "traumatic form of interpersonal violence which can lacerate the spirit, scar the soul, and puncture the psyche" (p. 25).

More recently, Hardy (2017) also uses the term ***sociocultural trauma*** to speak about the ways in which bias, discrimination, and marginalization evoke trauma responses. This term acknowledges that people who identify in other marginalized social locations (other than race or ethnicity)—including gender identity, sexual orientation, ability status, religious orientation, and so forth—are also vulnerable to trauma response as a result of everyday assaults from bias and discrimination. Sociocultural trauma results from "some form of domination coupled with inequities based on differential access to power, influence, and resources" (Hardy & Laszloffy, 2005, p. 13). Adding insult to these injuries, we sometimes hear voices in larger society dismiss as unreal this notion that one can experience trauma as a result of bias and discrimination. Of course, this micro-invalidation is an additional assault to one's sense of self.

While all of the trauma symptoms described in Chapter 4 may be present for those who experience sociocultural trauma, Hardy (2013, 2017) emphasizes internalized devaluation, an assaulted sense of self, and internalized voicelessness as the *hidden wounds* of sociocultural trauma. Hardy says that when one experiences repeated assaults to one's dignity, shame and humiliation result; it is like sitting in "perpetual discomfort and [having] the perception of being less than" (personal communication, September 22, 2017). For those who sit in marginalized social locations, these messages of devaluation are repeated over time and become internalized. Thus, the first hidden wound of sociocultural trauma is *internalized devaluation*. Sadly, this often shows itself in self-destructive behaviors. For example, Hardy and Qureshi (2012) point out that the misuse of substances among urban African American youth is deeply rooted in the invisible wounds of devaluation. It also can lead to disruptions in the very communities that one needs for support, a profound experience of loss, and rage (Hardy & Laszloffy, 2005). In the therapy room, these experiences of chronic devaluation translate into a hypervigilance about gaining respect, an understandable sensitivity to messages that are experienced as disparaging, a reticence to trust the therapist, and barely restrained expressions of underlying rage.

An *assaulted sense of self* results from a culmination of recurring experiences of devaluation, including internalized devaluation (Hardy, 2013). It is difficult to formulate a healthy sense of self when one is constantly exposed to damaging social messages about who one is, particularly when those messages are juxtaposed to a relative absence of positive messages. This puts people in marginalized social locations in an untenable position of feeling anger at the repeated experiences of injustice and at the same time needing to suppress this anger as it then is used as "proof" of their inadequacies. When one experiences micro-aggressions and other forms of bias, "he either speaks up and risks appearing to be threatening or remains silent and has his sense of self further assaulted" (Hardy, 2013, p. 26). Hardy (2013) identifies this *voicelessness* as the third hidden wound of sociocultural trauma. Voicelessness results from a diminished or eroded ability to defend oneself from the barrage of unjustified and debilitating messages that one experiences when located in a marginalized social location. As we know, when anger is constantly in need of suppression, it does not go away. Instead, it continues to grow. Suppressed anger, Hardy & Laszloffy (2005) remind us, often grows into rage and violence. Misguided clinical interventions, often from well-intended therapists, often focus on these symptoms of rage rather than on the underlying wounds of unacknowledged sociocultural oppression. Hardy (2013) recommends interventions that include acknowledgment and affirmation, naming and creating a space for conversations about experiences of oppression, and working to externalize and counteract the client's experience of devaluation. We will speak more about the use of externalization shortly, and in Chapter 10, we return to this topic of sociocultural trauma in our discussion about deconstructing conversations.

DEFINING CULTURAL COMPETENCE

Very generally, *multicultural competence* refers to the knowledge and skills needed by clinicians for working with clients from diverse cultures (Hook et al., 2016). Similarly, the concept of *cultural competence* is used in reference to the knowledge and skills required to work with people from a wide range of social and cultural groups, particularly those in marginalized social locations. Having offered this very general definition, it is important to point out that in the literature, definitions of cultural competence can be somewhat obscure, and they vary considerably (Fields, 2010). This is largely because cultures are not clearly defined categories, and definitions and understandings about race, culture, and other social groups can be rather confusing. Added to this, a wide variation of individual differences exists even within categorical social group identities, meaning that universal "understandings" about members of a particular social group may not apply to all individuals within that group (Monk et al., 2008).

With these ambiguities, it is difficult to imagine how anyone could have "competence" regarding any particular culture, race, ethnicity, or social identity group. In fact, the whole notion of having *competence* regarding work with others, particularly with large groups of individuals, is misleading, as it suggests that competence is a definable stage or level of achievement. Competence is simply not that concrete. It is also difficult to imagine that cultural competence could be described as a set of interventions and techniques that are specific to work with members of specific social groups. Here again, we are left with a rather elusive idea of what exactly is meant by cultural competence. Acknowledging these important caveats, we will attempt to unpack, just a little more, what is meant by cultural competence in the field of mental health.

Very generally, cultural competence might be thought of as a set of attitudes, beliefs, knowledge, practices, policies, and structures that enable professionals to work effectively and respectfully with people who locate in various cultural and social groups. However, most authors point out (e.g., Arredondo et al., 1996; Collins & Arthur, 2010a; Hogan-Garcia, 1999; Sue, Arredondo, & McDavis, 1992; Sue & Sue, 2003) that cultural competence has more to do with awareness and the development of certain attitudes and knowledge than it has to do with a specific skill set. Because culture exists in a complicated and unjust sociopolitical context, Tomlinson-Clarke (2013) points out that an integral part of cultural competence is that clinicians must be willing and able to confront bias when they see it. Emphasizing this point, Monk et al. (2008) say, "if counseling practice is not based on addressing the effects of power relationships, we don't believe it is adequately multicultural" (p. 39).

Founded on the work of Sue, Arredondo, & McDavis (1992) and Arredondo et al., (1996), the American Counseling Association's multicultural and social justice counseling competencies, or MSJCC (Ratts et al., 2015) outline cultural competence in the developmental domains of *counselor self-awareness*, *client worldview*, *counseling relationship*, and *counseling and advocacy interventions*. Within these domains are descriptions of competence in regard to counselor *attitudes and beliefs*, *knowledge*, *skills*, and *actions*.

The intent of this model is to map out the intersection of counselor and client social identities within the context of power, privilege, and oppression. We will explore each of these domains in more detail.

COUNSELOR SELF-AWARENESS

The American Counseling Association's MSJCC model (Ratts et al., 2015) begins with a call to counselors to be aware of their own social identities and the attitudes, beliefs, privileges, assumptions, and biases that are associated with those identities. It calls on counselors to make a commitment to actively develop their knowledge and skills around social identity. To this end, counselors need to be engaged in a process of questioning and challenging their own biases, negative reactions, and preconceived notions about others, and they also must be able to recognize their own limitations (Arredondo et al., 1996). The presence of bias is often signaled by a feeling of discomfort; working with people who identify in social locations that are different from

Photo 2.1 *We don't always see ourselves in the ways that others see us to be.*

our own requires us to be uncomfortable. A key point here is that clinicians must explore their own discomfort around difference and seek consultation and supervision at all times.

CLIENT WORLDVIEW

In the MSJCC framework (Ratts et al., 2015), the second focus is on the worldview of the client. Here the emphasis is on the importance of being aware of the assumptions, attitudes, values, and experiences of power, privilege, or oppression that may be associated with the client's worldview or social location. Understanding the client's worldview compels counselors to be active in acquiring knowledge about the historical and sociopolitical factors that shape people's lives and to understand the experiences of marginalization that clients may experience in regard to their social location or identities. Skills in this domain include acquiring culturally responsive assessment, critical-thinking, theory-application, analytic-thinking, conceptualization, and communication skills. In terms of action, clinicians must always work to increase their own self-awareness (Ratts et al., 2015). Arredondo et al. (1996) remind us that cultural competence is strengthened when we engage with individuals from various social locations or social groups. That is, we can develop cultural competence through having meaningful personal relationships with people who are culturally different from ourselves. This is an important suggestion, as it compels us to take personal action to broaden ourselves culturally by stepping out of our own comfort zone and into the lives of people whom we perceive to be different.

COUNSELING RELATIONSHIP

The therapeutic relationship is not immune to the effects of power, privilege, and oppression. In fact, we know that these systems of inequities can easily be reenacted in therapy. The MSJCC model (Ratts et al., 2015) calls on counselors to be aware of how their own attitudes and beliefs are juxtaposed to those of their clients, particularly in the context of power, privilege, and oppression, and to be aware of how all of that plays out in the helping relationship. Beyond awareness, counselors should also be open to diverse approaches to helping and expand their cross-cultural communication skills. The MSJCC model also asserts that counselors need to be committed to updating their knowledge about the different cultures and social groups within which their clients identify, and the model points out that these understandings should include the ways in which history, politics, and current issues affect the everyday lives as well as experiences of therapy for clients. Collins and Arthur (2010b) emphasize that collaboration should be the guiding principle when working with clients who identify in social locations that are different from the therapist's, and particularly when clients identify in social locations that are marginalized in larger society. A foundation of mutual trust and respect, Collins and Arthur point out, is at the heart of effective cross-cultural helping relationships.

COUNSELING AND ADVOCACY INTERVENTIONS

To attend only to the most visible artifacts of a client's cultural or social identity misses the important point that identity is also created in a social context that for many includes oppression and discrimination (Collins & Arthur, 2010b). When we are witness to the adverse effects of social forces on the lives of our clients, advocacy may be the most appropriate helping strategy. As mentioned in Chapter 1, advocacy refers to actions that are aimed at the social and/or institutional challenges and the barriers that interfere in people's lives. The final component of the MSJCC model (Ratts et al., 2015), then, calls for clinicians to act with or on behalf of their clients at all levels, as necessary.

Advocacy has to do with assuming the role of change agent—it is about speaking up and speaking out (Bemak & Chung, 2005). For example, Bemak and Chung (2008) point to a charge in the literature for school counselors to "move beyond the use of traditional services by implementing more proactive approaches to ameliorate the academic achievement gap" (p. 373). Here the recommendation is to focus on the social and institutional barriers that make it difficult for children in marginalized social locations to succeed. Lee and Rodgers (2009) describe advocacy in this way: counselors must

> move beyond the passivity often inherent in counseling as "the talking cure" to become active voices and conduits for social/political change at the macrolevel of intervention. … The ultimate goal of counselor intervention at this level is to increase public awareness, affect public policy, and influence legislation. (p. 285)

Photo 2.2 *Advocacy is about lifting others up.*

In the MSJCC model (Ratts et al., 2015), advocacy may include work on the intrapersonal and interpersonal levels as well as institutional, community, and larger public policy work nationally or globally.

Lewis, Arnold, House, and Toporek (2002) emphasize that the distinction between acting *with* versus acting *on behalf* of others has to do with the locus of responsibility for decisions and action. When advocating *with* a client, it is the client who makes decisions and takes actions; the role of the clinician is to assist in these processes. So, the clinician may help the client identify the problem to be addressed, participate in brainstorming various solutions, and set goals with the client. Ultimately, however, it is the client who makes the decisions and takes action. Acting on *behalf* of a client has more to do with doing *for* rather than *with* the client. Clinicians would only assume this role of acting on behalf of someone when that person is unable to make a decision, unable to take action by himself, and in other unique circumstances.

As an example, let us look at when Alaya came to Ms. K, a school counselor, to talk about a fight she had with her mother. Ms. K talked to Alaya about the situation and asked Alaya how she thought the situation should be handled. Alaya pointed out that the fight was based on a misunderstanding and said that she wanted to see if she could clear up the misunderstanding with her mother that night when she got home from school, even though she indicated that she wasn't sure what exactly to say to her mother. Ms. K had a good relationship with Alaya's mother and thought that she could make a quick call to ease the situation for Alaya, but, committed to taking a working *with* approach rather than on behalf of her client whenever possible, she did not offer to make the phone call. Instead, noting Alaya's comment that she wasn't sure what to say to her mother, Ms. K offered to briefly role-play the conversation with Alaya, and she checked in with Alaya a few days later to see how things went. If, on the other hand, Alaya had reported that her mother was physically abusing her, Ms. K would ethically and legally be obligated to report the allegation of abuse to appropriate social welfare authorities. In this situation, she would be advocating *on behalf* of her client. Even when working on behalf of others, however, it is important to work as collaboratively as possible, given the circumstances. In this case, Ms. K would probably talk to Alaya about her role as a mandated reporter, and she would be as transparent as possible regarding what was likely to happen after the report was made.

A caution is warranted here. It is critical that clinicians be aware of the ways in which acting with or on behalf of others can have unforeseen and adverse consequences. It seems straightforward that acting on behalf of a client who is suicidal and unable to protect himself, for example, is imperative in order to assure safety. However, speaking out on behalf of a client who has experienced racism is not as clear. In this example, is important not to expose clients to potential danger, particularly if they do not have sufficient information or ability to weather the aftermath of strong actions taken on their behalf. Also, as the above example with Alaya alludes, we must always consider the impact of our actions—with or on behalf of others—in terms of promoting agency. The point of advocacy is to give movement to systems that hinder healthy growth and development; taking action for someone may move systems but may also leave the client dependent on us for future actions. Engaging in collaborative decision making to the extent that it is possible, offering options, and promoting agency, even in those situations when it is clear that the clinician must take action for the client, should always be at the center of all advocacy actions.

Returning to the MSJCC model (Ratts et al., 2015), there are multiple options regarding the target audience for advocacy interventions: intrapersonal (individual), interpersonal (family, friends, peers), institutional (social institutions such as schools, churches, and community organizations), community, public policy, or international or global systems. Advocacy on the *individual level* focuses working with or on behalf of a particular individual in a specific situation. For example, you may help a client research a medication so that she can make her own decision regarding a prescription she received for depression. At the *interpersonal level*, you may organize a family meeting to discuss the next steps in their decision making regarding the care of an older family member. At the *institutional level*, you may work with your client to speak up about an injustice he has seen at his university. Or you may speak up anonymously and more generally on his behalf with university personnel regarding that particular issue. Advocacy at a *community level* may entail, for example, attending and speaking out at a public comment session of the city council that is focused on the closure of a homeless encampment where some of your clients currently reside. Addressing advocacy at a *public policy level* may include engagement in public awareness campaigns regarding legislative action and policy reform. At an *international or global systems level*, your advocacy efforts may include being educated and speaking out about world events regarding a particular subject, fund-raising for a specific cause, or engaging in volunteer or paid employment with a disenfranchised group.

POSITIONING THEORY

Positioning theory was first introduced into the field of psychology by Harré and his colleagues (see Harré & Moghaddam, 2003; Harré & Van Langenhove, 1991) as a way of examining how social interactions unfold according to local and typically unspoken rules of engagement and the processes by which individuals construct meaning (Harré & Moghaddam, 2003). Positioning theorists are particularly interested in how history, culture, and social context dictate the ways in which individuals are invited into and participate in social interactions.

Positioning theory is not typically included in clinical helping skills or counseling theory texts. That is probably due to many reasons, one of which is that it is more of a theory about interactions than it is a theory about development, personality, identity, or a clinical modality. It is included here, however, because understanding positioning theory and applying its principles to therapeutic clinical work is an excellent way to engage in culturally competent work with clients.

BASIC TENETS OF POSITIONING THEORY

One way in which positioning theory looks to understand human interaction is by focusing on how individuals participate in conversations (Davies & Harré, 1999). Of particular interest are the ways in which invitations to speak in conversations and social interactions are governed by unspoken social conventions (Harré & Moghaddam, 2003). To better understand what this means, let us look at some of the terminology used in positioning theory.

Position, sometimes referred to as *subject position*, refers to the relative authority or standing that one has in a social interaction. One's standing in a social interaction dictates the role that that person assumes (Drewery, 2005). For example, the director of an agency typically holds the responsibility for the decisions that are made in the agency and is typically afforded a wide berth to carry out those decisions. He typically calls meetings, sets agendas, and approves or disapproves final decisions. He is "the boss." The term *boss*, of course, is saturated in discourses that conjure an image of someone who is both in charge and holds power. This position of authority follows the rules and conventions of how we envision businesses or agencies to normally function.

Subject positions dictate *speaking positions*. Speaking positions are the "permissions" that people are granted in terms of how they are to act and respond in conversations in various social engagements. An individual who has the most authority or social capital in a particular social situation is positioned to dictate the terms of the social interactions and the kinds of conversations that will happen within that encounter. She invites others into discussions in particular ways and makes decisions about the direction of where those conversations will go. In many offices, for example, the boss decides what items will be discussed at team meetings, whose opinion is elicited, when the focus should shift to someone or something else, when the discussion is over, when the next meeting should occur, and what that next agenda should be. Of course, office cultures vary in the extent to which they promote authoritarian leadership, so the extent to which one person is in the position of issuing position calls depends on the setting.

We all step into different subject roles as we move from one environment or setting to another. That is, our subject position varies across the different social groups we inhabit. When the director of a human service agency goes home, she may have less speaking authority over her family members, and when she steps onto the curb of the street to hail a taxi, she may have little to no power whatsoever. She can only request, not direct, taxi drivers to stop and give her a ride.

A *position call* is an invitation to interact in a specific way in a particular social encounter. For example, when a client comes into the office to see a clinician, there are particular social dynamics that structure this encounter. Oftentimes, the client waits in a waiting room until he is called, and then the clinician typically initiates the encounter by issuing a position call—perhaps by introducing herself and then, maybe, by asking the client what he would like help with. Notice how position calls are structuring statements that communicate an expectation for a particular type of response. If the clinician wants to conduct an intake interview, a question/answer format position call is issued. If the clinician prefers to initiate the encounter in a more open-ended way, the position call may grant more leeway for the client to decide the direction of the conversation. For example, "What would be helpful to talk about today?" is a different call than "On a scale of 1–10, how would you rate your depression?" The point here is that mental health counseling sessions tend to be structured by certain rules of engagement that afford relative power to the clinician, enabling him to issue position calls. Some clinicians, of course, work to equalize these relationships as much as possible by being transparent in their work and inviting clients to participate in clinical decision making. Power dynamics may be enacted in other ways, as well. Other influences—from family members, loved ones, and insurance companies, for example—may exert pressure for clients to pursue goals and follow intervention plans that they may not wholeheartedly agree with.

When we have the status to dictate what happens in a social encounter, we are in what is referred to as an *agent position*. A *subjugated* or *passive position* results when we are invited into a compromised or stepped-down position (Drewery, 2005). For example, a teacher issues speaking rights in a classroom—students follow suit. A coach makes decisions about who will play the next game. At home, parents often make decisions about schedules, meals, and other activities of daily family life. And clients—not all clients, of course, but many—come into therapy with their disadvantaged positions heavy in tow. They may feel uninspired, trampled, helpless, or anxious, and they often inhabit subjugated speaking positions in some or many venues of their lives. Discourses saturated in power dynamics, positions of privilege, hierarchical social structures, and markers of social capital invite speaking positions and influence the rules of engagement in most social encounters. These positions on offer occur for clients, of course, both in and out of the clinician's office.

Importantly, position calls can be accepted or resisted (Van Langenhove & Harré, 1994). That is, any of us can resist a position call on offer. This is called *repositioning.* For example, a student who talks back to the teacher may be vying for a more powerful position in the classroom. A woman who refuses to answer an inappropriate question is taking a stand, and in doing so, she is challenging the position that is being offered in that social encounter. Similarly, a client who refuses to talk about a particular issue in therapy may be repositioning himself—may be stepping into an agent position—so that he is more in charge of what is discussed in therapy. This latter example helps us understand why it is so critical for clients to be involved in therapy decisions and why intervention plans must be constructed with rather than for clients.

DISCOURSES AND POSITION CALLS

A final important point here is about how social discourses play a role in how position calls are issued. Recall that discourses are "ways of speaking that reflect interwoven sets of power relations" (Drewery, 2005, p. 313). Discourses shape how individuals interact with each other; thus, they affect the offering of position calls in social encounters. For this reason, Drewery and Winslade (1997) argue that discourses are *prescriptive*.

For example, clinicians sometimes find that when they reveal to others that their day job entails being a therapist, those people—and on occasion this even happens with complete strangers—sometimes spontaneously begin to reveal their innermost secrets. Or conversely, other people may completely clam up, commenting that they don't want to be "analyzed." Therapy discourses are saturated with notions of Freudian psychoanalysis where the client reveals her inner dark secrets lying on a couch while a cold distant therapist listens and takes notes.

I am being overly dramatic, here, of course. But the point is that the work of mental health clinicians is storied by discourses, and many of these discourses are influenced by traditional notions about psychotherapy. We also

Photo 2.3 *Psychoanalysis on the couch still colors some therapy discourses.*

are witness to discourses about moms, for example, and these are different from doctor discourses—both clearly invite different expectations, different conversations, and different perceptions of social capital. Gay, straight, Black, or White markers of identity are also shaped by ideas and conventions—discourses—that are molded by social capital or power and that dictate different position calls in different social encounters. Of course, there are always multiple discourses operating in every social encounter and all of us have the opportunity to accept or decline subject positions on offer. But it is not hard to see the powerful and unquestioned influence that discourses have in shaping even the most benign encounters of everyday life—for us and for the clients we serve.

POSITIONING THEORY IN PRACTICE

Positioning theory offers a lens for understanding some of the situations that may be problematic for clients, particularly those who identify in marginalized social locations. It invites examination of the various *discursive positions*—position calls from discourses—that are on offer and gives us a language for speaking about the influence of discourses in everyday life.

Inviting clients to examine the discourses that offer unfavorable position calls helps in the resistance against these untenable power positions. Understanding the ways in which power dynamics are socially constructed creates a unique opportunity for influencing different conversations, different social interactions, and to grab hold of new and different identity conclusions. Having a name and a way to talk about all of this helps us engage in conversations with clients that have the potential to promote thoughtful and creative options for change.

Positioning theory also reminds us—as we have discussed—that position calls are issued and subject positions are taken up in clinical relationships as well. Even before the clinician and client meet, the clinical relationship is structured by discourses and practices from which the helping is negotiated (Winslade, Crocket, & Monk, 1997). The rules of engagement in most clinical relationships—the explicit rules, policies, and agendas—are typically based on conventions that privilege clinician knowledge, insight, education, training, and skill over that of their clients. And these relationships also credit clinicians with do-good social capital (i.e., "how wonderful that they are helping others who are less fortunate") as well. In contrast, clients often arrive at the clinician's office with their named deficits in hand—positioned, sometimes, as needy, damaged, and unstable. These positions on offer typically invite limited client agency in the helping process. So, when clinicians appropriately attend to power influences in the therapeutic relationship, they can invite their clients into agency by putting them in charge of clinical decisions and thinking about how to carry those decisions into life outside of the office. The helping skills discussed in Section II of this text are skills that can be used to invite agent positions in the helping process.

CASE EXAMPLE OF POSITIONING THEORY

Omar is a 17-year-old young man living with foster parents and attending a local high school. He has been living in and out of foster homes for much of his life as his parents struggled to maintain sobriety and to care for him. He has been in his current foster home for 3 years, and it has been going fairly well. Parental rights were terminated a year ago, and for continuity reasons, his current foster family agreed for him to live in their care until he turns 18 and graduates from high school. In therapy, Omar and his therapist often address difficulties that he has had both at school and at home related to what many refer to as "anger management problems." The last "blowup" occurred when Omar fumed out of a meeting with his foster mother, social worker, and school counselor during a discussion about future planning. Omar had dreams of moving across the country, attending college, and perhaps playing intercollegiate soccer. These hopes were parallel to those of many of his peers at school. At that meeting, the school counselor pointed to his poor academic record and suggested that "due to his difficult background, it might not be such a good idea to be so far away." Instead, the school counselor suggested that Omar go to a local community or state college first to raise his grades and perhaps play soccer, and then apply to one of the other colleges on his list. Upon hearing this suggestion, Omar shouted, "When are you going to stop calling me a 'freak' and telling me what I can*not* do?" He then ran out of the meeting. Later that day, when the social worker tried to talk to him about what happened, pointing out that running out of the meeting just reinforced what they were saying about his anger management problems and proved that he was not ready to leave home next year. Omar, again, resisted this story of deficit by sitting in silence refusing to say anything.

Let us stop here briefly to think about the possibility that discourses about children of alcoholics and foster children, however helpful they may be to some, may have issued position calls to Omar that he did not want. That his running from the room and sitting in silence were actions of resistance to the discursive position calls on offer. We might even imagine that if his ethnic identity further located him in a marginalized social location, he likely also experienced some forms of sociocultural trauma. At the same time, expressions of anger in response to these experiences of sociocultural trauma could easily be dismissed as psychopathology related to his other experiences of trauma (recall Hardy's (2013) concept of *voicelessness*). In this scenario, we might notice, too, that all of the adults in the room during the meeting exerted some form of power over Omar's life. The position calls on offer to Omar appeared to be saturated with ideas around incompetence, instability, not being ready or able to realize the hopes and dreams he had for himself. However true these prognoses might someday turn out to be, they amounted to some form of a subjugated position call to Omar. His running from the room and later sitting in silence may not have been hugely effective, but we can see that a refusal to participate in these conversations allowed him some power in the moment. These actions might be thought of as Omar's attempts to reposition himself.

In recounting this incident with his therapist at a later time, Omar said, "I hate being 'not normal.'" The therapist asked him to talk a little bit about the effects of "not normal" on his life. They discovered that Omar had been living under the influence of "not normal" for a very long time and that when "not normal" is around, he often gets angry and does things that get him in trouble. He also said that he sometimes regrets that he loses control and causes problems for himself and those who care about him. The scripted positions on offer about children of alcoholics, being a foster child, carrying a diagnosis of attachment disorder, and the experiences of internalized devaluation conjure a story of Omar as deficient, angry and potentially violent, or perhaps, someone well deserving of our pity. Certainly there are few positions on offer from these narratives that invite Omar into a position of strength or success.

As Drewery (2005) pointed out, discourses can become the organizing plot for how individuals come to see themselves, the world around them, and also for how they are seen by others. In our example, we see that even Omar's actions of resistance—his refusal to engage in conversations that did not fit with his own hopes and dreams—were woven back into the stories of deficit. He had "anger management problems." With a dominant story line of being somehow damaged due to the effects of the circumstances of his life and the silencing of experiences of sociocultural trauma, the story of "not normal" is a huge force in Omar's life. It easily becomes the lens that is used to explain Omar's behavior and offer prognoses on what his future holds.

In our example above, you may notice the therapist's use of *externalizing language* (White & Epston, 1990) when he asks Omar to talk about the effects of "not normal" in his life. This is an approach used by Michael White and other narrative therapists to speak about problems as being located outside of people. It signals an understanding that a person is not solely identified as the problem he is facing. Asking Omar about the effects of "not normal" on his life suggests that his difficulty is something temporary like a cold or blister on his foot and separates the problem from who he is—from his identity. As will be discussed more in later chapters, this practice of externalizing has the effect of reducing blame and defensiveness and enables clients to become self-reflective and engaged in critical thinking about the problems they face (Freeman, Epston & Lobovits, 1997). The therapist in our example might also become curious about the ways in which Omar resists "not normal"; how shouting and leaving the room might show that Omar knows that he is not—stay with me here—that Omar knows that he is *not* "not normal." Instead of offering strategies for how Omar could better manage his outbursts, because offering such strategies positions the therapist as an expert, the therapist might wonder out loud what it says about Omar that he was so eager to fight against the idea that he was not normal.

It should be pointed out that foster child discourses, for example, may invite Omar to see himself as damaged, but they also have the potential to tell a story about strength, overcoming adversity, or simply that one's identity is not simplified into one aspect of their experience. That is, one can have challenges in their life and also just be like everyone else at school—what Omar thinks about as "normal." As Freedman and Combs (1996) point out, there are many possibilities for interpreting one's experiences in the world, yet it is often the case that a single narrative can dominate one's perception of self and make it difficult to see oneself in any other way. *Deconstructing conversations*, which are discussed in more detail in Chapter 10, invite clients to interrogate the stories that are told about them as well as the discourses that belie those stories. They invite clients to see themselves and view experiences from different perspectives and to construct alternative meanings and preferred identity conclusions (Freedman & Combs, 1996).

To this end, in our example the therapist might ask Omar how it could be possible that he has lived "normally" with his foster family for so long if he wasn't normal. He might also be curious about what kinds of things Omar does to make the foster placement so successful. Let us suppose that Omar reports that he contributes to the household by helping make dinner, mowing the grass, watching his younger sister, and going on family camping trips. The therapist might wonder if there might be a little bit of "normal" with the "not normal" in his life? The therapist could ask Omar to bar graph the extent to which "normal" inhabits his life in comparison to "not normal." They might also explore the times and circumstances which enable "not normal" to creep its way into Omar's life and make him feel so angry and do things he later regrets. This is not to say that Omar's experiences of marginalization are not real, it is just to help him become aware of when they trigger him and to help him become more agent in determining his own identity—to how he wants to define himself (i.e., *his* identity conclusions) and how he wants to be seen by others.

Positioning theory, then, gives us a language for speaking about the influence of problematic stories and discourses in people's lives. Inviting clients to examine the stories and discourses that have untenable positions on offer helps them resist the effects of these stories and opens up space for clients become more agent in their own lives.

CHAPTER SUMMARY

In this chapter, we discussed the ways in which identity is constructed from beliefs, values, and experiences in the social and cultural contexts of our lives. These contexts also include formidable external forces, including discourses that rise from uncontested systems of power and privilege. When clinicians understand how the everyday experiences of disempowerment and lack of social capital influence people's beliefs, values, hopes, and behaviors, they are better able to understand the challenges that many clients bring to therapy. Cultural competence was described as a process rather than skill that includes awareness of self, other, and worldview. It also includes being able to develop a therapeutic relationship that recognizes social context and using counseling and advocacy approaches to effect change in clients' lives. Positioning theory was introduced as a model for understanding the effects of disempowering discourses in people's lives and for navigating complex social relationships, including the therapeutic relationship.

REFLECTION QUESTIONS

1. What are the various social locations you inhabit? What discourses exist about these social locations?

2. What can a therapist do to equalize the distribution of power in the therapeutic relationship?

3. How might a therapist encourage clients to step into agent positions in their social relationships with others outside of therapy?

CHAPTER

Ethical Principles for Therapeutic Relationships

Chapter Outline

INTRODUCTION

The counseling relationship is distinctively nuanced, creating challenges that can sometimes be difficult to navigate. Even very experienced and well-intentioned clinicians encounter complicated situations that present ethical and legal challenges. Mental health professional organizations have codes of ethics that articulate the moral principles and ethical responsibilities of clinical helpers in their various disciplines. In addition, clinicians must abide by agency rules and policies as well as state and national legal statutes that also guide their clinical decision making. These policies, codes, and laws are designed to provide a degree of accountability and assurance to the consumer, and they also serve as a road map for clinicians, guiding them through some of the complexities that may arise in helping.

We begin the discussion in this chapter by defining key terms related to ethics in helping. Then we proceed with a discussion about the basic moral principles that underlie the codes of ethics in mental health professions as well as a review of some basic ethical and legal concepts that are important for all clinical professionals. We end with an outline of a moral decision-making model that can help clinicians navigate complicated ethical and potentially legal challenges.

DEFINITIONS OF KEY ETHICAL TERMS

The word ***value*** is often used colloquially in reference to the personal preferences and ideas that we view to be salient in our lives. Values might be thought of as our fundamental beliefs about what is important. For example we might say that we "value the environment" or that we "value the sanctity of marriage." These are examples of what Kitchener and Anderson (2011) referred to as *personal values*. How these personal values fit into our professional roles, however, can be a little complicated. For example, Kitchener and Anderson (2011) point out that while individuals are free to hold their own personal values, when they choose to identify in a particular profession, they are obliged to adopt the values that are promoted by that profession. *Professional values*, then, are the ideas and ideals that are considered appropriate or tolerated within a particular profession. In the words of Kitchener and Anderson (2011), "by becoming a member of the profession, a psychologist or counselor forgoes the right to hold certain values by virtue of his or her place in a larger system" (p. 9).

Morals refer to ideas held about the character and conduct of self and others (Kitchener & Anderson, 2011). The term comes from the concept of morality and is generally used in reference to an expectation about what is appropriate within a particular social group (Gert, 2012). That is, morals are ideas about what is right, wrong, good, and bad. ***Ethics*** goes beyond the evaluation of what is good and bad, and so forth, and addresses questions about how people should act toward each other—the moral responsibility that people (and especially professionals) have in social and professional encounters (Kitchener & Anderson, 2011). Although these terms—*values*, *morals*, and *ethics*—are often used interchangeably, Kitchener and Anderson (2011) clarify that "normative ethics does not merely describe moral ideals held by human beings but asks which ideal is better than others, which ideal is more worth pursing and why" (p. 3). Ethics, then, address the question "What shall I do?" (Barnett & Johnson, 2015, p. 4). Thus, ethics might best be thought of as the action arm of personal and professional values and morals; ethics help us decide what is right or wrong and how to act accordingly (Corey, Corey, & Callanan, 2003).

A ***code of ethics*** is the application of normative ethics within a professional discipline for the purpose of structuring behavioral expectations (Kitchener, 1984). Codes of ethics represent a sort of "cumulative wisdom" (Kitchener & Anderson, 2011, p. 18) within a profession and attempt to establish a set of rules or guidelines for practitioners. Often also called *professional ethics,* ethical codes provide a map for how to navigate complex ethical territories. Sommers-Flanagan & Sommers-Flanagan (2004) assert that "a good code of ethics defines the professional knowledge base, describes the activities sanctioned in the profession, and provides a clear picture of the boundaries of professional activity" (p. 17). Professional codes of ethics, then, might also be thought of as the embodiment and articulation of the values held by a particular professional organization. In the professional disciplines of helping, they also articulate who one is as a professional counselor, social worker, psychologist, school counselor, and so on.

It is important to point out that while codes of ethics serve as an embodiment of a professional identity and serve to guide for professional behavior, most professional organizations also pose consequences to clinicians when they breach their professional code of ethics. For example, one's membership in the organization may be revoked as a result of a breach in professional ethics. The imposition of consequences is a way for professional organizations to monitor the behaviors of practitioners—an action intended to protect the rights of clients. We will return to this idea shortly.

Laws and policies are related to ethics as they also dictate behavioral expectations for helpers and they guide clinical practice. ***Laws*** are the rules that are established by courts or legislative processes that govern particular activities within society. They are, theoretically, created to maintain order. ***Policies*** are the rules and principles that articulate and guide the practice in a particular agency, organization, or business. As we know, a failure to abide by legal mandates may carry legal consequences. Many agencies have consequences for breaches in their policies as well, but these consequences are governed by the organization, not the legal system. For example, most mental health agencies have specific policies regarding the format of and time lines for completion of client records. A failure to abide by such policies may result in being terminated from working within the agency, but it is not likely to have legal consequences unless a particular law was also violated.

Table 3.1: Helping Ethical and Legal Definitions

CONCEPT	DEFINITION
Values	The fundamental beliefs about the importance or relative worth of something. Personal values are those ideas and beliefs that are held individually; professional values are those held by a profession, institution, or affiliated group.
Morals	Ideas about character and conduct—what is considered right, wrong, good, and bad. An articulation of an expectation about what is appropriate within a particular group.
Ethics	The evaluative branch of a personal or professional belief structure that is the foundation for rules regarding behavior or actions.
Code of ethics	An articulated set of principles established by a particular group that structures behavioral standards for members within that group.
Laws	Rules about behavior that have been established by courts or legislative processes. They carry legal consequences if violated.
Policies	Articulated rules of conduct established by agencies, businesses, or organizations. The consequences for rule infractions are governed by the agency (business or organization).

We began this chapter with mention of personal values because our own personal values as well as our own personal worldview affect how we understand and respond to ethical situations and decisions (Davis, 2015; Dollarhide & Saginak, 2012). This is one of the reasons we have professional codes of ethics. Professional values, codes of ethics, policies, and laws are designed to assure that the work we do in clinical helping is client-focused, appropriate, just, and safe for the clients who are in our care.

It can be helpful to think of ethics as a focus on what one *should* do. Laws, on the other hand, might best be thought of as what one *must* do. Ideally, what one must do is the same thing as what one should do. For example,

Photo 3.1

murder is clearly an unethical and illegal behavior. Cheating on an exam is not illegal; however, in most circles it is clearly considered an unethical behavior. But, clinical helping is complex and these distinctions are not always clear. The codes of ethics of many mental health professional organizations attempt to clarify complex ethical questions. They are also hugely influential to the state licensing of mental health practitioners. So, professional codes of ethics may have enforcement potential through employers, laws, and/or according to legal precedent, if litigation is involved. This is another reason why it is important for helpers to be knowledgeable about and follow both the ethical mandates of their profession and local, state, and federal laws that are related to their work.

MORAL PRINCIPLES FOR HELPERS

The helping professions discussed in this text have a set of standards articulated as codes of ethics that, as mentioned, attempt to address the ethical responsibilities of practitioners in their specific disciplines. Kitchener (1984) points out, however, that there often are "inherent contradictions and gaps in codes of ethics which give the professionals minimal guidance when faced with a decision of ethical consequence" (p. 43). We know that professional codes of ethics are not perfect, and clearly, it is not possible for them to address every specific dilemma that a practitioner may encounter.

Fortunately, the professional codes of ethics in the various mental health disciplines are grounded in underlying ethical theories or foundational moral principles (Beauchamp & Childress, 2013). Understanding these moral principles is helpful because they articulate the values that are most salient to that particular discipline. As such, they add an additional layer of guidance in the application of codes of ethics to clinical decision making, particularly in complicated situations. As Urofsky, Engels, and Engebretson (2008) point out, moral principles provide a helpful bridge between theoretical and practical ethics.

The moral principles outlined by Kitchener (1984; these are further clarified in Kitchener & Anderson, 2011) are foundational to the codes of ethics in many mental health professional disciplines. Although these ideas are generally referred to as "Kitchener's moral principles," they are actually based on the work of Beauchamp and Childress (1979; also see Beauchamp & Childress, 2013), who worked in the field of biomedical ethics. The American Counseling Association (see American Counseling Association [ACA], 2014) and the American Psychological Association (see American Psychological Association [APA], 2017), for example, both link their codes of ethics to Kitchener's moral principles. The code of ethics of the NASW is based on "core values" of the profession, many of which parallel these same moral principles (for more on the core values and code of ethics in the profession of social work, please see NASW, 2008). Similarly, the codes of ethics for school counselors (see American School Counselor Association [ASCA], 2016) do not stray far from these underlying principles (Glosoff & Pate, 2002). This is true for the codes of ethics in psychiatry (see American Psychiatric Association, 2010) and school psychology (see International School Psychology Association, 2011) as well. Here we will frame our discussion of moral principles on the five moral principles known as "Kitchener's moral principles." They include autonomy, nonmaleficence, beneficence, justice, and fidelity (Kitchener, 1984; Kitchener & Anderson, 2011). The additional principle of veracity is included in this discussion, as it is an additional moral principle that is fundamental to the American Counseling Association Code of Ethics (ACA, 2014).

AUTONOMY

Autonomy, in the field of mental health, refers to the principle of respecting a client's freedom of choice and freedom of action (Kitchener & Anderson,

2011). In general, it has to do with respecting a client's right to make informed and un-coerced decisions (Kitchener, 1984). This concept comes from the Greek word *autos*, which refers to "self," and *nomos*, which means "rule or governance" (Beauchamp & Childress, 2013). In the area of helping, examples of client autonomy include a client's right to decline services, to decide not to follow treatment recommendations, and to choose to see another clinician if she wants. Clients can marry the person they love, drop out of school, and quit their jobs, even if their therapists don't think that these are good ideas.

Autonomy is complex, however, so it is important for us to examine the fine print of this concept. First, autonomy refers to the client's right to make her own decisions, even if the clinician disagrees with those decisions and even if the clinician holds to a different set of values and beliefs. It means that the client gets to decide. Kitchener (1984; Kitchener & Anderson, 2011) points out, however, that autonomous decision making implies that the client is able to use *rational* deliberation to make *informed* decisions. These components of autonomy mean that a client must be lucid or competent enough engage in rational deliberation. It also means that a client's ability to make decisions in therapy must be based on having the appropriate information that is needed to make a particular decision. Thus, the principle of autonomy compels clinicians to provide informed consent about the work that they do, and it also speaks to an important role that clinicians play in helping their clients become informed as they engage in decision making.

Second is Kitchener's point about *respect*. As mentioned, clinicians must respect the right that clients have to make their own decisions even if they do not agree with those decisions. However, there is an important caveat here: A client's autonomy must be respected *as long as the decisions being made do not infringe on the rights of others* (Kitchener, 1984; Kitchener & Anderson, 2011). So, intervention may be required—and is legally required in some cases—if it is likely that the client's decisions will bring harm to others.

Third, Kitchener (1984; Kitchener & Anderson, 2011) notes that the principle of autonomy also extends to respecting clients' privacy. This latter protection is also a matter of federal law in the United States. Only in situations of duty to warn and a need for protection are clinicians legally and morally obligated break client confidentiality. We will speak more about this shortly.

NONMALEFICENCE

The principle of nonmaleficence emphasizes the helper's commitment to do no harm (Beauchamp & Childress, 2013; Kitchener, 1984; Kitchener & Anderson, 2011). Nonmaleficence means that clinicians should not intentionally harm their clients, nor should they engage in actions that might risk harming their clients. So, nonmaleficence refers to intentional or unintentional actions that can hurt clients.

Of course, harm is sometimes difficult to ascertain in a profession that entails having difficult or uncomfortable conversations. For example, when is harm different from discomfort? Or stress? Is it harmful for clients to cry in therapy? Is it harmful to request that a client tolerate exposure to the object of their phobia? The answers to these questions are: maybe. Sometimes. Discomfort in the moment may lead to long-term benefit. But in situations where a client is extremely vulnerable or has very poor affect-regulation skills, the discomfort in some interventions may be extremely harmful. They may require the clinician to work with the client to develop affect-regulation skills first, for example, or wait until the client is in a more stable and less vulnerable position. So, the principle of nonmaleficence requires us to carefully consider how much discomfort is justifiable. We must think clearly about when discomfort crosses the line to harm.

Another important implication of nonmaleficence has to do with practitioner competence. Clinicians have the duty to provide appropriate services and to protect their clients from faulty or negligent practices. That is, clinicians should never offer services that are not appropriate or that will make a situation worse. They also must refrain from engaging in practices for which they are not fully trained.

BENEFICENCE

Beneficence refers to engaging in actions that are aimed at contributing to the welfare and best interest of others (Beauchamp & Childress, 2013; Kitchener, 1984; Kitchener & Anderson, 2011). Kitchener & Anderson (2011) point out that while the general public does not have an ethical obligation to promote the welfare of others, helping professionals do. The very foundation of helping professions compels clinicians to hold fast to a commitment to only engage in actions that are beneficial to their clients.

Operationalized, this means that clinicians should only offer and engage in practices for which they are fully trained and competent and to use helping approaches with their clients that they are reasonably confident will produce effective outcomes. It should be noted that beneficence takes precedence over client autonomy in instances of harm to self or others. This means that clinicians must protect clients when they are in danger of harming themselves and in situations when there is a clear threat of danger to others. The principle of beneficence in these situations requires the therapist to intervene to protect the welfare of the client (or an identified other), even if the client is expressing that he wants to make his own decision (autonomy) about self-harm (or harm to others). More information regarding how to intervene in situations of harm to self or others will be discussed in Chapter 10.

JUSTICE

In helping relationships, the principle of justice refers to a commitment to fairness—to provide "fair, equitable and appropriate treatment" (Beauchamp & Childress, 2013, p. 250). Just to clarify, this principle relies on Aristotle's perspective on fairness, which is about "treating equals equally and unequals unequally, but in proportion to their relevant differences" (Kitchener, 1984, p. 49). This concept, then, rests on the idea that fairness does not simply equate to equality. That is, the moral obligation of justice does not mean that everyone gets the same. This important distinction is emphasized in the fact that Barnett and Johnson (2015) use fairness rather than justice in their discussion of the principles underlying the American Counseling Association Code of Ethics.

To tease out this notion of how fairness is different from justice, I will start with a very concrete example from my personal life that is unrelated to therapy. When my children were preparing to go back to school after summer break one year, my daughter said that she needed new soccer cleats for the upcoming soccer season. My oldest son needed new jeans, and my middle son needed new boxers and socks. My youngest son, however, wanted to stretch the summer along as far as possible and said that he needed nothing. We knew he would need a new winter jacket to get through the snow season at some point, but he insisted that he needed nothing. All of the children needed something at some point, but none of them needed the same thing. So, their needs would eventually get addressed *fairly*, but not *equally*.

Now consider the laws related to protected categories. In many of the United States, sexual orientation is a legally protected category, meaning that it is against the law to discriminate against individuals who identity as gay or lesbian. We can say that being treated in a nondiscriminatory way is an implied and respected right for people who identify as straight; they do not need this legal protection related to sexual orientation. People who identify as gay or lesbian warrant such protection by law, however, because they regularly experience injustice and threats to their safety due to their sexual orientation. So, this law addresses what is *fair*, even if it is does not apply to all. (Of course, protected category classifications exist for people who locate in other marginalized social locations as well, and these protections exist for the very same reason.) It should be pointed out that this concept of legally protected categories does not provide additional or special rights to just some people; it just assures that we are all clear that the laws of justice apply to everyone—even those in marginalized social locations. Kitchener's principle of justice, then, means that we must strive to be fair to everyone (Kitchener, 1984; Kitchener & Anderson, 2011). Because we live in an unjust society, assuring fairness may mean that we may not treat everyone the same.

This second example above related to protected categories illustrates the way in which the moral principle of justice is sometimes intertwined with legal actions and mandates. As Kitchener (1984) points out, rules and procedures are often needed in a civil society to adjudicate claims of fairness. So, agency policies and legal systems often take on the responsibility for assuring justice.

FIDELITY

A final principle outlined in Kitchener's work is fidelity. (Fidelity was not part of the original model presented by Beauchamp and Childress; Kitchener added this principle in her 1984 model.) As a moral principle guiding the work of clinical helpers, fidelity refers to being honest, trustworthy, loyal, and honoring the commitment of the helping relationship (Kitchener, 1984; Kitchener & Anderson, 2011). The helping contract is a key way in which the principle of fidelity works its way into therapeutic practice. As we mentioned in Chapter 1, the helping contract outlines agreements regarding the services that will be offered. Fidelity is a principle that assures that the clinician will do everything in his power to honor that commitment. Examples of this include being available at the arranged time for an appointment and following through on phone calls, referrals, billing commitments, or information promised. Kitchener points out that fidelity also means respecting client autonomy, providing informed consent, being truthful and honest, maintaining confidentiality, and not engaging in deceptive practices.

VERACITY

Although not included in Kitchener's outline of moral principles, the concept of veracity refers to the commitment for clinical helpers to be truthful. While Kitchener includes this concept of being truthful in her description of fidelity, the American Counseling Association Code of Ethics (ACA, 2014) is somewhat more assertive in separating out this important moral principle. The ACA notes that it is the professional responsibility of counselors to "aspire to open, honest, and accurate communication" (Barnett & Johnson, 2015, p. 55) in their communications with clients, other professionals, and in public.

Table 3.2: Moral Principles for Helping Ethics

KITCHENER'S MORAL PRINCIPLES	DESCRIPTION
Autonomy	The commitment to respect the capacity of a rational individual to make informed and un-coerced decisions.
Nonmaleficence	The commitment to do no harm.
Beneficence	The commitment to engage in actions that contribute to the welfare of and are in the best interests of the client.
Justice	The commitment to be fair. Fair does not always mean equal.
Fidelity	The commitment to honor the agreements of the helping contract that include providing informed consent, being truthful and honest, maintaining confidentiality, and not engaging in deceptive practices.
Veracity*	The commitment for clinical helpers to be truthful.

Based on:

Kitchener, K. S. (1984). Intuition, critical evaluation and ethical principles: The foundation for ethical decisions in counseling psychology. *Counseling Psychologist, 12*(3), 43–55. https://doi.org/10.1177/0011000084123005

*Barnett, J. E., & Johnson, W. B. (2015). *Ethics desk reference for counselors* (2nd ed.). Alexandria, VA: American Counseling Association.

KEY ETHICAL AND LEGAL CONCEPTS

We have just reviewed critical moral principles that underlie the codes of ethics in many mental health disciplines. Before moving on to a model for navigating moral dilemmas, we will discuss some key topics that are pertinent to any discussion about ethical and legal issues in clinical practice, and they are relevant across the various clinical mental health professional disciplines. In this discussion, we include the concepts of informed consent, helper competence, confidentiality, protection from harm, duty to warn, and nonprofessional or dual relationships.

INFORMED CONSENT

As mentioned in Chapter 1, informed consent defines the parameters of the therapeutic relationship (Barnett & Johnson, 2015; Wheeler & Bertram, 2012). Conceptually, informed consent is anchored in the best interests of the client and is in line with principles of autonomy, respect, collaboration (Barnett & Johnson, 2015; Henkelman & Everall, 2001), and veracity. Informed consent is the process that assures that clients have adequate information to be able to decide if they want to engage in therapy. This is also important because client engagement in clinical decision making invites client responsibility in the therapeutic process (Beahrs & Gutheil, 2001) and consensus around the goals of therapy strengthens the therapeutic alliance (Gaston, 1990; Norcross, 2010).

The duty to provide informed consent to potential clients is both a legal and an ethical duty for all mental health practitioners and should be discussed explicitly prior to initiating any services (Trachsel et al., 2015). The process of informed consent, Barnett and Johnson (2015) remind us, should continue throughout the course of therapy, as goals and intervention strategies may change over time. The specific required components of the informed consent vary by agency, institutional policies, state licensing laws and requirements, and Health Insurance Portability and Accountability Act (HIPAA) requirements (Sommers-Flannagan & Sommers-Flannagan, 2007; Wheeler & Bertram, 2012).

As mentioned in Chapter 1, informed consent guidelines put forward by various mental health professional organizations (e.g., American Association for Marriage and Family Therapy [AAMFT] Code of Ethics, ACA 2014 Code of Ethics, American Psychological Association: Ethical Principles of Psychologists and Code of Conduct, National Association of Social Workers: Code of Ethics, National Board for Certified Counselors: Code of Ethics) vary. Most, however, include some or all of these components, outlined by Wheeler and Bertram (2012): a statement indicating whether participation in counseling is voluntary or not (if relevant); expectations regarding client engagement in therapy; an outline of the therapists credentials and what services she will be providing, including therapeutic approach or modality; a statement clarifying that desired results are not guaranteed and the risks associated with therapy; confidentiality polices, including exceptions to confidentiality and a statement about engagement in social media; information about the counselor's supervision and consultation practices; a statement about ethical codes that guide the therapist's practice and what clients can do if they have concerns or complaints; therapist credentials; information about records, fees, and insurance reimbursement; and emergency procedures. Wheeler and Bertram also recommend that clinicians engage in a discussion with clients about the benefits and risks of mental health diagnoses, if that is relevant. The compensatory aspect of the helping contract should be clearly articulated prior to its initiation of service, even when such discussions are not negotiable and articulated between billing agencies and insurance companies. All informed consent conversations and documents should be "transparent and customized" (Trachsel et al., 2015, p. 776) to the specific needs of the client and services the clinician is trained to and willing to provide.

As mentioned, consent for engaging in therapy is something that can only be provided if and when a client is able to make decisions voluntarily and with appropriate information and understandings about the therapist and therapeutic process (Henkelman & Everall, 2001). This compels clinicians and the agencies for whom they work to provide information at a level and language that is understandable to the client, and it compels clinicians to discuss the various aspects of the contract prior to obtaining consent (Barnett & Johnson, 2015). In situations when clients may not fully understand the language used in the helping contract, the clinician should arrange for translation or interpretation services or find other ways of promoting comprehension prior to initiating services (Barnett & Johnson, 2015).

While most professional ethical standards apply to work with youth under the age of 18 (Wheeler & Bertram, 2012), it is important for clinicians to know that in most situations, parents or legal guardians hold the legal right of consent for their children to participate in clinical services. So, in these cases, informed consent is a process that is articulated and agreed upon with a minor client's parents or guardians. Upon consent from parents or guardians, information about the therapeutic process should be discussed with the child or adolescent client in language that is appropriate to his cognitive capacity. The point is that although most minors can only give assent (agreement), not legal consent (permission) for services, they still need "to be able to understand the ramifications of their decision and possess the ability to understand and make a sound decision" (Henkelman & Everall, 2001, p. 119).

Finally, informed consent typically looks a little different in a school setting. While it was already pointed out that parents hold the legal right to consent for their children to participate in counseling services, there is some debate in the literature and in practice regarding the need for consent in schools when the expectation is only for minimal participation in such services (Davis, 2015; Dollarhide & Saginak, 2012). For example, is consent needed before a school counselor can talk to a child she finds crying in a school hallway? Davis (2015) and Dollarhide and Saginak (2012) point out that the scope of services provided by school counselors is quite broad, including therapeutic, educational, guidance, and advocacy, and some districts have policies regarding consent in these various situations. Classroom developmental guidance, for example, is not considered a therapeutic service in many schools because it is part of the educational curriculum for *all* students, so consent is not typically required. In contrast, in many schools when individual and small group counseling services occur over a period of time or if they move over some invisible line that then considers them to be "therapy," parental consent is typically required. Consent here, of course, includes information regarding the purposes, goals, and techniques that will be used in counseling and information regarding confidentiality. And, of course, consent must be discussed with parents and students in culturally and developmentally appropriate language (ASCA, 2016). Regardless, it is always prudent for school counselors to inform and/or seek consent from parents or guardians regardless of the services offered, when possible and as appropriate, as this helps to build collaborative relationships that are in the best interest of students (Davis, 2015; Dollarhide & Saginak, 2012).

CLINICIAN COMPETENCE

The field of mental health service delivery is very broad—clinicians work in a vast variety of settings and with diverse populations. It is unrealistic to think that one clinician can work with every client or on every issue that comes in the door. So, being competent requires us to be aware of and work within the parameters of our level of training and experience (Barnett & Johnson, 2015). It also requires a commitment to offer high-quality services; keep abreast of new developments in the field; gain the knowledge, skills, awareness, sensitivities, and dispositions necessary for providing culturally competent services to clients from diverse populations (Barnett & Johnson, 2015); and it means protecting clients from harm. In a school setting, professional responsibilities include being able to work with parents, teachers, and school administrators. In addition to counseling, school counselors must be able to offer consultation services, engage in classroom instruction (often called "developmental guidance"), work with other professionals to provide coordinated services, and perhaps provide screening, evaluation, guidance, and advocacy services as well (Sommers-Flannagan & Sommers-Flannagan, 2007). So, what exactly constitutes professional competence depends on the setting.

But across the board, clinical competence is principally related to the moral principles of beneficence and nonmaleficence. We must serve the welfare of our clients and we must do no harm. To ensure that one is providing competent services, clinicians should regularly monitor the effectiveness of their work, consistently renew or upgrade their skills, participate in regular supervision, and seek consultation, particularly when working in new areas of practice (Barnett & Johnson, 2015). Obviously, counselors should also not provide services that are not requested, not offer services that are unethical or illegal, or breach their professional code of ethics in any other way.

The issue of working within one's area of training seems obvious, but in everyday settings, it can be a little tricky. One quandary is when a clinician is asked to provide professional advice in a nonprofessional setting. For example, what happens when the friend sitting next to you on the bleachers as you watch your children play basketball asks for professional advice? This innocent invitation for help puts you in a position of providing professional services without a helping contract (and it violates the conventions of dual relationships, which we will get to shortly). Yet, the social conventions of conversations warrant that you offer something to this friend of yours that is struggling. What are your responsibilities and what happens if your excellent expert advice falls flat and the problem gets worse? The moral of the story, of course, is that it is always best to attend to your friendships while you are in public, and save your professional expertise for your clients in the office. In reality, though, these seemingly disparate aspects of clinicians' worlds are sometimes not all that far apart.

A second quandary regarding competence is in regard to these notions of training and expertise. What constitutes training is one part of this challenge. Does one need to attend one workshop in order to put a particular modality into practice? Or, is more extensive training and supervision required to be able to use a particular technique? Probably the latter is the most prudent response to this question, but the larger issue is when, exactly, does one know if she is competent enough to use a particular helping modality? The second part of this quandary has to do with the ways in which experience offers a powerful learning experience. When does experience in a particular area connote competence? It seems obvious, for example, that those of us with no formal training in working with children should avoid working with children and not offer parenting advice to our clients. But what if we have raised our own children and worked with parents in our professional practice for over 20 years? When does experience equate to competence?

The truth is that professional knowledge comes from a wide variety of sources—most of us get better at what we do as we work in the field; we glean bits of information and training from various workshops, and participation in supervision and consultation is extremely informative. So, while it sounds obvious to say that clinicians should work within their scope of training and practice, the notions of training and expertise are not altogether clear-cut. Boundary rigidity—just working in one way, regardless of who the client is and what problem is being discussed—and the allure of being an "expert" also complicate the ways in which we draw lines around the parameters of our professional practice. And these can be as equally dangerous as having a loose definition of what one has actually been trained to do. The point here is that when we are expanding our area of expertise, we must do so with diligence. And, most importantly: When we are in these gray areas, it is always best to consult a supervisor.

CONFIDENTIALITY

As discussed in Chapter 1, maintaining confidentiality is a cornerstone of ethical practice in helping relationships. The ethical mandate around confidentiality is to protect a client's basic right to privacy.

Protecting confidentiality begins with the obvious prohibitions and protections around insuring that the information clients discuss in therapy will not be disclosed to others without the client's explicit consent (Barnett & Johnson, 2015). In fact, even revealing to others that a client is in a clinical therapeutic relationship is not appropriate. For example, counselors should refrain from acknowledging a client in public unless they are approached first by that client. Clinicians must also be cautious when engaging in social and professional communication that may be used in relation to their work—phones, computers, e-mail, and the Internet—because these all have the potential to put a client's privacy at risk (Barnett & Johnson, 2015). Protecting confidentiality also includes some less obvious nuances. For example, clients have the right to determine the conditions around self-disclosure. That is, clients get to decide when, where, and what they will disclose in therapy. Clinicians should be careful about eliciting private information from clients that is not specifically relevant to their clinical work with those clients (Barnett & Johnson, 2015). Barnett and Johnson remind us that the right to privacy in helping relationships extends to past, current, and prospective clients. Keep in mind, too, that the protection of client privacy is applicable to all of the all communications between client and counselor—verbal, written, and third-party conversations.

Maintaining confidentiality can be understood as a manifestation of respecting client autonomy and acting with fidelity. Confidentiality helps insure that the client is acting on his own accord—free from the influence of others. By protecting this right, the clinician is being faithful and loyal to the helping contract. The ethics around confidentiality also reflect a commitment to the moral principles of beneficence and nonmaleficence—the obligations to protect the welfare of clients and to do no harm.

Protecting confidentiality is an ethical dictate that is also regulated by legal mandates in some situations. Most notably, when a client appears to be at risk of harm to self, when a client has ideas of harming an identifiable other, and when there are suspicions of neglect or abuse of a child or a vulnerable individual, clinicians have an ethical and legal mandate to break confidentiality in order to protect safety (Barnett & Johnson, 2015; Sommers-Flanagan &

Sommers-Flanagan, 2007; Wheeler & Bertram, 2012). This is also true in some situations involving client terminal illness or in situations when the counselor is aware that a client has a life-threatening and contagious disease that puts an identifiable third party at risk (Barnett & Johnson, 2015). However, it is important to note that laws governing confidentiality vary considerably by state. The important point is that the ethical commitment to confidentiality is mediated by a legal mandate of protection from harm. In fact, laws regarding harm to self or others do not just suggest that clinicians *should* breach confidentiality in situations of threat or harm to self or others; they mandate that clinicians *must* do so. It is always appropriate for clinicians to consult with colleagues so as to best determine the validity of harm concerns and the need to break confidentiality.

State laws and agency policies around the sharing of case notes and other information related to therapy vary considerably, and issues related to third-party reimbursement for therapy services require careful attention (Sommers-Flanagan & Sommers-Flanagan, 2007). Having said this, there are two important federal mandates that govern the ways in which client information is provided to outside parties and all therapists, regardless of where they work, must adhere to these laws. The first is the Family Educational Rights and Privacy Act (FERPA) of 1974, which outlines the legal requirements around the sharing of student records in a school setting—so this law is relevant for school counselors. The parallel Health Insurance Portability and Accountability Act (HIPAA) of 1996 is a federal law that protects the privacy of patient's health information and is relevant for counselors working in clinical settings. These laws protect the confidentiality of written records, and HIPAA also has mandates around informed consent policies.

Laws around the extent to which clinicians are allowed privileged communication with their clients—meaning that they can maintain confidentiality regarding their work with a particular client, even if they receive a subpoena to speak in a court of law—vary from state to state. Legal privileged communication status tends to be issued according to professional affiliation, so some mental health professionals have the right to privileged communication whereas others do not. Clinicians should become familiar with the legal mandates regarding confidentiality and privileged communication in their state (Wheeler & Bertram, 2012). In general, however, if a clinician receives a court order to disclose confidential information about a client, that clinician should seek written informed consent from the client whenever possible, and attempt to attenuate the impact and potential for harm from such disclosures (Barnett & Johnson, 2015). It is always best to seek legal or professional consultation or supervision around issues of confidentiality, suspicions of harm to self or others, and in cases of court subpoena (Barnett & Johnson, 2015).

Situations involving mandated clients—clients who are required to participate in clinical services without choice—are complicated. One of the most challenging aspects of working with mandated clients is that they are not freely able to grant or deny consent for counseling, and confidentiality is not necessarily guaranteed. However, even in these circumstances, who the clinician can, should, and must report to and the general nature of these disclosures is something that should be discussed with clients prior to the initiation of service delivery and throughout therapy (Barnett & Johnson, 2015).

As mentioned, parents or guardians typically have the legal right to grant consent for their children to be involved in therapy, although the exact legal requirements for such consent varies widely across states and depending on the types of services in question (Barnett & Johnson, 2015; Glosoff & Pate, 2002; Kerwin et al., 2015). State laws also vary in regard to the extent to which parents are able to access information about their children who are receiving mental health services (Wheeler & Bertram, 2012). So, decisions regarding how much information to share with parents can be challenging. In these situations, counselors must balance the ethical rights of their minor clients regarding confidentiality on the one hand, with, on the other hand, parental (or guardian) rights to be informed about their children and to make decisions on their behalf (Barnett & Johnson, 2015; Glosoff & Pate, 2002; Wheeler & Bertram, 2012). To make these decisions, clinicians must have up-to-date information regarding agency policies, as well as state and federal laws that govern these issues of consent and confidentiality in regard to minor clients. Clinicians should also consider the age and maturity level of the minor client, the extent to which disclosure to parents will benefit or harm the client, and the potential for harm if the disclosure is not made (Wheeler & Bertram, 2012). To help navigate the challenges of how, when, if and why a therapist should share information about minors with their parents or guardians, Barnett and Johnson (2015) suggest that therapists work to establish healthy and collaborative relationships with the parents of their minor clients from

Photo 3.2

the start of therapy, and they recommend that children and adolescents be involved, as appropriate, in discussions regarding disclosure of information to their parents and guardians. In situations of suspected danger to self or others, or if a minor client is a victim of harm, of course, the clinician must break confidentiality to secure appropriate help so that the child is safe. This may or may not happen in conjunction with informing the parent of such actions.

PROTECTION FROM HARM AND DUTY TO WARN

Protection from harm refers to the ethical and legal mandate that we have been discussing—the mandate that clinicians have to secure the safety of clients who appear to present a threat to themselves or in situations where a client may be a victim of harm by others. The wording here is intentional—protection of harm is relevant in situations where clients *appear* to present a threat to self or who *may* be victims of harm. This means that even if there is uncertainty, it is the counselor's *duty* to do all that she can do to protect that client. The concept of **duty to warn** refers to situations in which a client issues a credible threat about harming another person. In these cases, when there is an identified potential victim of this threat of harm, it is the *duty* of that clinician to notify appropriate authorities and to notify the potential victim of harm. These legal mandates can be adjudicated in either state or federal courts.

Wheeler and Bertram (2012) explain that the concept of duty in the professional counseling relationship refers to an "obligation to act in the best interest of the client" (p. 15) using a *standard of care* that is consistent with one's level of training, skill, and the ethical practice of professional peers. Importantly, the omission or the failure to act also must not cause harm to the client or her potential victim. These mandates are based on a legal precedent in the 1976 *Tarasoff v. Regents of the University of California* case, compelling clinicians to break confidentiality and notify police and any identifiable victims when they are aware of potential threats of harm made by their clients to others (Corey et al., 2003; Davis & Ritchie, 2003; Isaacs, 2003; Wheeler & Bertram, 2012).

Mandated reporting is the legal requirement that clinicians and others working in helping professions must inform appropriate authorities when they have suspicions that minors or vulnerable adults are victims of abuse or neglect. Here "vulnerable adults" typically refers to people who have disabilities and to elders (Welfel, Danzinger, & Santoro, 2000). Clinicians also have mandated reporting obligations, as just mentioned, in situations of potential harm to identifiable others (Barnett & Johnson, 2015).

"Appropriate authorities" would be state social service agency personnel who are in the position to receive such reports—typically, those working in the child or vulnerable adult divisions of state departments of human services, as well as local, state, and federal law enforcement officers. Remember that it is up to the state social service agency, not the clinician, to investigate, substantiate, and, if substantiated, take appropriate action on these reports. The specific reporting procedures vary by state, and clinicians must keep up-to-date with these legal mandates (Barnett & Johnson, 2015; Brown, Brack, & Mullis, 2008; Sommers-Flanagan & Sommers-Flanagan, 2007; Welfel et al., 2000). It should be noted that in most states there are legal consequences for mandated reporters who fail to report their concerns around child or vulnerable adult abuse and neglect (Brown et al., 2008; Welfel et al., 2000). Again, within this legal mandate, it is up to the mandated reporter to report any *suspicions* of harm or neglect, even if it is not verifiable that abuse or neglect has actually occurred (Brown et al., 2008; Sommers-Flanagan &

Sommers-Flanagan, 2007; Welfel et al., 2000). These are specific areas, then, where the duty to warn and the mandate to protect supersede clients' rights to confidentiality.

A second concept that is relevant to our discussion regarding protection from harm is the legal concept of the **age of majority**. This refers to the chronological age when minors cease to be considered children, at least from a legal perspective. This concept is important because it speaks to the age at which youth are able to assume control over their persons, actions, and decisions—it is when the legal control and responsibilities of an individual no longer belongs to one's parents or guardians.

In the United States, and in many other countries throughout the world, the legal age of majority is set at age 18. This notion of the legal age of majority should not be confused with the legal age of drinking, voting, driving, marriageability, or sexual consent. These various activities, rights, and civic duties are sometimes set at a different age than the age of majority. Clinicians are legally accountable to the laws of their state in regard to issues of consent and confidentiality, as mentioned, and they should also be familiar with other laws that are designed to protect youth, especially laws related to statutory rape—laws related to ages at which minors can legally consent to sexual activity—as they may be in a position of mandated reporter in these situations as well.

NONPROFESSIONAL AND DUAL RELATIONSHIPS

The ethical mandate around establishing appropriate professional relationships is that clinicians must avoid acting in overlapping roles, duties, and relationships with their clients. When clinicians are not able to effectively manage the boundaries around the professional client/therapist relationship, their clients are at risk of harm, exploitation, or other potential adverse consequences (Barnett & Johnson, 2015; Wheeler & Bertram, 2012). This compels clinicians to do all that they can to avoid being in some other kind of relationship with their clients while they are providing professional clinical services. More concretely, counselors should not provide therapy to their friends or coworkers, they should not go out for drinks with their clients, and they should avoid other types of social relationship with their clients, including, of course, sexual relations. Sommers-Flanagan and Sommers-Flanagan (2007) also point out that dual relationship complications also may ensue in situations that include gift giving and receiving, self-disclosure, and physical touch.

This basic ethical principle regarding nonprofessional relationships and boundaries is important because helping relationships are not mutual, nor are they equal relationships. The helping contract is one that positions clinicians in a role that has some degree of power over the client. This unequal distribution of power has the potential to compromise client autonomy, and it can potentially be used in harmful and malicious ways. For example, a patient sitting in a dental chair as her dentist hovers with a drill in hand may not feel comfortable denying a request for a date—at least not at that moment. Similarly, a client who has revealed all of his inner insecurities to his clinician may not feel confident enough to reject that clinician's request for a ride home after therapy.

A quick perusal of the codes of ethics in most clinical mental health disciplines shows clear articulation of prohibitions regarding dual relationships. For example, Standard III.4.2 of the Principles of Professional Ethics for school psychologists (National Association of School Psychologists, 2010) requires school psychologists to "refrain from any activity in which conflicts of interest or multiple relationships with a client or a client's family may interfere with professional effectiveness" (p. 10). Similarly, the conflicts of interests clause (Conflicts of Interest, 1.06) of the Code of Ethics *of the National Association of Social Workers* (NASW, 2008) instructs social workers to avoid engagement in dual or multiple relationships, adding, "In instances when dual or multiple relationships are unavoidable, social workers should take steps to protect clients and are responsible for setting clear, appropriate, and culturally sensitive boundaries" (n.p.). In terms of prohibitions regarding intimate relationships with clients, the Code of Ethics of the American Counseling Association (ACA, 2014) specifically states that romantic relationships between a counselor and a client or any member of the client's family are prohibited for a period of 5 years after the last professional contact. For psychologists, the same ethical standard exists, although the prohibited period is only 2 years (APA, 2017).

The prohibition against dual relationships also extends to more seemingly benign and sometimes serendipitous situations. For example, I once delivered my child to his day care center only to find that a client I had been working with for some time was recently hired to work at this center. We were both surprised by this unexpected coincidence. Similarly, client autonomy may be compromised when a school counselor, for example, is also given the responsibility to investigate truancy in her school or is hired to be a coach of the soccer team. In these situations, students are potentially compromised because their behavior in one situation may affect their ability to receive fair services in the other. They also are potentially affected by what the helper may know about them and how information is shared. The problem is that information from one situation potentially informs services and relationships in the other, and this is particularly inappropriate in the context of relationships that have inherent uneven power differentials. Bartering for therapeutic services may sound like a fair way to offer services to individuals who otherwise may not afford them. But even these situations are potentially fraught with peril, as it may be difficult to accurately or fairly assess the value of bartered services, and questions about what to do if one of the parties is not satisfied with the services received can be complex (Barnett & Johnson, 2015).

Dual and/or multiple relationships are deceptively complex. Clients are sometimes not even aware of their own compromised position when they are put in a vulnerable position or when a boundary is violated. Sometimes it may even seem that a client is actually seeking out a dual relationship. They may, for example, enjoy the therapeutic intimacy of the counseling relationship so much that they may seek out opportunities to spend more time with their counselor. Or some clients may be so grateful for the help they received, they are eager to repay the clinician by offering a gift of some kind, not recognizing that the ways in which gratitude is expressed in social relationships may not be appropriate in helping relationships. The issue around multiple relationships is also difficult because in some cases a client may benefit from some aspect of a dual relationship (Barnett & Johnson, 2015). For example, attending a client's graduation or engaging in activities related to a particular cultural or religious community in which the client is also a member may be beneficial to the therapeutic relationship with the client and may not be harmful. However, Barnett and Johnson (2015) point out that the counselor owns the burden of proof in demonstrating that participation in these types of activities are truly beneficial to the client. The bottom line is that it is up to the professional clinician, not the client, to guard the sanctity of the therapeutic relationship and protect the client.

A final issue that is worth brief mention here is what to do when a clinician has reason to believe that a professional colleague is engaged in an unprofessional relationship with a client or has otherwise violated this or any other ethical standard. While this issue is complicated and goes beyond the scope of this introductory text, Barnett & Johnson (2015), citing the ACA Code of Ethics (ACA, 2014), assert that when a clinician suspects that an ethical violation has occurred in a colleague's work, the clinician should first attempt to resolve the issue informally with the other clinician. But if more substantial action is needed, and especially if substantial harm has occurred, the clinician should take further action that may include referral to the appropriate institutional authorities and the state or national professional ethics committee or licensing board. During this reporting process, the confidentiality of the client must be carefully protected to the extent possible. In this and all cases when a clinician is not sure how to proceed, consultation with other practitioners who are knowledgeable about ethics or with legal experts is always prudent and highly recommended.

Table 3.3: Key Ethical and Legal Concepts for Helpers

KEY ETHICAL/LEGAL CONCEPTS	DESCRIPTIONS
Competence	The commitment to work only in the area of one's competence. Clinicians must not offer or attempt to provide services for which they have not been trained.
Informed consent	Informed consent is an outline of the agreement of service provision between client and counselor. It also refers to providing information to potential clients regarding the services the clinician is trained to offer.
Confidentiality	The clinician must not disclose information (verbally or in writing) to third-party others without (written) consent from the client. Confidentiality may be broken in cases of harm to self or others or due to court order.
FERPA	The Family Educational Rights and Privacy Act of 1974 is a federal law that protects the privacy of student educational records.
HIPPA	The Health Insurance Portability and Accountability Act of 1996 is a federal law that protects the privacy of individual's health information.

(Continued)

Table 3.3 (Continued)

KEY ETHICAL/LEGAL CONCEPTS	DESCRIPTIONS
Protection from harm	Clinicians have a responsibility to get appropriate help for a client who poses a threat to himself or who is in danger of being harmed by a third party.
Duty to warn	Clinicians have a responsibility to inform authorities and potential victims if a client threatens to harm another identifiable individual.
Mandated reporter	Clinicians are required by law to inform appropriate authorities if they have any suspicions of child abuse and neglect or elder/vulnerable adult abuse.
Legal age of majority	This is the age, according to law, when minors cease to be considered children—when they are able to assume control over their persons, actions, and decisions.
Dual or multiple relationships	It is the responsibility of clinicians to avoid engaging in overlapping duties, roles, or relationships with their clients.

ETHICAL DECISION MAKING

One might think that this discussion about moral principles, legal mandates, and the existence of a written code of ethics for virtually every clinical helping profession would make it easy to navigate potentially complex ethical dilemmas. Unfortunately, this is not so. Traversing ethical decisions can be challenging, even with sound codes of ethics in place. For this reason, many professional organizations recommend a systematic process for ethical decision making. The model presented here is based largely on the work of Barnett and Johnson (2015), in addition to recommendations by the American Counseling Association (ACA, 2014), Forester-Miller and Davis (1995), and Corey et al. (2003). The purpose of decision-making models such as the one presented here is to help clinicians consider a broad scope of relevant information while making clinical decisions.

1. **Clarify the problematic situation.**
   Good decisions are those that are made carefully and from a well-informed perspective. The first step in ethical decision making, then, is to slow down and gather as much information as possible about

the situation of concern. Barnett and Johnson (2015) recommend thinking through the nature of the situation, working to identify the primary conflict or problem, gathering as many relevant facts as possible, and reviewing relevant ethical and legal issues and professional obligations. It is important to document all of this information as it is considered.

2. **Determine who may be affected by the situation.**
   Barnett and Johnson (2015) also point out that many ethical dilemmas have far-reaching effects, and so they remind us to consider the potential impact on the full range of people who may be affected by the problem. The point here is to be mindful of obligations and to be centered on the best interests of all persons who are involved—both directly and peripherally. Related to this, clients should be informed when there is a potential ethical problem, they need to know the dictates and boundaries that govern the clinician's work, they need to be informed of their rights, and they should know if they may potentially be affected by any actions the therapist may need to take to resolve the ethical concern. When discussing the dilemma to the client, it is helpful to use concrete language, rather than complex professional jargon or vague references to ethical or legal mandates. For example, if your client who has minor children in the home is living with a registered sex offender, you are bound by law to inform appropriate authorities. This legal obligation does not, however, preclude a discussion with the client about needing to take such actions.

3. **Consult the professional code of ethics (profession specific) and moral principles.**
   An important part of the ethical decision-making process involves careful consultation with the written code of ethics published by one's professional discipline or organizational body. Barnett and Johnson (2015) also recommend that clinicians keep in mind Kitchener's moral principles of autonomy, nonmaleficence, beneficence, justice, and fidelity—as well as issues related to privacy. These underlying principles can provide additional guidance, particularly when the situation is ambiguous or is not addressed specifically in

the code of ethics. Again, it is important to document all of this information, listing the specific codes that are relevant.

4. **Consider relevant legal statutes, agency policies, and best practice standards.**
   As mentioned, most states have legal mandates related to confidentiality, mandated reporting, duty to warn, informed consent, record keeping, and licensure, and it is a professional responsibility of all clinicians to keep informed about all of the legal statutes that are relevant to their work in their particular jurisdiction. When state or federal laws appear to be relevant to a particular ethical or therapeutic dilemma, it is a good idea for clinicians to obtain legal consultation, as this will help clarify the clinician's legal obligations as well as identify any potential legal consequences of actions taken (Barnett & Johnson, 2015). It is also important for clinicians to keep up-to-date on agency policies as well as professional research and literature in their field, as these offer guidelines for appropriate practice and standards for care. Clinicians should also document all relevant ethical, legal, and contractual information at this stage of decision making.

5. **Reflect on personal reactions, feelings, and competence.**
   Barnett and Johnson (2015) offer the suggestion that therapists should take time to think and self-reflect after gathering the important information already mentioned. The purpose of self-refection is to become aware of any thoughts and feelings that are aroused in the situation, including personal and professional feelings that the therapist may be experiencing. This is critical because it is possible that worries and concerns could prevent a therapist from appropriate action. Additionally, the therapist should consider his level of competence to handle the situation effectively.

6. **Consult with a professional colleague.**
   Best practice dictates that clinicians should always seek consultation or supervision when facing a potential ethical or legal dilemma related to their work (Barnett & Johnson, 2015). This is because

consultation or supervision offers an additional perspective, it can help reveal any missed information or nuances in the situation, and it offers additional protections if the situation ends up in adjudication. It is important to select a consultant based on her experience related to the situation or client population, familiarity with professional ethics and related legal implications, and, of course, the consultant should be one who has good judgment, is honest, straight-forward, and able to respect confidentiality (Barnett & Johnson, 2015). When seeking consultation, you should prepare by organizing your ideas and key information, including facts, your thoughts about the ethical or legal issues of concern, and possible courses of action. Be careful to document every consultation sought. This documentation should include the name of consultant or supervisor, date, a brief summary of what was revealed to the consultant, and all of the recommendations provided by the consultant or supervisor.

7. **Identify potential actions with full consideration of possible outcomes.**
   All of the information gathered in the preceding steps should point the clinician in one or a few directions regarding what actions should be taken. Clinicians should take time to consider a range of possible actions. And for every potential action identified, they should consider its feasibility as well as any related legal and ethical ramifications (Barnett & Johnson, 2015). The point is that it is helpful to think broadly and to avoid making quick or uninformed decisions.

   This list of potential actions should be written and each item on the list should be linked to possible risks and benefits (Barnett & Johnson, 2015). Having one's supervisor or a consultant review this list can be extremely helpful. And again, here it is important to preserve this list as documentation of the decision-making process.

8. **Make a decision and monitor its outcome.**
   Once a course of action is decided, it is important to be clear and firm in communicating that decision with the client and relevant others, as appropriate (Barnett & Johnson, 2015). This lets others know that you are taking full responsibility for the decisions you

have made. In discussing the decision with the client, it is important to be sensitive to how any decisions or actions will affect her, and it may be appropriate to offer support and referrals, if necessary. Finally, it is important to carefully monitor the decision, when appropriate and possible, and to be willing to review and modify decisions at a later date, if needed (Barnett & Johnson, 2015). As was the case in all of the previous steps in this decision-making model, it is important to clearly document the decision that has been made and any communications you have had with others regarding its resolution.

9. **Secure written documentation regarding your decision-making process in an appropriate confidential file.**

Table 3.4: Steps for Ethical Decision Making

1. Clarify the problematic situation.
2. Determine who may be affected by the situation.
3. Consult the professional code of ethics and moral principles.
4. Consider relevant legal statutes, agency policies, and best practice standards.
5. Reflect on personal reactions, feelings, and competence.
6. Consult with a professional colleague.
7. Identify potential actions with full consideration of possible outcomes.
8. Make a decision and monitor its outcome.
9. Secure written documentation regarding your decision-making process in an appropriate confidential file.

Based on:

Barnett, J. E., & Johnson, W. B. (2015). *Ethics desk reference for counselors* (2nd ed.). Alexandria, VA: American Counseling Association.

Forester-Miller, H., & Davis, T. E. (1995). *A practitioner's guide to ethical decision making.* Alexandria, VA: American Counseling Association.

CASE EXAMPLE OF DECISION MAKING

Let us embellish the earlier example of discovering one's client at morning drop-off at the day care center. Let us say that Serena, the client—not a true name nor true circumstances—had been grappling with issues of prescription substance misuse (pain medication), although she had been clean for approximately 9 months, and that the clinician knew Serena would be having minor surgery in 2 months. The two of them had spoken in therapy about

Serena's worries related to her upcoming surgery and using pain medications. Serena had reported that she was not confident that she would be able to remain clean after the surgery if she used the pain medication that would be prescribed. Serena had not been working, due to the substance misuse issues, but she had recently told the clinician that she was seeking employment. The clinician did not know, however, that Serena was applying for positions in day care settings. Upon dropping his child off at the day care one morning, the therapist was met by Serena—both not anticipating the encounter. Careful to protect confidentiality and in line with what the two of them had discussed early in therapy about any potential chance encounters in public, the therapist pretended it was the first time he had met Serena, and Serena followed suit. We will use the decision-making model above to discuss how this dilemma might be managed.

Clarify the problematic situation

- The client and clinician are now in a dual relationship.
- The client has access to personal information about the clinician (and his child).

Photo 3.3

- The clinician has access to personal information about his child's caregiver that could potentially affect the caregiver's employment status now or in the future.
- The clinician could potentially become aware of information in the future (if the problem with substance misuse resurfaces) that could put his child and others at risk.

Determine who may be affected by the situation

- The client
- The counselor and his child
- The other children and staff at the child care center
- The owner of the child care center

Consult the professional code of ethics (profession specific) and moral principles
Using the ACA 2014 Code of Ethics (ACA, 2014), these ethical principles are potentially relevant:

- A.6.b Extending Counseling Boundaries
    - Counselors consider the risks and benefits of extending current counseling relationships beyond conventional parameters.
- A.6.c Documenting Boundary Extensions
    - If counselors extend boundaries as described in A.6.a and A.6.b., they must officially document, prior to the interaction (when feasible), the rationale for such an interaction, the potential benefit, and the anticipated consequences for the client or former client and other individuals significantly involved with the client or former client.
- B.1.c. Respect for Confidentiality
    - Counselors protect the confidential information of prospective and current clients. Counselors disclose information only with appropriate consent or with sound legal or ethical justification.
- B.1.d. Explanation of Limitations
    - At initiation and throughout the counseling process, counselors inform clients of the limitations of confidentiality and seek to identify situations in which confidentiality must be breached.

- B.2.a. Serious and Foreseeable Harm and Legal Requirements
  - The general requirement that counselors keep information confidential does not apply when disclosure is required to protect clients or identified others from serious and foreseeable harm or when legal requirements demand that confidential information must be revealed.
- B.2.e. Minimal Disclosure
  - To the extent possible, clients are informed before confidential information is disclosed and are involved in the disclosure decision-making process. When circumstances require the disclosure of confidential information, only essential information is revealed.
- C.2.e Consultations on Ethical Obligations
  - Counselors take reasonable steps to consult with other counselors, the ACA Ethics and Professional Standards Department, or related professionals when they have questions regarding their ethical obligations or professional practice.

Consider relevant legal statutes, agency policies, and best practice standards

- This counselor is in private practice and participates in regular supervision with a trained and qualified counseling supervisor.
- The counselor does not have legal privileged communication status in his practice jurisdiction.
- The counselor is a legally mandated reporter in cases of suspected harm or risk of harm to children or vulnerable adults.

Reflect on personal reactions, feelings, and competence

- The counselor was initially uncomfortable when he unexpectedly ran into the client at the child care center, but upon picking his child up at the end of the day, the child seemed happy and appeared to have had limited interaction with Serena, as she had been working with children in another age group.
- The counselor had some worries about what the client might think about his parenting abilities if his child had a bad day or some other problems at day care.

- The counselor had a strong relationship with the client, and the client was doing quite well in therapy. They lived in a rural town, and the client did not have access to transportation and therefore would have difficulties transferring to another therapist, as there were no others practicing in the community.

Consult with professional colleagues

- When this issue surfaced, the counselor called his supervisor immediately for consultation.

Identify potential actions with full consideration of possible outcomes

The counselor and supervisor outlined these potential actions:

1. Transfer the child to a new child care setting.
   This option would be difficult for the counselor, as there were few child care options in the rural setting where he lived. Also, most day care centers had long wait lists for openings, so he suspected that it would be difficult to switch the child soon. Also, there was the dilemma of how to explain to the child care center and others the reason for a change, if he opted to move his child from the center.

2. Terminate therapy and make a referral for the client to see a different therapist.
   This option would be problematic, as there were no other practicing psychotherapists in the community, and the client had limited access to transportation.

3. Have a discussion with the client including these points:
   - Process the experience of seeing each other and invite the client to discuss her experience and concerns.
   - Discuss the ethical concerns as identified above.
   - Outline the extent to which confidentiality would be maintained and circumstances when it would need to be broken—such as if substance misuse initiated again and if there were any other indications of risk associated with working with children that could potentially put the children in the center at risk of harm. The counselor would outline the process for how this report would be made and who would have to be notified if mandated reporting was required (as per B.2.e.).

- Make a mutual decision (client and counselor) regarding how to proceed. If the decision was to continue with therapy and not make any employment or child care changes, they would also need to discuss how they would acknowledge each other at the day care center.

Make a decision and monitor its outcome

The counselor, with the support of his supervisor, selected option 3. This option was selected because there was no current discernable risk to the children at the child care center and the client and counselor had a strong relationship.

The counselor decided that he would arrange to avoid going to the day care center in the next few days prior to his next appointment with the client when they could discuss the dilemma in person. He would be able to do this by asking another family member (while maintaining confidentiality) to assist in the child care drop-off/pick-up schedule.

Secure written documentation regarding your decision-making process in an appropriate confidential file

Documentation of the above conversations were created and maintained in the private and confidential client file. Additionally, it might be reasonable for the client and counselor in this situation to develop a signed contract outlining the contingencies discussed above should the substance misuse problem surface again.

CHAPTER SUMMARY

We started this chapter with definitions of key terms related to helping ethics and legal issues in counseling. Next, the broad moral principles that underlie codes of ethics in many of the clinical helping disciplines were presented. Key ethical and legal concepts salient to most clinical helping situations were also discussed. An ethical decision-making model that can be used to help clinicians navigate challenging therapeutic situations with potentially ethical or legal implications was offered with a case example at the end of the chapter.

REFLECTION QUESTIONS

1. Discuss the ways in which Kitchener's five moral principles are undercurrent in your discipline's code of ethics. Are there additional components

of your professional code of ethics that are not based on these principles? If so, what are they, and what underlying moral principles are foundational to these additional ethical mandates?

2. We know that not every clinical eventuality is mentioned or addressed in professional codes of ethics. What cues might alert a clinician that a particular situation is ethically murky?

3. In the case example discussed in the last section of this chapter, sections in the ACA Code of Ethics were identified as an example of guidelines that were relevant to the case example. Use the professional code of ethics from a different professional organization to identify sections of that code that are relevant to this particular example.

CHAPTER

Neurobiology Basics for Clinicians

Chapter Outline

INTRODUCTION

The focus of this chapter is on the connections between the central nervous system and human behavior. First, we begin with a brief discussion on what is meant by interpersonal neurobiology and then move into a basic review of brain structures and synaptic functioning. Next, we will explore how these brain functions affect stress response, empathy development and perspective taking, trauma response, and emotional regulation. Although this information is often not included in basic skills text, it is offered here to provide the reader with a basic explanation of some of the more common challenges that clients bring to therapy and why some of the strategies reviewed later in this text are helpful.

INTERPERSONAL NEUROBIOLOGY AND HUMAN BEHAVIOR

The *mind* is a word and concept that has worked its way into colloquial language in a variety of contexts within and outside of the field of mental health. We hear people speak of "being of two minds." Or that someone has "lost his mind." The word *mind* is often used synonymously with *brain*, or at the very least, something that is located within the brain. Merriam-Webster ("Mind," n.d.) defines the *mind* as "the element or complex of elements in an individual that feels, perceives, thinks, wills, and especially reasons … the organized conscious and unconscious adaptive mental activity of an organism." Offering simple clarity to all of this, Walsh (2004) refers to the mind as the "software" (p. 27) of the brain machine—that which makes the brain function.

Siegel (2012) makes the point that the mind is a process rather than a thing, and he goes on to describe the mind as "an embodied and relational process that regulates the flow of energy and information" (p. 2). Siegel means here that mental processes extend throughout the brain and are activated by and in turn activate communication patterns and relationships with others. That is, while we have long intuited that brain processes influence individual behaviors, researchers are now beginning to understand how brain structure, neural connections, and even the expression of human emotions are shaped by a variety of *external* processes, including interpersonal relationships (Coan, 2008). The study of these connections—mental processes such as meaning making, neurobiology, experiences of culture and family, and interpersonal relationships—is what Siegel (2012) refers to as *interpersonal neurobiology*. Interpersonal neurobiology "presents an integrated view of how human development occurs within a social world in transaction with the functions of the brain that give rise to the mind" (Siegel, 2001, p. 67). Understanding interpersonal neurobiology, Siegel argues, enables us to better understand and promote overall well-being.

BRAIN ARCHITECTURE

Before moving forward, a short tour of relevant brain structures helps provide some context. The commonly used term *brain structures* suggests that the brain is an organ, somewhat like other body organs such as the kidney or heart. However, here brain structure actually refers to closely intertwined neural clusters in the brain that are organized and categorized according to various levels of complexity (Siegel, 2012). For this reason, the brain is

ANATOMY OF THE BRAIN

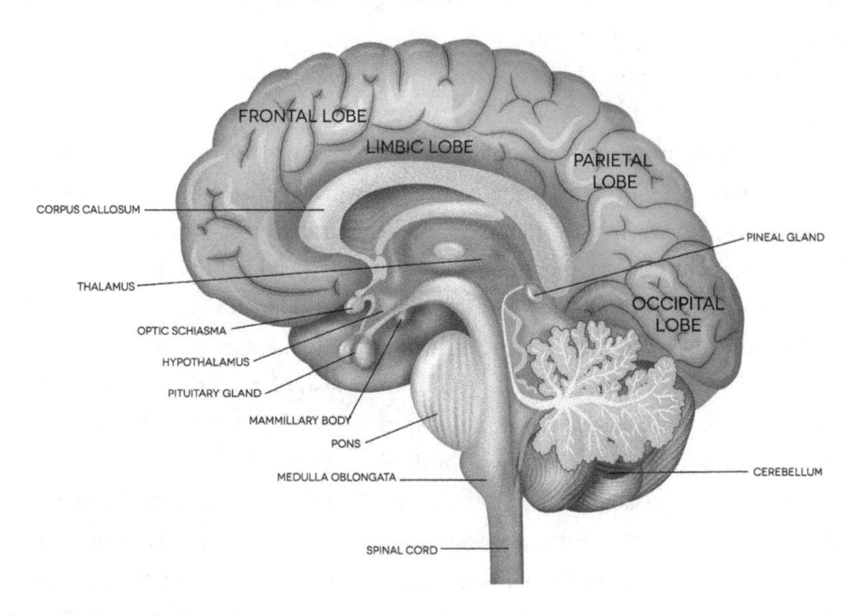

Photo 4.1

technically called the *central nervous system*. Figure 4.1 offers an image which may be helpful to understand this concept.

The **brain stem**, sometimes also called the *lower brain structure* or the *inner core of the brain*, is where are neuron clusters regulate energy flow, arousal, and physiological states of the body such as body temperature and breathing (Cozolino, 2014; Siegel, 2012). The *thalamus,* located in this lower brain region, is a neuron cluster that regulates sensory information and conscious awareness (Siegel, 2012). This is where information from the various bodily sensations flows into meaning-making structures in other parts of the brain. The *hypothalamus* is located in the very upper part of the brain stem and has extensive connections with other brain structures (Cozolino, 2014; Siegel, 2012). Thus, it functions like a command center for the brain. The hypothalamus works closely with the amygdala, located nearby in the central brain, communicating with the body through the autonomic nervous system, and controlling bodily functions such as breathing, blood pressure, and heartbeat; the hypothalamus, amygdala, and pituitary together play a critical role in how the body responds to stress and the processes around establishing physiological equilibrium or homeostasis (Cozolino, 2014; Lupien, McEwen, Gunnar, & Heim, 2009; Siegel, 2012).

The **central brain**, also known as the *limbic region* of the brain, houses neural clusters that are known for a variety of functions, including memory, emotion, learning, and the regulation of basic approach–avoidance responses (Cozolino, 2014). The limbic system is where emotion, motivation, and goal-directed behavior are mediated and integrated with other basic mental processes, including the cognitive processing of social cues and the activation of emotional responses (Siegel, 2012). Two critical clusters of neurons in this portion of the brain related to the processing of social cues and stress response are the *hippocampus* and the *amygdala*. They also play a critical role in coordinating neural activity across multiple regions of the brain (Siegel, 2012). The hippocampus is the part of the limbic system that regulates memory. The amygdala is associated with emotion. These two "structures," along with the pituitary, where key hormones are produced, work closely to interpret, mediate, and assign emotional responses to the sensory input that comes in through the brain stem (Lupien et al., 2009; Siegel, 2012). For example, say that you are walking in the woods and you come upon a potentially dangerous snake in your path. The sensory input registers the visual image of the snake, and the mind works quickly to assign appropriate meaning to what has been seen. The interpretation of snake, based on your memory of the concept of a snake, is what mediates your emotional response. If you hear and notice a shaker on the snake's tail, which you remember to be a telltale sign of a poisonous rattlesnake, the *hypothalamic-pituitary-adrenocortical* (HPA) axis will probably release the ACTH (adrenocorticotropic hormone) hormone, which, in turn, releases another hormone called *cortisol*. Cortisol is what regulates the body's response to stress (Baron-Cohen, 2011; Cozolino, 2014). On a physiological level, the cortisol causes a flooding release of glucose and inhibits its uptake, causing a narrowing of the arteries and an increase in heart rate. This is the sensation that compels you to feel fear and move to safety—it is a physiological response to stress—and key to what we refer to as a *stress response*. If, on the other hand, there is no rattle on the tail of the snake and if you remember that there are no dangerous snakes in the part of the country where you are walking, the stress response is inhibited. In this case, the physiological process goes back to its normal homeostatic level once the appropriate assignation that there is no danger is registered. Thus, the neuron clusters in the central brain are particularly important in the assignation of meaning and the triggering emotional and physiological responses in the stress response system.

Neuroscientists have also found that the hippocampus and the amygdala also mediate how social cues are interpreted (Coan, 2008; Cozolino, 2014; Siegel, 2012). This is because we generate understandings about the signs and symbols of human interaction through our memory of meanings and previous encounters, including earlier emotional responses. The HPA axis is affected by early parent–child interactions, attachments, and experiences of stress and trauma (Cozolino, 2014; Lupien et al., 2009; Siegel, 2001; Siegel, 2012). So, the hippocampus and amygdala are both affected by and also play important roles in how we make sense of our environment, how we interpret the behaviors of others, and in our emotional response to those around us.

The **cerebral cortex**, also known as the *upper brain structure,* is the outermost layer of the brain. It is appears as folded layers of cellular mass that are columns of neural clusters that allow for complex cognitive functioning (Siegel, 2012). Communication between the neuron columns in the various parts of cerebral cortex is critical to higher level information processing such as advanced perceptual and abstract representations, critical-thinking and reasoning abilities, and it is also where sensory, motor, and conscious experiences are organized (Cozolino, 2014; Siegel, 2012). These columns develop from back to front and over a long period of time and do not reach full maturity until early adulthood (Casey, Jones & Hare, 2008; Siegel, 2012; Walsh, 2004).

Within the cerebral cortex, the *frontal lobe* is engaged in complex mental processes, and most notably is involved in executive functioning—the cognitive processes that govern motor behavior, language, and abstract reasoning (Cozolino, 2014). It is this part of the brain that enables one to use past experience and knowledge to guide future behavior (Crews & Boettiger, 2009). The *parietal lobe* works closely with the frontal lobe to influence motor behaviors (Cozolino, 2014) as well as visual perception, and reading, writing, and computational tasks. The *temporal lobe* is generally thought to be involved in processing sensory input, particularly auditory perceptions, visual processing, and memories (Cozolino, 2014)—thus, it is involved in important speech and language processes. The *occipital lobe* is largely responsible for visual processing (Cozolino, 2014). The *cingulate cortex* has two sections (the posterior and the anterior cingulate cortex) and is involved in the integration of multiple brain processes, including cognition, sensory perception, emotional processing, and motor functioning (Cozolino, 2014).

The portion of the cerebral cortex that is located behind the forehead in the front part of the brain is the *prefrontal cortex.* This section of the brain is associated with memory, attention, and higher level cognitive abilities, including decision making and cognitive control, which is the ability to modulate attention and limbic impulses (Casey et al., 2008). The prefrontal cortex also is associated with self-awareness, empathy, emotional regulation, and attachment behaviors—these parts of the prefrontal cortex that integrate with the limbic system are sometimes referred to as the *paralimbic cortex* (Siegel, 2012). A cluster of neurons in the prefrontal cortex and the cingulate cortex enable *executive function skills*, which have to do with many of the skills used by therapists, such as cognitive flexibility, managing attention, goal setting, problem solving, impulse regulation, and complex information processing and organization (Cozolino, 2014; Crews & Boettiger, 2009; Siegel, 2012).

We know that the development of executive function is based on a complex interplay of many variables, including genetic makeup and environmental factors such as parenting, nutrition, play, educational experiences, trauma, environmental toxins, and stress (Masten et al., 2012). The long maturation time required for full functioning of the cerebral cortex helps explain the limitations that children and adolescents often have in regard to cognitive complexity, their ability to manage impulses and reactions, make sense of feelings, and maintain attention (Casey et al., 2008; Walsh, 2004). Walsh (2004) likens adolescent brain development to a new car with a high-powered engine and no breaks. He says, "Adolescence is a heck of a time for the impulse control center—the prefrontal cortex—to be under construction" (p. 65).

THE CENTRAL NERVOUS SYSTEM AND MEANING MAKING

As mentioned, Siegel (2012) describes the processes of the mind in terms of energy and information flow. These processes occur through a complex map of neural connections. Each neuron in this system has *synapses* and *dendrites* at its ends, enabling it to reach out to and connect with other neurons (Cozolino, 2010; Cozolino, 2014; Siegel, 2012). The synapses and dendrites facilitate the connection between tens of thousands of neurons throughout the whole central nervous system. Through these connections, electrical impulses are exchanged via the release of a chemical called a *neurotransmitter* (Cozolino, 2010; Siegel, 2010). Neurotransmitters are received through the dendrites of companion neurons, in a communication system typically referred to as *synaptic connections*. A neurotransmitter, then, is the hormone that facilitates the transfer of sensations between neurons.

When sensations are perceived through one, some, or all of the five senses they move up from the brain stem via synaptic connections. As the neurotransmitters connect and transfer energy between neurons across the various parts of the brain, "mental symbols" (Siegel, 2012, p. 8) or representations of information are patterned. Over time, the patterns of neurons that fire together form what is known as the *neural net profile* (Siegel, 2001, 2012), which gives rise to concept formation and meaning making. This complex web of synaptic connections linking sensory information to thought processes and physical responses is the foundation of the brain at work. Walsh (2004) aptly uses the metaphor of a complex electrical system to describe this process of the "thinking" mind.

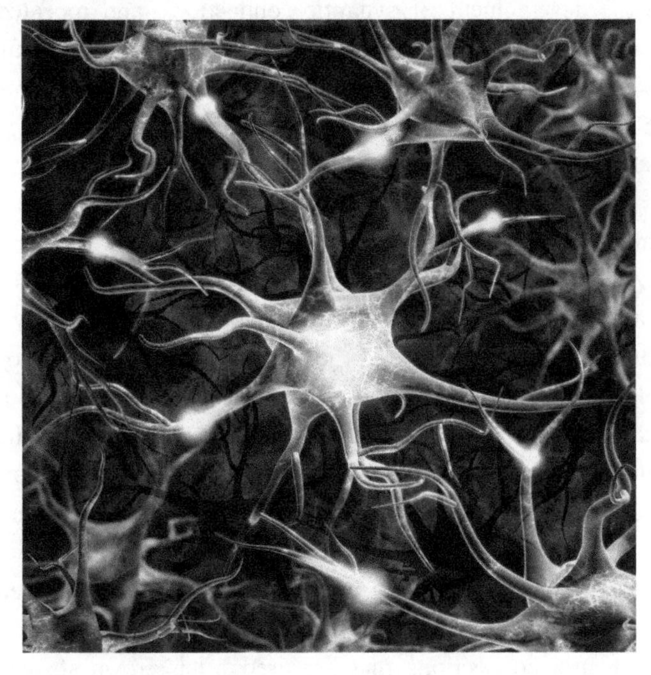

Photo 4.2

To better understand how this all works, let us return to our earlier example of being on a walk and suddenly coming upon a snake. Seeing the snake—this visual perception—stimulates a series of neurotransmitter firings across various parts of the central nervous system, coming together in a neural net profile to form the concept of a snake. Transmission of information through hippocampus enables this interpretation based on memory, and passage through the amygdala allows the assignation of emotional response. The identification of this long twisty reptile, then, is aided by our memory of what a snake is and all the possible connotations of having snake in our path. Our emotional reaction is mediated by how we understand the concept of snake. When the concept of snake is interpreted as a danger, the stress response system is triggered, likely causing a fright, flight, or freeze response reaction.

NEURAL BLOSSOMING AND PRUNING

An infant is born with an abundance of neurons, but at birth there are few synaptic connections between them. Everyday life experiences are what stimulate the development of synaptic connections, and repeated experiences over time activate and strengthen the development of certain neural pathways in the brain (Siegel, 2012). This is a process called *neuroplasticity* (Siegel, 2001), *axon elaboration* (Knudsen, 2004) or *neural blossoming* (Walsh, 2004). Gallagher (2005) points out, for example, that children's experimental play with various objects is one way in which synaptic connections begin in early childhood. Imagine that a child picks up a yellow toy and her caregiver labels it by color. When this experience repeats over time—a yellow pail, a yellow flower, and a yellow crayon are all identified specifically by color—a connection begins to be made, and the concept of *yellow* begins to develop. All of this is to say that the processes of neural development in the brain are stimulated by experiences in the environment (Blaustein & Kinniburgh, 2010; Gallagher, 2005), and these processes occur throughout the life span (Siegel, 2001, 2012). To fully understand the larger implications of this concept of neuroplasticity, the study of *epigensis* investigates the ways in which neural firings can alter genetic expression for future generations (Siegel, 2012).

Just as neural connections that are used often grown stronger; those that are not used will atrophy and disappear. This process is referred to as *parcellation* (Siegel, 2012), *pruning* (Siegel, 2012; Walsh, 2004), or *synaptic elimination* (Greenough, Black, & Wallace, 1987). More colloquially, Siegel (2012) calls this the "'use-it-or-lose-it' principle of brain development" (p. 22), although Gallagher (2005) asserts that even unused synapses remain intact within the central nervous system and thus are available for later learning.

IMPLICATIONS FOR MENTAL HEALTH

Siegel's (2012) concept of interpersonal neurobiology speaks to the ways in which the events in our lives and our everyday experiences within our community, family, culture, and other interpersonal relationships affect, on a neurobiological level, how we process information and respond to stress. This concept also addresses how these processes, in turn, affect our interactions and relationships in the social world. Here we take a look specifically at how experiences of trauma and stress affect mental health functioning, and how early life experiences can impact affect regulation, empathy, and perspective-taking skills.

COMPLEX TRAUMA

Siegel (2001) argues that the attachment relationship between young children and their caregivers affects neurobiological processes that promote healthy or unhealthy development. Indeed, research suggests that a history of minimal responsiveness on the part of one's caregiver during childhood, and especially the experience of harsh or unpredictable care or trauma during childhood, can have lasting neurological effects on later emotional functioning and behaviors (Baron-Cohen, 2011; Blaustein & Kinniburgh, 2010; Cook et al., 2005; Johnson, 2005; Mertin, 2014; Perry & Szalavitz, 2006; Rathus & Miller, 2015; Siegel, 2012). These effects may include limited complex cognitive functioning abilities; difficulties maintaining attention or focus, comprehending social cues, and negotiating interpersonal relationships; chronic stress response symptoms, including persistent emotion and behavior regulation difficulties, hypervigilance, difficulties in self-soothing, emotional vulnerability, and changes in the central nervous system; and diminished self-concept. Conversely, research also indicates that when children experience prosocial caretaking behaviors during childhood, such as grooming or physical contact, for example, these experiences can weaken stress-related dysfunction (Coan, 2008).

Chronic stress, experiences of abuse or neglect, exposure to domestic violence, war and forced displacement, traumatic loss, and exposure to community violence can leave children with what is typically referred to as *complex trauma* (Cohen, Mannarino, Kliethermes, & Murray, 2012; Cook et al., 2005). Like the effects of compromised caregiver–child attachments, complex trauma can affect children in the domains of attachment, cognition, affect-regulation, self-concept, behavior control, disassociation, and even in motor control, balance, and physical health (Cook et al., 2005). The long-term effects of living with chronic stress can be seen on cognitive functioning and mental health and interpersonal difficulties (Marin et al., 2011). Blaustein and Kinniburgh (2010) use the concept of *neuroplasticity* to explain how this happens. They argue that since our brain changes and develops in response to experience, the patterning of synaptic connections that occur from experiences of trauma prioritize the development of survival-related tasks, such as a heightened stress response system, and interfere with the development of other social and cognitive tasks. Hardy (2013, 2017) and Hardy and Laszloffy (2005) remind us that chronic stress and complex trauma can also result from experiences of devaluation, disruption of community, an assaulted sense of self, internalized voicelessness, and rage related to experiences of sociocultural trauma (such as experiencing micro-aggressions and other forms of racial or cultural oppression).

As it turns out, there are specific times in the development of the brain when neural activity is particularly sensitive to interpersonal and external experiences. It is during these *sensitive periods* of brain development, which occur largely during infancy and early childhood, that the environment of the young child has a particularly strong "instructive influence" (Knudsen, 2004, p. 1422) on neural circuit performance (Greenough et al., 1987; Johnson, 2005; Knudsen, 2004, Siegel, 2012; Walsh, 2004). According to Cozolino (2014), these sensitive periods of development are when there is rapid growth in the right hemisphere of the brain, influencing sensory and motor development as well as the basic structures for attachment and emotional regulation. Because the extent of neural growth that occurs during this time is so great, the interpersonal experiences that affect brain development are profound and have long-term development and well-being implications (Cozolino, 2014). For example, research suggests that stress and trauma during sensitive periods can lead to restricted emotional expression, a heightened susceptibility to stress, and more generally, compromised well-being (Kindsvatter & Geroski, 2014; Zeanah, Gunnar, McCall, Kreppner, & Fox, 2011).

As mentioned, the difficulties associated with chronic stress and complex trauma during childhood often extend into adulthood (Cook et al., 2005), but fortunately, we also know that the brain appears to have some capacity to modify neural connections throughout the lifetime (Doidge, 2007; Perry & Szalavitz, 2006). This is important because it suggests that damage from adverse childhood experiences may be repairable with intentional intervention.

Trauma-informed care is the term used to describe the constellation of services that are recommended for working with clients with a history of trauma. A critical component of the work with children who experience complex trauma is developing caregiver capacity to support affected children. According to Cook et al. (2005), the Complex Trauma Workgroup (CTWG) of the National Child Traumatic Stress Network identified the core components of intervention planning for working with complex trauma to include insuring safety; teaching and enhancing self-regulation skills (in the domains of affect, behavior, physiology, and cognition); strengthening attention and executive functioning abilities; resolving traumatic memories; enhancing coping skills; repairing faulty attachment relationships; and enhancing perceptions of self-worth, self-esteem, and positive self-appraisals. (See Cook et al., 2005, for more on these components of intervention planning. Also, see the ARC model of working with complex traumatic stress in children [Blaustein & Kinniburgh, 2010)] and dialectical behavior therapy [DBT] for children and adults [Linehan, 2015; Rathus & Miller, 2015]).

AFFECT REGULATION

Affect regulation refers to the ability to manage one's emotional response to a situation with flexibility (Eisenberg, Hofer, & Vaughan, 2007). As mentioned, the cycle of emotional response begins with a triggering event or experience that arouses some emotion. For example, a client lost his job, ended his marriage, or moved to a new city. The triggering event is interpreted in the brain, based on long- and short-term memory functions, and from this interpretation, emotional and behavioral responses are generated (Beer & Lombardo, 2007; Gross & Thompson, 2007; Siegel, 2012). The final part of emotional regulation is the return to homeostasis afterward (Courtois & Ford, 2013; Westphal & Bonanno, 2004)—this is when we calm down after experiencing a strong emotion. The cycle of emotional expression, then, includes a trigger, appraisal, emotional expression, and then a return to homeostasis or baseline functioning. Underscoring the connections between perceptions, emotional expression, and subsequent behavior is Gross and Thompson's (2007) point that emotions don't just "make us feel something, they make us feel like doing something" (p. 5).

The ability to manage or self-regulate one's emotions is thought to be learned during childhood in the context of positive caregiver–child attachments (Cozolino, 2010; Eisenberg et al., 2007; Stegge & Terwogt, 2007) and in the absence of experiencing stress and trauma, particularly during sensitive periods of development (Cozolino, 2010; Blaustein & Kinniburgh, 2010; Kindsvatter & Geroski, 2014). Affect regulation is important for intrapersonal and interpersonal mental health and functioning (Gross, 1998; Gross & Thompson, 2007). For example, an *overregulation* of emotion occurs when there is an inflexible restriction on the expression of affect. This may lead to rigid or avoidant behavior—a client may refuse to leave her house to avoid a perceived danger, avoid intimate relationships to evade the uncertainty or fear of being hurt, or try to plan and manage everything in her environment to prepare for every eventuality that may possibly happen in the future. *Underregulation*, on the other hand, is the lack of ability to manage the expression of emotion or difficulties in returning to homeostasis after feeling strong emotions. For example, aggravation becomes a physical altercation, a letdown becomes a catastrophe, or someone is in a chronic state of overarousal, unable to sit still or feel peaceful calm. Specific strategies used by helpers to help clients better regulate affect are outlined in Chapter 10.

EMPATHY AND PERSPECTIVE TAKING

Empathy refers to having the unique ability to understand and respond to the experiences of another person (Lamm, Batson & Decety, 2007). As was pointed out in Chapter 1, it is the ability to understand another person's perspective. This kind of perspective taking is associated with complex reasoning abilities, the ability to engage in social relationships (Heagle & Rehfeldt, 2006), and improved attitudes toward people who are different (Vescio, Sechrist, & Paolucci, 2003). Epley, Morewedge, and Keysar (2004) argue that most people understand others by first anchoring their perceptions in their own experiences. That is, we use our own experiences to anticipate or construct theories to predict future actions or situations involving others (Epley, Keysar, Van Boven, & Gilovich, 2004; Keysar, Lin, & Barr, 2003). For example, we typically reflect on our own experience of, let's say, an event that has just happened, and we use this reflection to hypothesize that a friend will probably have a similar experience. Increasing sophistication allows us to recognize that we are different from our friends, and we can accommodate for those differences by altering our perspectives.

The concept of *mirror neurons*, which are located in the frontal and parietal lobes of the cerebral cortex, was a serendipitous finding that neuroscientists now use to explain how this self-to-other process works (Baron-Cohen, 2011; Gallese & Goldman, 1998; Siegel, 2012; Spunt & Lieberman, 2012). Researchers noticed that the neural activity that was present when a monkey ate a peanut was similar to the neural activity when the monkey witnessed a researcher eat a peanut. This revealed a connection between a perception and intentional motor action. These mirror neurons, it is hypothesized, create a neural image of the mental state of another person (Siegel, 2012; Spunt & Lieberman, 2012). Siegel (2012) describes it as "the first stage of compassion, or 'feeling with' other persons" (p. 166).

Baron-Cohen (2011) uses the phrase "the empathy circuit" (p. 20) in reference to the complex neural firings that are part of the expression of empathy. He believes that mirror neurons alone do not account for the full empathy circuit (Baron-Cohen, 2011; Spunt & Lieberman, 2012). Pointing to MRI research indicating the activation of the amygdala when asking subjects to make judgments about the emotional and mental states of others, Baron-Cohen highlights the important role of the amygdala in the perception of empathy. In fact, neuroimaging research indicates that neural activity in the prefrontal cortex, amygdala, and the cerebellum underlies the cognitive and affective components of empathy (Baron-Cohen, 2011; Lamm et al., 2007; Masten, Eisenberger, Pfeifer, Colich, & Dapretto, 2013). So, while the mirror system enables us to identify emotional-relevant events, a complementary neural system called the *mentalizing system* supplies the meaning-making or attributional process to those perceptions (Spunt & Lieberman, 2012). The neural activity associated with the mentalizing system is located in a different set of cortical brain regions. And, because the neural clusters in the cerebral cortex mature over time, this cognitive component of empathy develops more complex sensitivity with puberty (Masten et al., 2013).

The neurobiology of these complex processes related to perspective taking, social cognition, and empathy are still not completely understood by neuroscientists (Siegel, 2012), and more discussion about this topic is well beyond the scope of this book. The point is that understanding the experience of others and adjusting one's behavior in response to social cues is a complex process that requires interaction among sensory perceptions and emotional and cognitive attribution and reasoning processes. These are all part of complex neural processes within the central nervous system. And, because the cerebral cortex develops over time, these abilities are not fully developed in children and adolescents.

CHAPTER SUMMARY

This chapter focused on how neural activity in the brain is both stimulated by and influential to interpersonal human behavior. We began with a review of basic brain structures and neurobiology and then spoke about how these concepts are related to experiences of stress and complex trauma, affect regulation, empathy, and perspective taking. While this information is relevant to our work with clients, it is also important in the discussion about helper self-awareness, self-management, and self-care, which are the focus of the next chapter.

REFLECTION QUESTIONS

1. If the expression of emotion is largely a function of synaptic connectivity in the central nervous system, how can therapists actually help clients who grapple with affect regulation difficulties such as mood disorders and anxiety?

2. What symptoms or behaviors might give you a clue that a client has experienced trauma or prolonged stress during childhood?

3. If you were working with a family of a young child who experienced a traumatic event, what does this chapter tell you about what might help that child avoid experiencing the effects of complex trauma?

CHAPTER

Personalization Issues, Self-Awareness, and Practitioner Self-Care

Chapter Outline

INTRODUCTION

A clinical helper works a bit like a ship captain navigating through the calm and stormy seas of therapy. To be a captain in therapy, all of the factors mentioned in Chapter 1 are required—the captain must have professional competence, including appropriate clinical knowledge and skills, and the captain must also be empathic, be able to establish a therapeutic alliance, work with intentionality, and have the capacity to instill hope and promote agency. While navigating the sea of therapy, the clinician must also be able to tolerate the discomfort and setbacks as the ship tosses and pitches in heavy wind and

Photo 5.1

unpredictable seas. Too, the counselor must be patient during long periods of calm as the client works to make meaning and decide to take action. To do this work, clinicians need to be steady on their feet, have their radar working, and be willing to hang in there through blustery times.

While the therapeutic *process* may, at times, be like a calm and stormy sea, the *goal* of therapy is always to enhance the life of the client. So, unlike the captain of a cruise liner whose job it is to make all of the guests happy, the therapist is in the business of enabling clients to become healthy and competent in managing their lives. This type of journey is not always fun and happy. A critical component of navigating the seas of therapy is that the captain must also be able to drive the ship without taking over the helm completely. These skills of shared navigation require a unique captaining skill. They require an awareness of when it is safe and in the best interests of the client to back off and let the client take charge. To this end the counselor must be able to separate her own drive instincts so as to honor those of the client—as long as they lead to the identified goal. And the captain of therapy must be able to do this even when the path chosen by the client is different from the one favored by the captain. The ship captain of therapy must remember that she is in the journey because of the client—that the goals of the journey are about the client, and the actions to realize these goals must also be taken by the client. With a watchful eye on client safety and an appropriate level of humility, the captain of therapy works in the interest of promoting agency for future navigations and must be willing to see and acknowledge that she is a shared partner in the successes that are obtained.

This business of therapy is complex. It is not a job for the faint of heart!

In this chapter, we will explore some of the ways in which clinician beliefs, experiences, and behaviors can have a profound impact on their therapeutic work, making the already challenging work of navigating the ship of therapy even more complex. First, we explore how personalization issues, including how clinicians' early life experiences, everyday stressors, the stress of the work itself, and the clinician's values, beliefs, and biases affect their therapeutic work. We end the chapter with a review of the literature regarding self-awareness, self-regulation, and self-care. The overriding point in this chapter is that self-awareness and self-management are critical in order to be fully present and focused on the needs of the client.

HELPER MENTAL HEALTH AND PERSONALIZATION ISSUES

Pieterse, Lee, Ritmeester, and Collins (2013) point to a long-standing implicit understanding in the helping professions that the personal processes and reactions of the therapist—traditionally referred to in psychodynamic circles as countertransference—affect the course of therapy. Of course, in psychoanalytic therapy as well as in other therapeutic modalities, countertransference is a therapeutic tool that is used with intentionality to affect the therapeutic process. However, it is also the case that the personal processes and reactions of the therapist can be detrimental to therapy and damaging to a client. Bernard (1979; Bernard & Goodyear, 1998) uses the term *personalization* to represent some of the ways in which a clinician's own personal life and health can impair his work with clients. We begin here with an examination of various components of personalization and later will move into the ways in which they affect therapy.

One set of personalization issues that is potentially impactful to professional functioning is generally referred to as **unresolved issues** in the therapist's life. These may be festering or complex family conflicts, difficult family of origin dynamics (Pieterse et al., 2013), and other "histories and vulnerabilities"

(Barnett, Baker, Elman, & Schoener, 2007, p. 604), including those related to early experiences of stress and trauma or other mental health difficulties. For example, Hersoug (2004) reports that clinicians' parental relationships (i.e., their relationships with their own parents) and negative introjects (i.e., their negative feelings about themselves) affect their ability to develop a strong therapeutic alliance with their clients and their use of therapeutic exploration techniques. Interestingly, Barnett et al. (2007) suggest that some clinicians may actually be attracted to the field of helping due to their own personal experiences of trauma or dysfunction and an unhealthy desire to provide care to others.

Even in the absence of significant early life stress or trauma, everyday experiences of **stress** and acute personal challenges such as, for example, a breakup with a partner or a significant financial loss, can affect a clinician's mental health and interfere with her ability to be fully present and therapeutic in the office (Barnett et al., 2007; Smith & Moss, 2009). Personal stress does not always adversely affect performance, of course. But, when stress continues with little melioration and when it moves into personal impairment, it can be deleterious to clinician competence and contaminate the therapeutic process (Barnett et al., 2007). These authors identify the following as potential indicators of stress impairment: frequent experiences of frustration, impatience, or anger toward a client; boredom; a lack of focus in one's work; and an increased or inappropriate reactivity to triggers. For some clinicians, experiences of fatigue, decreased motivation, and feelings of inadequacy or a lack of fulfillment can also signal distress. Finally, engagement in unhealthy coping behaviors such as increased alcohol or drug use and unhealthy food consumption are potential signs of impairment.

The concept of personalization also refers to the ways in which clinicians' **feelings, belief systems, values, and cultural biases** can potentially contaminate their work with clients. Borrell-Carrió and Epstein (2004), for example, assert "errors often result not from a lack of knowledge but from the mindless application of unexamined habits and the interference of unexamined emotions" (p. 310). As discussed in Chapter 2, we live in a society that is saturated with discourses about social identities, many of which are inaccurate to the lived experience of people within those groups. The subtle and ubiquitous nature of social discourses means that they often emerge outside of rational thought. Even if these ideas stand in opposition to how we were socialized in

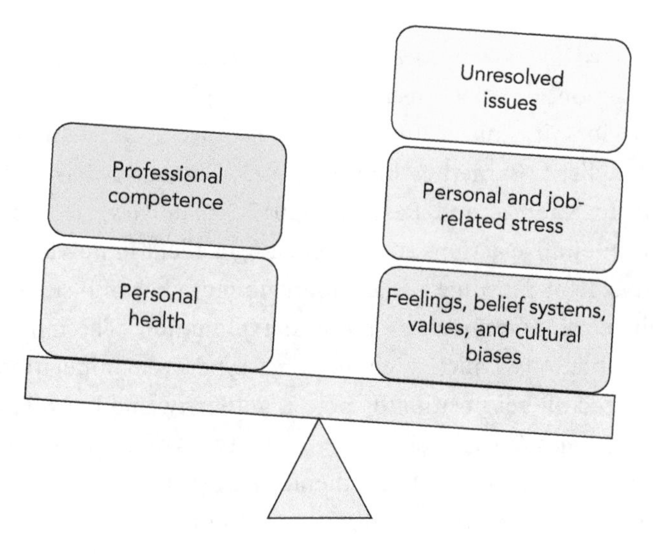

Figure 5.1 *Personalization Issues in Counseling*

our families, they exert a mighty force on how we understand or interact with others. The discussion below about implicit memory and bias helps explain how this happens at the interpersonal neurobiological level.

The final way in which personalization issues affect clinical helping has to do with the challenges and stresses inherent to the work of helping—I think of these as the **occupational hazards of helping**. If clinicians are not vigilant, the toll of their stressful work can have implications for their work as well as their personal lives. Often referred to as vicarious traumatization, burnout, emotional exhaustion, and compassion fatigue, these occupational hazards may make it difficult for clinicians to create sound therapeutic relationships and adhere to their intended intervention protocols, and these experiences can even affect their personal relationships outside of work (Barnett et al., 2007; Charlemagne-Odle, Harmon, & Maltby, 2014; Killian, 2008; Smith & Moss, 2009; Waltman, Frankel, & Williston, 2016). We will discuss these in more detail later when we turn our attention to the emotional toll of helping.

THERAPEUTIC CONTAMINATION AND BOUNDARY VIOLATIONS

The term *therapeutic contamination* is used by Barnett et al. (2007) in reference to the ways in which personalization issues such as those mentioned above can have an adverse effect on therapy. Related to this, *boundary violations* are actions or situations in which a therapist is engaged in unprofessional behaviors; it is most often used in reference to behaviors that harm or exploit a client (Barnett & Johnson, 2015; Thomas & Pastusek, 2012). According to Thomas and Pastusek (2012), boundary violations range from nonexploitative actions such as greeting a client in public or meeting a client outside of scheduled office hours, to more harmful situations that include financial, emotional, or physical exploitation. The more extreme boundary violations typically entail some type of manipulation by the therapist based on her position of power, authority, and knowledge about the client (Thomas & Pastusek, 2012). These types of boundary violations serve the interest or needs of the therapist over those of the client, and typically result because the therapist's position of power is be perceived so strongly by clients that they agree to things that are clearly inappropriate. As mentioned in Chapter 3, when a clinician suspects that a colleague has committed a harmful or exploitative boundary violation, he should take his concerns to that clinician. Depending on the situation, he may also need to report his concerns to institutional or law enforcement authorities or take his concerns to the state or national professional ethics committee or licensing board.

It is important to note, however, that some flexibility is necessary in regard to boundary crossings in therapy (Barnett & Johnson, 2015; Thomas & Pastusek, 2012). Extending a session, conducting a home visit, touching a grieving client on the forearm, for example, may be therapeutic in some situations and with some clients. But when these behaviors are not consistent with the helping contract or intervention plan, or when they are not in the best interests of the client, they have the potential to be harmful. For this reason, Thomas and Pastusek (2012) caution that a lack of awareness of or attention to even these minor or seemingly inconsequential boundary crossings puts one at risk for engaging in more serious violations.

INTERPERSONAL NEUROBIOLOGY AND THERAPEUTIC CONTAMINATION

We have identified a range of personalization issues that have potential contamination effects on a clinician's ability to appropriately provide therapy. Here we will draw on Siegel's discussion of interpersonal neurobiology to help us understand, briefly, how personalization issues can become hazardous in therapy.

EMOTION AND MEMORY

Research indicates that the ways in which sensory information is coded in memory influences how memories will be activated at a later date (Siegel, 2012). Siegel illustrates this point with an example of someone on a trip to Paris who visits the Eiffel Tower. During the trip, the visual image of the Eiffel Tower makes an impression and is encoded and stored in memory. Later, that visual image of the Eiffel Tower surfaces when that person recalls his trip to Paris. According to Siegel, this is because the memory of the trip to Paris is partially encoded through a visual perception of the Eiffel Tower—the neural net profile or concept of Paris includes the visual image of the tower. Now let us say that the visitor was bitten by a dog during the trip to Paris. In this case, his recall of the Eiffel Tower may be surprisingly shaped by anxiety or fear, related to the traumatic dog bite incident. This is because, Siegel (2012) says, traumatic memories are often stored in the amygdala-related memory systems and recalled unintentionally. Memories merged with emotion are often re-experienced emotionally.

This is magnified in the case of memories that are associated with early childhood experiences of stress and trauma. Remember that during the sensitive periods of development there is extensive neural growth in the brain that is particularly sensitive to interpersonal experiences, particularly those of trauma, stress, and caregiver–child attachments (Cozolino, 2014). So, we might say that early experiences of trauma are mapped into early brain development. In addition, as mentioned in Chapter 4, the HPA axis, which includes the hippocampus and amygdala, is affected by early parent–child interactions, attachments, and experiences of stress and trauma (Cozolino, 2014; Lupien, McEwen, Gunnar, & Heim, 2009; Siegel, 2001; Siegel, 2012). So, for some people, memories of childhood may be regaled with powerful emotional sensations, and this may happen out of conscious awareness.

Our discussion about interpersonal neurobiology in Chapter 4 was helpful in pointing to ways in which mental health issues can be affected by central nervous system development and functioning. Here the point is that all of this happens for clinicians as easily as it does for clients. So, when a clinician is triggered by something that happens in therapy and has unresolved issues related to early stress or trauma, he will be particularly vulnerable to emotional dysregulation. This is not to say that all clinicians who experienced stress or trauma in their early lives lack affect regulation abilities, and it certainly does not imply that they cannot be excellent therapists. It is just to say that the triggering that can occur with personalization issues may be deeply rooted in brain circuitry and may require careful and intentional awareness and management in trigger situations.

DUAL MEMORY PROCESSES

We have been talking about the important role of memory in the process of affect regulation. Here we turn our attention to the ways in which memory also plays a role in identity development and the transmission of culture. In this conversation, we will focus on the dual memory processes of *explicit* and *implicit memory*. Understanding these two processes helps us understand the ways in which one's assumptions, values, and beliefs affect interpersonal behaviors, including therapeutic helping.

Explicit memory, according to Cozolino (2010), is where information acquired from semantic (language), sensory, and motor input is stored. This information is acquired from conscious experiences and learning processes, and typically it is easily accessible for later use. For example, Angel was taught how to ride a bicycle by her mother, who told her how bikes work, had her sit on the bicycle, and then initially held the bike steady as Angel learned how to use the pedals and brakes and figured out how to balance herself while moving. As Angel began this new skill of bicycle riding, she coached herself to "move into the sway" and to "pedal and glide," just as her mother had taught her. These instructions and actions were stored in her explicit memory, and she was easily able to recall them when she was first learning to ride.

Implicit memory contains "unconscious patterns of learning stored in hidden layers of neural processing, largely inaccessible to conscious awareness" (Cozolino, 2010, p. 77). According to Mancia (2006), implicit memory is the place where emotional and affective experiences—many of which were even preverbal and presymbolic and the result of early parent–child relationship experiences—are stored. Although the process of acquiring and storing information in implicit memory is largely out of our conscious awareness, the information stored there still influences our thinking processes.

By way of example, let us return to little Angel and her bike-riding lessons. Instead, however, let us say that Angel was being taught to ride her bike by her father, who had a moderate fear of bike riding himself related to a bike accident he had as a child. This early accident seemed to create a general anxiety about parenting for Angel's dad; he sometimes worried that his daughter would get hurt when she was outdoors or trying something new. Determined not to let any of these fears rub off on Angel, however, the dad often tried to engage Angel in new activities. When it seemed that Angel was ready for riding a two-wheeled bike, her dad dutifully taught her all that he knew about how to ride a bike. As they were practicing riding the bike, however, his anxiety was, understandably, present. He did not see how slow he was to release her handlebars as she tried to ride on her own. He was not aware of the many cautions he called out to her as she started to ride. And his habit of trying to run alongside her to shelter any fall left him breathless and feeling guilty each time she did swerve or fall. Fortunately, Angel was coordinated and quickly became successful in pedaling the bike on her own. But, weeks later, she appeared reluctant to ride the bike. When her father asked her why she wouldn't ride bikes with him, she commented that bike riding was pretty scary and she was always afraid that she would fall or have an accident. So, while the dad's intentions were noble and his verbal instructions also sound, his nonverbal contradictory messages appeared to have silently worked their way into little Angel's implicit memory.

Explicit and implicit memory systems are located in different areas of the brain, Cozolino (2010) tells us, and these different locations influence how and what is retrieved and encoded in each system. Explicit memory is located near the hippocampus and develops more fully later as the cerebral cortex matures. Given this location, the explicit memory is more generally ruled by spatial and temporal information processing systems (Cozolino, 2010). It interacts with complex cognitive and logical thought processing and is sometimes called *rule-based* memory (Boysen, 2010).

Implicit memory, on the other hand, is hosted in the amygdala, thalamus, and the mid-frontal cortex section of the brain and appears to begin recording experiences even before birth (Mancia, 2006). Remember that the amygdala is largely responsible for the emotional component of memory functions. It plays a "'behind the screens' role in creating emotional bias in conscious processing" (Cozolino, 2010, p. 81). Boysen (2010) refers to

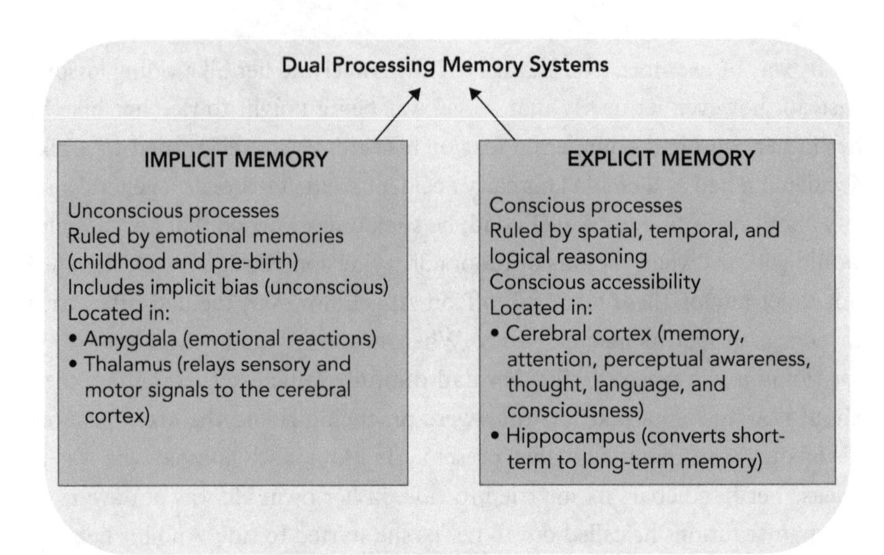

Figure 5.2 *Dual Processing Memory Systems*

this as the *associative* memory process. Together, they create a complex and broad cognitive appraisal system, which Boysen calls the *dual processing* memory system.

IMPLICIT BIAS

It is Boysen (2010) who helps us understand how assumptions, values, and beliefs stored in implicit memory unconsciously influence the practice of helping. Remember that information stored in both memory systems is accumulated from repeated experiences over time. As an example, let us think about some of the rituals associated with spiritual practices such as attending a temple, mosque, or church. When one regularly participates in a specific faith practice, and particularly when one has emotional experience associated with that practice, memories form in the dual processing memory system. Concepts and ideas form in explicit memory from the overt teachings of the practice. They also form in implicit memory systems from the emotional and other nonverbal experiences of participating in that practice. The learning that occurs in association with these explicit and implicit memories will inform that person's beliefs, values, and assumptions in any number of ways. I have met many people who unquestionably accept that Allah exists, others who have an unwavering belief that there is a God in heaven, and others who insist that there are multiple gods and spirits all around in everyday life. In addition, I have met many who deny the existence of any god, Allah, or spirits that inform life and existence, even after a long history of participating in a particular faith practice. And for many of these people, these beliefs—whatever they are—are merged with emotion and spoken with passion. Explicit and implicit memory systems are an important part of how the beliefs, values, and emotions associated with early or repeated faith practices, for example, influence everything from daily routines, behaviors, and dreams to engagement with others and worldview.

Also, remember that information stored in the implicit memory, typically associated with somatic and emotional content, is a part of a process of concept formation that happens out of conscious awareness (Boysen, 2010). As it turns out, memories of experiences can lie dormant in implicit memory over long periods of time and then suddenly appear, as if from nowhere, and influence our understandings or reaction to something. This process is what Boysen (2010) refers to as *implicit bias*, and it helps us understand how what we have learned and experienced in our own life can surface and influence our thinking in therapy, even when we no longer consciously subscribe to those ideas.

We are all raised in families and social communities that have ideas, beliefs, values, and assumptions about the world. When particular ideas or notions are articulated and demonstrated in a variety of ways over time, the synaptic connections of concept formulation become quite strong. These ideas and values are processed and stored in dual processing memory systems, meaning that they are activated in and out of conscious awareness.

Even though these processes of concept formation occur in both implicit and explicit memory functions, Boysen (2010) explains that explicit memory processes are not as quick and automatic as implicit memory systems. That is, the images and visceral messages that are stored in the implicit memory—implicit biases—are easily triggered; they are not constructed through rational thought. This means that implicit bias is our automatic go-to filter for interpreting experiences. It is the filter through which we process new information before we actually have time to think.

For us as clinicians, the implication of this lag time in explicit memory processes is that when we are working with clients, it is our own biased beliefs, values, and attitudes that will initially and more effortlessly inform our cognitive appraisal processes. And, because implicit memory processes occur largely out of conscious awareness, we are often unaware how our own personal ideas, values, beliefs, attitudes, and experiences bias how we think about and how we interact with our clients. This means that our own filters sit between us and our clients.

THE EMOTIONAL TOLL OF HELPING

We now turn our attention back to the earlier discussion about occupational hazards that are inherent, sometimes, to the work of mental health clinicians. *Vicarious traumatization, compassion fatigue, secondary trauma, secondary traumatic stress, empathic strain*, and *burnout* are terms that are sometimes used interchangeably to discuss the ways in which helpers experience an emotional reaction to the stories of or witnessing of someone else's stress or trauma (Ledoux, 2015; Merriman, 2015; Rzeszutek & Partyka, 2015). Although these terms are sometimes used interchangeably, there is merit to understanding their differences. We will also discuss the ways in which they can burden the helper and the therapeutic relationship.

Vicarious traumatization is a term that refers to the negative psychological effects on clinicians from their exposure to their clients' stories of trauma, pain, and suffering (Courtois & Ford, 2013; Rzeszutek & Partyka, 2015; Skovholt, 2001). Secondary trauma and secondary traumatic stress typically refer to this same concept. *Compassion fatigue* and empathic strain result from facing continuous and prolonged contact with clients who have profound difficulties in their lives (Ledoux, 2015). These experiences are compounded, according to Fahy (2007), with additional factors such as working in an environment or profession that is chronically devalued. *Burnout* is the term that describes the experience of being overloaded by work with chronic and complex problems or working in an environment that is overdemanding and chronically devalued. Here we will discuss these three concepts in more detail.

VICARIOUS TRAUMATIZATION

According to research, repeated and prolonged exposure to the trauma experience of others—whether that is by actually witnessing trauma inflicted on someone or by hearing someone's account of trauma—can result in short- and long-term changes to how we experience ourselves, others, and the world around us (Rzeszutek & Partyka, 2015; Smith & Moss, 2009). Hearing clients' accounts of sexual assault, abuse, accidents, and violence, for example, particularly when these stories are graphic, can cause emotional reactions in therapists that parallel post-traumatic stress disorder (Rzeszutek & Partyka, 2015; Smith & Moss, 2009). Thus, Rzeszutek and Partyka's (2015) definition of vicarious traumatization: "personal transformations experienced by trauma workers that stem from a cumulative empathic engagement with another's traumatic experiences" (p. 213).

A variety of symptoms are associated with vicarious traumatization, including tension or preoccupation with the client's stories or experiences, a perpetual oversensitive or hyperarousal state and invasive thoughts and images; or conversely, an avoidance of conversations and topics related to the trauma experience altogether (ACA, n.d.b; Trippany, White Kress, & Wilcoxon, 2004). Helpers who experience vicarious trauma may engage in avoidance, numbing, and hypervigilance; they may feel vulnerable, inadequate, and mistrustful of self and others; and many experience a sense of emptiness, inhibiting their interpersonal and personal intimate relationships (Smith & Moss, 2009; Trippany et al., 2004). Obviously, these responses can compromise a clinician's ability to be fully present and functional in therapy, and they also can affect his personal life. It is important to remember that these symptoms are not indicative of incompetence or any other fault of the clinician; they result as a way of protecting oneself and coping with the damage resulting from witnessing stories of trauma (Rzeszutek & Partyka, 2015).

COMPASSION FATIGUE

Compassion fatigue refers to when clinicians experience emotional and physical exhaustion as a result of working over time with clients who have extremely difficult lives (Ledoux, 2015; Rzeszutek & Partyka, 2015). It might be thought of as an experience of moral distress or a condition of deep empathy, rather than a result of direct exposure to trauma stories (Ledoux, 2015). Compassion fatigue is a deep psychological burden, spiritual exhaustion, or emotional pain that results from witnessing countless stories that have in common a plot line of stress, trauma, challenge, and difficulty. Clinicians who experience compassion fatigue often feel a deep awareness of the suffering of others and also feel frustration and hopelessness about their ability to affect change (Killian, 2008; Merriman, 2015; Rzeszutek & Partyka, 2015).

The symptomology of compassion fatigue is quite variable and also overlaps with the symptomology of vicarious traumatization and burnout (Merriman, 2015; Rzeszutek & Partyka, 2015). Clinicians experiencing compassion fatigue may display markers of post-traumatic stress, such as anxiety, stress response behaviors (i.e., hyperarousal and intrusive thoughts), fatigue, concentration and sleep difficulties; and they sometimes have difficulties regulating anger or frustration (Killian, 2008; Merriman, 2015). They may also experience burnout, or feeling overwhelmed by one's work (Ledoux, 2015; Rzeszutek & Partyka, 2015); they may have difficulties separating their work and personal lives or maintaining appropriate boundaries with clients; and they may also develop a lack of confidence in their abilities or lose passion for their work (Merriman, 2015). Also like those who experience vicarious traumatization, symptoms of compassion fatigue often overflow into the clinician's personal life in the form of communication and intimacy difficulties (Merriman, 2015).

A number of risk factors are identified in association with compassion fatigue. These include having a high caseload (particularly when that caseload includes a number of clients who have experienced trauma), a lack of access to regular supervision, professional isolation, an unsupportive work environment, poor habits of self-care, and a lack of self-awareness (Killian, 2008). Students in training to become therapists and new clinicians are particularly susceptible to compassion fatigue (Merriman, 2015), as are clinicians who have their own personal experiences of trauma or mental health difficulties and those who lack experience in the area of trauma therapy (Rzeszutek & Partyka, 2015).

BURNOUT

Another occupational hazard for clinical helpers is burnout. This refers to mental and physical exhaustion attributable to working with chronic and complex problems in an environment that is unrewarding, unsupportive or otherwise challenging (Fahy, 2007; Trippany et al., 2004). According to Skovholt (2001), burnout is a "slow erosion" (p. 106) of motivation and one's sense of competence and a "profound weariness and hemorrhaging of the self" (p. 107). Unlike vicarious traumatization, burnout is more related to stress related to the workplace rather than exposure to trauma or severe client issues. It exists in work environments where perceived demands outweigh perceived resources (Merriman, 2015) and tends to be a process that occurs over time (Fahy, 2007).

Symptoms of burnout typically include emotional exhaustion, fatigue, frustration, stress, depersonalization, hopelessness, and a reduced sense of personal accomplishment (Killian, 2008; Rzeszutek & Partyka, 2015; Skovholt, 2001). More visibly, clinicians who experience burnout may display poor work attendance, be highly cynical, and may report physical ailments with more frequency than normal (Fahy, 2007). James and Gilliland (2001) describe burnout as a process that begins with depersonalization, which is a separation of one's feelings and experiences from oneself. Depersonalization may appear as cynicism and negativity, and be experienced by others as rude or insensitive. This is followed by diminished sense of personal accomplishment. There is a sense of being ineffective or a lack of self-efficacy—the belief in one's ability to affect change. In the end, burnout can lead to emotional exhaustion, sleep difficulties, and other symptoms of depression. Attendance problems may surface and the clinician's engagement with others may be affected. Burnout, like vicarious traumatization and compassion fatigue, has implications on a clinician's therapeutic functioning as well as overall

Photo 5.2

well-being. Fahy (2007) cautions that in many contexts, the concept of burnout has a clinician-blaming connotation. But it is important to remember that the symptoms of burnout are related to the complexities of working in circumstances that are extremely challenging.

As a result of any or all of these occupational hazards, distress may manifest in serious physical or mental health challenges such as panic attacks, shakiness, appetite, hair and weight loss, exhaustion, and sleeping difficulties. Smith and Moss (2009) report that substance misuse is not uncommon and that depression, sometimes with suicidal ideation, is a leading reason for psychologists to seek their own therapy. Sadly, adding to these challenges, Charlemagne-Odle et al. (2014) report that some practitioners believe they should not talk with other professionals about the ways in which these occupational and personal stressors are affecting them, fearing that they will be stigmatized as having their own mental health issues.

SELF-AWARENESS

It is not difficult to understand the need for clinicians to be mentally fit and able to manage their own lives in this challenging work of helping others (Donati & Watts, 2005; Kottler, 1991). In fact, this emphasis on mental wellness is directly noted or alluded to in the codes of ethics in most helping professions (e.g., American Psychiatric Association, 2010; ASCA, 2016; International School Psychology Association, 2011; NASW, 2008). In short, counselors have a responsibility to be aware of signs of clinical impairment (Wheeler & Bertram, 2012). Yet, what actually constitutes clinical impairment is under considerable debate in the literature (Smith & Moss, 2009). Definitions of clinician impairment range from professional incompetence or poor clinical skills to unethical behavior, to not being healthy enough to properly care for others. Simply put, clinical impairment is when therapy is contaminated by the clinician's personalization issues and/or when boundary violations are harmful or exploitative.

Most agree that self-awareness is one way in which clinicians can begin to manage themselves and their personal reactions to the work that happens in therapy (Borrell-Carrió & Epstein, 2004; Pieterse, Lee, Ritmeester, & Collins, 2013; Waltman et al., 2016). Pieterse et al. (2013) define self-awareness as "a state of being conscious of one's thoughts, feelings, beliefs, behaviours and attitudes, and knowing how these factors are shaped by important aspects of one's developmental and social history" (p. 191). They believe that clinician self-awareness must include both a psychological openness and self-communication or metacognitive abilities. Self-awareness also includes, according to Borrell-Carrió and Epstein (2004), the ability to detect when one is activated, emotionally saturated, operating on cognitive distortions, or when one has made an error that needs to be corrected. It enables us to be attentive to the risk factors and warning signs of therapeutic contamination.

Pieterse et al. (2013) offer the integrated model of self-awareness to help clarify what is needed in terms of clinician self-awareness. In this model, they focus on these components of self-awareness: relationship and personality style, family of origin dynamics, spiritual/religious orientation, social class affiliation, racial/ethnic identity, and gender and sexual orientation. This model expands the notion of self-awareness, then, to include not only the clinician's experiences, but also aspects of one's identity and social location, as these also affect counselors' perceptions of and reaction to their clients.

Relationship and personality style have to do with the counselor's emotional style of engagement with the client—the degree to which the therapist is understanding, affirming, supportive, and able to facilitate affect expression and attend to the affective experience of the client (Pieterse et al., 2013). There is not one type of personality that is best suited to clinical mental health counseling, but these authors argue that all clinicians must, at the very least, be able to engage psychologically with their client. The focus on ***family of origin*** in the integrated model of self-awareness refers to the ways in which the therapist has developed patterns of communication and social connections that are associated with early experiences in family and with other central figures in early childhood (Pieterse et al., 2013). Here the focus is on having the awareness of how this component of personalization affects the therapeutic process. These authors are particularly attentive to how one's own family of origin influences one's ability to differentiate and have boundaries. They also believe that clinicians must be flexible enough to engage in a variety of relationships across roles and situations.

The integrated model of self-awareness also addresses the ways in which ***racial and ethnic identity*** and ***social class status*** influence therapeutic work with clients (Pieterse et al., 2013). Here it is also important for clinicians to be aware of the beliefs, values, and attitudes they have learned through racial, ethnic, and social class socialization. This includes not just cultural norms passed down through generations but also an awareness of the social positions that are on offer to us as a result of discourses, power differentials, and experiences (or lack of experiences) of bias and discrimination. Along these lines, Pieterse et al. (2013) also point out that ***spiritual and religious beliefs*** influence clinical decision making. Clinicians' values and beliefs around faith also extend to ideas about morality and decision making—all areas that are interwoven into many therapeutic conversations in one way or another. ***Gender identity*** and ***sexual orientation***, the two final components of the integrated model of self-awareness (Pieterse et al., 2013), are similarly seeped in contextual norms and discourses that have the potential to influence the therapeutic relationship in helpful or harmful ways. For counselors, awareness is critical for mediating the socialization we all have experienced around race, ethnicity, gender identity, social status, and sexual orientation. As Sue, Arredondo, & McDavis (1992) and Arredondo et al. (1996) assert, it is the responsibility of clinicians to bring one's biases into more conscious awareness, and to work to eliminate the ways in which bias contaminates our work with others. Clinicians need to be aware of the biases they carry into their work, the biases that sit in the social context of their work, and they must force a process of critical thinking into their work at every step along the way.

BEYOND SELF-AWARENESS: SELF-REGULATION AND SELF-CARE

It is important to point out that self-awareness alone does not make a therapist healthy and fully functioning (Barnett et al., 2007; Smith & Moss, 2009), nor does it assure that one's personalization issues are not contaminant to therapy. In fact, Smith and Moss (2009) tell us that even when clinicians become aware of concerns, they often neglect their own needs and do not engage in adequate self-care practices. So, in addition to cultivating self-awareness, we must also *actively work* to engage in healthy lifestyle practices and routines. Here we will discuss two components of how counselors can actively work to mediate the effects of personalization issues. First is to develop emotional regulation skills. Second is to engage in self-care practices.

EMOTIONAL REGULATION

As mentioned in Chapter 4, the connections between thought processes, emotional responses, and behavior (including physiological responses) is held together by complex balance of external stimuli and neural functioning. When the hippocampus is not imposing logical order and structure effectively on information processing systems within the brain, emotion and memory functions can cause physiological and behavioral responses consistent with what is often referred to as *emotional dysregulation*.

Emotional regulation is the process of influence over the expression of emotion (Gross, 1998; Westphal & Bonanno, 2004); it is about "manipulating when, where, how, and which emotions we experience and express" (Beer & Lombardo, 2007, p. 69). Having said this, it is important to note that we all have different thresholds of tolerance for emotional arousal and the "rules" and social consequences of emotional expression vary across gender lines and cultural norms (Butler, Lee, & Gross, 2007; Eid & Diener, 2001). So what exactly constitutes appropriate emotional regulation is a difficult question to answer. Yet, we can see that the free expression of emotion is not always appropriate in every setting. And this is particularly true for clinicians when they are in the office providing therapy to clients. Appropriate emotional regulation, according to Eisenberg, Hofer, and Vaughan (2007), is the ability to respond to the varying demands of one's emotional experiences with flexibility. Well-regulated individuals are not over- or undercontrolled; they are able to initiate and manage their emotional responses as appropriate to the particular situations at hand.

The process of emotional regulation begins with awareness: This is a **recognition of being triggered** emotionally. "Being triggered" refers to having an emotional experience or physiological or behavioral response to something that exceeds or is in danger of exceeding what would normally be appropriate. Again here, there are no hard and fast rules about what "appropriate" really means. But for therapists, it might be helpful to think about appropriateness in response to these questions: Is my response to this situation or to this person healthy? Does my reaction to this client or what is being discussed in therapy compromise my ability to be productive in our work? Is the therapeutic direction I am taking with this client about me or is it about my client? When we are aware of our personalization issues; our explicit and implicit biases (to the extent that we can be aware of implicit biases); and triggers associated with vicarious trauma, compassion fatigue, or burnout, that awareness helps us become more vigilant in monitoring our responses to the content of therapy, the clients we work with, and our interventions.

The second part of emotional regulation is the **ability to recover** or the recalibration of our stress response to homeostasis after the expression of emotion (Courtois & Ford, 2013; Westphal & Bonanno, 2004). It is the ability to reach *emotional homeostasis*—an appropriate balance in the frequency, intensity, and duration of an emotional experience. Here again, what is considered an ideal state of emotional homeostasis depends on a number of factors, including the type of emotion expressed, its effect on self and others, and it is also a function of individual, cultural, and situational variables. Most importantly in terms of the focus of this chapter, is the issue of whether a clinician is in a position to recover adequately after a personalization trigger, and thus be able to work effectively.

Most agree that appropriate emotional self-regulation is essential for personal health and interpersonal functioning (Gross, 1998; Gross & Thompson, 2007). And, apropos to the subject of this chapter, appropriate emotional regulation is especially important for those who are working in helping roles (Courtois & Ford, 2013). Although emotional regulation skills, as mentioned, are first developed at a young age in the context of parent–child relationships, experts in the field of trauma indicate that instruction in self-regulation strategies can be helpful for children and adults who chronically display emotional dysregulation (Blaustein & Kinniburgh, 2010; Linehan, 1993; Shearin & Linehan, 1994). Similarly, those in the helping professions can learn to regulate their own emotional responses to clients to avoid some of the occupational pitfalls discussed in this chapter. The affect regulation skills outlined by Gross (2008) and Gross and Thompson (2007) that are discussed in Chapter 10—situation selection, situation modification, attention deployment, cognitive change, response modulation, and also the inclusion of the skill of distress tolerance (Stasiewicz et al., 2013)—are good strategies that clinicians can use to manage their own emotional responses to the difficult work of helping others in need.

SELF-CARE

Pieterse et al. (2013) remind us that the therapist herself is the instrument of clinical helping. With such a critical component of one's ability to help others relying on the very being of the therapist, it is obvious to point out that the instrument of self must be well maintained and kept in tune. We can take our lead here from musicians who know that taking good care of one's instrument is crucial to being part of the orchestra. In the context of clinical helping, a failure to manage the complex tasks and many demands of our personal and professional lives may result in unintended harm to our clients, ourselves, and others in our lives (Barnett et al., 2007).

Of course, therapists are human, and I am not the first to point out that therapists do not need to be perfect. For example, Loganbill, Hardy, and Delworth (1982), who are recognized researchers and authors in the area of counselor supervision, point out: "It is our belief that people who are really effective [as helpers] generally go through a process of letting go of the belief that everything is all right with them" (p. 7). Experiencing troubles and stress in one's life does not necessarily mean that a clinician is impaired. However, distress left unchecked can have disastrous consequences on both therapist and client (Barnett et al., 2007).

So, what exactly constitutes adequate mental health or personal adjustment for therapists? First, as mentioned, navigating the potential minefields of personalization issues, implicit bias, and the occupational hazards we have discussed here begins with helper self-awareness. Second, being able to manage emotional reactivity when it appears in the therapy room is critical. Third, clinicians must be open to opportunities for supervision, consultation and professional development, and also be willing to alter their own practices when they are not helpful. For example, if we notice that we are regularly experiencing fatigue at work, we might want to establish a better bedtime routine, engage in physical activity, and be sure that we are not in the regular habit of taking work home with us. If we notice that we are constantly angry at a client who is grappling with an issue that we have also struggled with, it might be time to seek therapy ourselves. This last point is related to the final point: the importance of engaging in a regular regiment of self-care (for more on this see Barnett & Cooper, 2009; Barnett et al., 2007). In the words of Smith and Moss (2009) "overall, it is simply self-care that is most important in preventing or diffusing distress and impairment" (p. 9).

At work, clinicians can take care of themselves by taking regular breaks, by engaging in a diversity of professional activities, by managing their workload so that it is varied and paced, and by being careful to avoid temperamental mismatches between themselves and their clients (Barnett et al., 2007; Donati & Watts, 2005). Clinicians should also maintain professional boundaries, understand their own professional and personal limitations, work to increase their own professional knowledge and competency, use the ethical and professional guidelines of their discipline, engage regularly in clinical supervision, participate in personal therapy and peer support as needed, and be careful to avoid financial hardship as well as professional isolation (Barnett et al., 2007; Smith & Moss, 2009; Trippany et al., 2004).

In terms of combatting burnout, James and Gilliland (2001) point to the importance of receiving an appropriate orientation and training that includes suggestions regarding task management, insight into personalization issues, and managing professional boundaries. While an orientation to these topics at the start of a new position may help prevent burnout, engaging in regular supervision and receiving support from agency administrators around these issues is also critical during one's tenure in an agency. James and Gilliland (2001) also encourage a small degree of therapeutic detachment and an ability to modulate idealism—particularly if one is working in the area of crisis response. These authors also stress the importance of participating in continuing professional development, particularly regarding burnout and interventions in the face of impairment, and wellness promotion that includes establishing healthy work routines and making adjustments in work as needed.

Away from the office, clinicians should be mindful of attending to their own emotional, physical, relationship, and spiritual needs. This should include practicing self-care by getting adequate rest and exercise, having a sense of humor, spending time with friends, setting personal boundaries, and perhaps engaging in some type of spiritual practice that enables a renewed sense of meaning, connection, and hope (Barnett et al., 2007; Smith & Moss, 2009; Trippany et al., 2004). In short, Trippany et al. (2004) advocate that helpers develop systems of wellness that include a balance of play, work, and rest.

It is easy to get lost in a long list of suggestions. The point here is that this work of helping is not easy. Since the clinicians themselves are the instrument of helping, that instrument of self must be well-maintained and cared for. Clinicians do not need to be perfect, but they do need to be healthy. There is not one way to engage in self-care—all clinicians need to find what works best for them. What we do know is that not engaging in self-care will have adverse effects on the clinician's personal life as well as professional competence. It is best to begin self-care routines early and before one is stressed—that way they will be in place to serve as an important buffer when times are difficult.

CHAPTER SUMMARY

This chapter began with an exploration of the ways in which our personal experiences, emotional reactions, assumptions, beliefs, and values affect our work in helping relationships. This discussion led to an exploration of memory systems and underscored the ways in which implicit bias affects helping. We also discussed how vicarious traumatization, compassion fatigue, and burnout affect our ability to be emotionally present with others. Helper self-awareness, self-management, and self-care habits are important components of any professional practice of helping.

REFLECTION QUESTIONS

1. In this chapter it was pointed out that experiences in life that are stored in implicit memory are the foundation of many unquestioned ideas that are what we come to know as normal or as truth. Speculate about how repeated exposure to media images that evoke strong emotions may affect memory and emotion functions as well implicit bias. How might this affect your work as a clinician?

2. Is it appropriate to expect clinicians to engage in wellness practices such as those listed here? Why is what they do "off the clock" so important?

3. What commitments can you make at this time to establish health self-care practices?

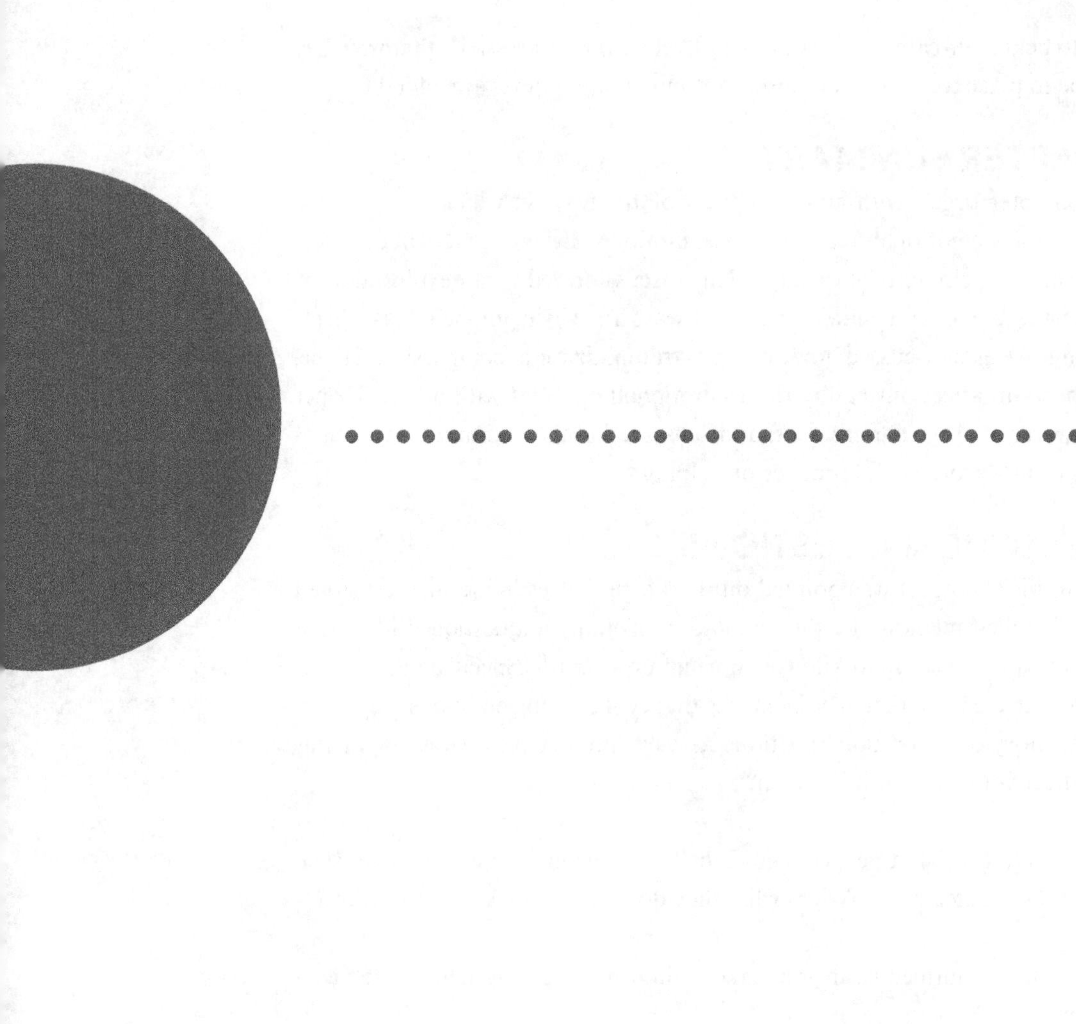

SECTION II

COUNSELING SKILLS

CHAPTER

Welcoming and Therapeutic Listening

Chapter Outline

INTRODUCTION

Remember that we enter into the lives of our clients when they are not at their best. They may be in pain, feel stuck, feel shame about something they have said or done, or for whatever reason, things are just not going well. It is truly an act of bravery for many of us to admit that we need help. Unfortunately, there are no easy answers for the challenging problems that clients bring into therapy, and for clinicians, there is no sure-bet formula for helping. Therapy is hard work—hard for the client and hard for the clinician. This chapter is intended to orient us to two fundamental components of helping: welcoming and listening. These engage clients from the start in a way that respects their hardship and honors their courage. Regardless of who the client is, what he is grappling with, and what type of counseling modality we will use, welcoming and listening are essential.

How we start therapy—the first moment of the therapeutic encounter, my colleague Dr. Kurt Kraus tells us—sets the course for how the therapeutic relationship will unfold. How we welcome clients into therapy is formative to what happens next and how therapy develops over time. So, in this chapter, we will examine the behaviors that communicate welcome. We then move into discussions about listening. This, too, is a critical yet underrated therapeutic skill. Listening, like empathy, is a skill that is not easily measureable or seeable, but we know when it is there. We end this chapter with the important topic of broaching conversations—this has to do with clinicians' ability to initiate conversations about race and other social locations, and to position themselves in ways that communicate that they want to understand the social context of clients' lives. In the chapters that follow, we will explore more advanced counseling skills that rest on these foundations of welcoming and listening, grounded in what we already know about empathy.

WELCOMING

Sometimes clients will come to us with an articulated concern or clearly identified problem and an equally measured resolve for change. Others are less clear. As mentioned, many clients struggle under the heavy weight of a problem that has entered into their lives and may feel embarrassed, uncertain, or fearful about change. Coming to therapy can feel shaming. For these reasons, David Epston's concept of *respectful welcoming* (Masterwork Productions, 2002) comes to mind as an important way to extend toward a new client at the start of this critical first encounter in therapy.

Many clinicians extend in this way by beginning therapy with an invitation for the client to tell her own story—typically some version of "Can you tell me what brought you here?" This kind of respectful curiosity and welcoming communicates that the counselor is interested in and has respect for the client's personal stories, skills, and knowledge. It is an extension of what Michael White (2005) referred to as a *de-centered* position, meaning that the client is at the center of the relationship. Even if the therapist has heard about the problem from someone else or read the tomes of information written about the client in a file somewhere, getting the client's perspective is both respectful and informative. Miller and Rollnick (2013) remind us that "people are the undisputed experts on themselves. No one has been with them

Photo 6.1

longer, or knows them better than they do themselves" (p. 15). A de-centered position puts the client's perspective in the center of the helping process.

Many counseling sessions do not actually begin with the client meeting the counselor in person. They often start with a phone call, e-mail, or some other communication that may not even be between the potential client and future therapist. Sadly, many clients have their first experience of therapy initiated by a terse conversation through a window that is opened at the discretion of the receptionist, and with concerns that others in the waiting room will overhear personal information about them. In schools, counseling meetings are often precipitated by some sort of disciplinary action or a referral by someone other than the student. All of these make for a most inauspicious beginning to the therapeutic relationship. According to research, when potential clients have long waiting times between initial contact and a first appointment for therapy and also between an initial intake interview and the first appointment, they are likely to not follow up or return for therapy (Carter et al., 2012; Claus & Kindleberger, 2002). Long waiting lists, being put on telephone hold for seemingly long periods of time, and waiting for calls to be returned do not feel welcoming to potential clients—especially those who may already be ambivalent about engaging in therapy. If these are the experiences that new clients bring to the first meeting, it is important that they are recognized, that apologies are offered, and that the clinician articulates a commitment to do what he can do to avoid those kinds of experiences in the future. This is critical, even if the therapist was not the one who committed the initial transgression. The bottom line is that a respectful welcoming needs to be communicated—albeit it in different ways—from individuals at all points during the intake process.

Welcoming a client also entails providing information to the client about the therapeutic process—this speaks to the informed consent process, discussed in Chapters 1 and 3. These conversations set the stage for establishing appropriate expectations and communicate respect for the client—understanding that she may not be familiar with the world of therapy. Even if an intake process has occurred prior to this first meeting between therapist and client, inviting the client to articulate her needs from her own perspective establishes a client-centered environment.

THERAPEUTIC LISTENING

Seasoned professionals can make therapy look simple, but the truth is that knowing what to say and how and when to say it is extremely complex. What most seasoned professions do know, however, is that effective therapeutic responses are based on careful listening.

Hearing is a central nervous system process of receiving sensory input through the ears. *Listening* is the related process of making sense of what has been heard. The process of listening, especially, requires multiple and complex cognitive processes. But, because these processes happen deep within the structures of the brain, clients may not know that we hear and understand them unless we actively communicate our understandings with them. The term *active listening* is used in clinical training in reference to the ways in which clinicians position themselves to listen to their clients and communicate back what they have heard. This term invites us to think about listening as an active process of engagement with the client. Therapeutic responses flow directly from what we have heard, as well as what we understand about a client and his life experiences, our own ways of making meaning, and our training in helping, and in alignment with the identified goals for helping. This all begins with therapeutic listening—adequately grasping the content of what is being said and also understanding its situated meaning. It is the context of the client's life that illuminates the meanings of his words.

As I have so far illustrated, it is difficult to talk about listening without also talking about responding—listening and responding are enmeshed in the communication process. Having said this, we will try to focus primarily here on this very important skill of listening. In the following chapters, we will review numerous strategies for communicating what one has heard and engaging in conversations that open up new understandings and possibilities for change.

NONVERBAL AND MINIMAL VERBAL TRACKING

There is no one right or wrong way to listen, of course. In everyday conversations, however, people typically use **nonverbal gestures** to signal their attention and register their comprehension of what has been said. This is sometimes called *tracking*. For example, we smile when someone says something pleasant, we have a look of surprise when we hear something unusual, and most of us have some version of a cringe to communicate that we understand someone's awkward or difficult situation. Clinicians also use **minimal verbalizations** as they listen to clients—this is a way of tracking what has been said and communicating a basic level of understanding. Minimal verbal responses include comments such as *"yes," "okay," "mmmm,"* and *"uh huh"* that are inserted into the flow of the conversation.

LISTENING POSTURES

Egan (2010) is typically credited for developing the SOLER acronym to represent a number of listening postures that clinicians use to communicate that they are listening. We will review them here, but it is important to remember that nonverbal communications are highly nuanced and culturally and socially normed, so these specific listening postures may not be appropriate in all situations. Also, rigidly adhering to these or any particular set of behaviors is not advised, as doing so can make conversations contrived or awkward and can easily lead to a communication failure. We review these SOLER behaviors here, however, because they offer a general picture of what therapeutic listening might look like.

S = Sit Straight and Square: Siting straight and squarely toward the client allows you to be able to hear well and to see the client's facial expressions as

Photo 6.2

he speaks, and it communicates that your complete attention is being given. Of course, you will want to maintain a socially and culturally appropriate distance, and it may not be appropriate to sit directly facing the client, so it is important to adjust your listening posture accordingly. The intent is to communicate attention but not to raise the intensity by your proximity or position, making the client uncomfortable. Use verbal and nonverbal feedback from the client to adjust your position as needed.

O = Open Posture: The O in SOLER represents the intent to communicate openness. Being open to what the client says is, of course, a nuanced and culturally and socially determined communication; there is no one way to describe the most appropriate open posture for therapists. In most therapy sessions, however, an open posture tends to be associated with a assuming a professional yet relaxed position as the client talks. For some, this is translated into a sitting posture where arms and legs are not crossed. But, sitting without crossing one's arms or legs, particularly when one is sitting for a long period of time, can look and feel unnatural. The bottom line is that clinicians should be aware of the social and cultural norms of their settings, and make decisions about how they want to position themselves within those contexts. For example, in our larger social context where gender tends to be oversexualized and laden with power differentials, therapists should think carefully about how they sit when they are in cross-gender helping situations. It is also important to consider that clients who have experienced boundary violations, who have some mistrust of others, or who do not have a clear understanding of the parameters of the clinical relationship may have difficulties "reading" the body language of the counselor. In these cases, clinicians may decide to default to more formal sitting postures. The point is to communicate openness physically, without sending a conflicting, confusing, or uncomfortable message to the client.

L = Lean Forward: Leaning forward or toward the client helps secure attention and communicates that you are listening. However, given the power differentials in the therapeutic relationship, this also has the potential to make some clients to feel scrutinized or uncomfortable. So, the cautions mentioned above also are appropriate here. It is perfectly natural to move around in your seat, leaning forward and then back again, as appropriate to the conversation and to manage intensity appropriately. The emphasis here is that you want to communicate to the client that she is important and has your focused attention.

E = Eye Contact: It is, of course, appropriate to look at the client when talking to him or when he is talking to you. But eye contact in most conversations typically fluctuates between looking at the person and then also looking away, and then back again. So, this should also be the norm in therapy. Clearly, directly staring at a client is inappropriate, and you should never obligate a client to make direct eye contact back to you when you are talking. Also, when a client seems uncomfortable, is talking about something particularly sensitive, or is very emotional, it is probably appropriate to not look at him directly, or at least not for a long period of time. Other times, however, direct eye contact can communicate a clinician's confidence and competence; this might be comforting when a client is struggling. Norms around eye contact are socially and culturally nuanced, and an important part of cultural competence is to become aware of the ways in which eye contact is perceived in the client's culture and/or family system. Most importantly, eye contact should facilitate emotional connection and empathy and should not create anxiety, communicate power, or be used to coerce the client to say or do anything against her free will.

R = Relaxed Stance: The R in SOLER reminds us to be relaxed. A high degree of formality may communicate competence in some social settings, but in therapy, formality and stiffness often translates as emotional distance or a lack of caring. Being extremely casual, on the other hand, works with some clients, but not with others. In some contexts, being too relaxed is interpreted as unprofessional. So, what constitutes being relaxed and how relaxed a clinician should be will vary considerably, depending on the cultural and social context of the client, the counselor, and the norms in the clinical setting and larger community. The point is that clinicians should assume a posture that puts the client at ease and that leaves her feeling understood and respected.

EMPATHIC LISTENING

Empathy, as mentioned in Chapter 1, is one of the most critical components of therapy. Yet, the experience of empathy is individual, personal, and somewhat elusive; it is difficult to describe empathy as a concrete behavior. Halstead, Wagner, Vivero, and Ferkol (2002) suggest that empathy might best be thought of as a kind of therapeutic engagement—one that connotes a willingness and desire to understand and help—rather than a specific skill. Breggin (2008) describes empathy as treating someone's feelings with "exquisite tenderness" (p. 43). These suggestions invite us to think of empathy as a therapeutic position of concerned caring, which is consistent with Brown's (2013) observation that empathy is the experience of connection.

Positioning oneself to understand, care about, and stand in connection with a client, especially when the client is in discomfort, requires a particular kind of attention to the client. At the same time, empathic understandings are guided by one's own experiences. As discussed in earlier chapters, we use ourselves as a guide for what may be happening for the client. So, the challenge here is to be focused on both self and other, but not so focused on the self that we lose sight of or inaccurately understand what is happening with the other. To do this, we must be fully present, free from the influence of personalization issues, and emotionally available.

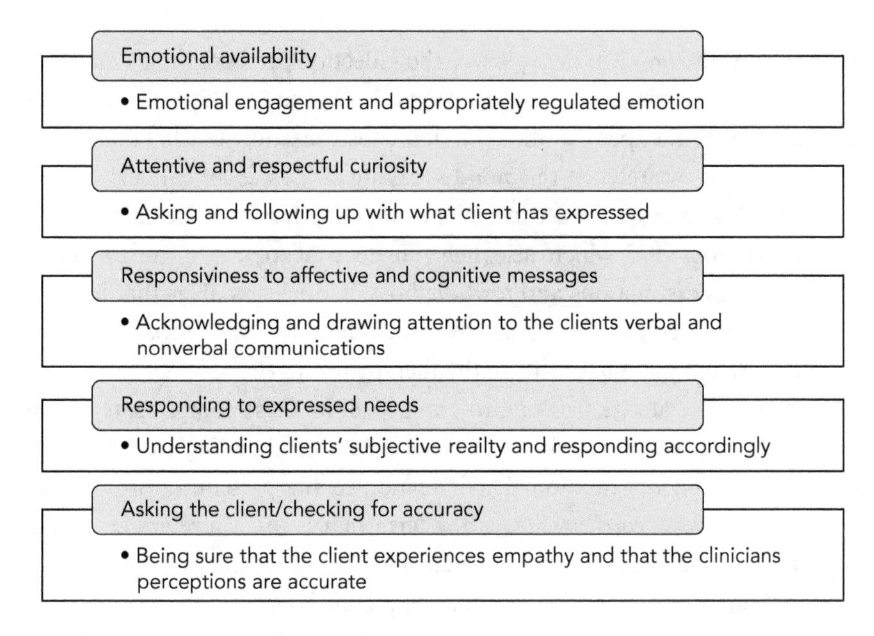

Figure 6.1 *Expressing Empathy*

Empathic listening also requires, as mentioned in Chapter 1, a nonjudgmental presence (Rogers, 1975). This is not to say that we must agree with what our client says or thinks. But, when the focus in the moment is on being with and understanding, there is no room for evaluating. Our therapeutic hunches, ideas, and other opinions are best saved for a time when they will be readily received or when it is therapeutically appropriate to offer them. Recall Frankel's (2009) description of empathy as a three-part process that includes the initial empathic opportunity from the client; the counselor listening, feeling, and communicating an empathic response to the client; and looking for a response from the client that the empathy was felt. The expression of empathy entails a complete feedback loop of communication. We can never assume that a client knows what we feel, what we think, and what we are experiencing in the moment. These components of empathic communications are summarized in Figure 6.1.

WHAT TO LISTEN FOR

Consider for a moment all that happens in normal everyday conversations. There is the content of the conversation—*what* is being talked about.

Then there is the *how* it is being said—the inflections and emphases that give meaning to the words used. Conversations also require both parties to listen carefully to the other person while simultaneously listening to what their mind is telling them—we refer to this mind speaking as *metacognition*. Also, there are the stories and experiences in each person's life that sit in the background of conversations and which also help create context and meaning. Then add in various distractions and a whole host of other variables that happen in and around everyday conversations. All of these variables, too, are at play when counselors listen to clients in the therapy room.

Clinicians are always working to manage all of these components of the therapeutic conversation, with particular focus on attending to the significant themes and information that is related to the presenting problem or goals of therapy. A *core message* is the term that is used in reference to the important themes that are undercurrent in therapy. In this section, we will explore the parts of conversations that help clinicians better infer core messages in therapy. These include verbal, nonverbal, and inconsistent messages; using context to understand significance; discursive positioning; and client meaning-making processes. These different components of listening are also summarized in Figure 6.2.

VERBAL MESSAGES

Verbal messages are, of course, what the client says. Listening to what the client tells us is the most straightforward way to comprehend what he is saying. However, verbal messages do not always point to important messages, understandings, or key meanings. A client may not be sure about what she is saying—she may actually be using the conversation to make meaning as she speaks. She may also be confused and have mixed or conflicting thoughts or feelings, and what she says may have unique meanings within her own context that we do not fully understand. So to help us navigate all of this, listening to verbal messages requires paying attention to the content or subject of what is being said, as well as word choice, frequency, intensity, and client-specific meaning attributions.

Obviously a client's **choice of words** can tell us something about the significance of what is said. For example, when a client says that she "kind of likes" something, that connotes something different than when she says she "loves" it. Something that is "awesome" is different than it being "okay."

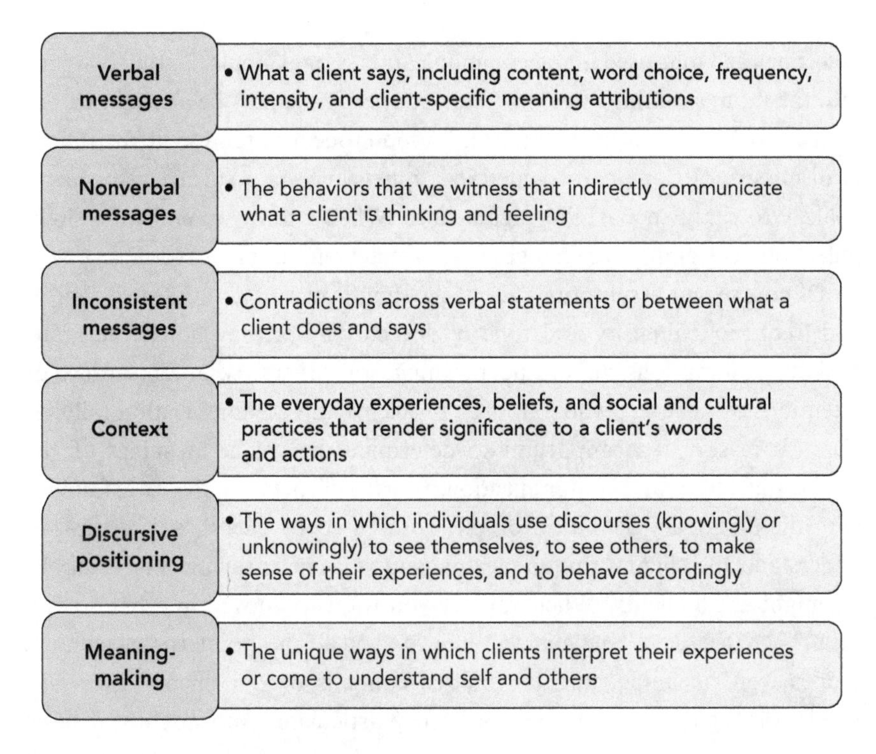

Figure 6.2 *What to Listen for*

Word choice, of course, also reflects regional, social, and cultural nuance. This brings us to the importance of **context.** Here we are talking about the social meanings of words and spoken expressions in a conversation. Context shapes word choice and meaning in obvious and also very subtle ways. "Hooking up" in contemporary youth culture, for example, means something different than it did 40 years ago, when it was part of colloquial dialogue to signify a casual and nonsexual meeting. Similarly, the comment "fine" is different when its articulated in the context of how someone is feeling than if it is intended to be a comment regarding someone's appearance.

Another cue to the significance of a message is **expression frequency**. When client uses a particular word or statement frequently, this probably means that there is something important about that word or idea. For example, if a client tells us that he is "not looking forward to Friday" a few times, it is important to explore the significance of Friday. Message **intensity**, too, signals significance and is often communicated in word choice, frequency, and in the

inflections and tone used in the communication. For example, if someone runs into the room shouting "fire" in a hurried speech, we may be alerted to a potential problem that is being reported. A loud tone may represent frustration. A dismissive "I don't care" stated in a quiet voice in a suicide assessment, is likely to carry an alarming significance. When a sentence ends in a slight inflection, its significance changes from a statement into a question.

Of course, our assumptions about the significance of certain word choices and frequency, intensity and tone of speech may or may not be accurate. Making assumptions about the meanings of others' communications or intentions can cause a whole host of problems and communication failures. For this reason, it is important to determine the **unique meanings** of the words, statements and communications of each client. Even if we are familiar with the dictionary-definition of the words used by clients, it is critical to understand the client's unique meanings in what he is saying. For example, we might ask a client: "When you say you want to 'move on,' what do you mean?" "What does 'anxiety' feel like for you?" The point is that context shapes word meaning, and the unique contexts of our clients' lives give rise to the significance of the words they articulate. We must not assume we completely understand our clients; it is always best to ask clients what they mean.

NONVERBAL MESSAGES

We know that nonverbal communications are those that are communicated without voice. The things that a client *does*—the behaviors that we witness—tell us something about what that client is thinking and feeling. For example, if a client's eyes tear up when she speaks, we assume that she is sad. If she looks away or does not offer eye contact, these behaviors may also signal significance. Or not. Does chronic tardiness mean reluctance, or is it an artifact of navigating public transportation? The truth is that we never know what others feel and think; nonverbal messages offer a cue, but they do not necessarily reveal fact. The best way to determine the significance of someone's behavior is to ask them. This may be done with a direct question, such as "Why are you always late for our appointments?" or more indirectly using reflection skills, such as "I see your eyes tearing up as we talk about this." These questions and reflections will be discussed in more detail in the following chapter.

INCONSISTENT MESSAGES

After we get to know people, we begin to understand their style of speaking, the meanings of their words, and the social and cultural context of their lives. Of course, we must always check out our assumptions, but when there are consistent patterns across stories and themes, this helps us generate more accurate understandings. Sometimes, however, we experience mixed communications—inconsistencies between the various "voices" of communication. For example, we may notice **conflicting verbal statements**. This is when the client says one thing and then contradicts it by saying something different. A client may say, for instance, that he likes someone and then later assert that he doesn't like that person at all. A second type of inconsistency is a **lack of congruence between verbal and nonverbal messages**. For example, the client tells us that she enjoys coming to counseling appointments but has missed almost half of the appointments that have been scheduled. Or, she says that she is happy, but her nonverbal messages appear to communicate sadness. Similarly, a client may falsely report doing something. For example, a parent reports that she monitors her teenage son but then admits that she does not ask him where he is going when he goes out at night, does not know most of his friends, and has no limits regarding when he should be home. Another version of this type of inconsistency is apparent **inconsistencies between reported values or beliefs and behaviors**. For example, a client tells us that he has a high level of respect for women, but he was recently arrested for domestic assault.

Mixed or inconsistent messages are very confusing to interpret. They may reflect reluctance or dishonesty, but it is equally possible that they may be due to confusion, mixed feelings, a lack of awareness, a lack of trust, a low level of motivation, anxiety, worry, etc. Therapeutic prudence compels us to avoid judging the intent behind discrepant messages and to instead assume a position of respectful curiosity and engage in collaborative exploration with the client. We can never be sure of the meanings of inconsistencies if we do not attend to them. We will speak in the next chapter about some of the response skills that can be used to explore inconsistencies in therapy—reflections, paraphrases, questions, and especially immediacy and confrontation. All of these skills are based on the clinician's attentive listening abilities.

CONTEXT

We have spoken about the ways in which context renders words significant. That is, the ways in which words are used to communicate thoughts, feelings, and intentions is a function of how a client has learned to speak and the unique meanings of those words in their particular social, family, and cultural habitats. For example, I learned that use of the reflexive verb in Spanish does not imply a lack of personal responsibility and that the concept of family in some places is very different from the blood-related nuclear family that means "family" in the region where I was raised in the United States. Similarly, nonverbal gestures are learned behaviors that reflect the norms of or particular context or environment. When I lived in Honduras, Central America, I learned to use a lip-pointing gesture rather than point my finger to someone or something, which was perceived to be rude in that culture. When I lived in Liberia, West Africa, I witnessed the significance of learning the hand shake, slide, and snap greeting. It became apparent to me that using this small gesture was one way of communicating my respect for the host culture in which I was living.

These are mere examples of the contextual meanings of words and behaviors in various cultural settings. I offer them to illustrate the point that context gives meaning to verbal and nonverbal communications. If a counselor doesn't know the context from which a client is positioned, it is possible that she will not fully understand the meaning of his communications. When working across cultures, it is helpful to have an informant or social broker to help you understand the significance of nuanced behaviors. Also, recall Arredondo et al. (1996)'s reminder that cultural competence is strengthened when we have social and professional relationships with individuals from various social locations or social groups, particularly those who identify in groups that are different from our own. Even so, when we are not sure, we can ask clients to clarify the context of their experiences and communications. It is inappropriate, of course, to ask clients to speak for the social group within which they identify or to educate us on characteristics or the history of a whole culture or social group. All of that is homework that we should engage in outside of the therapy office. Even when working within one's own culture, the other factors of people's lives—family, community, social location, personal abilities and experiences, interests, and beliefs—serve to create unique understandings and meanings. So, clinicians must honor clients' expertise regarding their culture, social group, and their experiences in life, and clinicians should also work to understand the distinct meanings of their clients' communications.

DISCURSIVE POSITIONING

In Chapter 2, the term *discourse* was introduced in reference to cultural and social ideas about how things should be done; what is important, good, bad, or "normal"; and how people should behave. Discourses are the taken-for-granted structuring ideas that shape everyday understandings in our lives. Winslade (2005) points out that "any utterance in a social interaction (including those in counselling conversations) calls upon a discursive background in order to make sense" (p. 354).

The concept of discursive positioning calls attention to the ways in which individuals use discourses (knowingly or unknowingly) to see themselves, to see others, to make sense of their experiences, and to behave accordingly. The relevance of this for clinical helpers is the reminder that when our clients' understandings about self, others, and their experiences in the world are based on ideas or stereotypes that are irrelevant, unhelpful, or even toxic, the positions they offer can be very destructive. This example from Geroski (2017) is intended to illustrate this point:

> David is talking to his counselor because he has experienced depression and has had suicidal thoughts in the past. As the conversation progresses, it is clear that David is beginning to question his sexual orientation. He has never been attracted to women, and he is beginning to see that he experiences glimmers of attraction to a few male classmates at college. However, the counselor learns that in David's family as well as the school and community where David grew up, homosexuality was considered a sin. This idea of sin is paralleled in historic and current contemporary discourses that invite us to think of homosexuality as a form of mental illness or a choice—a bad choice (e.g., Nuckolls & Baker, 2003). David, it turns out, has even witnessed verbal and physical violence perpetrated against individuals who identify as gay. With this backdrop, David struggles with making meaning of his attraction to men, and it may be that the depression and suicidal gestures are indications of internalized self-hatred. In this case, it seems obvious that David's

alignment with discourses of intolerance and expressions of hate influences how he is making sense of his developing awareness of his own sexual orientation.

It is important to note that in this situation mentioned above, David's concerns are not imagined; the social context of people's lives have a profound influence on how they think, how they feel, and the decisions they make. As this example shows, discourses are not neutral. Discourses have very real effects on people's lives. David's concerns about emotional and physical safety in his home community and, perhaps, family of origin, are valid concerns. This is true even if David is living in a local college community where sexual orientation discourses position him less harshly (p. 182).

Here again, we are talking about the ways in which context influences meaning-making processes. The best way to fully understand the unique meanings that clients attribute to their experiences and the ways in which those meanings are constructed from discourses, is to ask clients to share their understandings, insights, and interpretations with us. To this end, we might ask questions and engage in deconstructing conversations, which are discussed in more detail in later chapters of this text.

MEANING MAKING

In his book *Acts of Meaning*, Jerome Bruner (1990) describes people as interpretive beings—always working to make sense of their experiences. He was particularly intrigued by the ways in which people use stories organized along an underlying plot to interpret new information. For example, Laticia believes that teachers, in general, are always well-meaning and fair. When she found a few grading errors on her mid-term exam, she pointed them out to the teacher and the teacher quickly corrected her errors. Laticia interpreted the teacher's mistakes along the existing plotline that her teacher was generally fair and good, and called the mistakes "honest mistakes." In fact, she later told her parents that her teacher "made a few grading errors on her exam," which she said "were honest mistakes because she was working too hard and obviously needs a break." On the other hand, Manuel had a similar experience with mistakes in the grading of his exam. In this case, however, Manuel had had a number of incidents in class with the teacher, and he believed that the teacher was prejudiced against the boys in the class. His interpretation of the grading errors fell in line with the plot of teacher bias, and his explanation of the situation was that he was being discriminated against. This, then, became a new piece of evidence in his story of bias and would likely be used to generate future understandings and interpretations of interactions with his teacher. The earlier discussions in this text around interpersonal neurobiology and memory functions help us understand the complicated interplay between interpersonal experiences and central nervous system functioning. In both examples here, we can see how the concepts of "teacher," groomed from personal experiences as well as, we can assume, social discourses, shaped the ways in which the grading incident was perceived (differently) by Laticia and Manuel.

With meaning-making processes so intertwined with personal and interpersonal experiences, we probably should respect the suggestion that the meanings we have for the events in our lives are not part of some objective reality or universal truth. Winslade (2005) reminds us that with such a wide range of potential meanings that flow from discursive contexts, "we often find ourselves in the middle of a contest about which meanings shall prevail" (p. 354). We can never fully know the unique ways in which people will understand or interpret their experiences. This puts an extra burden on therapists, then, to work to understand the unique meanings that clients have for words, phrases, and thoughts that they express in therapy.

TWO LISTENING VOICES

Therapeutic listening is not social listening; is intentional listening. It requires us to listen carefully to all of the obvious and not so obvious communications from the client. It also requires us, at the same time, to think about how we will respond or intervene. Therapeutic listening is listening while also thinking. It is as if we are listening to two voices that are simultaneously speaking to us. The *first voice* is that which is communicated verbally and nonverbally with the client in the moment. The *second voice* is our own internal voice that helps us interpret what we hear and guides our thinking processes—earlier we called this metacognition. This is the voice of the mind at work. It is the *thinking voice*.

This thinking voice has two functions. The first is the **meaning-making** function. This is the interpretive work of the mind working to make sense

Photo 6.3

of the verbal and nonverbal messages that are being communicated by the client. For example, when a client displays a cluster of symptoms that include excessive talk about worries, restlessness, and difficulties with concentration, our mind may be searching through memory functions to piece together the differential diagnostic criteria for anxiety disorder. As it does this, it also informs us about what it is noticing. "Anne, she seems very anxious—she is tapping her hands, speaking quickly, and remember last week she said she wasn't able to sleep? Maybe she has symptoms of an anxiety disorder and that's why she 'shuts down'?" This internal dialogue is talking to us while the first voice is engaging in conversation with the client.

As the thinking voice works to make meaning of what the client tells us, it also calls upon **executive functioning** to guide our responses. This part of the thinking voice is instructional—it coaches our reply. For example, as our client tells us about her worries and an idea of anxiety disorder starts to materialize in our mind, executive functioning advises us on how to proceed. Here our mind may say something like, "It looks like she is starting to spiral with anxiety. Ask her to stop for a moment and take a deep breath. Point out the entry point of the anxiety spiral."

All of these voices are important, but they are a lot to listen to! These important thinking processes can distract clinicians from being fully present with clients. Some clinicians use brief note-taking—just a word or two jotted down in the moment—to help manage the thinking voice so they can be more fully present in the moment. For example, writing down "trauma?" as the client displays symptoms of anxiety might be a good prompt for you to remember to ask questions about a history of trauma later when the moment is right. Another strategy used by some therapists is to pace themselves. That is, they may use summaries, paraphrases, and reflections, which are discussed in the next chapter, to slow the conversation down and provide time for clearer thinking. And always, it is okay to take a quiet minute in therapy to think before saying anything. If this seems awkward, you can let the client know that you need a minute to think by saying something like, "What you are saying is really important. Give me a minute to think—I want to be sure I have it right."

OBSTACLES TO LISTENING

We have all probably had the experience of being with others who are not great listeners. They completely miss what we have said, fail to pick up the nuances in our tone, may change the focus to something unrelated, or ask us a barrage of questions that we don't want to or can't even answer. Even when one's intentions are good, an inability to really listen can easily lead to a conversational failure. Conversation failures, a concept mentioned by Wynn and Bergvik (2010), can look like a pause in the conversation, a reluctance on the part of the client to continue talking, or may be signaled when a client repeats himself frequently, has to reformulate what he is saying, recurrently corrects the therapist, or when there is an abrupt change of subject.

Most people don't set out to be poor listeners, of course, and clearly, professional helpers hope to be good at listening. But many things can interfere with these aspirations. **Being tired**, for example, can easily impair our listening abilities. **Distractions**, too, can impede proper listening. Some clinicians may even find themselves **rehearsing** what they want to say so that it comes out as intended. But this, too, can make it difficult to be attentive and really hear what the client is saying.

Feeling **hurried and pressured** to get work done or to come to a solution can also be a distraction that leads to inadequate listening (Halstead et al., 2002).

Photo 6.4

Related to this, **filtered or evaluative listening** can impair the clinician from being fully open and present to what a client has to say. According to Skovholt (2005), filtered listening can even result from trying to adhere too rigidly to a particular theoretical frame of reference or orientation. That is, when we try to shape what we are hearing into preconceived notions, it influences what we attend to and what we actually hear. For example, if we are convinced that an attachment disorder explains a child's behavior, we may miss the cues that the child is in a compromised or dangerous day care situation. Or when our listening is filtered through single mom discourses, we may miss the abilities and strengths of the single mom who comes to us for input on how to parent her young child.

Another obstacle to listening is **sympathetic listening**. This is when we get caught up in the client's story and have an emotional reaction that impedes our ability to be fully present (Skovholt, 2005). For example, upon hearing a story of a recent challenge, we may feel badly for a client. This reaction, if we feel sorry for the client, may make us want to do something to try to make

Figure 6.3 *Obstacles to Listening*

things better, when what our client really needs, let us say, is empathy or encouragement. Sympathetic listening is what happens when our own reactivity makes it difficult to attend to the needs of the client in the moment. Different from empathy, sympathy can cause disconnection (Brown, 2013).

BROACHING CONVERSATIONS

As we focus on the notions of respectful welcoming and therapeutic listening in this chapter, this is a good time to introduce the idea of broaching conversations. As discussed in Chapter 2, two key components of working with individuals who identify in marginalized social locations include (a) having an understanding of how heritage, culture, or group affiliation forms identity; and (b) comprehending how systems of power and privilege benefit individuals from different social locations unequally (Andersen & Collins, 2004; Pieterse, Lee, Ritmeester, & Collins, 2013). As Weinrach and Thomas (2002) point out, "How one is defined and treated by others is just as important as how one choses to define himself. … How others perceive an individual may have profound and, at times, tragic effects upon that individual's self definition" (p. 27).

According to Chu (2007), clinicians must be able to develop a "cultural exchange" (p. 39) in therapy that includes an ability to engage in an open discussion about cultural assumptions and experiences of marginalization. *Broaching conversations* is a concept developed by Day-Vines and colleagues (2007) that has to do with creating a space in therapy for dialogue about one's experiences within the context of their social or cultural identity. Broaching conversations reflect a clinician's ability to understand and address the ways in which sociopolitical issues affect clients' lives and the issues they bring to counseling.

Unfortunately, many clinicians are reluctant to raise issues of race or discuss topics that have to do with a client's social location. This is especially true when the client's social location is different from the counselor's and when the client appears to locate in an identity status that is marginalized in larger society. Discomfort with difference often means discomfort with one's own privilege and can also reflect a denial of oppression. All of these can result in a clinician's reluctance to see and address these issues in therapy (Day-Vines et al., 2007).

Being "colorblind" to difference enables clinicians to enjoy a relative position of safety and privilege; it also does not adequately address the needs of clients who identify in social groups that are marginalized (Smith, Geroski, & Tyler, 2014). In the words of the participants who self-identified as lesbian, gay, bisexual, and queer in a study by Quiñones, Woodward & Pantalone (2017), "Because therapist silence about sexual orientation might communicate naïve or negative views of sexual minority identity or life experiences, or general therapeutic neglect, culturally competent therapists should address sexual identity and affirm non-heterosexual identities as valid and non-pathological variants of human sexuality" (p. 197). Knowing that silence is complicit with other forms of marginalization, Day-Vines et al. (2007) emphasize that it is the responsibility of the clinician rather than the client to broach conversations about race and other social location identities. That is, rather than waiting for clients to bring up issues related to social location and marginalization, clinicians must initiate these discussions. Doing so communicates an openness to engage in conversations about how culture and other identity characteristics such as race, ethnicity, gender, gender identity, sexual orientation, religion, ability status, and socioeconomic status are experienced by that client. It also communicates that the clinician understands that for some, identity is located in a context of marginalization. It invites conversation in the place of silence.

Day-Vines et al. (2007) introduced five broaching styles and behaviors that reflect clinician's attitudes and proficiency in addressing diversity issues with their clients in therapy. It should be noted that the work of these authors focuses primarily on race, but they also suggest that clinicians should also broach conversations about one's experiences related to identity and experiences within other marginalized social locations. So, in our discussion we will consider broaching more broadly in reference to work with anyone who identifies in one or a few marginalized social locations.

The *avoidant* broaching style is characterized by a resistance to discuss diversity issues at all (Day-Vines et al., 2007). Avoidant counselors make no attempt to broach cultural issues in therapy, perhaps because they just do not understand how one's social location is relevant to client's lives and experiences in the world. They also struggle to understand how issues brought to counseling may be related to cultural background, social discourses, experiences of subtle or overt discrimination, and power and privilege. In fact, many avoidant counselors think that ignoring race or other social locations is appropriate. This may, of course, reflect a desire to not make anyone uncomfortable—particularly themselves.

Therapists who work from an *isolating* broaching style may briefly raise issues related to social location, but they tend to do this in a simplistic or superficial way. For example, they may ask a client if he is gay or what his ethnic background is, but then not follow up with any additional discussion or even suggestion on how that may be relevant to other issues discussed in therapy. It is as if the race box is checked off on the intake form and therefore no further discussion is required. The *continuing/incongruent* broaching style is described by Day-Vines and her colleagues (2007) as an invitation to explore how social location affects counseling issues. These therapists appear comfortable in discussing social location. But they tend to have a limited skill set in terms of being able to adequately explore the issues in a meaningful way, or they lack the skills that can be used to empower their clients. For example, continuing/incongruent clinicians may have visible artifacts around their office that suggest that they are open to understanding diversity issues, and they may even appreciate being with others with different orientations and worldviews. However, these understandings often lack nuance. For example, these therapists may make assumptions about individuals based on group affiliation stereotypes, or they do not have a critical understanding of how social location affects everyday experiences in people's lives. Even more dangerously, some continuing/incongruent therapists assume that they understand more about their clients and about diversity issues than they really do.

In the Day-Vines et al. (2007) model, counselors with an *integrated/congruent* broaching style are competent in bringing up issues related to race or social location throughout therapy, not just in an intake interview, they comprehend how social location shapes one's personal and social-political experiences, and they have integrated these understandings and behaviors into their professional identities. An integrated/congruent broaching style requires a nuanced understanding of the complexities around social location and an ability to distinguish between culture-specific behaviors and unhealthy functioning. These therapists encourage clients to explore and discuss their experiences in light of their own unique social identity or identities.

The final broaching style in the Day-Vines model (Day-Vines et al., 2007) is referred to as an *infusing* broaching style. Here, clinicians are not just committed to broaching because it is appropriate professional practice, but they tend to address diversity issues as a way of life. This requires grasping social location and all of its complexities with nuanced and critical-thinking abilities, having a solid commitment to social justice and what it means to be an agent of change. These therapists do what we might colloquially refer to as "walking the talk."

So, what does all of this look like in practice? There is no recipe for broaching conversations, of course. But often broaching conversations begin by asking the client directly about his social location—social location defined, again, most broadly to include race, culture, religion, socioeconomic status, sexual orientation, gender identification, disability status, and so on. This should come up in the intake interview or early in therapy. For example, a counselor may ask, "Do you practice any formal religion?" or "I noticed on the intake form that you checked the box indicating that you identify as bisexual. Can you tell me a little more about that?" This can be followed by additional questions—at that moment or later—that clarify the ways in which the identified problem in counseling is affected by one's social or cultural identity and related experiences. For example, "Shakira, can we talk about the ways in which being a woman of color in an overwhelmingly White workplace is related to the anxiety you have at work?"

If a client locates in a social location that is marginalized, it is critical that the counselor recognize that the client has experienced some bias and discrimination. So, in this case asking too many questions too early in the relationship may be counterproductive. The clinician must be careful not to create a climate that feels like an interrogation or make the client feel responsible for educating the clinician about group identity characteristics. Of course, it is also very important to respect the client's decision to engage in this conversation or to opt out. "Okay, I hear that you don't feel like talking about this right now. If it's okay with you, maybe we can check back in on this at another time. Okay?"

Broaching race or other social locations is important for many reasons. First, as Van Ausdale and Feagin (2001) point out, even children as young as preschoolers are aware of implicit racial dynamics in their immediate environment. They remind us that young children of color who are minorities in their environment often experience subtle forms of racism and may feel isolated. And this is even in schools where staff are vigilant about issues related to race. We also know that there are huge racial disparities in the utilization of mental health services across racial groups (for more on this, see Cabral & Smith, 2011; Duncan, 2003; Hayes, Owen, & Bieschke, 2015). These are in part due to mistrust, concerns about misdiagnosis, the cultural competence of the clinician (or lack thereof), and a variety of cultural norms related to privacy and worldview (Hayes et al., 2015). Not addressing cultural issues in therapy runs the danger of perpetuating bias and may constitute a microaggression. We know that when counselors broach race, their clients of color find them to be more competent and credible (Day-Vines et al., 2007).

CHAPTER SUMMARY

This chapter might have also been called "the seemingly small things that are big" in therapy. It is easy to overlook the importance of establishing a therapeutic position that engenders trust and confidence, but the research is clear that therapeutic alliance and expressing empathy are necessary factors promoting success in therapy. So, initiating therapy with a warm and receptive welcome is critical. We also talked about the important ways in which clinicians can be attentive to their clients, beginning with really listening to what they say and do in therapy. This can be challenging, as we also are governed by our own personal meaning-making and executive function processes as we listen. And these, too, are a critical component of listening. We ended the chapter with a discussion of the importance of therapists being able to broach conversations about social and cultural identity. A number of broaching styles were introduced, highlighting the important point that not only do clinicians have a responsibility to initiate conversations about social location; they must also remain engaged in these conversations when they are significant to the everyday lived experiences of their clients. The skills that are discussed in the following chapters complement these initial welcoming and listening skills.

REFLECTION QUESTIONS

1. How can a clinician be respectful and welcoming if she finds that she does not really like the client? What should she do?
2. How does a therapist know if his "thinking voice" is leading him astray?
3. What should the clinician do if she broaches a particular social location that she believes is pertinent to the therapeutic issue but the client does not seem to want to discuss it?

CHAPTER

Basic Responding Skills

Chapter Outline

INTRODUCTION

Cutting across most therapeutic practice modalities are a number of basic counseling skills that clinicians use to build and maintain the therapeutic relationship and carry out specific treatment modality protocols. These skills are the fundamental ingredients of therapy. In this chapter, we will discuss reflections, paraphrases, questions, and the importance of witnessing, acknowledging, and offering affirmations. In the next chapter, we will move to discuss interpretation, confrontation, feedback, self-disclosure, and immediacy.

REFLECTIONS AND PARAPHRASES

Reflections and paraphrases are two of the most basic skills used in clinical therapeutic helping conversations. Surprisingly, given their ubiquity, there is not one uniform definition for these terms, and they are often used interchangeably in the literature. For example, even though Brammer and MacDonald (2003) identify reflections and paraphrases as separate skills, they point out that they are very similar. Hutchinson (2012) and Ivey, Ivey, and Zalaquett (2010) suggest that a content reflection is the same thing as a paraphrase. Egan's (2010) concept of advanced accurate empathy is similar to Young's (2013) concept of reflection of meaning, and both are what many would call an interpretation rather than reflection or empathy. Despite this lack of clarity in terms of what these skills are called, being clear about how and when one might use them is most critical—it promotes therapeutic intentionality. Intentionality is an important undercurrent of our discussion here.

REFLECTIONS

Like a mirror, reflections illuminate what the client has said or done. They are the repeating back, almost verbatim, of what the client has communicated.

A **content reflection** is the reproduction of a key idea, articulated in the same words used by the client. For example, a client says, "I am so lost and confused; I need some time to think, or maybe I just need some help. I just

Photo 7.1
Copyright © 2014 Depositphotos/hibrida13.

don't know." The clinician uses a content reflection to mirror back key content in what the client has said: "You feel lost and confused. You need some help." Notice that the content reflection is a restatement of the exact words articulated by the client, offered in a condensed form.

Content reflections are used to shift the focus onto a significant part of a client's message—to highlight or focus on something that has been said by the client and insert it back into circulation. In effect, then, they typically keep a conversation in place rather than moving forward. Content reflections are also used for *tracking* in a conversation. Tracking is a minimal response form that entails repeating small pieces of what has been communicated by the client with the intent of communicating that she has been heard. It is used when the clinician does not want to shift the focus away from what is being said or interrupt the flow of the conversation.

A **behavior reflection** is used to focus on a particular behavior or something that the client *does* in the moment. For example, as a client reports that he is "lost and confused," his eyes tear up. The clinician responds: "Your eyes are tearing up." Behavior reflections call attention to nonverbal behaviors with the therapeutic intent of focusing on a significant but unspoken message. The purpose is to deepen the conversation. Calling attention to an unstated communication renders it important and invites further exploration. It also raises intensity and has the potential to make a client feel watched or monitored. So this is a skill that should be used judiciously and with intentionality.

A **feeling reflection** is the mirroring of a feeling that has been communicated by the client. Of all of the reflections, this may be the most tricky, since we can never really know how someone else is feeling. One way to reflect a feeling is to simply repeat the feeling word that the client uses. For example, a client says, "When she did that to me I was so mad." "You were mad," is a simple feeling reflection.

Of course, clients don't always articulate their feelings by name, and some clients lack a sophisticated feeling vocabulary. So, feeling words are often hard to come by. Clinicians can use verbal cues to infer client's feelings. Word choice is one clue about emotional content—sometimes clients use strong and evocative words. Intonation in the client's speech is another. For example, "I was delirious" or "ecstatic" suggest more than "I felt okay." A lull in the sentence when the client reports that he is "happy" may suggest something other than happiness.

Clinicians also use nonverbal clues to help them identify a client's feeling. For example, if a client is tapping his hand or pulling at his hair when he speaks, there might be an emotional connection to what he is saying. Of course, relying on nonverbal cues renders a feeling reflection somewhat speculative. It is easy to get it wrong. For this reason, it is important for therapists to be appropriately tentative when offering a feeling reflection. For example, a client has been talking about leaving his wife, who has had a long history of physical and mental health problems. He turns red and breaks eye contact as he says "I have been thinking about it for a while." In this scenario, the content is fairly obvious—the client is considering the idea of leaving his wife. Here the clinician may decide that she wants to add something to deepen the conversation around this difficult decision that the client is contemplating. So instead, she offers a tentative feeling reflection, based on her observation that the client would not look at her and seems to have turned an embarrassment red. She says: "You feel guilty even thinking that. Is that right?" Adding "Is that right?" at the end of this feeling reflection is a way of being tentative—inviting the client to disagree. And this is important here, of course, because the suggestion that the client may feel guilty is based on a hypothesis or assumption that may or may not be true.

Another way to construct a feeling reflection is to begin by reflecting a behavior. In this two-part reflection, the behavioral reflection serves to segue into a hypothesis. In effect, it offers some evidence or an explanation for why the therapist is identifying a particular feeling. For example, in the above example, the clinician might say, "Your face got red and you looked away when you said that. I'm guessing you feel ashamed of even thinking that." Offering this additional "evidence" positions the client to understand why the counselor has identified that particular feeling.

Feeling reflections tend to slow conversations down. They can help clients become more aware of their affect and prompt meaning making. Affect awareness is important for many reasons. First, emotions provide information about the outside world (Rathus & Miller, 2015). For example, when I was walking to visit a friend one night, I became tense and fearful when I walked past a scene where two cars had bumped into each other. Voices had become hostile as an argument broke out between the drivers and bystanders began to gather. Being alert to my feeling of fear warned me to be careful, as the situation could become volatile, and to keep moving. Emotions, then, can motivate us to act in certain ways (Rathus & Miller, 2015).

Emotions, too, are a source of communication (Rathus & Miller, 2015). When I frown, others can read the expression of disappointment or sadness just as easily as they might interpret a smile to mean happiness or joy. Related to this, we can see that the expression of emotion also influences the behavior of others (Rathus & Miller, 2015). For example, you may notice that toddlers often look at the face of the adult who is with them when they fall or experience some other type of minor mishap. It is as if they read the adult's expression for a cue about how they should react. In the world of therapy, this happens as well. Clients may lack awareness about the ways in which their expressions of emotions affect their interpersonal relationships. So, attending to affect may be a good way to help a client increase her awareness of emotions. Client emotion can also influence the behavior of the therapist. For example, a client's tears may signal a need for caution—that there might be something that is difficult for the client. So, in this case, the clinician knows to be mindful of regulating the intensity in that moment. Client emotion may also trigger therapist reactivity. For example, a client may be very angry, and this anger makes the counselor uncomfortable. So, the intervention on the part of the therapist may be to appease the client or change the focus. When this happens, we can say that personalization issues rather than therapeutic intent are in the driving seat during that particular therapeutic moment.

A few words of caution about using feeling reflections are in order here. First, remember that most people typically experience multiple feelings simultaneously. So, the counselor has a strategic decision to make: whether to reflect the feeling that he wants to emphasize or to attempt to reflect all of the likely feelings that are present, allowing the client to decide where to focus next. A simple way to reflect multiple feelings is to name some of the emotions that seem present and speak with appropriate tentativeness. For example, "You say that you are happy, but I sense some frustration as well." Or, "Part of you is happy. I wonder if part of you is also frustrated?" Another way to capture multiple emotions is to use a combined behavioral and feeling reflection. For example, "You say that you are happy. I notice that you are hitting your fist on your leg. I may be wrong, but I wonder if you might also be frustrated?" Notice the use of "I wonder…" and "I may be wrong…" as a way of introducing tentativeness in these examples. Tentativeness invites the client to confirm or deny the feeling that is being suggested. In most cases, getting the exact name of the emotion is not hugely important. What is important is the way in which the conversation has shifted to a focus on the affective content. Even if the emotion was improperly named, calling attention to the emotion—whatever it is called—can open up space for the client to discover the emotion he is feeling.

The second caution is that reflections can be problematic if the counselor reflects something that is not significant or pertinent in the conversation. In this case, an inaccurate feeling reflection can focus the conversation in a direction that is not intended or not helpful. For this reason, therapists must be attuned to the nuance in client communications. Counselors should also use appropriate tentativeness and check out the accuracy of emotional reflections.

Third, remember that feeling reflections have a tendency to increase emotional intensity, especially when they are paired with a behavioral reflection. For example, when we point out to a client that her eyes are "tearing up" and speculate that she is very sad, this draws our immediate attention to emotion, and it may also make her feel that she is being watched. Expressing emotion is not inherently good or bad, but when a client does not have the abilities or resources to regulate intense emotionality, a feeling reflection may not be appropriate. Therapeutic decisions around raising the intensity in a session must be guided by intentionality in the context of the ethical responsibility to do no harm. If it is therapeutically appropriate to focus on affect when working with a client who has difficulties regulating emotion, therapists may need to co-regulate with the client. This can be done by pacing the conversation slowly, breathing in and out with the client, inviting the client to be aware of his emotional state, taking breaks from the intensity, and checking in to see if he is okay. Of course, even when a client has adequate affect self-regulation abilities, emotional expression may leave clients feeling vulnerable. In general, counselors should have an adequate relationship with a client before using feeling reflections, and they also must be attentive to providing a safe emotional space when clients are emotional. Providing an appropriate emotional space often looks like sitting in an empathic silence as the client emotes and, perhaps, offering minimal verbalizations and supportive messages such as "Yes, yes" or "This is so hard."

The last thing to say here is that while reflections are fairly simple to use and can be surprisingly additive and effective in offering focus and inviting the client to take direction, excessive use of reflections can be very awkward and ineffective in advancing the direction of therapy. Let's face it, clients do not want to just hear you repeat over and over what they have already said! If reflections are offered in a rote or mechanical way and if they are not expressed with true respect and empathy, they will probably not add anything to the therapeutic conversation. Reflections should always be used with intentionality and care.

PARAPHRASES

A paraphrase recapitulates what the client has communicated, but it is stated in the clinician's words. It is not a verbatim repeat; instead, a paraphrase is based on the counselor's understanding of the client's message. The purpose of using paraphrases is to clarify, summarize, or emphasize a particular idea. Paraphrases may be used to slow down a conversation by focusing on a particular idea or situation so as to promote further inquiry. They also may be used to add something—to bring a particular idea or feeling that was present but not entirely in focus—into the conversation.

Table 7.1: Reflections and Paraphrases

REFLECTIONS	PARAPHRASES
Repeating back verbatim what client has said.	A summary of what client has said, articulated in the clinician's words.
Content reflection: A reproduction of the key ideas as articulated in the client's words.	**Paraphrase format** 1. Use an **introductory phrase** that communicates **tentativeness**.
Behavioral reflection: Calling attention to the client's nonverbal behavior.	2. **Summarize** the key words, phrases, feelings or concepts.
Feeling reflection: Calling attention to a feeling that has been communicated verbally or nonverbally by the client.	3. **Check in** with client to assess the accuracy of the paraphrase.

Here is an example that illustrates some important components of paraphrases. Let us say that a client speaks for a few minutes about things that have happened in his home over the past week. He says: "Geez, I've had a doozie of a week. I don't even know where to start. There was that car thing—just a minor accident but it will be costly, I think. And that's left me relying on public transportation to get to work and here and everywhere—public transportation is always such a hassle. And then, I had my hands full with Harriet again. She wanted to go to her boyfriend's house to do her homework, and Patrick told her it would be okay. You know, I love Patrick, but sometimes his parenting skills are not very good. Why does Harriet need to go out on Monday and Tuesday night to do homework all of a sudden? And when I pointed this out—that maybe she was going out a little too much, Patrick didn't back me up. Again. And then...." After a while, the therapist responds by saying, "So, let me see if I'm getting this right: It's been a rough week. First the car broke down and getting it fixed will be expensive. And then, there were some of the challenges we have discussed with your daughter. And also, it did not feel to you like your partner was very supportive to you."

A paraphrase is an intervention of condensing and repeating, and some things are included while others are not. The content of a paraphrase is based on what the therapist thinks is therapeutically appropriate to emphasize, given the client, the topic, the goals, and the theoretical modality or direction that is guiding the therapist's work. For example, in the above example, if the therapeutic goals and the focus of therapy were about a work-related issue rather than family or relationship issues, the clinician may have been using the paraphrase to summarize the conversation for closure and then move on to the more relevant topic. Let us say, however, that the therapist summarized the client's initial story in this way: "So, it was a stressful week, and here is this conflict with Patrick again." This paraphrase takes a decidedly different focus than the earlier one. Rather than offering a summary that captures a few of the points, this paraphrase is more narrowly focused on the client and his relationship with his partner, Patrick. Therapeutic intent guides paraphrase construction, and this intent is based on clinical intuition and therapeutic goals.

At the risk of belaboring the point, let us briefly examine a different paraphrase that might have been used in the example above. Let us say that the therapist responded with: "So, here again this week, you are feeling overwhelmed with the difficult tasks of work, parenting, and your relationship. This is even worse when a few unexpected things happen like the car issue." This paraphrase, like the first one, seems to accurately capture the main points that were mentioned by the client. We see, however, that here the clinician took the liberty of including "feeling overwhelmed" in the paraphrase. Because emotions are part of so many conversations—in and out of therapy—it makes sense that paraphrases would also include a hypothesis about what the client is feeling. Doing so, however, requires us to listen carefully to the verbal and nonverbal cues and the context that give meaning to the client's words. In this example, it might be that the client articulated the story in such a way that communicated a feeling of being overwhelmed. Or it may be that feeling overwhelmed was a recurrent theme across the multiple stories he brings to therapy. Or it may have been articulated initially as the problem he wants to address in counseling. There are multiple clues that help us understand the emotional and content messages communicated by our clients.

It is the clinician who decides what to include and omit in a paraphrase. For this reason, it is important to remember that paraphrases are a form of interpretation. Paraphrases are rarely described as interpretations in most skills texts, but I do so here to emphasize a caution. We can never fully know client's intentions, thoughts, and feelings. So, the clinician's choices about what to include and what to omit in a paraphrase are based on hypotheses, "educated guesses," or interpretations. This does not mean that clinicians should not add their own subjectivity and clinical intuition into paraphrases. But it is just to acknowledge that the truth and accuracy of a paraphrase is never assured.

THE CONSTRUCTION OF A PARAPHRASE

Paraphrases typically begin with an **introductory phrase** such as "I am hearing you say" or "It seems like." These are intended to reflect a tentativeness that invites the client to correct the paraphrase if it is inaccurate or misses something important. Next is an articulation of the gist of what the client has said. This recap should include some of the **key words, phrases, feelings, or concepts** that were communicated by the client. Sometimes the clinician may even bring in something from an earlier conversation or situation to clarify or connect important themes. For example, early on in the session, the client says, "I don't want to do it." Later, she says, "I am not sure if I should do it." And then later, "I think I should do it." The clinician responds with a paraphrase that captures all of these communications: "First you said you wanted to and now you are not sure. It's very confusing to know what to do." Again, here, the clinician offers a recapitulation of what the client has said, but he also uses his own words and understandings rather than a verbatim reflection. Note that in this example, the client never *said* that she was confused, but the mixed messages were evident. So, confusion is interpreted by the clinician to be an essential part of the message, and for this reason he included it in the paraphrase as a way of capturing the dilemma more fully.

Because a paraphrase is a communication that filters what has been said or intimated through the lens of the counselor, the potential for misinterpretation always exists. For this reason, it is always a good idea to use **tentativeness,** as mentioned, and to include an invitation for the client to correct the paraphrase for accuracy. This is what I refer to as a **check-in**. For example, a client, Moses, told a therapist, "I am so vexed about this, I don't know what to do. I know that I should be happy about this offer, but I do not want to go. We had trouble last time I went." Deciding that a pure reflection would not fully capture Moses's sentiment, the clinician offered a tentative paraphrase. "Correct me if I'm wrong here, Moses, but I hear you saying that you are confused about what to do. Is that right?" Moses responded with, "Well, yes. Maybe. But I'm just so mad at her, too." "So," the clinician said, "you are mad and this is making you unsure of what to do. Is that right?" "Yes," Moses agreed, "I guess I really am confused and angry about what happened last time." Notice how meaning was constructed using a series of paraphrases rather than just one paraphrase in this interchange between Moses and the clinician. Also, the tentativeness in the first paraphrase allowed Moses to correct the therapist. Here we can say, then, that the paraphrases were used as formative rather than definitive statements. Clarity came from increasingly more accurate paraphrases and the dialogic process invited Moses to be the authority on what he was thinking and feeling.

Clients often make sense of their experiences through conversation—while they are talking. This means that they may not be putting forward a completed idea or they may not have full awareness of what they are saying in the moment. Paraphrases and reflections can be very helpful in these moments, as they slow conversations down, provide space for clients to think, and follow the direction of the client. Keep in mind, however, that when too much attention is focused on repeating what has been said or when the client is not sure what to talk about, paraphrases may not be particularly helpful. Also, when paraphrases are used to bring attention to important or undercurrent themes or to shift the focus to a particular aspect of the conversation, the conversation becomes clinician directed and even more interpretative. The more interpretative a paraphrase becomes, the more important it is to use tentativeness and to check out understandings.

Table 7.2: Purpose of Reflections and Paraphrases

REFLECTIONS	PARAPHRASES
• To communicate that the client has been heard • To keep pace in the conversation with minimal intrusion • To focus on what client is saying/ keep the focus on a particular topic • To bring clarity or invite introspection • To invite the client to make meaning or interpret what he is saying • To slow the conversation down	• To communicate that the client has been heard • To keep pace in the conversation with minimal intrusion • To focus on what client is saying/ keep the focus on a particular topic • To bring clarity or invite introspection • To slow the conversation down • Invite the client to clarify the meaning that the therapist has articulated • To suggest new meanings or ideas • To illuminate or point out themes

QUESTIONS

Asking questions, it seems, is the hallmark of what therapists do. Clinicians use questions to initiate conversations, to gather information, to focus on an important topic, to explore an issue in depth, to solicit client input, to check out understandings, to help avoid confusion, and to prompt clients to think in new directions. Here we will review a variety of question types that are used for different purposes in therapy. These include closed questions; open questions and open-ended focused probes; how, what, when, where, and why questions; inflection questions; and sequential questions.

CLOSED QUESTIONS

Closed questions are used to prompt yes/no responses or for gathering specific information. For example, "Are you okay?" "Do you want to do that?" "What day did that happen?" "How long have you been waiting?" Because closed questions are effective for eliciting specific and focused information, they are typically used with some frequency during intake interviews and in the assessment process. They are also used, of course, at other times throughout helping conversations when specific or factual information is needed.

It is important to remember that the person in a conversational interchange who asks a question—any type of question—steps into a directive or agent position. While some questions invite the receiver to expound in

Photo 7.2

any way they choose, closed questions frame a particular response set that is determined by the asker. For example, when I ask a client *if* she likes her teacher, this closed question prompts a yes/no response rather than nuance and explanation. It does not invite the person to elaborate, to take charge of the direction of the conversation, or to clarify or elucidate her response in any way. The caution about using closed questions is that when they are used too frequently or at inappropriate times—early in a relationship, when a client is reluctant or demonstrates a low level of motivation for change—they can feel interrogative and invasive and have the effect of closing down a conversation. For example, the client may refuse to respond to a particular question, or she may just answer a question without much thought, as if she is just trying to get through the conversation. Of course, this does not mean that closed questions aren't appropriate and should not be used in therapy. However, it is usually best to limit the use of closed questions, embed them into larger conversations, and use other question types, too. The rule of thumb is to ask closed questions when a specific answer is needed. Otherwise, it is usually best to rely on other question types.

OPEN QUESTIONS AND OPEN-ENDED FOCUSED PROBES

An open question is one that does not prompt a specific answer—it offers space for the conversation to be taken in any number of directions. For example, instead of asking a student *if* she likes her teacher, as mentioned in the example above, asking "Can you tell me about your teacher?" or "How are things going with your teacher?" invites her to take the prompt in any desired direction. So, even though they are initiated at the direction of the therapist, open questions invite the client to determine how she wants to respond.

Also, open questions tend to invite larger, what I refer to as *paragraph responses*, rather than brief answers. For example, clinicians sometimes begin therapy sessions with an open question, such as "What would you like to talk about today?" This question invites the client to initiate discussion about whatever he wants, rather than what the clinician thinks is important. Of course, for some clients, this type of question is too open—inviting the client to talk about anything he wants can misdirect the therapy sessions, overwhelm a client, or invite the client to avoid a particular topic that is hard to talk about. So, instead, many clinicians opt to use **open-ended focused probes.** This semidirectional form of an open question provides some direction but is open enough to allow the client latitude as well. For example, questions such as "Can you tell me what happened in school since we last spoke?" or "Can you tell me a little about your family?" invite clients to take the conversation *about the particular topic* in any direction they want. Open-ended focused probes are commonly used in therapy to elicit the client's perspective and promote more depth in the conversation related to a particular topic or theme.

HOW, WHAT, WHEN, WHERE, AND WHY QUESTIONS

No doubt you have already noticed that the introductory phrase leading up to a question shapes the kind of response that one is looking for. **How**, **what**, and **why** questions invite the client to offer her perspective or ideas on a particular topic. For example, when a clinician asks "*How* did that happen?," he is eliciting the client's perspective or understandings about a situation. Similarly, asking why something happened invites the client to explain her thinking processes. For example, "*Why* do you think Patience said that to you?" asks for the client to explain her thoughts. *What* questions, too, typically serve this purpose of eliciting meaning making. For example, "What were you hoping for when you asked your sister to help?" or "What do you think will happen?" invite client speculation, communicate a respect for the client's point of view, and provide insight into the client's thought processes.

How, what, and why questions are obviously not appropriate for times when we do *not* want to encourage the client to share his perspective. They are also not often very helpful in *eliciting* feelings. This latter point about eliciting feelings may seem a bit counterintuitive because we often use a how question colloquially to ask people about their feelings. For example, we often ask people, "How are you feeling today?" But this kind of question tends to prompt a one-word response, and it is often a socially acceptable response, such as "Fine" or "Good, how are you?" It is fair to say that people are not always completely honest in their responses to *how are you feeling?* questions, probably because contemporary social etiquette dictates that these kinds of questions are more of a greeting than a serious inquiry. Also, social etiquette tells us that when we are asked this question, we should offer a response that does not take up too much air time, and that we should not air our grievances in public. Of course, there are other reasons why these questions don't always work: People may not want to bring others down, sometimes people really don't know how they feel, and it may be that the person being asked how she feels honestly does not want to talk to that particular person about personal experiences and feelings. But when people do respond to these questions with some honesty, the response often is a thought about a feeling, not a feeling itself. For example, in response to the question "*How* do you feel about that?," a client may say, "I am feeling angry" and then launch into a helpful explanation: "I mean, when she said that to me, I just didn't like her attitude and tone." This is not necessarily an undesirable direction for a therapeutic conversation, but the point is that the *how* question about a feeling moved into story and a thought about a feeling rather than an expression of the feeling itself. So, if the intent is to move a client into a feeling state, a feeling reflection is probably often more helpful. Also, sequential questions, discussed below, peppered with reflections, can help clients move into and remain in an affective state.

When and *where* questions are similar to closed questions, as they tend to shape the response set toward specific details. For example, "When did you do that?" asks for a particular time or date. "Where do you live?" similarly asks for a specific piece of information. So, while these questions can elicit helpful information, they are very focused and directive. When used too much, they can easily create a choppy conversation or make a client feel interrogated.

INFLECTION QUESTIONS

An inflection question is a statement that is articulated with an inflection at the end so that it is spoken as a question rather than an assertion. For example, a raised pitch at the end of the statement "So you will go" turns this statement into a question. Inflection questions introduce tentativeness into a conversation. Also, because they are stylistically different than other question types, they can buffer the feeling of being interrogated when multiple questions are being asked. Like closed questions, though, inflection questions tend to prompt very specific responses—they are directive. So, clinicians who seek to have clients say more or be more agent in a conversation should use them judiciously.

SEQUENTIAL QUESTIONS

As mentioned, clinicians ask questions—it's just what they do! Asking too many questions, however, can hijack therapeutic conversations and also make clients feel interrogated. For this reason, we begin this section with a caution about using sequential questions. Having said that, the use of sequential questioning is an important therapeutic skill that, when used well and with intention, can be very effective in deepening a conversation.

Asking sequential questions is not just about firing off random questions. Instead, it is a skill that is used to direct conversations in intentional ways. For example, a therapist wants Elliot to examine his drinking patterns, but she also is aware that Elliot's parents have talked extensively to Elliot about his drinking, and they report that he is "very defensive" when talking about it. So the clinician decides to broach the conversation about drinking slowly, using sequential questions. First she asks Elliot, "Why do you think your parents are concerned about your drinking?" Angrily, Elliot begins to describe his parents as nosy and overinvolved in his life. "Can you give me an example of when they did that? That way I can get a better picture of what you mean," the therapist asks. As Elliot goes on to describe a scene from the past Saturday night when he came home drunk, the therapist tracks the conversation, asking a few closed questions, such as "What time was it?" and "You said you had how many drinks?" She also asks a few focused open-ended probes, such as "I wonder why your parents were so angry that night. Any idea?" and

"When you say it was a difficult night with your friend Tarnue, can you help me understand what you mean?" Finally, at the end of the story, the therapist opens up the conversation to elicit Elliot's understandings. She does this by asking Elliot what he thinks it means to have a drinking problem, and later she asks what it means to Elliot that his parents are so concerned about him. The intent of using this series of questions is to keep the focus on the topic of drinking, follow the story that is being told, gather a variety of information, and invite Elliot to offer his understandings about the situation as well as consider the perspective of others.

Following your shot is a metaphor that I often use to discuss how sequential questions can be used in therapy. This metaphor is based on the soccer position of "striker," the player whose main job is to score a goal. Strikers know that when they kick the ball toward the goal, they must stay alert for an opportunity to kick the ball in the goal a second time—this is in case the ball is deflected by the goalie. By following her shot, the striker is more likely to have her touch make it to the back of the net.

Using sequential questions, then, is a way of following your shot. First you ask a question. Then, after the client responds to the question,

Photo 7.3

you ask another question related to what has been said. This process of narrowing down questions enables the conversation to gather depth and serves to keep the focus on the goal. The point of the soccer metaphor is a reminder that a clinician should not fire off a question and then retreat. If questions are important enough to be asked in the first place, they probably require follow-through. Using a variety of question types with reflections and paraphrases is a good way to follow your shot and at the same time maintain a conversational flow in the discussion. There is a special art in using sequential questions in a way that promotes therapeutic intention without being too heavy-handed. It starts with therapist positioning—recall the discussion about positioning theory in Chapter 2. When the clinician assumes a position of respectful curiosity—asking questions because she genuinely wants to hear what her client thinks—than sequential questions are likely to be received well and are generally more helpful.

Table 7.3: Types of Questions

Type	Description
CLOSED QUESTIONS	• Yes/no questions or seeking specific details • Purpose: to seek specific information
OPEN QUESTIONS	• Nondirective questions • Purpose: to Invite client-directed exploration
FOCUSED OPEN-ENDED PROBES	• Semidirectional questions • Purpose: to invite exploration of a particular topic or theme
HOW, WHAT, WHEN, WHERE, AND WHY QUESTIONS	• Specific-purpose questions • Purpose: to invite client perspectives and communicate respect and interest
INFLECTION QUESTIONS	• Statements as questions • Purpose: to alter questioning formats and bring focus
SEQUENTIAL QUESTIONS	• Using a varied question set • Purpose: to probe deeper and "follow your shot"

WITNESSING, AFFIRMATIONS, AND ACKNOWLEDGMENT

Winslade, Crocket, and Monk (1997) point out that oppressive problems sometimes have the effect of isolating individuals from others in their families and communities. This is particularly true for those who experience the devastating effects of trauma, including sociocultural trauma. Trauma often happens behind closed doors and is often enveloped in shame, so it is not always easy to see. This shame can be so menacing that it even makes others uncomfortable—sometimes so uncomfortable that they avoid stepping in to help. So, the experience of trauma can be a very solitary experience. Hardy and Laszloffy (2005) point out that "loss of any kind is painful, but even more painful than loss itself is when it remains unacknowledged, unmourned, and therefore unhealed" (p. 92). Unacknowledged loss, they remind us, can lead to internalized *voicelessness*—a self-censoring of one's experiences and even a censoring of one's own feelings, particularly of anger. Voicelessness is a hidden wound that results when one's experiences in everyday life are denied or minimized by others (Hardy, 2013). Experiences of trauma and distress, as mentioned, can produce a severing of connections—connections with others and also a severing of connections within one's own internal experiences (Weingarten, 2003). That is, victims of trauma can become disconnected from their own feelings, beliefs, and values, as well as with significant others in the family and community (Hardy, 2013; Weingarten, 2003).

Affirmation and acknowledgment are identified by Hardy (2013) as the first step in the healing of the hidden wounds of sociocultural or racial trauma. In therapy, this speaks to the importance of not standing silent in the face of a client's stories of trauma or injustice. When clinicians create a space for stories of violation or injustice, and when they listen to those stories with openness, curiosity, and sensitivity, clients feel invited to speak the unspeakable. Racial storytelling, Hardy (2013) tells us, enables clients to step out of voicelessness, invites critical thinking, and is validating. This kind of validation offsets the devaluation and assaulted sense of self that comes with experiences of sociocultural trauma. Affirmation and acknowledgment are also used by many clinicians in their work with clients who experience other types of grief and trauma. Affirmations are messaged when clinicians use active listening and tracking behaviors, such as minimal verbal responses, reflections, and paraphrases. They also are inherent to expressions of empathy and to emotional availability in the consulting room.

Weingarten (2003) uses the concept of *compassionate witnessing* in reference to the ways in which one can acknowledge and stand with another person who has experienced trauma or distress. According to Weingarten, compassionate witnessing begins with a "doable" (p. 192) selected focus. That is, it is to work with the part of the trauma experience that is accessible in the therapy room. For example, while a counselor may not be present when a woman experiences sexual harassment, he can speak to the shame that the client must have experienced during the incident. He could also comment on the rage that one feels to be judged and manipulated in such ways. These, then, are the aspects of the experience of sexual harassment that he can witness—he can see the effects of harassment reflected in the client's feelings of shame and rage. The act of witnessing, then, means standing in the emotional space of distress with another person. It is to acknowledge their experiences and their pain in a way that lets them know that they are not standing alone.

Another component of witnessing is to reengage a client in conversations about the important beliefs, values, feelings, and relationships that were severed due to traumatic or distressing experiences (Weingarten, 2003). This is a process identified in narrative circles as *re-membering conversations* (for more on re-membering conversations, see Hedtke & Winslade, 2016; Russell & Carey, 2002; White, 2005). The concept of re-membering is based on the idea that people's identities are shaped by the significant people in their life. It has to do with helping people "re-organize the 'members' of their 'club of life'" (Russell & Carey, 2002, p. 2). Re-membering invites clients to think about who they want to be surrounded by—what people will help them stay close to the values, beliefs, and hopes that are important to who they are and how they want to live their lives. The practice of re-membering does not necessarily include having others physically nearby; it is about inviting the shared voices and the kindred spirit of those who are significant. It is a way of garnering support for and reengaging a client into "his people"—a community that is important to him. To do this, clinicians invite a client to examine the important influences in his life and to study what important people in his life have given him—how they have cared for him and shaped his life. In this process, the client begins to identify what is important to him, and he finds that in re-membering those people (in flesh or in spirit) into his life, he is better able to be influenced by their shared values, beliefs, and hopes for him. And, he also recognizes that when others are re-membered into his life, he is not standing alone.

In a similar vein, Hardy (2013) suggests that clinicians help clients who have experienced the isolating effects of trauma connect with a variety of emotional, psychological, and behavioral supports that will bolster their strengths and buffer against future assaults. For example, upon hearing a story of sexual harassment, the counselor might remind the client how competent she is, pointing to examples of this competence that he has seen or heard of. Or he might invite the client to think about others she knows in the community who, too, have experienced this kind of degradation, or who might also stand in support with her against the perpetrator. In these ways, the clinician is working to help the client reestablish connections of support and also to not allow this experience weaken her sense of self and competence.

CHAPTER SUMMARY

The various approaches to providing clinical mental health therapy vary considerably, but cutting across most of them is a set of fundamental counseling skills. When used appropriately and with intentionality, reflections, paraphrases, and questions can open up fruitful therapeutic directions. Witnessing, encouraging, and acknowledging were also discussed in this chapter. These skills can be used in a variety of therapeutic contexts and to address a range of client issues, but they are particularly helpful when working with people who experience chronic distress or trauma. In the chapters that follow, we will move into more additive skills and strategies that are used across many therapeutic modalities for deeper exploration and to address specific areas.

REFLECTION QUESTIONS

1. Reflections and paraphrases seem to just repeat what the client has said. Why are these useful skills, and when should they be used?

2. What can a clinician do if asking many questions causes the client to shut down or not respond?

3. Why is it helpful to acknowledge and witness someone's experiences of trauma? When might these interventions be unhelpful or potentially harmful?

CHAPTER

Additive Responses

Chapter Outline

INTRODUCTION

In this chapter, we continue our discussion of counseling skills to include a number of additive skills. While the skills in the previous chapter are largely used to better understand the client and to communicate that understanding, the skills outlined in this chapter are used to move therapeutic counseling conversations in particular directions. This is not to say, of course, that the basic skills discussed in Chapters 6 and 7 do not have therapeutic value and do not provide important direction; they are valuable in providing focus on something that has happened in a conversation, and they invite client direction. The skills outlined in this chapter are intended to move the conversation in a *new* direction, and they entail more directive engagement on the part of the clinician. Here we will discuss interpretation, confrontation, feedback, self-disclosure, and immediacy.

INTERPRETATION

Based on the psychoanalytic notion that psychic material stored unconsciously affects current functioning, interpretation has long been a therapeutic practice of promoting insight. While the term *insight* is currently used in the field in reference to a client's ability to recognize and understand one's own symptomology or functioning, the psychoanalytic focus on insight is somewhat unique. It is fair to say that the meaning and purpose of prompting insight through interpretation varies according to one's theoretical model of practice. It is also important to point out that engagement in interpretation for insight is not solely reserved for psychotherapy. Bruner (1990) points out that all human beings are interpretive beings—we are always engaged in a process of trying to understand or make meaning of our everyday experiences. Bruner's observation helps us understand, in part, why insight-oriented practices in therapy are heralded so strongly—the process of prompting insight as a therapeutic practice parallels personal practices that most of us engage in privately in our own lives outside of therapy. We always want to understand why.

In psychoanalytic circles, interpretation is aimed at revealing unconscious material—to help a client grasp the latent or concealed meanings of her words and actions (Johansson et al., 2010; Schermer, 2011). In other therapeutic modalities, interpretation is less of a process of uncovering underlying impulses and unconscious material and more about inferring meaning and significance, or understanding the implications of an event (Schermer, 2011). According to Schermer (2011), a phenomenological approach to the therapeutic use of interpretation is for the clinician to share her experience or ideas with a client and then invite discussion. When done in this way, the therapist is not centered as an expert, and the point is not to reveal unconscious material. Instead, the aim is to promote client awareness in a manner that invites a construction of meaning making between therapist and client. The shift here, it seems, has to do with clinician positioning.

From an existential perspective, interpretation entails a mutual and ongoing dialogue between client and therapist—"making the consciousness possible" (Schermer, 2011, p. 830) through thought, examination, and dialogue. In this frame, interpretation can be used to improve the client's ability to "be in contact with and to tolerate his or her mind as it is, so that the patient may develop independently" (Caper, 2001, p. 110), rather than to convince a client of the therapist's preconceptions or hypotheses. Across approaches, then, it is safe to say that interpretation is used to promote psychological development by helping a client gain insight into the connections among internal thoughts, confusions, conflicts, and past experiences, and how all of these affect everyday present relationships and personal well-being (Caper, 2001; Johansson et al., 2010). And in many approaches, it is a process that happens in dialogue between the client and counselor.

Even though it is used widely and can be very helpful in therapeutic practice, the use of interpretation as a therapeutic tool is tricky—it is easy to get it wrong. It is easy to lead a client down a misguided path. And because of the power dynamics inherent to the counselor–client relationship, interpretation can easily convince a client to think about something in a way that is not accurate to his own beliefs, values, and experiences. This is especially true when working with vulnerable clients. We never want to suggest to a client that we know him better than he knows himself. Interpretation is an advanced therapeutic skill that requires clinician sophistication, a solid therapeutic alliance, and grounded knowledge about the client and the context of his life.

INTERPRETATION CAUTIONS AND GUIDELINES

For the reasons mentioned above, there are some important cautions around the use of interpretation in therapy. First, again, we must recognize that we really do not know what the client is thinking and feeling, nor can we be sure of his motivations and intentions. We have only a glimpse into the client's life, and we can never be sure of why he does what he does. It is critical to remember that interpretations are never more than hypotheses. As such, interpretations should always be offered with an abundance of **tentativeness**. For example, a clinician asks a client, "*I am wondering* if you *may be* harboring a bit of anger about what happened in the past, which is being projected on to your husband?" The insertion of "I am wondering" and "may be" invites tentativeness—acknowledges that the clinician may be wrong. According to Schermer (2011), even Freud himself cautioned against making inappropriate interpretations and suggested that valid interpretations are those that can be verified by client response. This means that the validity of an interpretation is shown in how the client responds to it; the client will indicate its accuracy and whether it brings insight or affects change.

Another caution has to do with the tone and context in which an interpretation is used. Schermer (2011) recommends that in order for the interpretation to be fully assimilated, the therapist should include detailed **clarification or explanation**. That is, interpretation should not be executed as a delivery of truth but instead as an opening for mutual engagement in a meaning-making process based on evidence that is presented. So, adding to our example above, the clinician might say, "I am remembering that last week you mentioned that you sometimes have bouts of uncontrollable anger at your husband—anger that you don't fully understand. I wonder if you may be harboring a bit of anger about what happened in the past—the abuse you experienced at the hand of Peter, which is being projected on to your husband?" Dialogue happens best when the client fully understands how the clinician has come to the hypothesis offered.

Schermer (2011) points out that that a client's "internalization of what transpires may be more consequential than what the analyst says" (p. 818). So, here the focus is on how a client understands an interpretation. In fact, clients bring their own understandings into therapy and actively use these to make meanings, despite the gems of wisdom offered to them by their therapists. So, the recommendation here is to **check out** what or how a client has understood the interpretation offered. For example, adding "what do you think about that?"

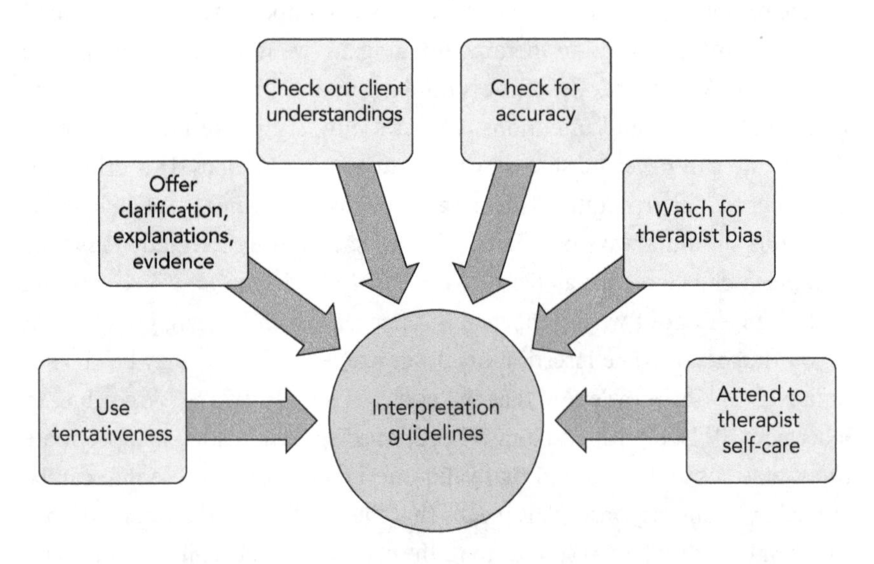

Figure 8.1 *Interpretation Guidelines*

to the end of the interpretation offered in the example above invites the client into discussion and thus is more fully engaged in the meaning-making process.

Finally, it is important to acknowledge that interpretations are highly susceptible to therapist bias. Of course, that is the point of therapy—a therapist's outsider perspective is very helpful in many situations. However, this also means that therapy, and specifically interpretations, are extremely vulnerable to clinician personalization issues. In emphasis of this point, Hersoug (2004) reported that the frequency of therapist's use of interpretations as well as the quality of interpretations is more closely associated with therapist characteristics rather than client need (Hersoug, 2004). That is, what we do in therapy is based on our own perceptions of what a client needs. If we are not healthy ourselves, or if we carry implicit bias that unknowingly becomes the lens through which we understand a client, we risk making errors in clinical judgment. Within the context of power inherent to the therapeutic relationship, what the therapist proposes is often taken as gospel truth. We must be careful about what we say in therapy. And doing this, as discussed in Chapter 4, requires that we take care of ourselves. **Self-care** is the underscored recommendation in regard to this final caution.

Photo 8.1
Copyright © 2013 Depositphotos/styf.

CONFRONTATION

Festinger (1957) pointed out that people are motivated by an inner drive toward consistency. This drive to be consistent, according to Festinger, is prompted by the experience of tension that happens when we experience a conflict between our beliefs, values, thoughts, attitudes, and/or actions. People are motivated to act in ways that reduce or avoid this tension, he proposed, and thus they will attempt to find alignment. Confrontation is an intervention that calls attention to inconsistencies. It has the potential to foster insight into the meaning and effects of one's behavior on self and others (Scaturo, 2002); to help clients be more accountable or make decisions that lead to a change in attitudes, behaviors, or decisions (Bratter, 2011); and to stimulate a process of self-understanding and self-evaluation.

Maslow (1967) justified the use of confrontation in therapy, coining the term—which in and of itself feels a little confrontational—"no crap therapy" (p. 28) as a way of being honest, clear, and straightforward with clients. He says:

> people are very tough, and not brittle. They can take an awful lot. The best thing to do is get right at them, and not to sneak up on them, or be delicate with them, or try to surround them from the rear. Get right smack into the middle of things right away. (Maslow, 1967, p. 28)

Maslow was not suggesting, of course, that confrontation be an attack; he did not promote the idea of therapeutic confrontation as an act of hostility. His point was that clients often need straightforward feedback to make change. In this vein, confrontation may best be thought of as giving the client feedback so that he can see himself as he is seen by others and gain insight into his actions and experiences (Kuntze, Van der Molen, & Born, 2009).

It is important to point out that there is a difference between social and therapeutic confrontation. Social confrontation is used among friends, colleagues, and sometimes complete strangers to give feedback. It tends to be about challenging someone or something because we don't like or don't agree with what they say or do. It is also an act of asserting power. When a social confrontation is delivered with frustration, anger, antagonism, and especially when it is delivered without consent, it can easily be perceived as an assertion of hostility. Even when delivered with care, social confrontation tends to be an expression of the desires of the person who is confronting rather than the needs of the person confronted; it is often stated because the deliverer wants it said.

Like social confrontation, therapeutic confrontation is a way of providing feedback. But in this case, the purpose of the confrontation is centered on the client. It is used to promote change in an explicit area that is linked to specific goals of therapy, which are part of the helping contract. Therapeutic confrontation is about helping a client move in the direction of the change that is the focus of therapy. There is never a place for social confrontation in a therapy.

The use of therapeutic confrontation has long been a staple in the work of substance abuse counselors. In this field, confrontation is frequently used to cut through denial, to reroute the clinical conversations from extreme expressions of emotion, to keep a focus on behaviors and thinking patterns related to the substance misuse, and to challenge a client "to take responsibility to change some aspect of their behavior or thinking that is detrimental to their recovery" (Polcin, 2003, p. 166). Although it is a commonly used tool to these ends, Polcin concludes that more research is needed to assess exactly how confrontation should be used in therapy and how to measure its effectiveness. He also points out, importantly, that confrontation and empathy are not mutually exclusive. That is, all therapeutic treatment must involve support and confrontation, but different clients require different levels of each.

Therapeutic confrontation is widely used across many counseling modalities, not just substance abuse counseling, and it is used address a wide variety of issues with powerful and effective results. But its use as a clinical skill also has a long and controversial history (Polcin, 2003; Strong & Zeman, 2010). Many of us can give personal testimony to the ways in which our own growth and change has emerged from experiences of being confronted; we can easily see growth potential from challenge. But, many of us have also had personal experiences of when confrontation was not delivered well, and for some of us, it has caused pain and unnecessary turmoil. If this happens in therapy, of course, progress will be hampered. And, one's own personal and professional experiences around confrontation cause anxiety for many clinicians.

Another reason why confrontation is such a formidable and complex therapeutic skill is because, as mentioned earlier, confrontation is an interactional communication through which power is enacted (Strong & Zeman, 2010). Confrontation will always trigger a response. The extent to which the response is productive for the client, according to Strong and Zeman (2010), has to do with the extent to which the clinician positions herself in a "power with" rather than a "power over" (p. 333) position. To this end, confrontations should be conducted as "dialogic" (Strong & Zeman, 2010, p. 332). Here, Strong and Zeman mean that confrontations should prompt a discussion between client and counselor, and not appear as an order or command that the client change. The therapeutic significance of a confrontation is not the confrontation itself; its powerful effect results from what happens *after* the confrontation (Strong & Zeman, 2010). When clinicians offer confrontations as social confrontations or from a position of power over, clients are likely to become defensive, angry, and foreclosed to conversation and change. In contrast, confrontation must always be conducted with empathy and respect, and with the intent of opening up a conversation rather than issuing an ultimatum or thinly veiled advice. A good way to initiate a confrontation is to notice and work with discrepant client messages. We will talk about this in more detail here.

WORKING WITH DISCREPANCIES

None of us is immune from communicating mixed, confusing, inconsistent, or contradictory messages when speaking to others. And, too, all of us have personally experienced discrepant feelings, thoughts, attitudes, and values. We sometimes say one thing and do something else. Or we say something one minute and then something contradictory the next. Sometimes we even do things that are inconsistent with our values, our intentions, and our best judgment. Despite Festinger's (1957) observation that humans crave consistency, the truth is that we are not always consistent. In therapy, the presence of inconsistencies offers a potential opportunity for change. When used as part of a dialogic process, confrontation is a very effective way to mine discrepancies for growth opportunities.

The following steps are recommended for conducting a confrontation by pointing out discrepancies:

1. **Point out the discrepancy with appropriate tentativeness, a position of power with, and with respectful curiosity.**

Use a paraphrase or reflection to identify the discrepancy you witnessed. Speak clearly, be straightforward, and speak with empathy. Do not interpret the discrepancy, merely point it out for further examination. For example, "Zach, you say you don't like her but it seems that you spend a lot of time with her." Or "Chloe, you say that you're not angry but I notice your fist is pounding the side of the chair as you speak."

2. **Invite discussion and exploration. Invite the client into meaning making.**
   Whenever possible, invite the client to explain or make meaning of the discrepancy before you offer an interpretation. This communicates respect and sets a tone for a continued conversation about the issue raised. This inviting can also lower the intensity of a confrontation, which can help bypass any resistance, embarrassment, or anger that may initially be part of the client's reaction. Also, inviting a client to make meaning or consider why she has said or done something promotes agency. Ultimately, we are almost always striving for the client to be able to solve her own problems, address her own challenges, and be able to make meaning from her experiences in life. Therapy is a fertile learning environment for these to happen. Comments that are likely to invite discussion after the initial confrontation include: "Help me understand why that happens?" "What do you think that means?" "I wonder if we could talk about this some more?"

3. **Offer your hypothesis or explanation, when and if appropriate.**
   After a client has had an opportunity to think about and try to understand the discrepancy that was pointed out, it may be appropriate for you to also offer a potential interpretation. This may be necessary when you observe that an issue you think is critical has not surfaced in the client's interpretation, when you want to expand the possibilities or invite the client to think in a new direction, or when the client is not able to offer a hypothesis or asks for your input. Because we can never really know what someone else is thinking and feeling, it is always appropriate for therapists

to offer their hypotheses with tentativeness and to invite the client to disagree. Remember that meanings are often constructed through conversation, and disagreements can help surface new ideas. Examples of how to articulate hypotheses so as to invite discussion include: "I wonder if ..." "Correct me if I'm wrong, but ..." "Could it be that ..." "Do you think that maybe it's because ...?" Also, a simple, "What do you think?" or "Is that right?" after offering your input communicates that you are open to discussion about your assertion.

CONFRONTATION CAUTIONS

As we know, power shapes clinical therapeutic relationships in many overt and subtle ways, and the use of therapeutic confrontation is an assertion of power. So, confrontation must be used with intentionality. Remember that the most important component of confrontation is "what the recipient does with it" (Strong & Zeman, 2010, p. 335). The effectiveness of confrontation, like any therapeutic intervention, typically lies in how the intervention is delivered and how the conversation is managed afterward. As Øyum (2007) points out, "To know how to confront, and at the same time be respectful and inviting, is both necessary and difficult" (p. 42).

One of the potential landmines around the use of therapeutic confrontation is that it can rupture or cause problems in the therapeutic relationship if it is not handled appropriately (Scaturo, 2002; Strong & Zeman, 2010). Confrontation should never leave clients with an inappropriate or paralyzing sense of guilt, embarrassment, anger, or shame. If a therapeutic confrontation results in a breach in the helping relationship, the therapist must work to repair the breach in a way that conveys genuineness and empathy, restores confidence, and promotes learning. Engaging in conversation and working collaboratively to explore discrepancies is the best way to promote an intact relationship after a confrontation and to assure client learning.

Another caution is that even when a confrontation is delivered well, the client may still not respond as hoped. He may not agree with the observation, may not want to engage in conversation about the discrepancy, or may feel vulnerable, ashamed, or angry. This is true for most of us—when we are called upon to learn or address something difficult or that contradicts our existing beliefs, we may resist or may select for attention only those pieces of the message that are consistent with what we want to believe (Dechawatanapaisal & Siengthai, 2006; Stone & Cooper, 2001). Therapists need to remember that we can't make people think in certain ways, believe everything we tell them, or do what we think is best. When the confrontation is not as effective as expected, be genuine and be patient. It may be helpful to use the skill of immediacy, which will be presented shortly, to point out the disagreement between you and the client and suggest that the discussion be continued at another time. Alternatively, it may be helpful to consider that your inclinations were not correct, let the issue slide until and if it resurfaces again in therapy, or apologize and invite the client to offer her own interpretation of the discrepancy or version of events. Finally, it is important to consider that your client is not ready to hear what you have to offer. In this case, increasing her readiness for change in other ways may be most appropriate. Remember that if something is important, it will resurface again at another time.

Table 8.1: Confrontation: Reasons and Guidelines

REASONS FOR USING CONFRONTATION	GUIDELINES FOR USING CONFRONTATION
• A way of offering feedback • To draw attention to and promote accountabilty for discrepancies in attitudes, behaviors, and decisions • To stimulate self-evaluation and foster insight • To create enough tension to motivate change	• Identify discrepant messages in clear, concrete, and straightforward language • Do not make assumptions about intentions • Be tentative when inviting discussion and meaning making • Attend to dialogic conversation and connection

FEEDBACK

When we hear the word *feedback*, we might be reminded of that shrieking sound that happens when a microphone is too close to its speaker.

This image conjures up the experience that many of us anticipate from being given feedback—a harsh noise that hurts our ears … and sometimes our feelings as well. But in the world of therapy, feedback is an important therapeutic tool that should not be experienced as harsh, noise, or hurtful.

Photo 8.2

The term *feedback* is sometimes used interchangeably in the literature with other terms such as *confrontation*, *interpretation*, *praise*, *reinforcement*, and *immediacy* (Claiborn, Goodyear, & Horner, 2001). It is an intervention of providing clients with information about their behavior from an outside perspective and is typically used to promote awareness of the effects of one's behavior on oneself or others (Claiborn et al., 2001; Morran, Stockton, Cline, & Teed, 1998). Like confrontation, feedback is used to promote new learning and self-examination, improve performance, or suggest and promote change (Smith & King, 2004). As a therapeutic process, feedback is typically called *feedback exchange*, reflecting its intent to promote a reciprocal dialogue (Claiborn et al., 2001). This process typically begins with the clinician's observation articulated to the client. Then the client responds and the clinician offers a rejoinder or in some way continues the conversation in a constructive direction, leading to dialogue about the issue or concern. Feedback exchange is frequently used in group therapy modalities because receiving feedback from one's peers is a powerful motivator for change (Claiborn et al., 2001; Hulse-Killacky, Orr & Paradise, 2006; Kivlighan & Luiza, 2005).

Feedback can be descriptive—describing what one experiences about the recipient—or it can be evaluative, such as providing information on how one performs on a particular task or deed. In therapy, descriptive feedback is more common; in a work or school setting used by bosses or teachers, evaluative feedback may be more prevalent. *Positive feedback* typically focuses on an accomplishment, and in therapy, it is typically related to a goal that a client hopes to achieve. *Corrective feedback*, which is also sometimes called negative feedback, refers to providing information—typically about behaviors—that are somehow problematic or that warrant further consideration. Here again, like in our discussion about confrontation, it is important to distinguish between social and therapeutic feedback. As mentioned, the general purpose of using feedback in therapy is to offer information to clients about some aspect of their behavior or their presence that is or may be problematic. It should never be about clinician irritation or offering random advice. Group leaders should never permit social commentary to be delivered to group members in therapeutic feedback exchange.

FEEDBACK EXCHANGE IN THERAPY

Feedback exchange is evocative and complex; it can easily trigger an emotional response (Ilies & Judge, 2005). Claiborn et al. (2001) underscore that it is the clinician's responsibility to manage the process of feedback exchange so that a client's level of arousal does not interfere with his ability to hear the feedback that is being offered. One way to manage feedback exchange is to consider the timing of offering feedback to a client. It is best to offer feedback in the context of a solid therapeutic relationship. Also, Morran et al. (1998) point out that offering feedback to people who are not ready or willing to hear it is not effective. So, it is important to assess the strength of the therapeutic relationship as well as the readiness and openness of the recipient to hear feedback. Feedback should be offered when it is therapeutically pertinent, but also when the timing is appropriate.

The way in which feedback is delivered also influences its hear-ability. Feedback should always be communicated in a clear, concise, and respectful manner. Research suggests that high-intensity feedback—feedback that is overly harsh, critical, or negative, and even when feedback is given directly—sometimes has the risk of impeding task performance (Smith & King, 2004). These authors, for example, found that clients who were highly sensitive to feedback performed better when they received low-intensity feedback. This means that clinicians need to be able to alter the intensity of their feedback, depending on the depth of relationship, client level of sensitivity, and the content of the feedback to be delivered. We also know that when feedback is offered in a "sequence of valence" (Kivlighan & Luiza, 2005, p. 259)—sequencing positive and corrective feedback—it is more likely to be perceived as credible and more acceptable (Kivlighan & Luiza, 2005; Morran et al., 1998). Related to this, Scaturo (2002) points out that offering too much feedback at one time can overwhelm the client. This compels us, then, to think carefully about what feedback we want to deliver in a given moment and to consider structuring feedback over time so that it is offered in small and hearable doses.

Experiencing cognitive dissonance for a short period of time is a good way to arouse movement in the direction of change (Dechawatanapaisal & Siengthai, 2006). Going to either extreme of avoiding any exchange of feedback at all or, on the other hand, delivering it in a way that is too harsh opens up the potential for harm to clients, both in individual and group counseling situations. It is important to remember that feedback exchange, like confrontation, is meant to be dialogic. Clinicians should remain engaged with the client after providing feedback, as this serves to maintain the therapeutic relationship and provides an opportunity for the client to make meaning from what she has heard (Morran et al., 1998). Finally, all of these ideas are relevant to the ways in which group leaders should structure the exchange of feedback among clients in group work (Hulse-Kilacky et al., 2006).

GUIDELINES FOR GIVING FEEDBACK

The steps listed below are recommended for offering feedback to clients in therapy. These steps can also be used in groups to structure feedback exchange or to coach clients in giving feedback to each other. Additionally, a version of these steps can also be used as a psychoeducational tool to teach clients how to participate in feedback exchange with others in their lives outside of therapy.

STEPS IN FEEDBACK EXCHANGE

1. **Ask the client if he would like some feedback.** The intent here is to prepare the client for feedback and also to ascertain client readiness

for hearing and engaging in a discussion about the feedback. For example, "Isaac, I have some feedback for you. Would you be willing to hear what I have to say and then we can talk about it?" Here it is important to point out that if the client says that he does not want to hear the feedback, it should not be given (at this time).

2. **Consider offering a feedback in a sequence of valence.** Recall the point made by Kivlighan and Luiza (2005) that sequencing positive and negative feedback increases client receptivity. For example, "Congratulations, Chris! I know that you have been working hard at speaking up and it seems that you are able to do that pretty well now. That is a major accomplishment! I am thinking that we now will want to work on tone. I notice that sometimes you have a bit of an edge—that you seem to be angry and it comes out in the tone of your voice. I am wondering if that might happen at work, too? Can we talk a little more about this?"

3. **Consider using a variation of the I-message when delivering feedback.** An I-message is to speak about your personal reaction to something the client has said or done as a way of providing feedback. The I-message format is: (a) describe the behavior of concern, (b) offer an accounting of the feeling or thoughts that were aroused in you as a result of the behavior—the effect of the behavior on you, and (c) you may include—but this is not always appropriate—an assertion of what you would like to see happen or change as a result of the feedback. For example, "Raphael, when you say, '*Some people* don't care about you,' with so much emphasis on *some people*, it makes me feel a little defensive and wonder if you are talking about me? Or if you mean some other people? Can you clarify who you are talking about?"

   Using I-messages can offer credibility to the feedback because one's personal reaction to what a person has said is less open to dispute than speculation about how others might react to what the client has said or done. Raphael and the counselor could debate for hours about whether others outside of the room are reactive to Raphael's tone and intent (i.e., "some people"), but when the counselor offers an honest and undeniable testimony to the effect that the comment has on her, there is less room for debate.

4. **Clarify that the client has accurately heard what you said.** Misunderstandings abound when emotions are high, and we already know that feedback exchange can be very evocative. For this reason, it is always a good idea to clarify that the client has accurately heard the feedback that was delivered. For example, "Lakshmi, before we move on, I want to be sure that you accurately heard what I said. Can you just repeat back to me what you heard me say?"

5. **Invite discussion.** As mentioned, therapeutic feedback, particularly descriptive feedback, is typically meant to be dialogic—to initiate conversation about something the client has said or done. And, as Claiborn et al. (2001) reminded us, it is up to the therapist to manage this discussion. Feedback discussion should center on working with the client to better understand the feedback, consider its validity and implications, and facilitate exploration of pertinent issues. Using tentativeness and empathy are critical for creating a safe environment that fosters this kind of honest discussion. For example, "Frank, it seems that my feedback might have felt a little harsh—I am really sorry about that. My intent was not to hurt your feelings, but to have a discussion about how these kinds of comments may affect your relationship with Tonya. Can we stick with this a little more and talk about what happens for you when you hear this feedback from me?" Or the counselor may redirect the conversation to "Can we discuss why, maybe, your communications sometimes have a tone that maybe you aren't aware of or don't intend to have?"

SELF-DISCLOSURE

Self-disclosure is when a clinician reveals personal information about himself to a client. That is, self-disclosure typically refers to when a clinician intentionally offers verbal information about something that the client would not otherwise know about him. This sharing often involves some level of risk or vulnerability on the part of the therapist (Burkard, Knox, Groen, Perez, & Hess, 2006). While our definition here of self-disclosure does not include nonverbal or unintentional disclosures, it is the case that clinicians may also reveal something of themselves unintentionally or inadvertently as well (Psychopathology Committee of the Group for the Advancement of

Psychiatry, 2001). It could be argued, in fact, that everything from the pictures on the wall, the ways in which the clinician dresses, and her mannerisms and content of speech all reveal something about the clinician. But here, we are limiting our discussion to the ways in which clinicians use verbal self-disclosure with intentionality for therapeutic ends.

A wide range of therapeutic modalities call upon clinicians to use some form of self-disclosure or transparency, but interestingly, many of these encourage its use for different reasons (Burkard et al., 2006; Roberts, 2005). For example, Burkard et al. (2006) point out that in some modalities, self-disclosure is used to promote genuineness and authenticity; to normalize client challenges; to provide feedback; to promote or describe the use of specific techniques, strategies, or effective coping skills; and to model the process of self-disclosure in relationships. It may also be used to promote a deeper level of client disclosure, to deepen trust in the therapeutic relationship, and to assert therapist credibility (Levitt et al., 2016). Roberts (2005) adds that self-disclosure is sometimes used to facilitate joining or therapeutic connections, to model certain ideas or behaviors, and to promote collaboration in therapy. He points out that self-disclosure is used in narrative therapy in the form of reflecting teams, therapeutic letter writing, and directly in therapy to reveal a therapeutic stance and to shift power dynamics. Similarly, and perhaps even more ubiquitous in the world of therapy, self-disclosure is commonly used in feminist approaches to therapy. In these modalities, self-disclosure helps to demystify the process of therapy, increase client–counselor collaborative work, deflate hierarchies, offer affirmation, and acknowledge the inherent power differentials in therapy (Roberts, 2005).

Another important application of the use of therapeutic self-disclosure is in work with clients who experience marginalization or sociocultural trauma. Burkard et al. (2006), for example, found that clinicians sometimes use self-disclosure with clients in cross-cultural counseling situations to reveal their sensitivity to cultural and racial issues with the intent of increasing trust and credibility and improving the therapeutic relationship. These clinicians reported that using therapeutic self-disclosure in this way to communicate empathy did have the effect of improving the therapeutic relationship, and it also helped clients feel understood and, they believe, promoted engagement in therapy. This point regarding the use of therapeutic self-disclosure as an expression of empathy parallels the point made by Hardy (2013) and Hardy and Laszloffy (2005) that it is critical for clinicians to acknowledge and witness clients' experiences of bias and discrimination.

SELF-DISCLOSURE CAUTIONS AND SUGGESTIONS

Despite all of these identified uses, Burkard et al. (2006) point out that therapeutic self-disclosure is actually not used with much frequency in therapy. In fact, Levitt et al. (2016) suggest that many clinicians have concerns about using self-disclosure because of the ways in which it can leave them feeling vulnerable and, thus, arouse anxiety. Indeed, there is considerable debate in the literature and changing attitudes toward the use of counselor self-disclosure in therapy (Levitt et al., 2016; Roberts, 2005). This restraint likely is due to the point made by Goldfried, Burckell, and Eubanks-Carter (2003): "There is a fine line between our personal reactions during the course of therapy and what we convey to our clients" (p. 555). Clinicians, rightly, have concerns about crossing that fine line. Indeed, caution about the use of self-disclosure in therapy is warranted.

One of the major concerns regarding the use of self-disclosure in therapy has to do with the potential it has for boundary violations (Roberts, 2005). While clients may experience self-disclosure helpful in one sense, it can also have the effect of redirecting the therapeutic relationship to focus on the counselor rather than the client. For example, when a client who has experienced sexual assault learns that her therapist, too, has experienced sexual assault, she may become worried or protective about the well-being of the therapist. In this case, the self-disclosure that may have been meant to convey empathy or connote the witnessing of pain may actually further overwhelm the client. So, the importance of assuring that the client's needs are central in the therapeutic encounter, especially when using self-disclosure, is emphasized.

Second, self-disclosures tend to have an embedded point of view. For example, if a clinician reports that he used a particular parenting strategy at home, this statement may—intentionally or not—influence the client's behavior. In the context of a power differential between the clinician and client, this kind of self-disclosure can have the effect of infringing upon or overtaking client agency or choice (Roberts, 2005). Clinicians using self-disclosure, then, should be attentive to the obvious and nuanced ways in which clients react to their self-disclosure. They can use transparency, if needed, to reconcile any adverse reactions or effects of their self-disclosure.

Finally, while research regarding the efficacy of using self-disclosure in therapy is beginning to appear in the literature, its therapeutic value remains inconclusive. For example, Burkard et al. (2006) cite research indicating that very generally, clients view self-disclosure to be helpful. Reportedly, this is because it offers a view of the clinician as someone who is real or "human," it appears to strengthen the therapeutic relationship, and it also has a normalizing effect—it helps the client feel that she is "normal." Similarly, Levitt et al. (2016) point to research indicating that self-disclosure in some cases is associated with improved symptomology and interpersonal relationships—it betters posttherapy functioning. At the same time, however, Burkard et al. (2006) report on some studies that indicate a neutral or negative effect from the use of self-disclosure in therapy. These mixed reports support the suggestion that the benefits of self-disclosure vary according to intervention modality, therapy setting, and client characteristics (Psychopathology Committee of the Group for the Advancement of Psychiatry, 2001). So, this calls upon clinicians to be intentional in their use of self-disclosure in therapy.

In the words of Geller (2003): "Intentional self-disclosures require interpersonal skills such as tact, timing, patience, humility, perseverance, and sensitivity. These soft skills cannot be learned from a manual" (p. 543). To position oneself in these ways, a clinician must engage in careful and empathic listening, have a good understanding of the client as well as the context of his life, and, importantly, maintain a secure hold on the therapeutic goal. Roberts (2005) suggests the following strategies in order to advance the therapeutic value self-disclosure: First, be sure that the use of self-disclosure as a technique is included in the informed consent process. Second, when using self-disclosure, be careful to divulge only a small piece of self-information at first, and then observe the client carefully for feedback on its usefulness. Further self-disclosure should then be based on how well initial self-disclosures were received. Third, clinicians should be aware of the potential that a self-disclosure may trigger their own emotional reactions. That is, revealing something about oneself to a client may cause a clinician to be sad, angry, distracted, and so on. This is particularly harmful when these reactions distract the counselor from being fully present with the client in the moment. Fourth, it is important that self-disclosures are offered as shared experiences or dilemmas rather than oblique suggestions or solutions that are intended as advice to the client. Finally, clinicians should always be careful about suggesting—intentionally or not—how the client should respond to them after a personal self-disclosure. The client should not be directly or subtly invited to take care of or attend to a clinician after a personal self-disclosure. In short, the rule here is that "anything shared should be in the service of sustaining them [the client]" (Roberts, 2005, p. 56).

IMMEDIACY

Immediacy is the name of the skill that refers to attending to or calling attention to what is happening in the helping conversation in the moment. It is used to invite the client to name, explain, or make meaning about what is happening in therapy. This concept of *immediacy* is sometimes used interchangeably with the terms *confrontation* and *feedback* (Claiborn et al., 2001). Immediacy, like these others, also has the potential to arouse a great deal of intensity (Hazler & Barwick, 2001), and like with interpretation, confrontation, and feedback, its primary intent is to open up a discussion. In the case of immediacy, however, the focus is on something that is happening immediately in therapy. For example, a clinician may point out that the client changes the subject every time he asks about the client's father. Or notice that a client appears distant after a strong confrontation the week prior. The immediacy in these examples, then, might be that the therapist wonders aloud about how the conversation often seems to change when dad is mentioned. Or, in the second example, he asks the client if she can talk about the distance that seems apparent in the room and how she felt after the last session.

Immediacy is used to promote insight about a particular issue or situation, to gain deeper understanding about the helping relationship, to address ruptures in the counseling relationship, and sometimes to model how clients can be assertive in their communications with others outside of the therapy room (Wheeler & D'Andrea, 2004). Immediacy can be used to address trust issues and client worries, to point out discrepancies, or to address other sensitive issues related to the counseling relationship. For example, "You mentioned that you didn't want to lie to me anymore, yet you haven't been 100% truthful with me about what happened last night. I wonder if there is some reason that it is difficult to be honest with me in here. Can we can talk a little bit more this?" Immediacy often uses self-disclosure and typically calls upon the counseling relationship or experiences in the room at the moment to promote deeper conversation.

TYPES OF IMMEDIACY

There are three types of immediacy that may be used in therapy (Wheeler & D'Andrea, 2004). ***Relationship immediacy*** is used to address issues, concerns, or ruptures in the therapeutic relationship. Here the clinician would use immediacy to check in, open up discussion about discrepancies, fortify the relationship, or repair potential damage. For example, after having to cancel a scheduled appointment with Kyong, the therapist noticed that Kyong seemed upset and closed. She addressed this through immediacy: "Kyong, I might be wrong, but it seems that something is not right between us. I am thinking that it must have been very hard for you when I canceled our last meeting—and I have had to do that before, due to the illness and passing of my father a few weeks ago. I apologize. I can understand if that was difficult for you to have me cancel at such late notice. I wonder if maybe we can talk about this a little?"

Here-and-now immediacy is when the clinician draws attention to something that is happening in the moment in the conversation. For example, "It seems like we are having a difficult time communicating right now. Can we talk about this?" Here-and-now immediacy is used to focus on something that may be relevant in the relationship or conversation—something that may otherwise go unspoken. It is typically used to open up discussion about a sensitive or challenging issue.

Self-involving immediacy is a form of self-disclosure. This is when the clinician shares her personal response to something that the client has said or done. For example, Mohammad tells a powerful story about the unexpected death of his twin brother. The clinician very genuinely responds by saying, "Oh Momo, I am so moved by your story. It brings tears to my eyes." And then slowly adds, "I am thinking about how hard it has been to talk about your brother in here—and how hard it must have been to keep this to yourself, too." Self-involving immediacy often begins with a genuine expression of empathy or a personal disclosure on the part counselor. Then it shifts the conversation back to the client to explore what has been said or a related topic in some way. The clinician needs to remember to keep the focus on the client in therapy and the therapeutic intent of using this intervention. In this case, one of the goals of therapy revolved around a feeling that Mohammad had of distance and a lack of authenticity in relationships. So, a little later, the therapist added this interpretation: "I might be wrong, Momo, but I wonder if holding back about your personal experiences is part of that distance you feel with others?"

GUIDELINES FOR USING IMMEDIACY

Immediacy can raise the intensity in the therapeutic conversation (Hazler & Barwick, 2001). For this reason, it should be used in the context of a solid therapeutic relationship, when the client (and the clinician) can handle the intensity that may ensue, and for therapeutic purposes. Immediacy is an intervention that is designed to elicit conversation, and its value largely comes from the conversation that follows. So, be sure that there is adequate time to follow through on a discussion when using immediacy.

A rough formula for how to articulate an immediacy intervention is as follows:

1. **Point out what you see, hear, or notice in the moment.** Example: "I notice that you are not saying very much today."
2. **Invite the client to offer a hypothesis or a comment about what you have said.** Example: "What do you think about this?"
3. **Share your hypothesis, if appropriate, and always with genuine tentativeness.** Example: "I was wondering—I am not sure, and I might be wrong—if you are wanting to keep things a little light this week because things were so intense last time we spoke?"
4. **Invite discussion and further exploration.** Example: "What do you think? Does that seem accurate, or is there something else going on?" or "Can we talk a little more about this?"

Table 8.2: Guidelines for Using Immediacy

REASONS FOR USING IMMEDIACY	• To give attention to an issue or situation • To initiate discussion about a particular issue or topic • To promote insight • To illuminate discrepancies and open discussion • To address ruptures, concerns, or issues in the helping relationship • To check in about the helping relationship
GUIDELINES FOR USING IMMEDIACY	• Be clear and direct • Monitor intensity • Be sensitive to impact • Attend to timing • Use with intentionality—only when it is therapeutically appropriate.

CHAPTER SUMMARY

The various modalities of clinical mental health therapy vary considerably, but cutting across most of them is a set of fundamental counseling skills. When used appropriately and with intentionality, these skills are the critical ingredients of good therapy. In this chapter, interpretation, confrontation, feedback, self-disclosure, and immediacy were introduced. In the chapters that follow, we will discuss assessment processes as well as additional basic change strategies that cut across many counseling modalities and are used to deepen therapeutic exploration or to address specific concerns.

REFLECTION QUESTIONS

1. Many cautions were given regarding the use of interpretation, confrontation, feedback, and immediacy. Why should a clinician even use these skills if there are so many cautions about using them? How does a therapist know when to use them (and when to not use them)?

2. In this chapter, it was suggested that self-disclosure was particularly helpful when working with clients who identify in marginalized social locations. Why is self-disclosure particularly helpful in these situations?

3. The skills in this chapter were identified as additive skills. How are they different, very generally, from the basic skills discussed in the previous two chapters?

CHAPTER

Interviewing and Intervention Planning

Chapter Outline

INTRODUCTION

Most people who seek clinical help do so because they are experiencing a problem of some sort. It may be a problem they want help with, a problem someone else wants them to get help with, or a problem that defies clear articulation and definition. Sometimes clients seek help because they are truly ready to make a change in their lives, and others seek help because they really want someone else to change. Some people want direction and answers, and most all seek validation and support in one form or another. What we can be sure of is that people end up in clinician's offices because something is just not right. And so, a key step first step in helping is to learn about the client and the problem or challenge that the client is facing. From these understandings, clinicians spend time thinking about and planning an appropriate intervention.

Although this discussion about interviewing and intervention planning is all the way back here in Chapter 9, it is important to remember that the therapeutic process actually **begins** with gathering information. We locate this information back here because the *how* of clinical interviewing and intervention planning is rooted in the basic counseling skills discussed in Chapters 6 and 7. The important skills of welcoming, listening, expressing empathy, broaching, reflecting, paraphrasing, and appropriately asking questions are used for clinical interviewing, problem assessment, and goal setting. Understanding the fundamentals about the helping contract, as discussed in Chapter 1, the nuances of social context and neurobiology, discussed in Chapters 2 and 4, and the ethical obligations of helping outlined in Chapter 3 are also foundational for how clinicians engage in clinical interviewing and intervention planning. So, this chapter is an application of the information that has come before it in this text.

THE CLINICAL INTERVIEW

Gathering information about the client and the specific concern that is being brought to therapy is a process that is typically referred to as a *clinical interview.* It is also sometimes called a *clinical diagnostic interview* or more colloquially among professionals, the *intake*, *intake interview*, or simply, the *initial interview.* Given this overlap in the use of these terms, we will use them interchangeably in this chapter. The purpose of the clinical interview is to learn more about the client and the problem that is being brought into therapy, and it is used to devise appropriate goal and intervention planning.

I hope you will notice the careful language used above. In this short paragraph I twice used some version of the phrase "the specific problem or concern *that is being brought to therapy.*" First, a comment about the word *problem*. According to Cameron and turtle-song (2002), problems that come to therapy are "major areas of concern for the client that are not within the usual parameters when compared with others from the client's same age group or as areas of client concern that can be changed through therapeutic intervention" (p. 287). Among other things, this definition reminds us that a problem is something that is of concern *to the client*. So while we might be asked to work with a client because someone else is concerned, it is important that we remain centered, as much as possible, on the issues and concerns expressed by the client. Second, notice that my introduction here locates the problem outside of the client, alluding to the point that problems rather than people are what we work on in therapy. As mentioned briefly in Chapter 2, Michael White and others in narrative therapy circles speak about this as *problem externalization* (White & Epston, 1990). By identifying a problem as something that is external to the client, space opens for the client to become agent in working to resolve it (Madigan, 1992). Externalizing problems opens up new possibilities that may have otherwise gone unnoticed, and it promotes the abilities, beliefs, and resources that clients already have to help them resolve challenges (Morgan, 2000). It avoids blaming, encourages collaborative work between client and counselor, and promotes optimism and engagement (White & Epston, 1990). This point is especially critical as we tiptoe into the waters of diagnosis a little later in this chapter.

A clinical interview has two parts. The first is to learn about the client. The second is to learn more about the problem. This information will identify and clarify therapeutic goals and enable intervention planning. There are many ways of conducting a clinical interview, but most clinicians use some variation of a structured or semistructured format. These are sometimes also supplemented with a mental status exam, and, in many cases, more formal diagnostic assessment materials. Additional training and experience is required for using the formal diagnostic assessment tools, so they will not be covered in this chapter.

Also during the initial contact with the client in the intake interview, most clinicians and agencies give clients or potential clients a packet of information about agency or practice policies. This typically includes scheduling, cancellation, and payment/billing policies; emergency information and contact details; an informed consent statement outlining the scope of services provided by the agency or clinician and the clinician's qualifications and theoretical orientation; a statement about confidentiality (including policies around written and verbal information); and a release of information form that would be used, if needed, to secure consent for the clinician to speak to other service providers.

THE STRUCTURE OF THE INTERVIEW

A *structured* clinical interview is a formal interview and assessment process that entails asking specific questions in a certain order and recording the responses a particular way. This type of interview is generally considered to be a reliable and valid method of gathering information and is typically used for diagnostic decision making (Grills & Ollendick, 2002). Grills and Ollendick (2002) point out that little to no clinical training is required to give these highly structured interviews, because the interview protocol is designed to lead to clinical decision making without relying heavily on clinical judgment. Thus, these interviews can be conducted by intake workers who are not trained as mental health therapists. The caveat, however, is that these interviews tend to be fairly rigid and are easily experienced by the client as impersonal, thus hindering the establishment of early rapport. *Semistructured* interviews similarly are focused interviews with question prompts, but these types of interview protocols allow more leeway to the clinician to determine the manner and order of asking questions and the recording of responses (Grills & Ollendick, 2002). Some clinicians use an *unstructured* interview process that does not follow a predetermined set of questions and typically does not entail reading from or completing a form in the session itself. All of these interview approaches require the clinician to carefully document what has been learned through the interview process, including essential basic contact information about the client.

Children should be included in the clinical interview and other components of the assessment process, even when their parents or caregivers are the initial or primary interview informants (Grills & Ollendick, 2002; Macleod et al., 2017). It should also be pointed out that school counselors rarely conduct formal clinical interviews—these may be conducted instead by school psychologists or diagnosticians hired by school districts. However, a large number of school counselors engage in the practice of individual counseling (Burnam & Jackson, 2000), so they will need to gather sufficient information about a student and the concern prior to providing counseling services.

GENERAL CLIENT INFORMATION

The type of information solicited in the clinical interview varies across practice settings and clinical practitioners and tends to reflect the theoretical orientation of the clinician, the mission of the agency, and in some cases, funding source dictates. Having said this, most clinical interviews begin with the collection of personal details such as the client's name, address, phone number, and emergency contact information. Typically, insurance or billing information is also collected. All of this is important, as the clinician needs to be able to contact the client easily and also needs to know who to contact in emergency situations. The insurance information, of course, is important for billing purposes. All of this information, you will see, is included in the sample intake form in Figure 9.1 at the end of this section.

Besides basic contact information, most interviews also ask about social identity–related information that includes the client's race, ethnicity, gender identity, partner or marital status, and sexual orientation. Even if the client is asked to respond to these questions by checking a box on an intake form, it is critical that the clinician engage the client in a conversation about these social location categories. We know that heritage, culture, and social group affiliation all inform identity, and also that one's experience in a particular social location is shaped by discourses that are connected to systems of power and privilege in larger society. All of these affect how one is experienced and treated by others, are relevant to the experience of stress and challenge that people have in everyday life, and also affect how clients may experience the therapeutic relationship (Day-Vines et al., 2007). So, social location does matter, and it is the responsibility of the helper, not the client, to invite conversations about diverse identities (Day-Vines et al., 2007). This idea and suggestions on how to engage in broaching conversations about social location were discussed in Chapter 7.

As a part of the initial clinical interview, most clinicians also ask clients to identify and talk about the problem for which they are seeking services. This helps the clinician ascertain the client's understandings or perspectives on the problem—the intensity, history, background, triggers, effects of the problem in the client's life, and how the client makes sense of or interprets the problem. It is also helpful to know what actions or strategies the client has already tried to resolve the problem and the extent to which these strategies have been successful.

As the client articulates his reasons for seeking therapy, the clinician can draw out more information through conversational questions and other basic communication skills such as those included in Chapters 6 and 7. Scaling questions, often used in solution-focused brief therapy, or SFBT (for more on SFBT, see De Jong & Berg, 2008; de Shazer, 1985; de Shazer & Dolan, 2012; Sklare, 2014), can also be used to learn more about the problem. These kinds of questions ask clients to evaluate the problem by rating it on a scale of 1

X Agency for Therapeutic Services
Address
Phone, Email, Website

Client Intake Information

Name: ____
Address: ____
____

Phone: ____________________ Okay to leave message? (Y/N): ________

Emergency Contact Information
Name of who to contact in emergency: ____________________________
Relationship to you: ________________ Phone: ____________

General Information
Date of birth: ____
Gender: ____
Race/ethnicity: ____
Sexual orientation: ______________________________________
Marital status: ____
Religious/spiritual affiliation: ___________________________

Insurance Information
Insurance provider: ______________________________________
Policy number: ____
Name of policy holder: ___________________________________

Additional Information
Reason for seeking services:

What else would you like us to know?

Who referred you to us?

Figure 9.1 *Sample Intake Information Form*

to 10. Scaling questions can also be used to assess how bad the problem has been in the past and the extent to which the client feels supported, hopeful, or overwhelmed by the problem; they can also be used at any time during the course of therapy to invite the client to rate his sense of how well the therapy is progressing.

It can be difficult to conduct the initial clinical interview without bombarding the client with questions. Using a variety of question types and working from a position of genuine curiosity, however, can help create a positive atmosphere for exploring the dimensions of the problem. Formal and informal assessment and screening tools can also be used to learn more about the problem and for diagnostic purposes. These can be given to the client in advance of the initial interview or at any time during the intake or therapy processes. They allow the client to respond at her own pace (unless, of course, they are timed assessment instruments), and they offer a good alternative to a lengthy initial interview.

PSYCHOSOCIAL INFORMATION

Psychosocial assessment is the term that is generally used for the portion of the clinical interview that is aimed at gathering contextual and historical information about the client and the presenting problem. The particular questions asked in a psychosocial assessment vary across settings but may include questions about the client's past experiences very generally; medical and legal history; educational and employment information; current and past relationships, social connections, and family; substance use/misuse; experiences of loss, crisis, or trauma; strengths, coping mechanisms, and resources; and the client's previous experiences in counseling and any medication she is using for mental health–related problems.

Clinicians who work with youth may use drawing activities to elicit information and to understand their perspectives. The Kinetic Family Drawing (Kottman, 2002), for example, is an assessment tool that asks children to draw a picture of their family doing something together. The clinician typically asks the child to tell him about the drawing afterward. This then helps the therapist learn more about the client's family and, more generally, her perspectives and experiences. Similarly, asking a child to draw a self-portrait can elicit helpful information about how the child sees himself and his position in the world. Children can also be asked to draw a picture of school, of their friends,

X Agency for Therapeutic Services
Address
Phone, Email, Website

Psychosocial Assessment

Presenting problem:

Presenting mental status:

Is client in crisis? If so, document actions taken:

Personal/family/relationship current and history:

Education:

Employment:

Developmental/medical history:

Counseling history:

Loss/crisis/trauma history:

Substance use:

Legal history:

Stage of change:

Resources/strengths:

Clinical observations:

Collateral information:

Diagnosis:

Intervention recommendations:

Figure 9.2 *Sample Psychosocial Assessment*

and a host of other topics that may give insight into the difficulties they are facing.

Gathering collateral information—collecting information about a client or a particular situation from a third party—is another way that clinicians learn more about clients. For example, with consent, a clinician may talk with a counselor that the client has worked with in the past in order to gain insight into which modality might be useful. Or the clinician may talk with a psychiatrist or family physician working with a client to learn more about the medications that the client is taking. There is a caveat here, however. While collateral information can be very helpful, it also can bias the clinician in ways that might not be so helpful. For example, if you speak to a provider who labeled a client "noncompliant," this may set the stage for you to anticipate difficulties or problems before you even have a relationship with the client herself. So, remember that collateral information provides an additional perspective, but it is important for clinicians to use their own clinical judgment and other tools and to make sound clinical decisions. Written consent is needed to talk to others about a client, the problem, or anything related to the clinical work with a particular client, of course. Gathering collateral information about minor children requires written consent from the child's parents or guardians.

MENTAL STATUS

Clinicians sometimes include a mental status exam in the clinical interview, particularly when they have concerns about the clients' cognitive functioning, when they witness unusual or unexpected behavior, when there are questions about serious mental health concerns, when medical problems appear to affect cognitive or emotional functioning, and when there are concerns about harm to self or others. Physicians also sometimes use a mental status exam when they are making a differential diagnosis in complicated cases. The mental status exam is a structured assessment based on a series of questions and the clinician's observations of the client.

The mental status exam focuses on the client's appearance and general behavior; motor behavior and speech patterns; affect and mood; thought processes (i.e., coherence, connectivity between ideas, etc.) and content, including suicide ideation, perceptions (i.e., illusions, hallucinations, disassociation), and cognitive orientation; attention and memory processes; and abstract thinking abilities, judgment, and insight (see Brannon, 2016; Coverdale,

Louie, & Roberts, 2015; Daniel & Gurczynski, 2010). Many clinicians and other medical professionals receive training on conducting the mental status exam during their practical or clinical internships. A condensed versions of the mental status exam—the Mini-Mental Status Exam (MMSE; Folstein, Folstein, & McHugh, 1975) or the Modified Mini-Mental State Examination (3MS; Teng & Chui, 1987)—is frequently used when a thorough assessment of mental status is not required or when the clinical interest is primarily about the client's cognitive functioning.

ASSESSMENT OF HARM

Triage—deciding what needs immediate attention—is an important component of the clinical interview. If the client indicates that she is or otherwise appears to be suicidal, the clinician will move directly into a thorough harm assessment. The question about whether the client is a victim of harm or is in some way in danger of being harmed is also an important question to ask during the clinical interview. In cases of known aggression and apparent agitation, it is also appropriate to determine if the client has intentions of harming a third party. These concerns and the specific components of a harm assessment are explored in more detail in Chapter 10.

INVESTMENT IN CHANGE

In a landmark study of people involved in smoking cessation (Prochaska & DiClemente, 1982) and then later with individuals who were involved in outpatient psychotherapy and alcohol addiction (Prochaska & DiClemente, 1986), Prochaska and DiClemente discovered that people follow a fairly predictable series of steps when they are in the process of making a change in their lives, regardless of whether they are in therapy. These researchers and their colleagues transformed these findings into a therapeutic model for working with people who struggle with a multitude of different challenges. The model is called the *transtheoretical model of change* (Norcross, Krebs, & Prochaska, 2010; Prochaska, Johnson, & Lee, 2009), or more commonly, the **stages of change**. The stages of change model maps out a series of motivational processes that underlie clients' proclivity toward making a change of some kind in their life (Norcross et al., 2010; Prochaska & DiClemente, 1986; Prochaska, Norcross, & DiClemente, 1994).

The first part in the process of change for many people is a lack of recognition that there is a problem and a corresponding lack of motivation to change. At this stage, the client does not see or acknowledge that a problem exists and thus is not thinking about change. This stage is called *precontemplation* (Norcross et al., 2010; Prochaska et al., 2009). Next is *contemplation*. At this stage, the client may acknowledge that he is having difficulty and may be beginning to consider how this difficulty is adversely affecting his life. But, people in the contemplation stage often lack an understanding of the causes of the problems they experience, may not fully acknowledge the effects of the problem in their lives, and are not fully committed to making a change (Norcross et al., 2010; Prochaska et al., 2009). When a client is beginning to think about and make plans to take action about a problem, we say that he is in the *preparation* stage of change (Norcross et al., 2010; Prochaska et al., 2009). Clients in the preparation stage may buy a book about the issue they are struggling with, for example, or make an appointment to see a therapist. However, there is typically still some ambivalence at this point. The client is planning to act but not yet actively changing.

The *action* stage is next. As the name implies, this is when the person is actively engaged in change behavior—she is making choices and doing things differently (Norcross et al., 2010; Prochaska et al., 2009). Since change can be a very difficult process and tangible results from one's actions are sometimes slow to come, clients in the action stage need support, even though it appears that they are doing well. The final stage of the model is the *maintenance* stage. This stage is characterized by efforts to preserve changes that have been made (Norcross et al., 2010; Prochaska et al., 2009). Here the focus is on relapse prevention and continued client support.

The stages of change model is used across many clinical and nonclinical settings to guide clinical assessment, intervention planning, and therapy. The practice of *motivational interviewing* (Miller & Rollnick, 2013) offers a series of clinical interventions that correspond to each level of motivation in the stage of change model. The idea, as we will discuss in Chapter 10, is to match clinical intervention to the motivational level of the client. For clients who are in the precontemplative or contemplative stages, clinical responses focus on accepting where the client is at and trying to increase his motivation to change. When clients have sufficient motivation—when they are committed to

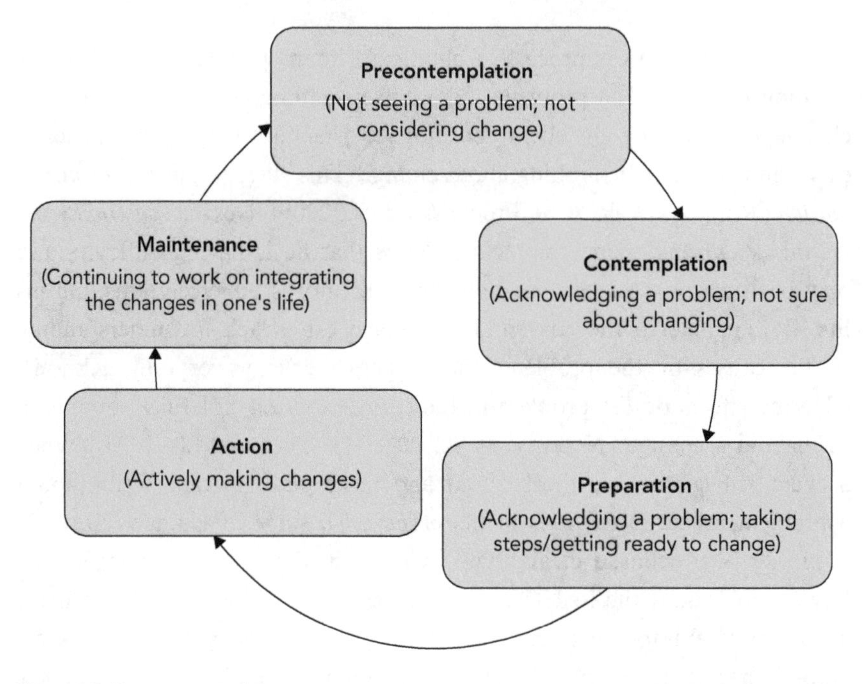

Figure 9.3 *Stages of Change*

Adapted from:

Norcross, J. C., Krebs, P. M., & Prochaska, J. O. (2010). Stages of change. *Journal of Clinical Psychology: In Session, 67*(2), 143–154. https://doi.org/10.1002/jclp.20758

Prochaska, J. O., Johnson, S., & Lee, P. (2009). The transtheoretical model of behavior change. In S. A. Shumaker, J. K. Ockene, & K. A. Riekert (Eds.), *The handbook of health behavior change* (3rd ed., pp. 59–83). New York, NY: Springer.

Prochaska, J. O., Norcross, J. C., & DiClemente, C. C. (1994). *Changing for good.* New York, NY: Harper/Collins.

the process of change—then therapists can move into more action orientated interventions.

DIAGNOSIS

In the world of mental health, the concept of diagnosis refers to a determination regarding a mental health condition; it is used by mental health and medical professionals to guide intervention planning. Coverdale et al. (2015) also point out that diagnoses can also be helpful in facilitating communications between client and clinician and with family members and other professionals, as appropriate. Diagnosis is also required for reimbursement by most insurance companies.

Typically, clinicians use a structured or a semistructured interview process, often accompanied by formal battery of mental health–related tests or screening tools, to arrive at a diagnosis (Coverdale et al., 2015). The *Diagnostic and Statistical Manual of Mental Disorders* (DSM), published by the American Psychiatric Association and now in its fifth edition, called the DSM-5 (American Psychiatric Association, 2013), is a catalog of mental health disorders that offers descriptions of symptomology and criteria used for diagnosis. The DSM is so widely used for the classification of mental health difficulties across clinical mental health and medical practice settings, in fact, that Earle (2014) calls the DSM a "kind of a bible" (p. 179) for diagnosis. It provides the language of diagnosis. Not all mental health practitioners subscribe to or use the DSM diagnostic classification system, but those who do need specific training in understanding the diagnostic categories within the DSM-5 and related clinical assessment processes. Accurate and helpful diagnosis is dependent on clinician experience and training.

Coverdale et al. (2015) point out that in some cases, a clinical diagnosis can do more harm to a client than good, largely because of the social stigmatization related to some diagnostic terms. I underscore here that a clinical diagnosis is a description of symptoms not a description of a person. It is not uncommon to hear professionals refer to a client as, for example, a "depressed," "anxious," "narcissistic" (or fill in any DSM diagnostic label) person. In fact, DSM diagnostic language is sometimes used colloquially among those with no training at all in the field of mental health in reference to their family members, friends, or complete strangers! The reminders here are first that while someone may demonstrate a cluster of symptoms that match a diagnostic category, those symptoms do not describe all of who that person is. People may experience problems, but that does not make them problem people. Second, as professionals we need to be thoughtful about if, how, when, and where we use DSM language in talking about our clients. And if we do use a diagnostic label, we need to talk through with our clients the meaning of the diagnostic categories we use as well as potential implications.

A final point about diagnosis is in order. Frances and Widiger (2012) cite a number of fundamental problems with the issue of diagnosis in general and suggest that the DSM be a "guide" (p. 110) rather than a bible for psychiatric diagnosis. The "art of diagnosis," according to Coverdale et al. (2015, p. 19), should take into consideration a range of biological, psychological, and social factors that shape the human experience. In the words of Lewis-Fernández and colleagues (2014):

> culture shapes every aspect of patient care in psychiatry, influencing when, where, how, and to whom patients narrate their experiences of illness and distress, the patterning of symptoms, and the models clinicians use to interpret and understand symptoms in terms of psychiatric diagnoses. (p. 131).

They remind us that people who identify as racial minorities and individuals in marginalized social groups often experience stressors associated with their social status, and these may be confused with or considered signs of psychopathology. They also point out that clinicians' diagnostic decision making can be influenced by stereotypes, discrimination, and other subtle forms of bias. Echoing this sentiment, Neighbors, Trierweiler, Ford, and Muroff (2003) report that research has consistently shown racial differences in mental health diagnoses, even when standard diagnostic criteria was used in the assessment process. So, caution is well advised. In short, there are many potentially harmful and long-term implications of receiving a mental health diagnosis (Kitchener, 1984). The uncertainty that surrounds our current understandings of mental illness as well as the bias that is a part of clinical interviewing and other aspects of the diagnostic processes compel us to be prudent when making diagnostic decisions and to be hypervigilant about the labels that we choose to describe the symptoms that affect the lives of our clients.

THINKING ABOUT PROBLEMS

The purpose of a clinical interview, as mentioned, is to gather information about the client, the problem, and the client's motivations for engaging in counseling and change. The clinician uses this information, along with knowledge about human development and an understanding of the cultural and social context that is the landscape within which the client lives, to make sense of the client and the problem that has been brought to counseling. From this, the clinician may arrive at a clinical diagnosis, if appropriate, consider various counseling or psychological theories, consult current literature, and map out an intervention plan. Before discussing the details of the intervention plan, we will spend a little time here talking about some ways in which clinicians can think about the problems that clients bring to counseling.

PROBLEM LOCATION

One way to examine a problem is to determine where the problem is affecting the client. The discussion here about locating problems is inspired by the work of Cohen and Smith (1976), originating in the field of group work, and is helpful in directing intervention planning. Based on this model, we will refer to the location of problems as problem *levels*.

Some problems take hold of clients at an ***intrapersonal level***. These types of problems are ones that affect the client singularly and directly—they are not intimately tied to a relationship with others nor are they in response to an obvious external event. For example, consider a situation where a client experiences anxiety so acutely that he is unable to leave his house. Here again, we must be intentional to avoid *totalizing* the person as the problem. This can be particularly challenging when the problem is located at the intrapersonal level because the implication is that the problem is within the person—often thought of *as* the person. In line with the notion that the problem is the thing that is causing trouble in the client's life, we might say, for example, that the client "struggles with depression" or "has difficulty controlling anger."

Interpersonal-level problems are those that are located between people. Examples include a conflict between two people, ineffective communication patterns within a family, or behaviors that happen within a group. In these examples, the problems exist among various people in a particular relationship, and again, they are not located within any one person. ***External-level*** problems are those that are situated outside of the individual affected. Sometimes we think of these as environmental influences on people's lives. Racism, for example, is a social problem that cannot be traced to something inherently wrong with an individual. Another example of an external problem is a crisis or disaster such as a flood, a fire, or a car accident. These are situations that happened out of the control of the individuals affected.

Of course, the effects of a problem at any one of these levels are often felt at the other levels. For example, a medical condition can have a profound effect on a person's own intrapersonal functioning and may also affect her interpersonal relationships. Conversely, we can see how interpersonal conflicts can affect one's individual well-being. And we can see how widespread social and institutional injustice, which would be considered an externally located problem, can affect interpersonal and intrapersonal functioning. Despite the overlapping effects of problems, however, thinking about problem level can help us begin to untwine the complicated web of how a problem takes hold in a client's life and help point us to an entry point for intervention. This is particularly important in situations where we must decide whether to move in the direction of counseling versus advocacy.

Let us discuss how this might work. As an example, a therapist was helping a client with a medical condition. Initial goals for their work were for the client to better understand his illness and to be more assertive in his medical care. An intrapersonal level intervention of providing the client with information about his medical condition was the first thing that the counselor helped with, and this helped alleviate some of the client's worries. It also helped him feel less anxious about telling his son about his diagnosis, meaning that it had an effect in the interpersonal level as well. Being armed with facts and information also provided the client with confidence and knowledge, and he was able to advocate for himself in medical decision making. A third goal was to have an improved relationship with his wife, as things had become complex in regard to living with his new medical diagnosis. As an intervention strategy, the clinician and client decided that a counseling session with the client and his spouse together—an interpersonal intervention—would help them begin to plan how they could cope with the illness that affected their relationship.

Now let us discuss how this might work in the case of an externally located problem. A child was being teased at school about having a disability, and the first-line intervention taken by the school counselor was to ask the assistant principal to intervene directly with the children who bullied this student. The counselor also launched a disability awareness and stigma reduction campaign in the school, which complemented the work he was doing to address the topic of bullying in all of his classroom-based psychoeducation programs. While these externally focused interventions were appropriate, the school counselor also intervened at the intrapersonal level with the student who was bullied by helping her find ways to cope with the overt bullying and micro-aggressions she experienced at school. Being clear about the source of the problem—social discourses about disabilities and the behavior of other children in the school rather than something inherently wrong with the client—helped the school counselor avoid the implication that the child was somehow responsible for

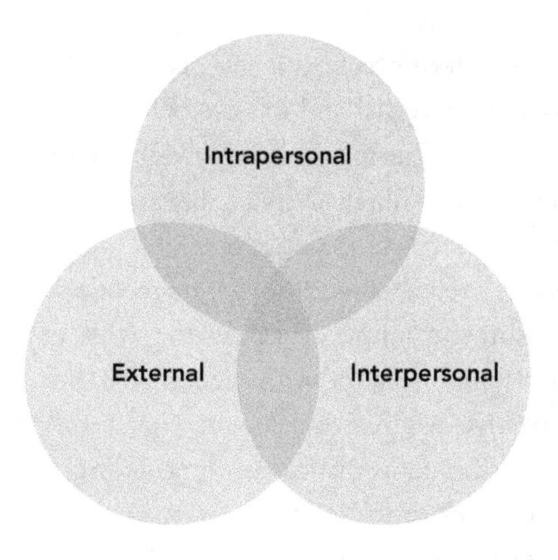

Figure 9.4 *Problem Levels*

the bullying she experienced at school. In their individual intrapersonal work, the focus was on helping the client see herself as agent and possessing the skills and abilities that could be used to stand up to this challenge, if needed, in the future.

A final example of how we might think about the overlapping levels of problems comes from work in the area of disaster response, which will be discussed in more detail in Chapter 12. It is not uncommon for a person who has experienced an external event such as a natural disaster to develop anxiety symptoms (intrapersonal). These might include an inability to sleep, incessant worry, and general irritability. These symptoms may also cause disruptions in interpersonal relationships as well. Understanding that these symptoms are a normal reaction to an external event can help guide intervention, even if the interventions we select are intrapersonal and interpersonal.

PROBLEM DOMAIN

Another way of thinking about problems is to consider the ways in which they affect how clients behave, think, and feel. Some problems, for example, show themselves in the ***behavioral domain.*** When thinking about behavior problems, images may come to mind of someone being out of control, displaying extreme or inappropriate behavior, or situations of harm to self or others. The DSM-5 (American Psychiatric Association, 2013) outlines a whole host of behavioral disorders that are characterized by acting out behaviors, including conduct disorder and intermittent explosive disorder. Here I want to broaden this discussion to include verbal and passive behaviors. For example, hitting someone is an aggressive behavior. So is being verbally abusive. Not being able to get out of bed in the morning is also a behavior, but it is not an aggressive behavior that so easily attracts the attention of others. Deliberately not responding to someone's repeated questions or someone's attempt to engage in a conversation is another example of a behavior—this, of course, is a passive behavior. It is a decision to respond with silence. Arguably, this latter example might even be a passive–aggressive behavior. But in this case, as with all of these examples, the context is critical in interpreting whether a particular behavior is appropriate or problematic.

While the complete assessment of behavioral challenges goes beyond the scope of this text and typically requires a multiteamed approach, applied behavioral analysis is one assessment method that has been used widely in educational institutions for decades (Gresham, Watson, & Skinner, 2001). A functional behavioral assessment (FBA) is, perhaps, the most widely used application of applied behavioral analysis. A FBA is the mapping out of antecedent and consequent events that reinforce a particular target behavior—it is an examination of what elicits certain behaviors and what variables enable problematic behaviors to continue. The FBA requires a fairly simple observation in a naturalistic setting and is particularly helpful, as it provides a useful map for intervention planning (Floyd, Phaneuf, & Wilczynski, 2005; Gresham et al., 2001; Waguespack, Vaccaro, & Continere, 2006). Even though there is considerable overlap between problems in the behavioral domain and the other domains, the FBA is designed to illuminate the context of problematic behaviors, rather than focusing on internal psychopathology (Waguespack et al., 2006). It is also used in some medical settings to assess medical and physiological concerns such as headaches, sleep disorders, nail biting, and various behaviors indicative of stress related to medical conditions (O'Brien & Carhart, 2011). Many recommend using other assessment tools in complement to the FBA for a more thorough assessment of behavior. These include behavior rating scales, questionnaires, structured interviews, self-report or self-monitoring instruments, and other forms of direct observation in a naturalistic setting (Floyd et al., 2005; O'Brien & Carhart, 2011; Waguespack et al., 2006). Using a variety of assessment tools can provide more detailed information about a problem behavior and the conditions under which it occurs.

There are a host of problems that tend to manifest in the ***affective domain***. Affect difficulties include problems with the regulation of emotion, limited emotional intelligence or knowledge, temperament-based emotionality, and the psychophysiological and neurological aspects of emotion and adjustment (Southam-Gerow & Kendall, 2002). A chronic state or patterned negative or positive affect may reflect temperament-based emotionality or a mood disorder (Brown & Astell, 2012), and the DSM-5 (American Psychiatric Association, 2013) includes a list of mood disorders, including depression, bereavement, acute stress disorder, anxiety, and others. Affect regulation difficulties are sometimes associated with more serious mental health difficulties (Hamilton et al., 2009; Lavender, Tull, DiLillo, Messman-Moore, & Gratz, 2017). Additionally, people sometimes use alcohol or other substances to cope with the symptoms of mood disorders, and conduct problems are often accompanied by heavy alcohol use (Brodsky & Ostacher, 2015). *Dual diagnosis* is a term that refers to when a client experiences mental health and substance misuse disorders simultaneously—these are also sometimes referred to as co-occurring disorders.

Because emotional state is difficult to see, many affect-related mood disorders are first identified by their behavioral components. It is those actions that often call attention to a problem. For example, a client with depression does not get out of bed. An anxious client has a habit of nonsuicidal self-harm. Problems in affect regulation are often noticed and assessed through observation (Adrian, Zeman, & Veits, 2011) as well as self-administered self-report questionnaires (Berthoz & Hill, 2005; Furukawa, 2010; Hamilton et al., 2009; Lavender et al., 2017). Clinicians may also use structured diagnostic interview protocols, rating scales, and more formal assessment inventories for the screening and assessment of anxiety and depression. In general, a thorough and multilayered assessment process conducted by someone trained in the area of diagnostic assessment should be used when there are serious concerns about mood disorders (Furukawa, 2010; Serrano Burneo, Bowden, & Simpson, 2016).

Problems in the ***cognitive domain***, many of which are referred to in the DSM-5 (American Psychiatric Association, 2013) as neurocognitive disorders, are typically related to difficulties in cognitive processing, maintaining attention, executive function, learning and memory, language expression or interpretation, motor skills associated with perception, and social cognition.

People who have cognitive difficulties may have trouble interpreting new, complex or unfamiliar information; challenges in being able to accurately interpret social cues, perspective-taking, and the expression of empathy; or they may have obsessional or intrusive thoughts, delusions, and hallucinations. More specific details about these cognitive challenges are beyond the scope of this book and the challenges that people face in these areas are often addressed in the work of a multidisciplinary team that includes neurologists, physicians, and medical-related therapists.

Most of these mentioned cognitive difficulties have some form of related behavioral component. For example, some people develop neutralizing behaviors such as ritualistic or compulsive activities when they have cognitive processing difficulties (Moulding, Aardema, & O'Connor, 2014) or emotional dysregulation related to high levels of anxiety. Cognitive difficulties are also sometimes comorbid with affective disorders such as depression or anxiety (Moulding et al., 2014). Individuals who have autism spectrum symptomology often have affective domain difficulties—identifying the bodily sensations associated with emotional arousal, for example, in addition to cognitive processing difficulties (Berthoz & Hill, 2005). Autism spectrum disorder is also typically associated with behavioral difficulties in the area of social engagement and nonverbal and verbal expression (American Psychiatric Association, 2013). The mental status exam is often used for initial screening of cognitive difficulties and a more thorough assessment process is required

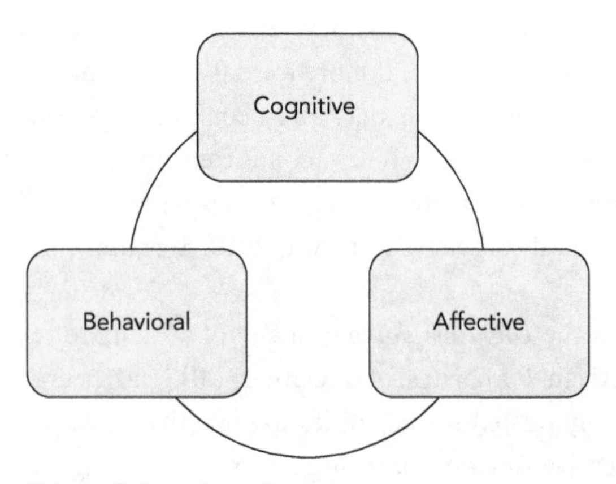

Figure 9.5 *Problem Domains*

for accurate diagnosis and treatment planning in complicated cases of cognitive domain disorders (Tombaugh, 2005).

THEORY AS A ROAD MAP

The definition of theory, according to *Dictionary.com* ("Theory," n.d.), is "1. a coherent group of tested general propositions, commonly regarded as correct, that can be used as principles of explanation" and "2. a proposed explanation whose status is still conjectural and subject to experimentation." With this in mind, then, we can say that theories might best be thought of as explanatory systems—ideas that offer information or explanation about something. We have theories for just about everything: molecular theories, economic theories, theories about the mind, and of course, more relevant to our discussion, theories about development and theories about intervention. These latter two—theories about development and theories about intervention—are often grouped together and called psychological theories. However, the difference between them is important.

Theories of development—human development and social theories—are the theories that attempt to explain how people develop and grow. As such, they formulate a clinician's **theoretical orientation**. Developmental and social theories help us make sense of how people are nurtured in the environment or internally programed—depending on the theory—to feel, behave and make sense of the world around them. These theories also help us understand what can go wrong in development, and why some people face extremely difficult challenges in their lives.

Often grouped into these categories: psychodynamic, ethological, humanistic, behavioral, learning, and feminist and other contemporary schools of thought, developmental and social theories vary considerably in how they explain growth processes and problem etiology. They also focus on different aspects of development. Some, for example, focus on child development, while others focus on the aging process. Some focus almost exclusively neurobiology, relational development, or on factors in the social environment that shape development. And still others look at identity development, cognitive development, or the processes around the development of social or cultural identity. While it is outside of the scope of this particular text to review even a small portion of the multitude of existing developmental and social theories, the point here is that it is important for clinicians to have a system of explanation that shapes how they understand their clients and the problems they bring to therapy. These theories do this for clinicians.

While developmental and social theories prompt thinking about clients and their challenges, **theories of intervention** dictate **counseling modality**. They might be thought of as the road map for what clinicians do in therapy. Theories of intervention vary considerably in how they map out strategies for change. For example, cognitive theories focus on addressing problems by altering one's thinking processes. Behavioral theories look to alter those things in the immediate environment that stimulate or reinforce certain behaviors. Psychoanalytic and psychodynamic theories tend to focus on promoting insight to facilitate change.

There are so many possible roads to take in therapy; selecting the best travel route can be very difficult. But, how clinicians think about intervention—the road they take in therapy—is based on how they understand the client and the etiology of the problem. For example, attachment theory, based on the work of Bowlby (1969; 1988) and colleagues (e.g., Ainsworth, 1979; Ainsworth, Blehar, Waters, & Wall, 1978), is a theory of development that focuses on the ways in which caregiver responsiveness during infancy and early childhood and creates attachment bonds that become *working models* for future relationships. This theory outlines a developmental trajectory for normal and unhealthy development, and is supported by years of empirical research (see Blaustein & Kinniburgh, 2010; Thompson, 2008; Weinfield, Sroufe, Egeland, & Carlson, 2008). Attachment theory, however, is not a counseling modality; it does not tell the therapist what to do with clients who have attachment or relational difficulties. The ARC model (**A**ttachment, self-**R**egulation, **C**ompetence; Blaustein & Kinniburgh, 2010), however, is a therapeutic intervention framework that uses attachment theory principles for working with children and families who have experienced trauma. The focus of the ARC model of intervention includes working directly with children and their caregivers so as to strengthening parent-child attachment bonds, foster children's self-regulation abilities, and promote children's competence. Unfortunately, not all theories of development are as seamlessly connected to intervention theories. But the point here is that the understandings we have about who our clients are and the etiology of the problems they bring to therapy will have a direct influence on what we do to help.

Circling back to the definition of *theory*, another point is important here. While clinicians need to understand human growth and development and have a sound theoretical underpinning for their intervention approach, it is also important to remember that theories are a set of ideas, they are not truths. They offer one perspective. If they are followed too rigidly, theories can easily introduce a singular perspective bias. Bias is not inherently bad, but bias can influence the work we do with clients in some very unhelpful ways. If a clinician rigidly believes that children pass through predictable and universal stages of development, for example, she may not attend to the important ways in which a child's current social milieu—harassment at school, for example, or living in poverty, may be causing problems. And, in these cases, a focus on the intrapersonal psyche of the client may misdirect important interventions that need to happen in the social or external environment. How we think really does matter!

We need to be clear about our values and beliefs, and careful about the ways in which these shape the work we do with others. We also need to be flexible in our thinking, and invite multiple perspectives and explanatory systems. For this reason, we turn next to the importance of using research findings to guide our thinking and intervention planning.

EVIDENCE-BASED PRACTICE

Research suggests that most accepted or standard clinical psychological interventions are very generally effective (APA, 2005; Lambert, 2013). That is, therapy usually helps people. However, therapy isn't always helpful for everyone, and successful therapy really is a function of multiple variables, including the clinician, the client, and the therapeutic modality being used and matched well with the problem it is designed to address (APA, 2005). The term *evidence-based practice* (EBP) refers to the "integration of the best available research with clinical expertise in the context of patient characteristics, culture, and preferences" (APA, 2005, p. 5). Although EBP is colloquially associated with the idea that best practice is that which is proven effective in in research studies, notice that the American Psychological Association definition quoted above broadens the concept of evidence-based practice to take into account clinical expertise and other variables in the determination of effectiveness (DiMeo, Moore, & Lichtenstein, 2012). So, it is important to note that intervention planning should be based on what research studies reveal, on clinical judgment and clinician experience, and also must be specific to the particular client and issue sitting before us in the office.

The movement toward evidence-based practice in mental health initiated with a commitment to boost clinician efficiency and accountability (Evidence-based practice in psychology, 2006; Nevo & Slonim-Nevo, 2011) but should also be understood as an effort to be transparent and collaborative (between client and clinician) in clinical decision making (Shlonsky & Stern, 2007). While Hubble, Duncan, Miller, and Wampold (2010) and Lambert (2013) conclude that the therapeutic relationship is the most critical factor in terms of promoting therapeutic outcomes—even more so than any one theoretical approach—other research findings do suggest that there are some specific intervention approaches are most effective for some particular client issues (APA, 2005). For example, in an extensive review of research studies regarding specific intervention approaches for working with anxiety and childhood depression, Chambless and Ollendick (2001) report that the use of behavioral and cognitive behavioral approaches with children, adolescents, and their parents—particularly when working with specific phobias, obsessive–compulsive disorders, and depression—is effective. Along these lines, Ehlers et al., (2010) argue that there is strong research supporting the use of trauma-focused cognitive-behavioral therapy in work with clients grappling with post-traumatic stress disorder (PTSD). Benish, Imel, & Wampold (2008), however, disagree with this research-based conclusion and suggest that a wider range of modalities may be effective when working with clients who struggle with PTSD. So, while it is imperative to be informed about current research data, we also know that research often offers contradictory findings. In fact, some conclude that because outcome research is so inconclusive and there are so many variables that influence success in therapy, it is not truly possible to claim that one treatment modality is superior to another, at least for working with adults in therapy (Wampold, 2010).

Indeed, despite their findings mentioned above, Chambless and Ollendick (2001) point out that rather than a using a single modality, a whole range of approaches may be effective for addressing mental health issues. Similarly, Roy-Byrne (2015) concludes, "It may well be that different kinds of individuals and problems demand different psychotherapeutic approaches rather than that there is one elemental Holy Grail that will be best for everyone" (p. 786). So, even with strong research findings, the results of what to use when, with what difficulty remains unclear.

In part, this debate in the literature regarding the use of evidence-based practices rests on concerns regarding the validity of outcome studies (Benish et al., 2008), the problem with confounding variables in research design (Wampold et al., 2010), and the fact that some intervention approaches—namely those in the affective domain—are difficult to quantify and thus research (Roy-Byrne, 2015). Also, there are concerns that evidence-based practice studies marginalize the important practitioner effects in the delivery of mental health interventions—they ignore the point that effectiveness is based on the clinician, not just the intervention modality (APA, 2005; Nevo & Slonim-Nevo, 2011). Finally, Chambless and Ollendick (2001) voice concerns that the evidence-based practice movement may overly restrict clinical mental health practice and lead to therapy being directed by managed care companies, rather than practitioners.

Regardless, the call is for clinicians to align their intervention plans with identified and proven strategies, as much as possible. A growing emphasis on evidence-based practice has found a recent resurgence as policy makers, funding sources, clients, and clinicians all search for the most effective approaches in working with mental health challenges. All clinicians have a professional responsibility to be engaged in professional development, and this includes learning from research data on effective practice as these data continue to grow and shape the clinical practice of mental health therapy. Therapeutic outcome research is an important tool for intervention planning in clinical mental health practice.

INTERVENTION PLANNING

THE PROBLEM LIST

When a client comes to therapy with an unclear sense of what the problem is or what is most pressing (when multiple problems are identified), clinicians typically create a problem list. The problem list normally includes all of the problems that are derived from the assessment, interview, and client history—this may include old and new concerns (Cameron & turtle-song, 2002). The problems on this list are often organized according to priority of what will be addressed first, second, and so on. For each problem identified on the problem list, one or a small number of goals will be articulated. These goals are then matched to intervention strategies and later will be assessed to determine if the therapy has been successful or if changes are needed in the direction of therapy.

GOAL SETTING

"The trouble with not having a goal is that you can spend your life running up and down the field and never score" (Copeland, n.d.). In therapy, the trouble with not having a goal is that you will run up and down and without any idea where you are going. Having goals in therapy is what gives direction to the work. Therapeutic goals might best be thought of as the anticipated accomplishment of therapy, the end point of the work, and the hope and the vision of life without the problem. Goals are the link between identified problems and intervention strategies.

IDENTIFYING THE CLIENT'S GOAL

Counseling goals should be directly connected to the problems identified on the problem list. It can be surprisingly difficult to move from the articulation of a problem to an identifiable goal, however. This is especially true when multiple problems are identified, when the client is "mandated" or in the precontemplative stage of change, and when the problem is identified *for* rather than *by* the client. For example, I once worked for a young man named Alec who was referred to me by a psychiatrist. The psychiatrist wanted me to work with Alec toward being compliant in taking an antidepressant medication. But, both Alec and his mother did not believe he experienced depression, and they were not in favor of the medication. When I asked Alec what he wanted help with, he said that he wanted to have friends at school. His mother wanted him to be happier and to behave better at school. When I consulted with school personnel, they wanted him to learn how to control his behavior. While I suspect that all of these versions of the problem were somehow related, I wanted to be sure to center our work on the concern that was most pressing for Alec. Our work began, then, with us trying to sort out why Alec was having difficulties making friends at school, and from there we were able to explore some of the other experiences that made him angry at school. In that practice setting, I was also able to work directly with school personnel to develop clearer and fairer discipline policies—for all students, not just Alec—as that became relevant to the challenges Alec faced in school. And in the final stages of my work with Alec, I worked with his mother to be clear about her expectations and the behavior management skills she was using (with some good success). I also helped her recognize her strengths and have confidence in herself as a mom. In a 6-month follow-up meeting with the psychiatrist, the psychiatrist reported that Alec no longer appeared to be depressed and there was no need for medication.

The point here is that it is important to be clear about the problems you are being asked to address and by whom, and to be sure that the client has a voice in the goal-setting process. We know that goal setting facilitates intentionality and is also associated with successful outcomes in therapy (Norcross, 2010). We also know that when therapists involve clients in the goal-setting process, the clients feel engaged and they report higher levels of satisfaction in the therapeutic relationship (Gaston, 1990; Norcross, 2010), which, as discussed in Chapter 1, is associated with positive outcomes in therapy (Hubble et al., 2010). So, being sure that the client is part of the goal-setting process is critical. Clinicians should also be careful not to address goals and attempt intervention strategies that are beyond the scope of their ability and level of training. If a clinician knows that he lacks the training or experience to work effectively on a particular goal, he should receive training and careful supervision at every step in the therapeutic process or make a referral to someone who is better situated to help in that particular area.

GOAL CHARACTERISTICS

Here we will discuss the characteristics of well-articulated therapeutic goals. These are also summarized toward the end of this section in Figure 9.6.

As already noted, clients are not always clear about why they have come to see us, or they may feel so burdened by the challenges they face that they are not able to even consider that things will get better, much less set a goal for therapy. Added to this, problems have a tendency to magnify when they have too much attention (Freeman, Epston, & Lobovits, 1997). That is, when all of our "helping" efforts entail talking about problems, warning about problems, and coaxing individuals to quit or change, clients can easily become overwhelmed. Extensive problem talk can also obscure clients' abilities, skills, competencies, beliefs, values, and commitments (Freeman et al., 1997; Monk, Winslade, Crocket, & Epston, 1997; Morgan, 2000), further hampering efforts to identify goals and strategies for change. So the more attention we give to talking about the problems that clients face, the harder it may be to generate goals and intervention plans. For this reason, framing goals in terms of what the client hopes to accomplish, rather than what he can't do is helpful. This is what we refer to as articulating goals in accomplishment language.

Accomplishment language, then, is about framing goals in terms of what the client wants for his life—what life would look like if the problem did not exist. This way of thinking about goals is often called the *miracle question* and is used by many clinicians, particularly those practicing solution-focused brief therapy, to help clients think more broadly about change, to remain focused on future and future possibilities, and to facilitate goal-setting (De Jong & Berg, 2008). Basically, the miracle question begins by setting up a hypothetical scenario where the client is to imagine that he fell asleep and that while sleeping a miracle occurred, erasing the problem from his life. The question then becomes what life would look like without the problem. This idea of encouraging clients to approach the process of goal setting by thinking about the world might look for them when the problem is resolved is an adaptation of Milton Erickson's "crystal ball" technique (de Shazer, 1985), but the miracle question itself appears to be discovered "serendipitously" by Inso Berg in her work with a client who was extremely discouraged in the face of weighty problems (De Jong & Berg, 2008).

In the example with Alec above, I used this concept to help identify our goals for counseling. I did this by noticing out loud that Alec seemed to have many people in his life who were concerned about him—his mother, the psychiatrist, and the school principal. "Mad at me, actually," he corrected me. Instead of asking him what they were mad at, which would have focused on the problem rather than the goal, I asked "Well, if things were going right in your life and if these people weren't mad at you, what would you be *doing*?" Alec was quick to tell me that if things were going right in his life he would have friends at school. Having friends became the first draft articulation of the goal he was interested in working on. By asking a client what he would rather be doing, thinking, feeling, or experiencing, the goal often emerges as a statement of intention that is meaningful to the client.

Next, since therapeutic goals are about what the client hopes for, they should be articulated from the **perspective of the client.** They should outline what the client will be thinking, doing, or feeling when all is said and done, and articulated in **clear, specific, and concrete language**, as much as possible. To this end, it is helpful to try to articulate goals in behavioral terms, as the concreteness of a behavior can showcase the desired result. In the example of Alec, above, then, it would be important to clarify what "friendship" means to him. To help, we might ask Alec what he would be doing with his friend if it were a true friendship? When we have concrete manifestations of the concept of friendship, such as "We would be sitting together during lunch" or "He would hang out with me on the playground," then we have a better sense of what we are working toward. This, too, helps us later determine if the goal was accomplished.

Asking what one would be thinking, doing, or feeling if the goal was accomplished are good prompts for focusing a goal statement in a **particular domain area**. For example, a goal about being able to *think* about a situation differently suggests interventions within the cognitive domain. A goal that has to do with *feeling* differently is in the affective domain. And a focus on *doing* something different suggests a potential goal in the behavioral domain. Of course, goals that are located in one domain may call for interventions in overlapping domain areas.

Similarly, it can be helpful to articulate goals in terms of the **level** at which the problem is manifest (i.e., intrapersonal, interpersonal, or an external). But here, too, there will be much overlap. For example, Faith was working with her school counselor because she was in a fight with another student at school. As it turns out, the fight was prompted by Faith's frustration about being the recipient of multiple racial micro-aggressions at school. In this case, Faith may have as a personal goal to not let racism make her feel bad about herself or not let racism shape her sense of self. The racism that she experiences at school is a problem that exists in the school environment, however. Faith is not responsible for fixing it, and it is not indicative of something that his wrong with her. It is an external-level problem, even though it affects her at the intrapersonal and interpersonal levels. And so while Faith can work to control her reactions to racism, the problem will likely continue to exist if it is not addressed by those who have control over the school environment—the teachers, administrators, students, and families. This is a good example of where advocacy meets therapy. Stopping the problem should be a goal for the school—calling for an intervention at the level of system change. It is not

Faith's responsibility to end racism in her school, and it should not be a goal in her intervention plan. Her goals should relate to what she can reasonably or realistically do.

This brings us to the next important characteristics of goal statements: Goals should be **realistic** or **attainable**. People tend to be motivated to work toward goals that they think they can accomplish. When goals are too large or overbearing, we can easily feel overwhelmed. This is true for both clients and their therapists—both can be discouraged if they are working toward a goal that is unrealistic. It can be helpful to divide larger goals into smaller concrete steps or subgoals as small steps taken toward a goal often have ripple effects (de Shazer, 1985; Sklare, 2014). That is, successful completion of smaller subgoals becomes steps in the right direction toward change. So, think big, but in small steps, one at a time.

We identified a goal for the school of ending racism in our example above with Faith. Here again, this is not an individual goal that should be passed on to a child who is the victim of racism, but it is an important and truly appropriate goal for the school—one that must be embraced in this and every school across the nation. The point about having goals that are realistic and attainable is at issue here. Is this goal is actually attainable? Personally, I would argue that this particular goal of ending racism is appropriate and attainable for every school and for every community across the nation and world-wide. Realistically, however, subgoals might be more appropriate, so that the larger goal is addressed one step at a time. To identify these subgoals, the counselor might ask: What would teachers, students, and staff in the school be doing if racism were not present? What would one see when they walked into a school with no racism? How would students, staff, and teachers be feeling if they worked in a racism-free environment? And, importantly, what is the first accomplishment that school personnel and students will commit to in their efforts to eradicate racism in their environment?

It is also important to have goals that are **measureable**. Therapy should not be a life-long event; when the therapeutic goals have been met the helping contract is complete and it is time to move on. Measurability has to do with how one knows if the goals have been met. It also alerts us if changes need to be made in the therapeutic process because the identified goals have not been adequately met. So, with each goal, it is important to consider what it would look like if the goal were attained. This is why using doing, feeling, or thinking language in goal statements is very helpful;

these terms point to domains within which we might expect and measure change.

Measuring goal attainment starts with having good baseline data regarding the status of the goal at the start of therapy. It is also important to identify success indicators—what it would look like if and when the goal is met. Formal assessment tools such as depression scales, for example, or surveys and questionnaires may be used to assess goals. Berg and de Shazer (1993) recommend using scaling questions to this end as well. *Scaling questions* ask the client to measure their perceptions regarding goal attainment on a scale from 1 to 10. Scaling questions, like the miracle question, were discovered somewhat serendipitously, and are used by solution focused therapists to help concretize clients perceptions about problems and solutions, to measure progress toward an identified goal, and for a whole host of other purposes

Articulated in accomplishment language

- The goal should state what the client would be doing, feeling, or thinking if the problem did not exist.

Client-oriented

- The goal is articulated from the perspective of what the client hopes to achieve.

Clear, specific, concrete

- The goal is articulated clearly and concretely.

Domain-specific

- The goal identifies the domain that will be the initial focus of intervention.

Aimed at appropriate level

- The goal addresses the level of problem manifestation (i.e., intrapersonal, interpersonal, or external).

Realistic and attainable

- The goal is something that the client is potentially able to achieve.

Measurable

- The goal statement is articulated in or includes language that facilitates outcome assessment.

Figure 9.6 *Goal Characteristics*

where it is beneficial to hear the client's perspective in fairly concrete terms (Berg & de Shazer, 1993; De Jong & Berg, 2008).

As a concrete example of establishing goals that are measureable, consider a young child, Roger, who learning to tie his shoe. The goal is for him to be able to tie his own shoe by himself. This is a goal that is simply stated, fairly concrete, and observable. To later assess if this goal has been accomplished, we note that little Roger was completely unable to tie his own shoe at the start of instruction. We might also note that he has expressed an eagerness to learn, thus apparently in the contemplative or even preparatory state of change. We decide to set a target of 4 out of 5 for the subgoal completion criteria. This means that we know that in order to move on to subsequent subgoals in shoe-tying, Roger would have to perform each subgoal task correctly 4 out of 5 times. Note that this criterion was set prior to starting instruction; it informs us that we can move to the next step in the learning process.

The first subgoal is that Roger will be able to cross the laces in an X. The next subgoal is that he will learn how to cross one lace under the other and

Photo 9.1

Goal: Roger will tie his shoes independently.

Subgoal 1: Roger will cross the laces in an X.

Subgoal 2: Roger will cross one lace under the other and pull tight.

Subgoal 3: Roger will loop one lace.

Subgoal 4: Roger will tuck a loop from the other lace in the wrap-around hole.

Subgoal 5: Roger will pull both loops tight.

Baseline observation:

- Roger is not able to tie his shoes at all.
- Roger is very motivated to learn to tie his shoes—he has repeatedly asked his father to teach him.

Success criteria:

- 4/5 rate of success in independent tries will allow movement to the subsequent subgoal.

Figure 9.7 *Sample Goals and Subgoals*

pull tight. After these two subgoals have been achieved—as demonstrated by Roger's success in crossing and pulling the laces in the simple cross knot four or five times independently, we move to the next subgoals. The third subgoal is that we expect little Roger to loop one lace, wrap the other around it, and tuck a loop in the wraparound hole. And then, finally, the last goal is to be able to successfully pull both loops tight—an effort, we know, that is sometimes more easily imagined than done. Our intervention plan might be to repeat instructions for each of these steps two times, demonstrate the task with our own hands and his shoe laces, put our hands over Roger's hands to attempt the task, and finally, observe Roger doing each step by himself and providing encouragement.

Of course, clinicians will rarely be working with their clients to tie shoes, and often therapeutic mental health goals are much less concrete. However, I offer this example of little Roger and his shoes because it easily illustrates the importance of organizing goals into small steps, articulating them in concrete and observable language as much as possible, and establishing a success criteria to guide the assessment of goal attainment. Goals that are realistically attainable and measureable offer a feedback mechanism to assess the course of therapy to better insure positive outcomes.

INTERVENTION STRATEGIES

In order to best meet the needs of their clients, Cameron and turtle-song (2002) point out that counselors need an organized method of planning, evaluating, and documenting the services they offer to their clients. Hubble et al. (2010) highlight the importance of structure and focus in therapy, linking it to positive therapeutic outcomes. All of this, then, has to do with clinical intentionality. Intervention strategies are the plans that the therapist will use to help the client reach her goals—they are the articulation of the therapists' intentions in the therapeutic work. We will speak shortly about how all of this becomes documented in a plan and case notes.

There is no one formula for providing therapy, as we have reiterated throughout this text. Intervention strategies are created from a complex mix of who the client is, the experiences he has had in life, his current situation, and the level of motivation he has to change. They are also based on the circumstances of the problem and the goals set out for therapy. Adding to the mix are the ways in which the therapist conceptualizes the problem and the theories and practices that the therapist believes are appropriate, given the identified goals. These are all factors that the therapist takes into consideration when making intervention strategy decisions.

WRITING THE INTERVENTION PLAN

Since decisions about specific intervention strategies are client and situation specific, we will focus here on how to *write* the intervention plan rather than its content. Recall that the goals, as much as possible, articulate what the client will be doing, thinking, feeling, when the problem is ameliorated. For each goal, then, the clinician will want to develop (and document) one or a small number of intervention strategies. These describe what the clinician will be doing to help the client achieve her goal. This structure is outlined in the sample intervention plan in Figure 9.8.

Remember that while goals identify a desired outcome, an intervention strategy is what the clinician will be doing to facilitate that outcome—it is the articulation of the counseling modality in juxtaposition to each identified goal. For this reason, intervention strategies are typically **written in third party language**, beginning with "Clinician will. ..." In cases when other professionals are involved in the therapeutic intervention, specific names may be included. When multiple strategies will be used to accomplish a particular goal, they

Date: 10/7/17 **Clinician name:** Anne M. Geroski

Client name: Cyrus Johnson
DOB: 5/16/03
Emergency contact information:
Mr. Ezera Johnson (father), 718-342-2118
Ms. Leona Brigg (mother), 718-344-1862

Identified problem:
Adjustment Disorder w/Anxiety 309.24 [DSM-5] (parent divorce within year)
R/O Social Anxiety Disorder (Social Phobia) 300.23 [DSM-5]

- Marked anxiety about social situations in school and other settings with peers, manifested in introversion, avoidance, failure to speak/participate, thus causing functional impairment and habitual rubbing/scratching along arms
- Concerns about negative peer evaluation re: anxiety
- Persistence of concern for approximately 9 months
- No other existing mental health/physical condition present

History summary:
Parents report that Cyrus "always" appeared "uncomfortable" among larger groups of children, but the anxiety symptoms increased markedly upon his move to middle school last year. Presently wants parents to be "on call" throughout the school day for when he has anxiety symptoms. Psychosocial evaluation completed. No hx medication/prior counseling. Parent divorce/recent change in visitation arrangements. Parent/child preparation stage of change—expressed motivation to engage in therapy, participated eagerly in psychosocial evaluation.

Intervention goal (include anticipated completion date):
Cyrus will attend school and social functions without experiencing anxiety. Re-evaluate: 6/15/17

Short-term goals/objectives (include anticipated completion date):

1. Parent/child will learn about the interrelated physiological, affective, cognitive, and behavioral aspects of anxiety. Completion: 4/15/17
2. Child will develop awareness of and develop control over the physiological signs of anxiety. 5/15/17
3. Child will develop awareness of and develop control over cognitive distortions that trigger anxiety symptoms. 6/30/17

Figure 9.8 *Sample Intervention Plan* *(Continued)*

Intervention plan (include responsible person):

1. Therapist assistant/educational consultant will meet with parents to educate them on the physiological, affective, cognitive, and behavioral aspects of anxiety.
2. Therapist assistant/educational consultant will offer bibliotherapy to parents regarding divorce triggers and the manifestation of anxiety.
3. Therapist assistant/educational consultant will conduct follow-up session with parents at 3 and 6 months.
4. Therapist will use bibliotherapy materials to explain the physiological, affective, cognitive, and behavioral components of anxiety to client.
5. Therapist will teach awareness and relaxation strategies to client and assign homework tasks to reinforce the use of these strategies between sessions.
6. Therapist will teach CBT model and "catch, check, change" strategies to client. Homework assignments will be given to reinforce the use of these strategies between sessions.

Review date:

Progress report:

Figure 9.8 *Continued*

should be **listed sequentially**, beginning with what the clinician will do first, second, etc. Keep in mind that if you are working with a client who is in a precontemplative stage of change or who is easily discouraged, it may be most appropriate to begin the clinical work with the strategy that is most likely to yield immediate success. Being successful early in therapy can engender continued investment in the therapeutic process. In other situations, it may be better to begin with strategies that are not deeply personal or intense as some clients may need some time to get used to the process of therapy or to get to know the counselor better before allowing themselves too much vulnerability. Finally, intervention plans should be **reviewed periodically and potentially revised** to determine if the client's goals have been met and if the strategies have been effective. For this reason, it is helpful to include dates or periods of time indicating when the intervention plan will be reviewed.

CLINICAL PROGRESS NOTES

Virtually all health service providers are required to provide a clinical record of their work. These records typically include assessment information, including summaries of the clinical interview, psychosocial assessment, and narratives from formal assessments or tests; documentation of the DSM diagnosis, if that is being used; the treatment or intervention plan; and clinical progress notes, which we will get to shortly. The purpose of these documents is to record the clinician's perceptions and plans, facilitate communication between professionals, create a legal record of the work, and to provide justification in cases of third party billing (Rosenbloom et al., 2011). Many practices are moving toward using some form of electronic health record system to facilitate communication between professionals and for ease in billing processes. In general, case notes support clinical decision making, provide accountability, and assure the delivery of appropriate services (Cameron & turtle-song, 2002).

Progress notes are the notes that clinicians write after each therapy session to stimulate critical thinking about the counseling session and to document the work that has occurred. Most clinicians review these notes prior to subsequent counseling sessions to help them recall what has happened in previous sessions and to help them begin the current session with direction and intentionality. While the specific format that clinicians use for progress notes varies across clinicians and agencies, SOAP notes (or some version of the SOAP note format) are used by many clinicians and other health care professionals. This model of note-taking is aligned with a problem-oriented medical record system, which is commonly used in the medical profession (Cameron & turtle-song, 2002).

The S in SOAP refers to the *subjective* information—information that is told to the counselor. This is where the clinician documents the client's concerns, thoughts, expressed feelings, plans, and perceptions about the intensity of the problem and how is impacts significant relationships (Cameron & turtle-song, 2002). Relevant comments from significant others, including family, friends, or other authorities, might also be included in this section. For example, the clinician might write here that the client reports feeling better and her daughter also observed that she is getting out of the house more frequently.

The O refers to *objective* data. This typically includes the therapist's observations and any documentation or reports that might be relevant (Cameron & turtle-song, 2002). Here it is important to avoid evaluative language and opinions, and use behavioral descriptions, as much as possible. For example, the clinician might indicate that the client appeared anxious as evidenced by quick speech and frequent movement, including occasional foot tapping and shifting in the seat. Or, an example given by Cameron and turtle-song (2002) is: "client smelled of alcohol; speech slow and deliberate in nature; uncontrollable giggles even after stumbling against door jam [sic]; unsteady gait" (p. 288) rather than saying that the client was drunk.

The A refers to *assessment* in the SOAP format. This is a summary of the clinician's critical thinking about the problem (Cameron & turtle-song, 2002). The assessment section synthesizes and summarizes the subjective and objective comments in the first part of the notes. When using the DSM system, this might be the clinician's diagnosis, or tentative diagnosis.

The final section in the SOAP notes model is the *plan*—that is represented by the P. Here the clinician documents the plan of action as well as a tentative prognosis (Cameron & turtle-song, 2002). A plan of action typically includes the date of the next appointment, a comment about the progress that was made in this section, and directions for the next session. Any comments about prognosis in the plan should include, as much as possible, concrete information. For example, the comment "the client is making good progress, as he appears to be going out more frequently and reports fewer sleep disturbances. Continued homework assignments are likely to continue this trend." includes information that supports the claim that progress is apparent. All case notes should be brief, concise, and limited to information that is relevant to the goals of therapy and the content of the counseling session.

A WORD OF CAUTION

Here we end with two cautions. The first is to remember that while all documents pertaining to clinical assessment, treatment planning, diagnosis, and progress notes are confidential; there are situations where they can, potentially, be read by others. For example, clients themselves may ask to see them. Also, if the clinician does not have legal privileged communication status, case notes may be requested in a court subpoena. In some practice settings, other professionals may have access to case notes about a particular client, particularly if they are part of an electronic health record and the client has given consent. Additionally, in some cases, law authorities may have access to the case notes written about mandated clients. And finally, insurance companies may also have access to clinical case notes. So, the caution here is to always be thoughtful, professional, and concise when writing case notes. Do not guess or speculate, and never use derogatory language or references.

The temptation is to say that clinical case notes should only include factual information. However, the second caution here really is a question about what is actually meant by "factual information." Swartz (2006) writes: "The wisdom of the poet lies in their knowledge that truth is not 'fact', that our clumsy attempts to make language represent reality in some transparent way lets loose exactly what we hoped to capture in our web" (p. 428). While the SOAP format carefully divides subjective and objective perceptions, we must acknowledge that if the therapist is the one writing the case notes, it is her perception of facts that will be recorded as truths. They are the documents that offer a story about the client—a story that is told by the author of the notes, not the client herself. Clinicians often hurry to write case notes after each therapy session, but the reminder here is that these clinical case notes become part of the record of the client. "Stories" about clients have the potential to take on a life of their own and to follow a client for years and years into the future—into realms of life that at the time of the writing are unimaginable. It is up to us as clinicians to be very careful about the information that we have about others, and to be thoughtful and intentional about the ways in which we document that information in writing.

CHAPTER SUMMARY

This chapter focused on clinical interviewing, assessment and diagnosis, intervention planning, and writing progress notes. Mental health clinicians use a clinical interview process to learn about their clients and the concerns they bring to therapy. In addition to asking questions of the client and others involved in his care, clinicians may also conduct a mental status exam, assess a client's level of motivation for change, and use other assessment tools, particularly if they are considering a DSM diagnosis. The skills reviewed in the previous few chapters are the tools that counselors use to conduct a clinical interview, especially: listening, empathy, reflection, paraphrasing, and questions. The clinical interview process yields information that is used to develop appropriate goals and intervention strategies for therapy. Clinicians are encouraged to engage clients in goal-setting processes, since it is important that therapy is focused on the concerns and needs of the client. Ideas for identifying goals and articulating them in helpful language were reviewed in this chapter, as were specific suggestions for how to write intervention plans. The chapter concluded with recommendations regarding the writing of progress notes to document each therapy session.

REFLECTION QUESTIONS

1. In this chapter, there is a strong emphasis on the goal-setting process being one that involves the client. Why is this important? Are there times when it might be appropriate for the counselor to set the goals and not involve the client in the goal-setting process?

2. Why the distinction between human development and intervention theories? Why is this important? How are the two related? Different?

3. In this chapter, the points were made that many therapeutic interventions have research evidence to support their effectiveness, and also that one approach is not necessarily better than another. How can these two juxtaposed and seemingly contradictory points be reconciled? What does this mean about theory-based and evidence-based practice?

CHAPTER

Transmodality Change Strategies

Chapter Outline

INTRODUCTION

In the previous chapters of this section of this text, we reviewed basic helping skills that are used across multiple intervention modalities. Here we focus our attention on some general helping strategies that are also used across multiple intervention modalities—thus the title of this chapter: transmodality change strategies. These are not specific skills; they are practices that fit with many different counseling approaches and are commonly used in a variety of helping situations.

Following up on our conversation about stages of change in Chapter 9, we begin here with a discussion about how to encourage and motivate clients to take action in their lives. This is an approach that is often used when working with clients who are somewhat ambiguous about therapy or reluctant to take steps toward change. Next, we move to a discussion about deconstructing conversations. Most texts on helping skills do not promote this as a general helping strategy. But following the thread interwoven throughout this text, when thorny problems are related to problematic social discourses or experiences of sociocultural trauma, it is important to help clients question the discourses and experiences that position them in untenable ways. This is the aim of deconstructing conversations. Next, we will review the use of psychoeducation and problem-solving strategies in therapy. These approaches can be used in combination with other approaches but also are called upon when a client lacks critical information, when the client does not know what to do, or when specific decisions are needed. We also will review a conceptual model for promoting self-regulation, discuss the use of mindfulness, and end this chapter with a return to the concept of advocacy.

ENCOURAGING CHANGE

The fundamental idea underlying the stages of change model, discussed in the previous chapter, is that meaningful change occurs when one is ready to change—research bears this out. Regardless of the particular focus of change or whether one is in therapy, clients move toward action when they are motivated to do so (Norcross, Krebs, & Prochaska, 2010; Prochaska & DiClemente, 1982; Prochaska, Norcross, & DiClemente, 1994). The practice of **motivational interviewing**, developed by Miller and Rollnick (2013), is a therapeutic approach that dovetails the stages of change model. In essence, motivational interviewing has to do with meeting a client at his level of motivation and then gently nudging him toward change.

According to Miller and Rollnick (2013), motivating change begins with **empathy**—truly understanding that change is hard. This is communicated to clients by listening carefully and accepting and honoring that the client is ambivalent about taking steps toward change. Miller and Rollnick point out that being empathic does not mean colluding with the client against change or agreeing with them about not needing to change. Instead, promoting change begins with accepting where the client is at in his own process of change.

For example, it was pointed out to Inez by her parents that her partying at night might be getting in the way of her studies in college. Inez told her counselor that she was upset about failing three of her classes, but she also did not agree with her parents that going out at night and sleeping through morning classes was the reason for her failures, and it made her angry that her parents suggested otherwise. She perceived that they were "controlling her life." The counselor expressed empathy by saying, "Inez, I can see that it makes you angry to hear people questioning you about going out at night. I'm guessing that it feels like people are telling you what you can and can't do, and I get that you don't want to hear that from your parents, nor from me or anyone else. I know that you also have a lot of pressure on your shoulders to do well here in school and this grade report is really disappointing. You are in a tough spot."

Another technique in motivational interviewing is to **develop discrepancies** (Miller & Rollnick, 2013). This has to do with amplifying the dissonance between what the client wants and the reality of the situation. Most often this entails pointing out that there is a discrepancy between what the client thinks or does and her goals or desires. In our example, Inez does not want to see that her social behavior is getting in the way of her academic success. The reality is that Inez needs to make some changes if she wants to succeed in school. Here the technique of developing discrepancies would be to point out these two competing issues and invite Inez to look at both of them in juxtaposition. The aim of this step is to promote awareness of a problem and to evoke dissonance so as to prompt the client to consider change. It is not to argue, coax or advise, as doing any of these would shift the focus from the problem that needs to change onto the therapeutic relationship, and would likely also evoke resistance or defensiveness. Instead, the clinician remains steadfast in emphasizing personal choice and continues to point out discrepancies.

For example, the counselor working with Inez says, "The social life at college is a lot of fun, and making good friends and having a good time is important. But also, it is clear that you want to do well in college—because of your parents and, of course, because this is something you have decided to do. You want to have fun and do well in your classes, but it looks like these too are not in balance." It is important to remember that it is up to the client to make a decision about change and the clinician must always respect the client's decisions and choices.

Resistance is a normal part of the process of change. **Rolling with resistance** is a technique that entails both acknowledging that there is something that makes it hard to take action and also accepting that the client is not ready (Miller & Rollnick, 2013). Reacting to resistance in all of the familiar ways of being angry, exacerbated, frustrated, or by giving advice or trying to coax, are often not very helpful. What is unique here about this stage of motivational interviewing is that therapists take the respectful position of standing *with* their clients and their reluctance rather than standing against clients when change is hard. Rolling with resistance, then, entails pointing out that change is hard, illuminating the decision that the client is not wanting to change at this time, and pointing out that not wanting to change is normal and understandable.

For example, Inez says "Everyone always makes a big deal about partying. That is not the problem here. It's that the classes are just scheduled too damned early in the morning. What do the instructors expect?" The counselor responds, "Inez, I hear that you are frustrated when people tell you to stop going out so much. No one wants to hear people telling them that they have a problem or that they shouldn't have fun. You want to find a way to have fun and to do well in your classes, but right now you are not wanting to do anything different and you are mad at the registrar for when classes are scheduled. This is a tough spot to be in right now." It is important to remember that for all of us, change is difficult. We should expect resistance. Clinicians need to align with the client and with the resistance in order to encourage change.

Supporting self-efficacy is the final principle in motivational interviewing (Miller & Rollnick, 2013). This step has to do with encouraging action through a genuine expression of hope or confidence. This is an expression of the belief that the client can and will change if she desires to do so. For example, the counselor in our example tells Inez, "I remember you saying that it took a while to sort out your social life and your school work when you were in high school and that you worked hard to retain your academic eligibility to play basketball. I suspect that some of those strategies could be used here, too, right?" Later he adds, "I predict that you will be able to find balance because I see you are smart and you have done this before. Of course, I am here to help, but it is clear that when you decide what direction you want to go in, you are able to make it happen." Here the clinician has to be careful not to position himself as someone who is dragging a client to do something that she does not want to do, not someone who tries to placate the client into action, and also the clinician must remember not to abandon a client who is not ready to change. The point is to be realistic, supportive, and focus on desires and hopes for change.

Motivational interviewing is a way of communicating respect and encouraging change; it is not a practice of talking clients into doing something that they do not want or are not ready to do. It is also not a step-by-step process, such as this brief outline suggests. Motivational interviewing is a cyclic process that entails gauging where the ever-changing client's motivations lie and intervening accordingly. This brief review is also outlined in Table 10.1. I encourage readers to receive more detailed instruction and practice in this model, as it is a helpful intervention strategy that complements most counseling modalities.

Table 10.1: Encouraging Change

EXPRESS EMPATHY
DEVELOP DISCREPANCIES
AVOID ARGUMENTATION
ROLL WITH RESISTANCE
SUPPORT SELF-EFFICACY

DECONSTRUCTING CONVERSATIONS

We know that experiences within family, the community, and larger society influence the ways in which we become known to self and others. They also structure the lens through which we view the world. Pointed out throughout this text, systems of power and privilege have a profound and normalizing influence on ideas that are seen as "truths." These truths influence people's behaviors toward each other, and they serve as building blocks for identity. In everyday life we adjust to the discourses that surround us, and we step into or away from the positions they offer—and all of this happens, sometimes, out of our own conscious awareness.

Deconstruction, in the context of therapeutic processes, refers to the interrogation of taken-for-granted assumptions that guide people's lives (Monk, Winslade, & Sinclair, 2008). It is a practice of inviting critical examination of ideas that have previously never been questioned (Freedman & Combs, 1996) with intent to "expose the biases, flaws, and inconsistencies" (Leffert, 2010, p. 8). Deconstructing conversations invite us to become aware of the influence of normative ideas (discourses) on our ways of thinking and how we live our lives. Ultimately, the aim of deconstructing conversations is to invite new possibilities.

Narrative therapists often use the term, *unpacking*, when speaking about deconstructing conversations (Freedman & Combs, 1996). Unpacking one's experiences, identity conclusions, and the discourses that support problematic positions enables clients to examine "different perspectives, to notice how they are constructed (or *that* [emphasis in original] they are constructed), to note their limits, and to discover that there are other possible narratives" (Freedman & Combs, 1996, p. 57). This, then, allows clients to challenge narratives that offer untenable positions and to begin to construct alternative stories that are more in line with how they see themselves and how they want to live in the world. In a sense, Freedman and Combs point out, engaging in the deconstruction of taken-for-granted truths opens up new possibilities and invites agency as the client takes a stand regarding certain ideas and practices in society.

Unsurprisingly, the idea of a suitcase full of clothes comes to mind for me when I think about unpacking discourses. Let us say that we have a suitcase filled with clothes for a trip. Before leaving for the trip, we thought about what we might need for the trip and packed the suitcase accordingly. We filled the suitcase with clothes that matched our ideas about which shirt should go

Photo 10.1

with which pair of pants and what we might wear on the various days and anticipated events during the trip. When we arrive at our destination, let us say that we sit with someone who asks us deconstructing questions about our suitcase filled with clothes. They might unpack our suitcase with us by asking questions about which shirt goes with which pants, and perhaps which socks might go along with one particular outfit over another. This person might also ask us why we always wear this particular shirt with that pair of pants and why we might wear one outfit to one special occasion but not another. These questions get at what we like to wear, of course, and our thoughts regarding what is appropriate in various situations. They also get at a more fundamental issue of identity—they begin to reveal how we are thinking about who we are, how we want to be seen by others, and our understandings about how things should be.

As mentioned, deconstructing conversations are used in therapy to invite new possibilities. Of course, there is nothing wrong with wearing the pale yellow shirt with the khaki pants and dark brown socks, as planned. But, when these choices restrict where we go, how we see ourselves, and how we are seen by others, it is important to give them a second thought. Sometimes just asking "Why the yellow shirt versus the blue one?" or "What impression do you hope to give to others?" can open up new possibilities.

The point is that deconstructing conversations question the unquestioned with the intent of inviting alternative ways of thinking. They might also inspire some people to take a stand against ideas that are not helpful or somehow limiting in their lives (Freedman & Combs, 1996). For example, it might be risky to show up in a T-shirt exposing a political statement, but doing so may allow the expression of one's beliefs at a time that seems important to do so. The point, of course, is not about what one wears and when. It is about working with clients to open up new possibilities, to encourage critical thinking and meaning making in regard to self, and also to invite critical inquiry into ones experiences in the world (McKenzie & Monk, 1997; Monk et al., 2008). When we invite a client to think about how he wants to manage his life in a way that is not controlled by the ideas, values, and behaviors of others, we invite agency.

Deconstructing conversations encourage clients to decide who they want to be, how they would like to be seen by others, and what identity they want to put forward as self in the world. To be clear, this intervention is not aimed *directly* at changing the conditions of context. But it is intended to help people be agent in how they want to manage their lives, given a particular context. It is a reminder to clients that while we cannot always change others, we can make decisions about the ways in which we are invited into positions by others and how we want to respond to discourses on offer around us.

DECONSTRUCTION IN THERAPEUTIC PRACTICE

The work of deconstruction in therapy is not for the faint of heart. It is difficult to challenge the very assumptions that are the foundation for how we have always lived. The role of the helper in this process is to offer meaningful questions from a position of tentative curiosity, and to assume a "deliberately naïve posture" (Monk et al., 2008, p. 130) rather than assume a position of expert. This guiding happens through posing questions for which there are no concrete or specific answers—no objective truths. Again, deconstructing conversations are designed to invite the client to consider options and to open up un-seen possibilities. The following discussion offers suggestions—not meant to be rigidly followed or conducted in any specific order—for deconstructing conversations.

In the therapy room, deconstructing conversations typically begin with what Freedman and Combs (1996) refer to as ***deconstructive listening***. This is to listen to the client's stories with an understanding that they likely have many possible meanings. While listening, counselors need to respect that the client is recalling stories of lived experiences, but at the same time, the counselor does not necessarily need to accept the conclusions that the client has taken from those experiences. For example, a client may experience rejection by a parent, but that does not make the child unworthy of love. That is, clients do not need to accept the invitations on offer from experiences in life or unhelpful discourses of deficit.

Clinicians are also listening for aspects of the client's experiences that may be omitted from their stories, or for stories that sit outside a narrative thread. For example, is this client *always* sad? Bad? Anxious? This requires counselors to be listening for successes in stories of failure, resistance in the face of pain, or for untold stories of agency. A therapist who is listening for stories outside the narrative may be asking herself, "Was there a time when this client was successful at work?" or "Are there times when this client has been courageous in the face of fear?" Freedman and Combs (1996) also call on therapists to work to understand the unique meanings that adhere language to context, with an eye for opportunities to interpret events in alternative ways. What do "anxious" or "fearful" mean to this particular client? May a "resistant" client be appropriately wary of revealing too much too early in therapy? There are multiple ways of understanding events—never is there one reality or truth.

As clients begin to tell their stories, clinicians might offer a brief summary of what they have heard and **ask questions about the meanings** of particular words or events that are used or discussed. For example, a school counselor said, "So, Jamiliah, you want to go to the prom this year, but you hated it last year, right?" "When you said you hated it, what was it that you hated so much?" After Jamiliah responded, the counselor clarified what she heard to be sure it was accurate to Jamiliah's intent. "So, you hated what felt like competition for getting the best date, and also your parents were upset about the cost of getting the 'right' prom clothes. Right?" Next, the counselor invited Jamiliah to take a **critical examination of the issue** by asking additional questions. She asked, "I wonder what it is about going to the prom that is so appealing to you, even if your experiences don't quite match up?" And later, she said, "Can we talk about what it means to have the 'right' or 'best' date for the prom?" and "Let's examine for a minute what it means to have the 'right' prom clothes, okay?"

Again, the point is to **invite examination of discourses that may be undercurrent to the problem or issue**. If you have previously used the term *discourse* with a client than that term can be used again here. Otherwise referring to discourses as "ideas out there" or "stereotypes" may be more client-friendly. In our example, the counselor continued with "Jamiliah, we've talked about 'popular girl' discourses and how these can sometimes make it difficult to figure out who you are and how you want to be with others at school. Do you think that this issue with the prom is influenced by some of the 'popular girl' discourses?" Alternatively, the counselor might have said, "Jamiliah, I wonder if some of those ideas about what's cool sometimes trick us into thinking that we have to do things that don't really feel 100% like who we are or what we want to do?"

Next, the counselor in this example asked questions that invited speculation about the **validity or voracity of the discourse,** particularly in regard to how the client wants to see herself or live her life. In our example after

Jamiliah agreed that maybe this issue about the prom is related to the "cool girls" discourse, the counselor said, "So, what is it about 'cool girls' that is so appealing?" "Who gets to choose what is cool and what isn't?"

Discourses can also be examined in light of the **extent to which they influence clients' decisions and identity conclusions**. These types of relative influence questions get at the notions of agency and choice. For example, the school counselor might ask Jamiliah: "What effects do you think that the 'cool girls' discourse has on your life?" Or "What does 'cool girls' get young women to think about themselves if they really don't want to comply? What if they want to do something different?" " 'Cool girls' ideas are compelling—everyone wants to have friends. But would it also be helpful to decide the extent to which you want 'cool girls' to influence your decisions—to figure out how much 'cool girls' you want in your life?"

Finally, it is always helpful to **invite clients to consider counter narratives** or other discourses that they want to influence the ways in which they live their lives. Dominant discourses can obscure competing ideas on offer and thus effectively limit one's ability to see options. Inviting clients to see other options can open up new possibilities and avenues for change. For example, the counselor could ask Jamiliah, "What other options are out there for kids who don't want to be 'cool girls'?" Or, "I have heard you speak about 'cool kids,' 'nerds,' and the 'Goth crowd.' Are there any other options for young women your age?" This line of questioning is intended to invite exploration into the **beliefs, values, and hopes** that the client has for her life. This important discussion invites the client to be agent in making decisions about her life and in the construction of identity—figuring out who she wants to be rather than aimlessly following ideas set forth by others.

PSYCHOEDUCATION

In a 1997 address to the World Bank Conference regarding worldwide poverty and injustice, UN Secretary-General Kofi Annan (1997) said:

> The great democratizing power of information has given us all the chance to effect change and alleviate poverty in ways we cannot even imagine today.... Knowledge is power. Information is liberating. Education is the premise of progress, in every society, in every family." (pp. 2–3)

Also, in the context of therapy, providing information and knowledge can affect change in powerful ways.

Conceptualized as a therapeutic intervention, *psychoeducation* is to provide information to clients—information related to a specific issue of concern or about mental health, more generally. Psychoeducation is often used in mental health and medical settings with families and clients who experience medical and mental health conditions such as stress and anxiety (see Breitborde, Woods, & Srihari, 2009; Kolostoumpis et al., 2015; Nezu, 2004; Top & Karaçam, 2016). In a range of studies, psychoeducation has been found effective in promoting treatment compliance; in relapse prevention; and in promoting social and global functioning, client satisfaction, problem-solving abilities, family support, and more generally a higher quality of life for people, particularly with clients who struggle with serious mental health challenges (Lyman et al., 2014). Psychoeducation is also widely used by counselors in school settings to promote mental health and wellness, academic success, study skills, and social justice awareness; to address risk-taking behavior and relationship violence; and to promote advocacy (Glodich, Allen, & Arnold, 2001; Hall, 2006; Kayler & Sherman, 2009; Portman & Portman, 2002). Psychoeducation can be delivered in a group venue or in an individual counseling session.

Photo 10.2

Many of us have had the experience of being offered information we were not interested in, not ready to hear, did not fully understand, or did not know how to use. We also have experienced receiving information from a "helper" when what we really wanted was an ear or support. Conversely, many of us, too, have had the experience of needing but not receiving straightforward information when we really needed answers. When deciding about the efficacy of using psychoeducation in therapy, then, we must consider the helping contract as well as the client's needs and wants. We might ask ourselves: Does this client want or need this information? Will he benefit from me providing the information, or would it be more helpful if he seeks out this information on his own? When you are not sure, it is always good to ask the client. And it is extremely important, of course, to respect your clients' decisions about whether they want the information you are offering. If we think the information we have is critical but the client does not seem open to hearing it, we can let him know that the information is available when he is ready or interested in hearing it.

When providing psychoeducation to clients, clinicians will want to be sure to give **relevant** information that is **appropriate** for their developmental, knowledge, language, and/or reading level, and **not to overwhelm** them with too much information. In general, it is important to avoid professional jargon and complex research articles, unless the client is already familiar with this format of information. There is a plethora of information on the internet available for all audience levels—and this can be good information for clients. But we all know that the internet also warehouses extensive information that is not credible. So, be careful to **read any information before giving it** to a client to assure that it is accurate and relevant. The keys are to keep it **simple**, **clear**, **relevant**, and **minimal**.

Finally, to go back to the point about whether it is best for the clinician to provide information to a client or it is best for him to access it himself, I want to emphasize the reminder not to let any over-zealous intentions interfere with the other important components of therapy, including agency and self-empowerment. Sometimes it is far more therapeutic to invite the client to gather information on his own rather than provide it for him. In these situations, the role of the counselor might be to point the client in the direction of appropriate information, removing barriers, or creating access points such as creating a username and password or talking through the process of using a local library. Counselors may also discuss the information that the client has accessed on his own, to help him fully understand or utilize it constructively in his life. Circling back to the point made by UN Secretary-General Kofi Annan, information is power, and power has the potential to affect change. It's important not to underestimate the role of psychoeducation in therapy, regardless of what clinical helping modality is being used.

PROBLEM SOLVING

Problem solving is an essential life skill, and research suggests that an ability to solve problems contributes to social competence and overall well-being (Bell & D'Zurilla, 2009; Nezu, 2004). Along these lines, Nezu (2004) identified a reciprocal relationship between stress, emotional well-being, and problem-solving abilities—when people are stressed, they are prone to emotional reactivity and in such a state, it is difficult to make good decisions. Poor decisions, in turn, often cause consequences that lead to additional stress and emotional instability. So, according to Nezu (2004), many mental health challenges can be understood as resulting from inadequate problem solving skills. Helping clients make decisions may have a buffering effect on stress and can lead to improved functioning and a reduction of emotional distress (Bell & D'Zurilla, 2009; Nezu, 2004; Overholser, 2013).

Problem solving as a clinical intervention refers to the cognitive behavioral process of helping a client discover adaptive solutions to difficult situations (Nezu, 2004). Keep in mind that problem solving and insight-oriented approaches to therapy are not categorically exclusive; problems are often more easily solvable when we better understand them. It is possible, however, that a client may have good insight into what is not working in his life or into the etiology a problem, but that insight many not easily translate into action or change. Most of us can attest to the fact that knowing why we have a problem does not mean that we know what to do about that problem. This is why therapists sometimes help clients engage in the process of problem solving.

The literature suggests that an ability to problem solve has two dimensions (Bell & D'Zurilla, 2009; Malouff, Thorsteinsson, & Schutte, 2007; Nezu, 2004). The first is **problem orientation.** This refers to how a person thinks about (i.e., the cognitive schema) and reacts to (i.e., how one copes) a particular problem. For example, a client can appraise a problem to be an insurmountable challenge or she can think about it as an obstacle that is solvable. Trusting in our ability to solve a problem actually helps us find solutions because, Nezu (2004) suggests, being positive fuels motivation. This is what Malouff et al. (2007) refer to as *problem-solving self-efficacy*. **Problem-solving style** refers to the ways in which one goes about solving problems. The most functional approach to solving problems, what Nezu (2004) calls "rational problem solving" (p. 4), entails a systematic implementation of problem-solving skills. Outcome research indicates that using a problem-solving approach that includes *both* a problem-solving orientation and problem-solving style can be very effective with clients who experience mental health and chronic medical challenges (Bell, & D'Zurilla, 2009; Malouff et al., 2007; Nezu, 2004; Overholser, 2013). This suggests that problem solving with clients should address helping them think carefully about their problems, consider various coping strategies, and include teaching them how to go about finding a solution.

There is a familiar saying that is often cited as a Chinese proverb and sometimes credited to Anne Isabella Thackeray Ritchie's 1885 novel, *Mrs. Dymond*, that goes something like this: *If you give a man a fish, he will fish for a day. But if you teach him how to fish, he will eat for a lifetime.* This saying, perhaps, best captures the spirit in which problem solving is conducted in therapy. It should never be a process of telling a client what to do. Instead, the position of a therapist in the process of problem solving is to act as a

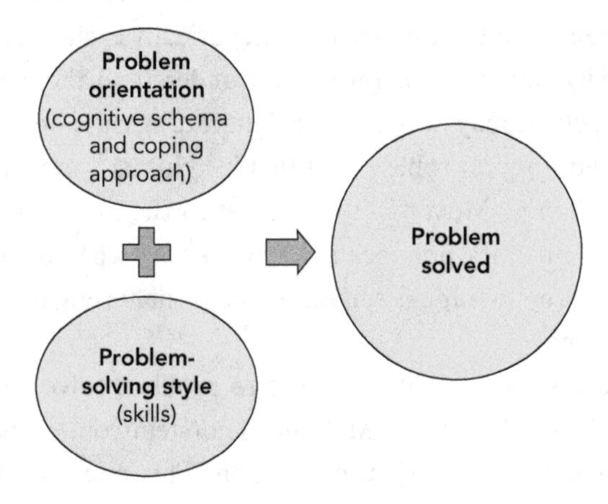

Figure 10.1 *The Two Components of Solving Problems*

guide in helping the client move toward an appropriate solution. The steps identified below are aimed at cultivating both problem orientation and style in problem solving.

PROBLEM-SOLVING STEPS

1. **Identify the problem.** People approach decision making in a variety of ways (Galotti et al., 2006), but being clear about the problem to be addressed is always the best way to start (Nezu, 2004). While it sounds easy, problems that are brought into therapy can be very complex—both for the client and for the therapist. When there is an overlay of emotion, understanding the problem can be even more complicated. The focus here, then, is to help simplify and isolate the key issues. While emotional reactivity can be helpful in spotlighting the nature of a particular problem, clinicians may need to help clients regulate their affect during the problem-solving process so that they remain calm, are not overwhelmed, and so that they can think clearly (Overholser, 2013). Helping a client see a particular problem as something that is external to himself (i.e., externalizing the problem; White & Epston, 2004) can tame emotional reactivity and position the clinician to be working with client against the problem. This also helps avoid blame and guilt, and instead encourages collaboration, engagement, and optimism.

2. **Gather information.** How individuals think about problems will determine how they go about solving them (Fink, Boersma, MacDonald, & Linton, 2012). Gathering as much information as possible about the problem and its context allows for a more complete picture of what has gone wrong and why, and it also may unearth possible solutions (Overholser, 2013). Therapists can facilitate this process by asking clients a series of open-ended, closed, and what, when, where, and why questions.

3. **Be aware of the goal.** A clear and realistic goal in terms of what the client hopes for in solving a problem should be the guide in determining how to go about addressing a problem (Nezu, 2004). When there are multiple problems or multiple parts of a problem, it is important to determine which ones need to be addressed immediately

and which ones can be ignored or can wait (Overholser, 2013). The point is that the counselor should be careful that the client doesn't take on too much at once, and he can help the client stay focused on issues related to the helping contract or goals in therapy.

4. **Generate solution options and evaluate each one.** The next step in the problem-solving process is to open up discussion about all of the solutions that are potentially available, and then to evaluate each option.

   First, the client and counselor should brainstorm potential solutions. In this process, it is important to encourage the client to be open to a variety of options, even if some of them don't seem realistic or viable—look for quantity rather than quality during the initial brainstorming process. Even if some of the choices are perceived to be suboptimal, knowing that there are options and choices to be made may be encouraging and, of course, sometimes unique and creative options offer clever solutions to tricky problems. Brainstorming a wide range of solution options increases the likelihood that the best solution will ultimately reveal itself (Nezu, 2004).

   It is sometimes appropriate for clinicians to offer additional options that the client may not have identified. Caution should always be used when adding new information like this, however, since the unequal power dynamic in the therapeutic relationship may sway the client in favor of something that the clinician has said, even if it is not what the client desires. So, if adding options to the list, the clinician should always present the information as a choice, invite the client to consider it carefully during the evaluation process, and indicate that the choice is up to the client. At the end of the day, it is the client who has to make and follow through with his decisions.

   The next step of the brainstorming process is to evaluate each option and cull the list of potential solutions down to the most viable options. Clients should be invited to consider both the short-term and the long-term effects of the options they are considering (Overholser, 2013). Because it can sometimes be difficult for clients to think through all of the potential consequences of the various options, especially if they feel stressed or hurried to act, the counselor should encourage thoughtfulness over speed in making a decision.

These open-ended questions may be helpful to both identifying and evaluating solution options:

- Have you had a challenge like this in the past? Do you know of other people who have had this problem? What solutions were used in those situations?
- Is this option likely to lead to the desired goal?
- Is this option realistic? Doable?
- How might this work in your situation? How do you think this decision would affect your relationship with X?
- Is this option consistent with the client's values and beliefs? How the client wants to live his life? How he wants others to see him?
- What are the potential consequences of each option?

5. **Choose a course of action and identify next steps to take action.** After a variety of options have been identified and evaluated, the next part of the problem solving process is for the client to make a decision. This decision must be made by the client, not by a family member, a loved one, or a teacher, and certainly not by the therapist (as tempting as this may be).

   Avoidance is a common obstacle to decision making (Nezu, 2004). Clients sometimes fail to understand that indecision *is* a decision, and they may need assistance and encouragement to actively make a decision. Even when clients are sure about a decision, they may be unsure how to implement it. Here clinicians can encourage clients to think in terms of small doable steps. They can also offer the opportunity for the client to practice or role play, they may need to help the client secure additional resources, and in some cases counselors may need to help a client draft a time-table for action.

6. **Follow up to assess success or to determine if alternative is needed.** The final step in the problem-solving process is to assess whether the selected solution has achieved the desired results (Nezu, 2004; Overholser, 2013). Remember that coming to a decision or identifying a solution to a problem is not the same thing as acting on that decision. This may be particularly true when a client is frustrated or embarrassed with their lack of success at initial attempts to implement something that has been agreed upon in therapy. So follow-up

is important. While this step may seem obvious, it can be easy to forget to check in with our clients at a later date.

When problem-solving efforts fail—for whatever reason—the counselor and client can easily return to the early steps in the decision-making process (Malouff et al., 2007). In fact, resolution may take multiple passes through the problem-solving process, and counselor may need to trouble-shoot next steps with clients at every step along the way (Malouff et al., 2007; Nezu, 2004). It is helpful for clients to understand that decisions made at one point in time need not be thought of as permanent and nonretractable—the process is dynamic and should also be flexible. Finally, we know that a strong therapeutic alliance is associated with client engagement in between-session activities (Owen, Quirk, Hilsenroth, & Rodolfa, 2012), so clinicians are reminded that clients may be more likely to follow through with identified steps when the therapeutic relationship offers them encouragement, support, care and empathy.

Although there are a multitude of models of problem solving, clinicians are cautioned against rigid adherence to any one process and to be careful not to rush through decision making too quickly (Overholser, 2013). When clients are fully engaged in the process of problem solving (rather than being told what they should do), they are more likely to feel responsible for the decisions that are made, to be accountable for their actions, and to feel good about their successes. Conversely, when clinicians are too forceful in offering solutions, they risk promoting inappropriate or untenable options, they may unwittingly take on some responsibility for the solution, they may encounter resistance or a lack of "buy-in," and they probably missed an opportunity to promote agency. Working *with* rather than *for* the client to solve a problem has the best potential for promoting agency and scaffolding change.

AFFECT REGULATION STRATEGIES

Affect regulation, as discussed in Chapters 4 and 5, refers to one's ability to effectively manage their emotional and behavioral responses in a situation that is triggering. As mentioned, this ability is connected to complex neurobiological processes that occur within the central nervous system. It is developed through experiences in life, particularly those in early childhood, in context of positive caregiver–child attachments and in the absence of chronic stress and trauma. As mentioned in Chapter 5, the process of self-regulation entails (a) having an awareness of potential triggers, (b) being aware of when one is activated, and (c) having the ability to calm oneself or return to homeostasis after emotional arousal. The self-regulation strategies we will discuss here, and which are outlined in Figure 10.2, are largely based on these premises. This model, offered by Gross (2008) and Gross and Thompson (2007), refers to each of the strategies mentioned as a point of entry into the process of affect regulation—it is not a sequential step model. These ideas can be easily and creatively translated into skills that can be taught or coached in therapy with children, adolescents, and adults.

Situation selection (Gross, 2008; Gross & Thompson, 2007) is the first entry point into emotional self-regulation that we will discuss. This has to do with *avoiding* a situation that triggers an emotional response. While the idea that one should avoid a situation that is emotionally triggered may seem obvious, it can be deceptively challenging. First, we must aware of what is triggering before we can avoid it. So, this strategy really begins with helping clients identify emotional triggers. A series of "activities" such as those outlined in dialectical behavior therapy (for more on this see Linehan, 2015; Rathus & Miller, 2015) and in cognitive behavioral therapy (for example, see Friedberg & McClure, 2009; Leahy, 2017) are often used to this end. Knowing what is potentially triggering, clients can begin to take charge of the decisions they make regarding where they are, who they are with, and what to avoid.

The use of situation selection as a strategy also implies that we have options regarding the situations we are in. While in theory we always have options, sometimes we do not see the options that lie before us. For example, a client may have never considered that he could leave an abusive husband. Another may not have thought about requesting to work in a different location. Of course, many of our clients find themselves in situations where options such as these are not possible. For many, options truly are limited. Many clients cannot afford to leave a job. They are not able to begin a new life as a single parent. So, while clinicians should always work to help clients see options, this must be done in a mindful and appropriate way. The work here, then, is to open up possibilities but also to help clients assess the viability of all options presented.

Clearly we are not always able or desire to avoid triggering situations. A second point of entry into self-regulation of emotion in the Gross model, then, is **situation modification** (Gross, 2008; Gross & Thompson, 2007). This refers to modifying rather than avoiding a triggering situation. The focus here is to manipulate the situation in some way so that the trigger does not have such a strong impact. For example, a client cannot, perhaps, avoid his job. But he can request that his desk be moved or that he work a different shift. Here again, this intervention is prerequisite upon client insight into what the trigger is, and requires an ability to come up with a feasible modification. The problem solving approach reviewed earlier in this chapter is an excellent way to help clients to explore modification options. In some situations, a clinician may need to step into the role of advocate to help clients establish appropriate modifications. For example, advocacy may be needed to address a bullying situation in a school. The school may need to be pushed to consider modifications such as moving a child from a classroom, making a change in a classroom environment, or instituting appropriate discipline policies.

Another strategy for managing emotion is **attention deployment** (Gross, 2008; Gross & Thompson, 2007). Here the client is taught ways to distract himself from the trigger in the moment. These strategies may include concentrating and, possibly, ruminating on something that is nontriggering, or using a basic distraction technique when one is triggered. Examples of these include teaching clients to count to 10 before responding, using a squeeze ball when they are upset, or engaging in self-talk to coach themselves through difficult times. Many CBT workbooks (e.g., Friedberg & McClure, 2009; Leahy, 2017) include a variety of strategies for helping clients manage their attention in moments of potential emotional triggers.

Intervening at the level of **cognitive change** is another point of entry in regulating emotion (Gross, 2008; Gross & Thompson, 2007). This approach calls upon the use of cognitive behavioral therapy (CBT) strategies. The idea is to regulate emotional reactivity by identifying, evaluating, and altering the cognitive appraisals that trigger strong emotional and behavioral responses. Here the counselor helps the client alter how he makes meaning of a situation or trigger. This change in meaning making then opens up new emotional and behavioral responses. CBT entails teaching clients to *catch* cognitive errors or distortions—I refer to these as "unhelpful thoughts" that trigger emotional reactivity—and to *check* whether these thoughts are valid and/or helpful.

When the client's cognitive appraisals are not helpful, the third step in this process is to help clients *change* how they interpret or makes sense of their experiences (Creed, Reisweber, & Beck, 2011). Here the idea is that when clients learn to think differently, they will feel and behave differently.

Although not part of the Gross and Gross and Thompson model, **distress tolerance** another strategy for managing unhelpful emotional reactions. This has to do with being able tolerate discomfort or withstanding adversity without acting impulsively (Bardeen, Fergus, & Orcutt, 2013; Rathus & Miller, 2015). Rather than changing the trigger or the cognitive appraisal of the trigger, as mentioned earlier, the focus here is on managing one's reactivity to a trigger in the moment (Stasiewicz et al., 2013). It is the ability to sit with discomfort or distress, and not feel compelled to respond. Distress tolerance requires having trust and patience that uncomfortable emotional sensations will resolve, and being able to refrain from action when uncomfortable. Distress tolerance is an important component of Dialectical Behavior Therapy [DBT] (for more on DBT see Linehan, 1993; Linehan, 2015; Linehan, Armstrong, Suarez, Allmon, & Heard, 1991; Miller, Rathus, Linehan, Wetzler, & Leigh, 1997; Rathus & Miller, 2015). In addition to the regulation strategies already mentioned, distress tolerance also includes implementing self-soothing strategies when in high-intensity situations, using rational thought to weigh the pros and cons in decision making so as to make pro-tolerance decisions, and engaging in mindfulness practice that includes accepting one's situation and recognizing that pain and discomfort are a natural part of life (Miller et al., 1997; Rathus & Miller, 2015). The practice of mindfulness will be discussed shortly.

Gross's concept of **response modulation** is the final affect regulation strategy recommended by Gross (2008) and Gross & Thompson (2007). This might best be thought of as prevention as it refers to engaging in on-going self-care practices—being healthy. Unlike the earlier strategies mentioned, this is work that happens in the landscape of life, rather than in the moment of distress. The focus here is on developing a healthy lifestyle, which then reduces one's vulnerability to triggers and emotional dysregulation. Wellness, according to Linehan (1993), refers to physical, emotional and social, spiritual, and intellectual health. A broad variety of strategies may be used here to encourage general wellness, including helping clients adopt healthy diet, exercise, and relaxation routines; avoiding stress when possible; engaging in caring communities; and engaging in activities that build self-efficacy and a

STRATEGY	DESCRIPTION
Situation selection	Avoiding a situation that triggers an emotional response. This requires awareness of what is triggering and an opportunity to avoid this situation. This typically includes identifying the trigger, identifying situation options, and assessing the feasibility of avoidance.
Situation modification	Altering a situation so that the trigger does not create emotional dysregulation. This typically includes identifying the trigger and problem solving to identify appropriate modifications. Advocacy may be required.
Attentional deployment	Distracting oneself from the triggering situation by refocusing, concentrating, or ruminating on something that is not a trigger and using distraction strategies.
Cognitive change	Altering one's cognitive appraisal of a situation or trigger so that it is not perceived in a way that elicits emotional reactivity. This entails identifying the thoughts that trigger emotional responses, evaluating the accuracy or utility of those thoughts in the moment, and altering those thoughts or thinking patterns so that they do not trigger a dysregulated emotional response.
Distress tolerance	Developing the ability to tolerate triggers and troublesome emotions without having to act impulsively on them. This includes distraction, cognitive change, self-soothing, rational decision making, and engaging in mindfulness practice.
Response modulation	Adjusting one's lifestyle so as to reduce everyday stress and strengthen one's reserve. This has to do with prevention.

Figure 10.2 *Affect Regulation Strategies*

Adapted from:

Gross, J. J. (2008). Emotion regulation. In M. Lewis, J. M. Haviland-Jones, & L. F. Barrett (Eds.), *Handbook of emotions* (3rd ed., pp. 497–512). New York, NY: Guilford.

Gross, J. J., & Thompson, R. A. (2007). Emotion regulation: Conceptual foundations. In J. J. Gross (Ed.), *Handbook of emotion regulation* (pp. 3–24). New York, NY: Guilford.

Photo 10.3

sense of competence. For some, response modulation may also include taking medication, if appropriate, or avoiding substances, if contraindicated.

MINDFULNESS

Reflecting on the passing trends of new words and concepts, Heffernan (2015) says that mindfulness is a hefty word that "can't readily be dismissed as trivia or propaganda" (n.p.). Indeed, the recent proliferation of mindfulness-based interventions that are used today in mental health and beyond is quite impressive. It seems more than just a passing trend.

With its roots in Buddhist traditions, mindfulness is a way of regulating one's attention so as to become aware of one's experiences in the moment, and doing so with curiosity, openness and acceptance (Eberth & Sedlmeier, 2012). It is about "paying attention in a particular way: on purpose, in the present moment, and non-judgmentally" (Kabat-Zinn, 1994, p. 4). Paradoxically, mindfulness is both simple and complex. Kabat-Zinn (1994), who is generally credited for bringing the Buddhist practice of mindfulness into the contemporary practice of mental health, suggests that mindfulness engagement is the ability to stop and be fully present in the moment. This includes being able to focus one's attention and concentration on one target, to let go and engage in a nonjudgmental presence with self and others, and to trust oneself and be self-accepting.

Some confuse mindfulness with being able to block out or empty one's mind of thoughts. On the contrary, mindfulness is about being aware of one's thoughts as they come and go, and accepting them without judgment (Siegel, 2010). Here, the emphasis is on awareness not diminishing or changing. Mindfulness is also not about being emotionless (Siegel, 2010). In fact, when we develop an awareness of all of our sensations, we may actually become more sensitive and emotional. The point is to not expend effort pushing away emotion, nor be critical of, rationalize, or try to make sense of one's emotions. Instead, mindfulness practice requires us to become aware of and just feel the emotions with unconditional acceptance. Siegel (2010) also points out that mindfulness is not about escaping pain, nor is it about seeking bliss. Again, it is about being with our sensations and experiences, whatever they may be. We do not need to withdraw from everyday life to engage in mindfulness practice—mindfulness is not about adopting a new religion, going on a special retreat, or spending an exorbitant amount of money. Instead, mindfulness is something that we can do in everyday life. In its most basic sense, mindfulness is about attending to our experiences in the moment (Siegel, 2010).

Mindfulness as a therapeutic modality is often used in the absence of adherence to its underlying Buddhist foundations and practiced using a variety of techniques, many of which have some meditative component (Academic Mindfulness Interest Group, 2006). Mindfulness-based stress reduction (MBSR) programs are roughly based on the Kabat-Zinn model include the three components of: mindfulness meditation, body scanning, and engaging in simple yoga postures (Eberth & Sedlmeier, 2012; Goldin & Gross, 2010; Keng, Smoski, & Robins, 2011). Beyond these programs, there are some therapeutic modalities that incorporate mindfulness practice as an integral part of the process of therapy—examples of this include mindfulness based cognitive therapy (for more on MBCT, see Kuyken et al., 2010; Ma &

Teasdale, 2004; Teasdale, Segal, & Williams, 1995; Teasdale et al., 2000) and Dialectical Behavior Therapy (for more on DBT, see Linehan, 1993; Linehan, 2015; Linehan et al., 1991; Linehan, Heard, & Armstrong, 1993; Shearin & Linehan, 1994). These modalities have a component of mindfulness that is conveyed in a skills-training approach. They focus on teaching clients how to develop intentional and nonjudgmental awareness of their sensations and typically include practice in listening and observing one's sensations and attending to basic movement and everyday bodily activities, including breathing and eating. Even without using these particular models and programs, many clinicians incorporate some mindfulness practices into their therapeutic work with some clients. For example, a clinician may teach a client who is anxious to become mindful of mounting worries or to become aware of thoughts that lead to unhelpful emotional responses or behaviors in certain situations.

Kabat-Zinn (1994) asserts that the development of a mindful practice requires commitment and vision, but, he adds, doing so will lead to a calmness and wakefulness to self, others, and our experiences in the world. Research suggests that mindfulness practice can be effective in improving pain, mood, anxiety, and overall general well-being (Academic Mindfulness Interest Group, 2006; Brown & Ryan, 2003). It has been found to increase metacognitive awareness, desensitize distressing emotions, and enhance attention, particularly when one is experiencing stress (Keng et al., 2011). Mindfulness-based stress reduction (MBSR) programs that are roughly based on the Kabat-Zinn model have been found to be effective in reducing stress and negative emotions, including depression and anxiety, improving concentration, and enhancing a sense of well-being (Eberth & Sedlmeier, 2012; Goldin & Gross, 2010; Keng et al., 2011). These programs have also been found to promote mental clarity and insight (Eberth & Sedlmeier, 2012), modify distorted thinking patterns, enhance emotional regulation (Goldin & Gross, 2010) and improve behavior regulation abilities (Keng et al., 2011). While mindfulness practices are widely circulated in professional trainings and nonprofessional venues such as the internet, they do require some specialized training to be used appropriately and therapeutically with clients. The reader is advised to receive additional training and supervision in the various components of mindfulness practice before implementing them with clients.

ADVOCACY

With some notable exceptions, much of what happens in the world of mental health therapy has to do with addressing challenges that are conceptualized to be within the individual. That is, addressing mental health challenges by changing how the client thinks, feels, or behaves. Yet we know that many clients grapple with issues that are external to them. For example, clients who identify in nondominant social groups often experience marginalization, disadvantage, and discrimination. As clinicians working with a wide variety of people, we know that systems of power and privilege influence the experiences of individuals, causing stress and pain that sometimes manifest in poor mental and physical health. When we are witness to these adverse effects of social forces, helping a client cope is often not enough. We may also need to "swim upstream" and address the cause of the problem. This is when clinicians become advocates.

As mentioned in Chapter 1, advocacy refers to acting with or on behalf of others at the individual, community, and/or societal levels to create change. This conception of advocacy is based on the work of Lewis, Arnold, House, and Toporek (2002), sometimes referred to as the *ACA advocacy competencies*, and was endorsed by the American Counseling Association in 2003 (Toporek, Lewis, & Crethar, 2009).

In the ACA advocacy competencies (Lewis et al., 2002), advocacy at the individual level focuses on providing direct support and services to clients with the aim of identifying and dismantling barriers that interfere with their success. This may include psychoeducation, counseling, planning, identifying allies, and making referrals when additional or unique support or assistance is needed. For example, at my university, faculty is required to contact the office of Affirmative Action when they have suspicions of bias, discrimination, or harassment. At the school and community level, advocacy may include working with community groups in identifying problems, gathering information or data, and engaging in goal setting, consultation, and collaboration with an eye on promoting social justice. An example of this is establishing a gay–straight alliance in a school. Advocacy at the societal or public level calls upon the clinician to collaborate with others at a broader level. Here the focus is on promoting justice by making policy and legislative change. For example, a clinician may become involved in advocating for legislation that affects marginalized populations, or attend rallies that speak out in support of certain issues.

Photo 10.4

Within each of these levels, Lewis et al. (2002) distinguish between working *with* versus *on behalf* of clients. Advocating *with* a client means that the clinician-advocate works collaboratively and, perhaps, behind the scenes to support the client in her efforts to advocate for herself. An important part of working from the *with* position is to assure that it is the client who makes the decisions and takes action. The clinician-advocate may help by identifying or clarifying the problem or issue, discussing the pros and cons of various courses of action, and discussing details regarding actions that have been decided upon (for example, who will do what, when, and how).

Acting *on behalf* is fundamentally different. Clinician-advocates who work *on behalf* of their clients are typically the ones who act, usually because for whatever reason, the client is unable to do so. It is important to emphasize, however, that working from an *on behalf* position still includes careful and collaborative discussion. The client still should be making decisions, as much as possible, about what the clinician-advocate can do for her. *On behalf* advocacy is not a license to go ahead and do whatever the clinician wants to do—it is an engagement with the client to make decisions together about what should happen and then for the clinician to do those pieces that are most appropriate for her to do.

These concepts of working *with* or *on behalf* of clients are very tricky and it is important to be aware of the potential disempowering effects of each. Funk, Minoletti, Drew, Taylor, and Saraceno (2006) point out that people with mental health and other disabilities are often presumed to "lack the capacity" (p. 71) to make their own decisions. This makes it easy for a clinician-advocate to make assumptions about the client's ability or inability to provide consent for the clinician to act on his behalf. Even in cases where there is clear consent from the client to work on his behalf, clinician-advocates should always consider the unintended consequences of doing so. It is possible that acting on behalf of a client may promote helplessness, diminish the client's sense of agency, or move in a direction that is not desired by the client. When advocating *on behalf* of a client, then, it is always important to find ways to ensure that the client is learning skills and able to assume agency where and when possible. Advocating *with* a client can also have adverse consequences. The clinician-advocate should always monitor the situation in which the client is advocating for himself to be sure that such actions do not expose the client to vulnerability and danger. Also, clinician-advocates can be helpful by providing clients who are self-advocates with sufficient information and support so that they are able to work from an informed position of strength.

Regardless of advocacy level and position, clinician-advocates need effective communication skills enabling them to speak up and to speak clearly, they need knowledge about the systems within which they are working and the particular issue that is being addressed, they could benefit from having information about appropriate models for creating institutional and system change, and finally, they need a good understanding of the culture of agency, school, community, or system where they are working (Beck, Rausch, & Wood, 2014). This work requires an abundance of patience—developing allies and partnerships can be long and slow work. It also requires vision and courage; advocates need to be prepared to be "fearless risk takers" (Beck et al., 2014, p. 372). Perhaps most importantly, being a clinician-advocate requires us to be fundamentally clear about our own personal biases and to have solid self-care practices in place. Counselors who need to step into the role of advocate should have additional training in leadership, advocacy, and systems change theories.

CHAPTER SUMMARY

We began this chapter with a discussion about how clinicians can work with clients who are in various stages of change. We then moved to the important work of helping clients think about discourses and situations that invite them into positions that are untenable. This work entails engaging in deconstructing conversations that help clients think critically about the ways in which they want to position themselves within various contexts to achieve certain goals. Next we moved to bringing information and skills into therapy through psychoeducation, problem solving, affective regulation strategies, and mindfulness practices. The final section in this chapter was a discussion about when counselors need to move into the role of advocates and offers a frame for how to think about this important work of advocacy. All of the strategies reviewed in this chapter are intended to be introductory—they are no substitute for the training that is required to put them fully into practice. The reader is encouraged to engage in further study of these practices prior to implementation and to use them under careful clinical supervision.

REFLECTION QUESTIONS

1. How does a clinician know when to use a problem-solving strategy versus an insight-oriented strategy, and might both of these disparate approaches be used at different times with one client? If so, what dictates what to use when, and why?

2. How might a counselor introduce ideas about discourses, positioning, and deconstructing practices into therapy without using hefty jargon and referencing abstract ideas?

3. How might a clinician encourage a client to use some of the emotional self-regulation strategies mentioned here if that client is not highly motivated or does not see that he has a problem?

CHAPTER 11

Basic Concepts for Leading Groups

Chapter Outline

INTRODUCTION

We begin our introduction with this simple working definition of group offered by Johnson and Johnson (2006): A group is "a number of individuals who join together to achieve a goal" (p. 5). This definition helps us conceptualize group work most broadly—a venue that includes more than one person. But, it also reminds us that the kinds of groups we are discussing here are groups that are conducted for a particular purpose—for achieving a particular goal. Group work can be powerful and dynamic, offering learning experiences that cannot happen in individual counseling sessions. This is largely because groups invite members to be exposed to feedback and learning opportunities that also arise from engaging with other group members. But, because groups are so complex, they are also challenging to lead. While many of the skills already discussed in this text are used by counselors running groups, additional knowledge and skills are also required for effective group leadership.

This chapter opens with a description of the various types of groups that are conducted by counselors, and then moves into basic group work concepts. Next, theories that help us make sense of the nuanced complexities of groups will be discussed. The chapter closes with a discussion of some specific skills that group leaders use for facilitating groups, regardless of group type. Keep in mind that this chapter offers just an introduction to the possibilities that can unfold when working in groups. As with most of the topics mentioned in this text, focused group work training and regular supervision is a must for running groups effectively.

GROUP TYPES

The Association for Specialists in Group Work (ASGW, 2000) describes these four categories of groups that are commonly used across a variety of therapeutic and related work settings: counseling, psychotherapy, psychoeducation, and task or work groups. Identifying these types of groups as distinct from one another helps illuminate the broad scope of opportunities that can be addressed through group work. However, Day (2007) points out that the "edges" (p. 9) between these types of groups often overlap. The distinctions between them often blurs in practice. For example, counseling, psychotherapy, and task groups sometimes include psychoeducation, and the differences between counseling and psychotherapy are often so unclear that the terms

Photo 11.1

are used interchangeably. Also, while these group types are named for their differing functions and each requires slightly different leadership priorities, the fundamental principles about group work and many group leader skills apply to all of these group types. We will get to group concepts and skills that are applicable across groups shortly, but first we begin by introducing the scope of group work practice that is available to clinicians in these different group types.

COUNSELING AND PSYCHOTHERAPY GROUPS

Psychotherapy groups (also called therapy groups) are typically aimed at addressing difficult, severe, and/or chronic personal and interpersonal mental health and related issues (ASGW, 2000). Their function is sometimes described as promoting "personality reconstruction" (Day, 2007, p. 9). These are the kinds of groups we often think of when we think about group therapy—they tend to encourage a high level of engagement and personal self-disclosure on the part of group members. Psychotherapy groups, for example, may be conducted for people who struggle with suicide ideation, complex trauma, addictions, or the perpetration of violence on others. They are often used in partial or full inpatient hospitalization programs.

Counseling groups also aim to address personal or interpersonal mental health challenges. But these types of groups tend to focus on transitory, episodic, somewhat common, and less chronic or severe stressors or challenges (ASGW, 2000; Day, 2007). They are used in a variety of settings and with clients who are likely to benefit from the opportunity to learn from others who face similar challenges. For example, counseling groups are often used by school counselors to address personal or interpersonal difficulties that appear to interfere with children's ability to be focused or appropriately benefit from instruction. Some school counselors conduct groups for children who have experienced loss, for children have difficulties regulating their emotions or behaviors, or for students experiencing changes at home. In a mental health setting, counseling groups may be used to address a variety of situations. For example, groups may focus on the needs of survivors of assault, for clients who live with loved ones grappling with substance misuse, or at-risk youth who have had run-ins with law enforcement.

PSYCHOEDUCATIONAL GROUPS

Like therapy and counseling groups, psychoeducational groups are often used to promote personal and interpersonal growth and development (ASGW, 2000). But, they tend to be more instructional and less interactive than counseling and therapy groups, and they are often used for prevention or remedial purposes. In fact, psychoeducational groups are sometimes referred to as "skills training" groups and they are often used by counselors to deliver a social-emotional curriculum in schools. Examples of psychoeducational groups in clinics or schools include groups that focus on helping individuals acquire skills for assertiveness, parenting, or for mediating conflict. Psychoeducational groups are different from counseling and therapy groups because they are structured, largely, around educational content. They often have a set of predetermined learning objectives and leaders tend to use planned activities rather than spontaneous interactions as the medium for engagement and learning (Chen & Rybak, 2004; Geroski & Kraus, 2010). Psychoeducation practices and other types of skills training modules are sometimes included in therapy and counseling groups when it is determined that some kind of structure is needed to accomplish certain group tasks or goals. Dialectical behavior therapy (DBT) (Linehan, 2015; Rathus & Miller, 2015) is a counseling modality, for example, that includes individual and group psychotherapy as well as skills training in its treatment protocol.

TASK OR WORK GROUPS

Task groups, also referred to as meetings, work groups, or teams, are another form of group work used by a variety of clinicians and other helpers, teachers, and administrators to accomplish a specific goal or task. For example, a clinician might be on a task force within his agency to address a particular issue or a teacher may engage in committee work in her school. Work groups tend to be time-limited and specific, with a focus on a particular task and identified goals (ASGW, 2000; Gladding, 2003). While there is overlap between psychoeducational and task groups, psychoeducational groups are typically designed for clients or students, they often focus on mental health or related issues, and they are frequently used for prevention. Task groups, on the other hand, tend to be more related to work issues (ASGW, 2000). A task group is something that a clinician might be involved in with his colleagues whereas a psychoeducational group is something that he might facilitate for his clients.

Photo 11.2

SELF-HELP GROUPS

While not identified as a unique group type by the Association of Specialists in Group Work, it is estimated that some 10 million Americans participate annually in some form of self-help group (Salzer, Rappaport, & Segre, 2001). Self-help groups tend to be leaderless groups that develop organically among people who experience similar challenges or difficulties. They offer appeal to individuals who tend to avoid traditional mental health services or do not want the help of a professional (Ben-Ari, 2002). Because these groups are leaderless, the role of clinicians with regard to self-help groups is often ancillary. She may help, for example, by providing initial organizational assistance, provide indirect consultation, or provide resources or referrals (Ben-Ari, 2002; Salzer et al., 2001).

BASIC CONCEPTS IN GROUP WORK

One of the things that makes group work so unique and such a powerful learning modality is that learning opportunities come from multiple and sometimes unexpected sources—from exposure to a variety of ideas and information offered by peers as well as the group leader, from having the opportunity to try things out, and from receiving in-the-moment feedback from various perspectives. Even in the most carefully planned and well-functioning groups, there will always be an element of the unknown; the leader can never fully control what group members say to each other and what they do in the group. These unplanned learning opportunities are part of why groups can be so potent. And they are also why groups can be so difficult to lead! Using a common language is how we will start to make sense of some of these group processes. Here we will discuss the concepts of group process, group content, and group dynamics.

GROUP PROCESS

The patterns of communication and interaction that happen within a group is what group workers call *group process* (Yalom, 1995). This refers to the ways in which group members interact with each other and with the group leader—all of which change over time and according to group type and topic. Group process is also sometimes referred to as the *how* of the group (Geroski & Kraus, 2010; Schwarz, 2002). That is, *how* members interact with each other and the leader, *how* members work together or not, *how* communication occurs, and *how* the work of the group moves forward—these are all a part of group process dynamics. The examples below show how behaviors, words, or actions in any one area or by any one group member affect the other members of the group. These are examples of group process dynamics.

- A student in a classroom makes disparaging remark to another student in the room. The teacher does nothing to intervene. This dynamic potentially inhibits other students from participating in class discussions.
- Clinicians and members of an advisory group were part of a work group assembled to study the climate of inpatient services at a large community mental health facility. At their first meeting, they were welcomed warmly by the director, thanked in advance for their commitment to the group and their work, and then asked to introduce themselves to each other and identify one thing they hoped to accomplish in their task. This way of starting the group was planned so as to engender a spirit of ease and appreciation at the start of the group.
- A new clinical social worker joined a seasoned colleague in facilitating a group for teen mothers considering giving their child up for adoption. The seasoned colleague, unhappy to have this inexperienced clinician as a coleader, often dominated the group discussions and decision making and sometimes contradicted what her coleader said in the group. Although members initially participated actively in the group, over time they seemed reluctant to share their experiences and voice opinions.
- Five fifth-grade children were participating in a changing families group conducted by a school counselor. The children were selected for the group because they all seemed to have difficulties this year in school. After 2 very quiet weeks in the group, a serendipitous thing happened. One child began to cry as she recounted the story of getting lost when walking to her father's new home. A second child spontaneously reached out toward this child and offered a hug. Seeing this, the counselor invited the others to reach out to the child who was in tears if they wanted, and almost immediately the girls were engaged in a group hug and sharing stories of parent visitation. In subsequent group meetings, the children talked more freely and openly demonstrated support to one another.

All of these examples of group process dynamics illustrate how the behavior of one member in the group can impact the behavior of others and, more generally, the functioning of the group. These examples also demonstrate how group leader behavior, including how he responds (or not) to group members, sets a tone in the group that impacts member decisions on if and how to participate. Ultimately, this, too, impacts what members will take from being in the group. While it could be argued that the group leader in this last group example above may have needed to do more sooner to affect the group climate, it is also important to remember that group process dynamics are a multifactorial; and some variables such as safety result from an experience in the group over time.

GROUP CONTENT

Group content is "what the group is working on" (Schwarz, 2002, p. 5)—the goals, tasks, subject matter, or purpose of the group (Geroski & Kraus, 2002; Gladding, 2003). It is what the group is about. For example, the work group mentioned above had as its goal to study the climate of the agency. The counseling group mentioned above with coleaders who did not work well together had as its goal to support these teens in their decision making regarding adoption. As these examples also illustrate, how and if a group realizes its content-related goals is a function of the group process dynamics. That is, the ways in which group members and leaders interact affects how and if the intended goals are eventually realized.

Most agree that group leaders must give dual focus and some sort of balance in attention to group process dynamics and group content goals in order for a group to function appropriately (Kraus & Hulse-Killacky, 1996). As Geroski and Kraus (2002; 2010) point out, however, the relative balance of focus on group process dynamics and content goals may vary by group type. For example, they point out that in psychoeducational groups in schools, the balance often leans toward group content goals. As a result, in these groups leaders often use executive function skills to manage the group process dynamics fairly tightly in order to keep the focus on content-related goals. So, group leader interventions in groups often vary according to the purpose of the group, the goals for members, and group type and setting.

GROUP DYNAMICS

Gladding (2003) points out social influences within a group compel members to act in certain ways. That is, being in a group causes people to adjust their behaviors, words, attitudes, and sometimes even their beliefs. These adjustments are largely due to group process dynamics (who else is in the group) and the purpose of the group. Some group members, for example, have concerns about how they might be perceived by others in the group. Others do not care about how others might perceive them. Some members bring experiences of being silenced or judged by others into their group experience and thus weigh their words carefully before putting them forward. We can see that some people embrace stepping into a position of power in some groups, while others may prefer to sit back and listen. And, of course, in any group there may be some members who are just not that interested in the content goals or other members of the group. These are just a few of the weighty factors that go into group member decisions regarding what they are willing to say and do in a particular group.

Interestingly, research suggests that when people are in a group with others they know, or with people they hold in high regard or respect, they feel more pressure and are more likely to be influenced by group dynamics than when in groups with people they do not know or identify with at all (Gladding, 2003). Bandura (1977) observed that people are easily influenced by those they perceive to have higher status, prestige, and power, and we know that this is a factor that is alive and well in many groups. Bandura also noted that people who have experienced rewards for emulating certain behaviors, who lack self-esteem, who feel incompetent, and who are highly dependent, are more suggestible than others (Bandura, 1977). So, these variables also factor into how one might participate in groups. Bandura's research intuitively makes sense—we care less about the opinions of strangers than we do of the opinions of people we respect or want to impress. It also helps us understand Raghubir and Valenzuela's (Raghubir & Valenzuela, 2010) finding that women and men are evaluated and rewarded differently in mixed-gender groups, reinforcing how group process dynamics are affected by the perceived social capital of various group members. All of these factors call attention to why careful and intentional leadership is necessary across group types. Group leaders have the task of facilitating group process dynamics in order to accomplish group content goals. So, when these underlying conditions and perceptions are at work in groups, they must be addressed by the group leader.

Photo 11.3 *Complex member interactions can create productive or unproductive group dynamics.*

THEORIES AND MODELS OF GROUP WORK

A number of theories are used explain the complex and powerful dynamics that happen when individuals join together in a group to accomplish a shared goal. Here we begin with a brief review of Irving Yalom's 11 therapeutic factors that make groups work (Yalom, 1995; Yalom & Leszcz, 2005). We then move to systems and stage theories of groups that provide insight into the complexity of group dynamics and how to most effectively navigate groups so that their intended learning objectives are achieved. Although many of these ideas were originally conceived for psychotherapy groups, it turns out that they are also applicable to the functioning of task and psychoeducational groups as well.

THERAPEUTIC FACTORS

As we examine Yalom's therapeutic factors for groups, it is helpful to understand Yalom's premise that a group is a social microcosm or recapitulation of the relationships that clients have with others outside of the group (Yalom & Yalom, 1990). That is, clients bring into the group their preexisting perceptions of self, their interactional patterns with others, and their understandings and experiences of the world around them (MacNair-Semands & Lese, 2000). Group members will behave in a group in the same ways that they behave outside of the group. This quickly gets complex, however, as we consider that each and every group member brings their own unique interactional patterns and understandings into the room at the same time. Yalom also believed that changes that result from interaction and feedback within the group are then transferred back into interactions outside of the group. This is what is meant by using the here-and-now of the group as a laboratory for learning and practicing new ways of being with others.

Yalom (Yalom, 1995; Yalom & Leszcz, 2005) identified a set of therapeutic factors—originally called curative factors—that are largely responsible for facilitating growth and change in psychotherapy groups. These factors relate largely to the ways in which leaders work with group process dynamics to influence goal attainment. Yalom's therapeutic factors are *universality* (recognizing that one's challenges are shared by others in the group), *altruism* (extending toward others), *cohesiveness*, the *installation of hope*, *imparting information*, *socialization*, *imitation*, *catharsis* (the release of strong feelings), *interpersonal learning* (gaining insights about oneself from feedback and interacting with others), a *corrective recapitulation of the primary family experience* (the reenactment of family dynamics in a corrective or healing manner), and *existential factors*, especially including accepting responsibility for one's decisions (Yalom, 1995; Yalom & Leszcz, 2005). Yalom hypothesized that the relative importance of these factors varies according to group type, group stage, and group membership (Kivlighan & Goldfine, 1991). The extent to which these factors contribute to the process of change in a group, however, depends on the group leader's ability to successfully activate and integrate them into the group process.

While there is some debate in the literature about the validity of Yalom's conclusions, these factors have been shown in multiple clinical and research studies to be the mechanisms of healthy and well-functioning groups (American Group Psychotherapy Association, 2007). According to Greene (2007), Yalom's core therapeutic principles and conceptualizations about the practice of therapy in groups "are among the best exemplars of a viable eclectic and integrative approach" (p. 552) to therapeutic group work. Greene's observation is shared by many; the voracity of Yalom's ideas about psychotherapy groups has generated innumerable research studies and commentary over decades of work in the area of group work. Although perhaps Irving

Yalom might disagree, Bernard et al. (2008) and others (e.g., American Group Psychotherapy Association, 2007) report that of all of the therapeutic factors identified above, group cohesion is the most significant for promoting growth and change in therapy groups. Group cohesion refers to the multiple alliances that exist in a group across members, member to leader, and intra-group alliances. Leader interventions that promote cohesion include encouraging a sense of belonging and acceptance among members of the group and promoting a sense of commitment or investment in the purpose of the group (American Group Psychotherapy Association, 2007). As we move through our discussion about group stage theory and group leader intervention skills, you will see this underlying influence of Yalom's therapeutic factors for effective group facilitation, regardless of group type.

SYSTEMS THEORY

Vetere and Dowling (2016) point out that "conceptualising people's difficulties in terms of patterns of interaction has been one of the most productive contributions of systemic thinking to the understanding and reconstruction of mental health problems" (p. 3). Systems theory, then, focuses on the ways in which individuals within various social systems or groups (such as a family, a community, or any other organized group) are interconnected, and how the functioning in one part of a group system affects other parts (Connors & Caple, 2005). Applying systems theory to group work illuminates how the interactional styles and the social and emotional needs of individual group members (and the group leader) influence group dynamics and goal attainment (Toseland & Rivas, 2005).

In systems theory, the complexity of groups is described as a collection of parts that interact together so as to operate as a whole (Schwartz, 2002). Within a group, all of the members are ***interdependent***—meaning, as mentioned, that each member plays a role in group functioning and what happens with one member effects other group members (American Group Psychotherapy Association, 2007; Bernard et al., 2008; Connors & Caple, 2005). The image of a body is sometimes used as an analogy for this notion of interconnectivity within groups. The body, we know, exists as a total of all of its organs, with each organ relying on and driving other body parts. For example, the heart depends on the lungs to pump oxygen into the blood. If the heart or the lungs inhibit the appropriate flow of oxygen, all of the body organs are potentially compromised—some more than others. The parallel

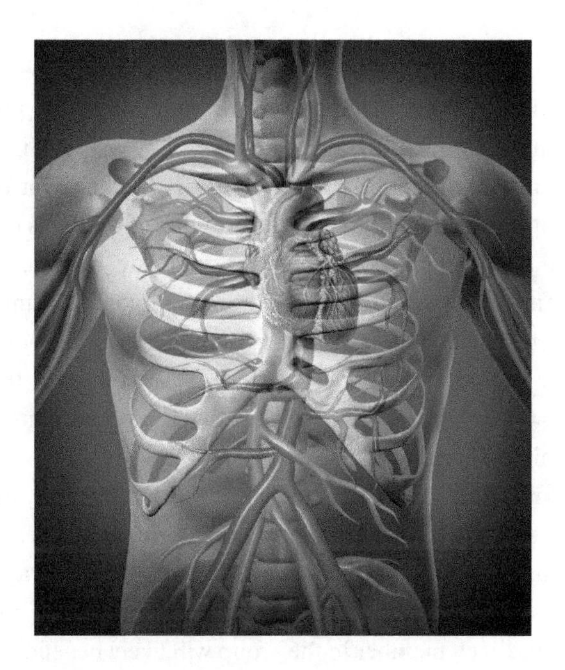

Photo 11.4

in groups is that individual members are always making decisions about how to participate in the group, based on how others in the group are behaving or functioning. If one group member is tangential, stops working, or is over-bearing or aggressive, the other group members will adjust their behavior accordingly. Some may respond, for example, by also becoming tangential or they may also stop working. Others may vie for power, try to repair the damage, take on the responsibility of task accomplishment, or shrink into the corner and avoid being drawn into the group in an active way.

This brings us to the concept of ***equilibrium***—a term that is sometimes used to describe the ways in which groups move toward order and stability (Day, 2007; Toseland & Rivas, 2005). This concept suggests that group members tend to organize themselves in stable and repeating patterns of behaviors. These patterns inform roles that members assume in the group; boundaries, alliances, and communication patterns between members; and the exchange of information and feedback within the group. Within this homeostasis the group moves toward resolution of its required tasks. This also means that groups tend to favor adaption over confrontation—particularly in early stages of group development. Group members will look for ways to adjust, accommodate, or compensate when one or a few members in the group are not functioning properly or not conforming to group norms. With an implicit goal of maintaining homeostasis, however, group norms can prohibit members from taking risks, growing and changing. For example, if one member dominates the group, others become voiceless. If the behavior of one group member cannot be accommodated in the group or if it affects others in ways that the group cannot manage, the whole group can become consumed by this problem and adequate group functioning and goal attainment are compromised. So, the concept of equilibrium is important for group leaders as it emphasizes the importance of every member's experience in the group and illuminates how destructive interpersonal dynamics can significantly alter group functioning (Connors & Caple, 2005).

A final point related to systems theory and using the body as an analogy for a group has to do with the importance of overall wellness to maintain proper body functioning. This is also true in groups. When a group is well taken care of—facilitated well by the group leader—the goals are likely to be accomplished and each member in the group will likely benefit. In fact, Kraus and Hulse-Killacky (1996) tell us that group leaders can evoke beneficial harmony in groups by maintaining an appropriate and flexible balance between group content goals and group process dynamics. Achieving this important balance is particularly important in times of conflict in the group.

In summary, systems theory reminds us that the power of groups lies in the ways in which individual members contribute to the growth and change in others, and that this learning happens when the group functions well as a whole. The extent to which individual members learn and contribute to the learning of others and the ability of a group system to function well is dependent on the careful facilitation of the group leader. The skills reviewed in the previous chapters in this book as well as those introduced in final section of this chapter are the important skills that leaders use to facilitate these dynamic and nuanced processes.

GROUP STAGE THEORY

Many group leaders suggest that group dynamics pass through a somewhat predictable process from the start of the group until the end (Birnbaum & Cicchetti, 2005; Tuckman, 1965; Tuckman & Jensen, 1977). These observations have led to the development of stage theories of group development. Stage theories propose that in order to develop appropriately toward identified group

Photo 11.5 *The balancing act of group leadership.*

goals, groups—group members and groups as a whole—must navigate the inevitable challenges that present themselves at various times. Tuckman (1965) and Tuckman and Jensen (1977) offer a model capturing this progression of group development that is arguably still the most widely used stage model of groups in the literature. The stages identified in the Tuckman model are: *forming*, *storming*, *norming*, *performing*, and *adjourning*. Tuckman (1965) proposed that movement through these stages is largely unavoidable and also necessary in fully functioning groups. We will review these stages here. Table 11.1 at the end of this discussion offers a concise description of each stage along with some basic suggestions regarding leader direction strategies in each stage.

FORMING

The first stage in the Tuckman model is called *forming* (Tuckman, 1965; Tuckman & Jensen, 1977); Tuckman initially called this stage *testing and dependence*. When in the forming phase, group members become oriented to the purpose or task of the group, its relevance to them and their own personal situations, and they begin to develop ideas regarding what is needed for task completion or goal attainment. It is a time when members begin to get to know each other and the group leader.

During this time, members observe each other and the developing group dynamics, and they begin to make decisions about their own investment and involvement in the group. They may be eager to connect with others in the group and even look for opportunities to do so. But also in this early stage, members may have concerns about how they will be perceived by others in the group. In general, in the forming stage, members tend to engage in safe patterned behaviors, are reluctant to take risks, and tend to look to the group leader for guidance and direction. According to Birnbaum and Cicchetti (2005), problems can arise in this initial stage when members perceive the group to be meaningless, when there is a lack of focus, when the members do not understand the group—how the group activities or agenda items are related to the purpose of the group, and also when members are encouraged to engage in conversations that are premature or perceived to be too personally risky at this early stage of group development.

Group leaders are tasked with a variety of responsibilities to get the group started in this early stage. These begin with setting up the physical environment and working to create an atmosphere of safety (Alvarez, 2003). Because safety comes, in part, from clarity about the purpose of the groups, leaders clarify expectations, outline group norms and rules, talk about what will happen in the first and subsequent group meetings, and clarify to members their own role as the group leader (Birnbaum & Cicchetti, 2005; Gladding, 2003; Toseland & Rivas, 2005).

In terms of group norms and rules, it is appropriate for group leaders to engage members in a discussion around group rules in order to set a collaborative tone to start off the group (Alvarez, 2008). There are some rules than may need to be introduced by the leader if they do not emerge organically during these early conversations—rules related to confidentiality and some basic ground rules such as asking members to turn off their cell phones. Gladding (2003) points out that leaders may also need to establish norms related to group participation so as to prohibit one or a few members from monopolizing the discussion, manipulating others, or being disengaged. These behaviors, if not managed early in the group, could set a tone that inhibits full participation from others. Leaders in this initial stage will need to be patient as members develop comfort, and they may also need to be active, as mentioned, in setting limits or structuring norms when necessary during this first stage of the group (Gladding, 2003; Toseland & Rivas, 2005).

An important group leader task for the early stages of any group is to promote positive interactions among members and address any apprehension they may have about the group (Gladding, 2003; Toseland & Rivas, 2005). To help members get to know each other, leaders should to attend to introductions, perhaps using a predictable round-robin structure so that members have a prompt for what to say and can anticipate their turn for speaking. This limits unpredictability and also sets a norm that everyone will say something. Additionally, offering guidance, instilling hope, and promoting universality, altruism, and cohesion among members are important early group stage leader tasks in early stages of group development (Kivlighan & Goldfine, 1991; MacNair-Semands & Lese, 2000). If members are already known to each other prior to the group session, subgroups—smaller and exclusive groups within the larger group—can threaten the development of group cohesion (Gladding, 2003). So, leaders should be prepared to attend to this early on by encouraging cross-group interaction and by setting norms related to inclusion. For example, if two work groups come together to form a task group, the members of each subgroup are likely to be more comfortable with one another and may resist reaching out to the other group members. The group leader may ask or assign these members to work with others that they do not know in the group.

STORMING

Storming is the defining characteristic of this next stage in the model of group development (Tuckman, 1965); this is a time of conflict. Storming happens because members have used the relative comfort of the forming period to begin to express themselves and to bring their own individuality into the group. When they engage more openly, competing interests and patterned interactions may begin to surface among group members. For example, a member may express a particular opinion that is insulting to another group member, or one member may be quiet and take few risks even if clearly upset with another group member. In this storming phase, we may see Yalom's point that the group is a microcosm of other social relationships—the idea that members bring a recapitulation of their relationships with others into the group (Yalom & Yalom, 1990).

In storming, group members begin to assess others and make decisions about asserting their own needs in the group. According to Gladding (2003), this initiates a process of *integrating with* and *differentiating from* others in the group. By this, Gladding suggests that the personal needs of group members (differentiation) may come in conflict with the competing need or expectation to integrate into the group. Members may also try on new behaviors and new roles or ways of interacting in this process. As a result of these dynamics, members may become more assertive, vie for a position of relative power, or may become defensive or argumentative. Others may feel anxious, defensive, or resistant to particular group members or to the general tasks of the group. Ironically, the storming stage may mark a time of deeper investment in the group, as group members may perceive that that they no longer need to be overly polite with each other and they become more honest and assertive. It is as if members have come to the point where they feel safe enough to be more authentic in the group (Harris & Sherblom, 2005). All of these storming dynamics arouse conflict among group members, as mentioned, and they also may inhibit the ability of the group to engage effectively with group tasks—ideas, structure, and direction (Toseland & Rivas, 2005). The group leader can easily become the target of the turmoil within the group during storming, as questions often arise from members about structure, power, and control of the group (Gladding, 2003). All of these behaviors are normal during this stage of group development.

As the expression goes, "the only way *to* is *through*"; most agree that the storming phase is necessary for the development of subsequent cohesion and cooperation in the group (Harris & Sherblom, 2005). According to Kurland (2006), "The ability to appreciate and accept conflict, to be more comfortable with diversity and the expression of difference are essential to good group work practice" (p. 16), and this is particularly true when muddling through the conflicts of the storming phase. The task of group leaders in this phase, then, is to help members resolve the disagreements and conflicts, engage with each other authentically and respectfully, and work together on group tasks or goals as much as possible. Leaders who are uncomfortable with this level of conflict may attempt to ignore, minimize, or avoid it. These responses will probably not work in resolving the conflict and may prohibit the group from moving on to productive dynamics and task completion.

Navigating this period of storming, then, means that group leaders will need to listen carefully and respectfully to the perspectives of *all* members in the group. It is the leader's job to insure sure that everyone has equal access to group process and goals, and that everyone has a voice in the group. Here the point is to support all members so that they perceive the group to be safe. The skill of leveling, mentioned in the next section, is particularly important in securing space for all members and equalizing power in the group (Gladding, 2003). Leaders can also encourage and model attentive and respectful listening and clear and direct communication, they can coach members to interact in ways that are open, nonjudgmental, and respectful of others, and they can guide group members so that the feedback they offer to others is both appropriate and respectful (Toseland & Rivas, 2005).

Another important leader intervention used in storming is to make *process comments*—recognizing and naming the conflict when it surfaces in order to help members better understand the new group dynamics that have arisen in this phase of the group (Toseland & Rivas, 2005). For example, upon noticing members of a therapy group become increasingly contentious with one another, the leader used this process observation: "It seems that we are at the place in this group now when many are becoming more comfortable with each other—comfortable enough, even, to disagree with each other. I am noticing that the conversation is starting to get very heated."

Group leaders can also call upon group rules to help members engage with each other in respectful and productive ways. For example, the leader in the group above reminded members about the earlier agreed-upon group rules "I think it is a good idea for us to pause a minute here," she said, "and take a minute to review the ground rules we decided on weeks ago. We have them posted on the wall over here," she added, pointing specifically to the rules about respect and not dominating the discussion in the group. "I want to be sure that we find a space in this group for everyone's voices, so I may sometimes ask one person to pause and I may invite others into the conversation. Also, let us be sure that we are using I-messages when offering feedback to others, as we agreed. And finally, I want to remind everyone to abide by our rule of being 'assumption-free' with each other." Later, the leader used leveling, which will be discussed later in this chapter, to help equalize the air time in the group: "Todd, let me interrupt a minute. I want to offer a space to someone who has not yet had a chance to comment on this before we move ahead. Francisco, would you be willing to weigh in on this?"

NORMING

When the conflicts begin to resolve in the group, a sense of cohesion often follows. This characterizes the next stage of group development called *norming* (Tuckman, 1965). In this phase, members begin to extend toward each other—they demonstrate an appreciation for each other's unique contributions and perspectives, subgroups or cliques typically dissolve, the group is able to refocus on its intended goals, and there often is a sense of support among members and cooperation in the group (Tuckman, 1965). Groups at this stage may develop boundaries around the group, blocking outsiders, and forming a coalesced sense of "we"—they may even become somewhat insular.

In therapy groups, honest personal sharing and openness becomes the new norm for the group at this time. In nontherapy groups, an open exchange of opinions and ideas emerge. In both types of groups, members become more willing to take risks and may engage in personal self-disclosure. Participants become more invested in the group, members communicate more openly and freely between each other, and norms around cooperation and a shared purpose are established to preserve a sense of harmony.

One role of group leaders in the norming phase is to monitor what is happening in the group. Here the leader wants to be sure that the new norms in the group are understood and shared by all group members (Gladding, 2003). The norm of respecting the views of others should always be implicit. If this is not happening, it is the responsibility of the leader to insure respectful engagement. For example, in a psychoeducational group that had been together for some time the leader noticed that one member tended to dominate the group. While there was no apparent conflict around this, it seemed that a norm had developed whereby the other members quietly waited this person out. The group leader decided to intervene by starting the next group with a more explicit discussion about norms and respect. He engaged members in a discussion about the importance of respecting one's own space in the group and he encouraged members to speak up if they felt that the norm of shared group time was not happening. Next, the leader introduced a model of how to engage in respectful feedback exchange and invited members to practice these skills. Learning how to offer feedback to others was also consistent with the content goals of the group, which focused on developing interpersonal skills.

The norming phase of the group begins a new phase of group functioning. As the group is able to focus on its intended objectives, the group leader can encourage and reinforce group member's efforts, promote clear and direct communication between members, and empower members to achieve the goals for the group (Gladding, 2003). To these ends, the skills of drawing out, cutting off, and leveling—all of which are discussed in the next section—are typically used to promote this level of engagement. Leaders may also introduce new content or activities within the group at this time (Toseland & Rivas, 2005) if appropriate to the direction of the group.

PERFORMING

As norms for engagement and task completion are established, the group is able to move into the *performing* stage (Tuckman, 1965). This is also sometimes also referred to as the *working stage* (Day, 2007; Gladding, 2003). In performing, members are actively engaged and invested in the purpose or task of the group, and thus this becomes the focus (Day, 2007; Gladding, 2003). Groups in the performing stage tend to be very productive (Tuckman, 1965)—the group functions with a sense of competence that was not present during the earlier stages of the group. The purpose or goals of the group consume the energy of group members. A sense of trust and safety invites a level of risk taking so that we often see members trying out new behaviors and learning from each other. Conflicts that arise in this stage are typically negotiated and resolved within the group.

For group leaders, interventions tend to focus on encouraging interpersonal process dynamics that facilitate task attainment. That is, leaders monitor member's adherence or commitment to the decided-upon norms and they may help members renegotiate rules and norms, if needed (Gladding, 2003). At this time, leaders may introduce new group tasks, if that is the nature of the group, but largely the focus is on encouraging and reinforcing group member efforts and contributions so that the group can effectively reach its goals or complete its intended purpose.

ADJOURNING

The ending of the group is typically signaled when tasks of the group or the group goals have been adequately met; this phase is called *adjourning* (Tuckman & Jensen, 1977). Interestingly, the adjourning stage was not included in the original Tuckman model, but is now included in virtually every group stage theory model that is used in the field. Gladding (2003) pointed out that in some groups, this final stage is embraced as a cause of celebration where members feel energized, hopeful and inspired. In other groups, members may feel indifferent, or even sad about the disbanding of the group. It is not unusual for members of some groups to want to avoid discussions about the group ending. They may express denial, or feel abandoned, disappointed, unsure, and angry as the group comes to an end (Toseland & Rivas, 2005). This may be especially true for members who were particularly engaged in the group and who took many risks. Group leaders, too, of course, may have mixed feelings about the ending the group—they may feel pride, worry, or even relief! Regardless of how the group leader may feel about the adjournment phase of the group, it is an important phase that needs careful leader planning and facilitation skills. In fact, Gladding pointed out that preparation for ending a group is so important that it really "begins in the planning stage" (Gladding, 2003, p. 180).

The tasks of the leader in this stage are threefold: First, to assess the extent to which the group was successful in meeting its intended goals (Toseland & Rivas, 2005). Second, leaders may need to help members to think about and, perhaps, articulate how their experience and learning that resulted from being in the group will transfer into their everyday lives outside of the group—sometimes referred to as the *transfer of learning* (Gladding, 2003; Toseland & Rivas, 2005). Leaders can promote these discussions by asking members to recall any critical incidents or experiences they had in the group, reflect on changes resulting from having been a member of the group, and, if appropriate, provide an opportunity for members to rehearse new skills learned in the group (Gladding, 2003), or they can simply talk about how the accomplished task will be used in the future. The final task for leaders in this stage is to bring closure to the group. In counseling and therapy groups this typically includes acknowledging the contributions of each member of the group and resolving any residual concerns regarding the interpersonal relationships that were part of the group process (Toseland & Rivas, 2005). Resolving any outstanding conflicts is also important in work groups, especially when members of these groups are likely to continue to work with each other in other tasks in the future (Keyton, 1993). Finally, Gladding (2003) emphasized the importance of structuring an opportunity for saying good-bye or in some way expressing farewell in the final group meeting.

Table 11.1: Tasks for Leaders at Various Group Stages

GROUP STAGE	DESCRIPTION OF STAGE	LEADER TASKS
Forming	Members are getting to know each other and the leader and getting oriented to the tasks of the group.	• Introductions, welcomes, setting members at ease • Facilitate connections between members • Review group tasks and goals • Establish rules • Set limits, if necessary
Storming	Conflicts emerge as members are more comfortable, begin to be honest, express themselves, and create an identity for themselves in the group.	• Provide space for all voices to be heard • Assure safety • Bring attention to interpersonal and group process dynamics • Use process observers and facilitate feedback exchange, if appropriate
Norming	As the group members express themselves and open dialogue begins, there is a new process of creating norms. Cohesion and mutuality develop, and the interpersonal dynamics become cooperative and supportive among members.	• Encourage discussion and renegotiation of rules, if needed • Monitor member commitment to the new norms • Encourage member participation • New content or tasks (related to the group goals) may be introduced
Performing	The new group norms give way to productivity, and the tasks of the group become the focus of the group.	• Continue to monitor norms and encourage participation and interpersonal engagement • Encourage members to use resources and make decisions • Offer support and resources as needed • Engage members to resolve conflicts, if necessary
Adjourning	Group tasks or goals are met. Learning is summarized, and members consider the transfer of learning to outside the group.	• Help members summarize and reflect on learning • Encourage transfer of learning • Address any unresolved issues • Lead the group in a process for expressing farewells

Based on the work of Tuckman, B. W. (1965). Developmental sequence in small groups. *Psychological Bulletin, 63*(6), 384–399. https://doi.org/10.1037/h0022100

A quick perusal of the literature around models of group development indicates that they have also been applied to the variety of group types (Berman-Rossi, 1993). Interestingly, Birnbaum and Cicchetti (2005) proposed that groups pass through a miniature parallel process of these stages within each group session (Birnbaum & Cicchetti, 2005). That is, each time a group meets, there is a period of preparation, a middle, and an ending phase. These mini stages, according to these authors, parallel the very same stages that are thought to characterize the life span of groups described in group stage theories. Of course, group processes are not be as linear and foreseeable as these models would suggest. Harris and Sherblom (2005), for example, caution that not all groups follow these stages and not always in the order expected. Toseland and Rivas (2005) point out that groups are often cyclic, moving from one stage to the next and then back again through earlier stages. Regardless, these models do describe group phenomenon that has been observed by many and across multiple group types, offering some degree of face validity. Stage model theories of groups are helpful because they offer a general sense of how a group is likely to develop and grow over time, enabling leaders to anticipate and respond to challenge more effectively.

GROUP LEADER BASICS

Groups offer a good venue for working on a variety of work and/or educational tasks, to achieve therapeutic goals, to learn from others, and to practice new interpersonal behaviors. All of these things are possible if the group has a skilled leader. To work with the kind of intentionality that is required to run a group properly requires careful study of the tomes of research and practice-based literature on facilitating groups. It also requires advanced group training opportunities and practice under supervision. Below are some general principles gleaned from this literature and applicable to a wide variety of group types. This chapter, however, is in no way intended to provide adequate training for effective group leadership; it is merely offered as an introduction.

GROUP PLANNING

Successful groups do not just happen—they are built on clear intentions and they are carefully planned in advance (Corey & Corey, 2006; Geroski & Kraus, 2010). Group planning starts with having a **clear set of goals** (American Group Psychotherapy Association, 2007; Bernard et al., 2008). The goals of the group

Photo 11.6

dictate the type of group that will be conducted and the leadership style that is required. Some groups are formed to address a specific identified problem, others to avoid potential problems, and still others to accomplish a specific task, impart certain information, or to provide an opportunity for socialization and interpersonal learning. Whatever the purpose of a group may be, its purpose is articulated as its *goal*. Group goals should be articulated in terms of what members will gain from being in the group; the outcome expectations for the group (Geroski & Kraus, 2010). In addition to having a clear set of goals, the structure and framework of the group—where, when, and any specific requirements or rules regarding participation, also need to be made clear at the start of the group (American Group Psychotherapy Association, 2007).

Clarity around the intention of the group will determine group **membership**—members should be invited into groups that are relevant to them and their needs. A number of questions can guide member selection for a particular group. First, will this potential member's challenges or needs be addressed adequately in this particular group (Toseland & Rivas, 2005)? Second, does this potential member have an appropriate level of knowledge and skill to be successful in this group (Schwarz, 2002)? These two issues get at the points that a member is appropriate for a group if it is in alignment with his therapeutic needs (in a therapy or counseling group) and if he has the ability to function productively in that group.

Clearly, group members benefit when their personal needs are congruent with the group goals (American Group Psychotherapy Association, 2007; Bernard et al., 2008), but the question also arises as to how much members need to be alike in order to benefit from the group? This is a question about group member *homogeneity*. Are similarities, particularly in regard to gender, culture, ethnicity, problem or sexual orientation, personality style and/or problem constellation, important in member selection (Toseland & Rivas, 2005)? Groups thrive when members bring to them diverse perspectives and skills, when they display some level of openness to other perspectives, and are generally interested in personal learning and change (Schwarz, 2002); membership diversity can increase learning opportunities for all group members. But when group members are too different from each other, it may be challenging to develop common goals or to facilitate group process across wide expanses in experience, knowledge, and personality style. Individual member needs may not be addressed. So the question of group homogeneity is an important one to consider when determining who will be in a particular group.

Another issue regarding membership is the extent to which potential members *want* to be in the group and are *able* to contribute and grow in meaningful ways. The American Group Psychotherapy Association (2007) asserts that therapy groups are helpful for clients who display interpersonal and intrapersonal difficulties and who are motivated and interested in being part of a group. Ideally, however, potential group members are also psychologically minded, are open to engaging in personal self-disclosure, and have some interpersonal skills (American Group Psychotherapy Association, 2007). When members are ill suited for a particular group, they may be unfairly asked to meet inappropriate expectations and their presence in the group may have unwanted and detrimental consequences for others in the group as well. The American Group Psychotherapy Association (2007) recommends that clients who present with anti-social tendencies or excessive anger may not be appropriate for group work unless the group is specifically designed for individuals who struggle with these issues. In general, if potential members are not able to engage interpersonally with others and have a very low capacity for insight, a group therapy format may not be appropriate. This is why **screening** all potential members prior to the first meeting is particularly important in the case of therapy and counseling groups. This screening process should afford group leaders and potential members the opportunity to decide appropriate fit.

Another issue to consider when thinking about group membership is the **format** of the group. *Closed groups* are those that maintain membership across a prescribed period of time. *Open groups* invite members to come and go freely without a firm commitment to regular attendance. Membership in closed groups should be based on one's ability to make a full commitment to be in the group across time, as irregular attendance can be very disruptive to group process in closed groups (Schwarz, 2002).

When and where a group is conducted—the **venue** of the group—is another important detail relevant to group planning. The physical environment—seating, space, room size, furniture, and so on—can affect group climate and goal attainment (Toseland & Rivas, 2005). For example, a task group may need tables, desks, and white boards to help members participate in brainstorming, and so they can create lists and write things down. A support group may do best in a private setting with comfortable seats and, possibly, dim lights. Therapy and counseling groups have a similar requirement of needing to offer members both comfort and, in many cases, some degree of anonymity to extend them privacy from outsiders not participating in the group. Additional consideration must also be given to some of the unique needs of the population served by the group. A group designed for single parents, for example, must be conducted at a time when these parents do not have childcare responsibilities unless childcare options are specifically addressed in the planning of the group. A work-related task group is probably going to be conducted during the workday. The point, of course, is that groups need to be held in settings and at times that suit their purpose and that are appropriate to the situations and needs of the group members.

The **number** of participants in a particular group is also an important variable to be considered in the planning phase of a group. Having too many people in a group may affect task engagement and render the group unproductive (Schwarz, 2002). For example, a grief and loss group of twenty would be very difficult to manage in a way that provides adequate time for all members. High numbers may inhibit the formation of support across members, which is typically one of the goals of this type of group. However, a psychoeducational group that focuses largely on imparting information may not be hampered as much by large numbers. In these groups, the leader can break the group into smaller subgroups if that is needed for some group tasks or activities within these larger groups. In short, groups should be based on practical constraints such as the purpose of the group as well as the size of the space, schedule, availability, etc. of the group venue (Toseland & Rivas, 2005).

Hagedorn & Hirshhorn (2009) assert that experiential activities can be a good way of engaging clients, particularly clients who are in the precontemplation and contemplation stages of change. The scope of potential **experiential activities** that can used in group work is quite broad, and includes psychodrama, Gestalt exercises, play therapy, adventure-based therapy, mindfulness exercises, art, music, and structured exercises. In groups for children, Gladding (2003) recommends using puppets, music, and artistic activities to promote self-understanding and interpersonal understandings. Others use written exercises (e.g., sentence completions, journals, listings), movement exercises (e.g., family/classroom sculpting, trust exercises, relaxation training, high-low level adventure-based activities, dance), arts and crafts activities (e.g., drawings, collages, clay sculpting), readings (e.g., read by leader/read by members), music, fantasy and guided imagery exercises, group decision making, consensus exercises or challenges, and rounds in groups with people of all ages. All of these kinds of activities are used in groups to promote a nonthreatening and fun tone. They also may facilitate engagement and provide an opportunity for group leaders to assess group member interpersonal skills (Gladding, 2003; Hagedorn & Hirshhorn, 2009; Jacobs, Masson, & Harvill, 2005; Kees & Jacobs, 1990). Hagedorn and Hirshhorn (2009) also suggest that experiential activities can help circumvent defense mechanisms or resistance that is sometimes present with clients who struggle with motivations to change.

While using experiential activities in groups may be fun, doing so may not be particularly therapeutic unless there is a strong match between activity, the goals of the group, and who is in the group—the membership. The purpose of using an activity in a group should always be to promote specific individual and group goals. Lieberman, Yalom, and Miles (1973), use the term *meaning attribution* in reference to ways in which group leaders help group members make meaning from what is happening in the group. When experiential activities are used, the link between activity and learning often needs to be explicit. "Processing" an activity is an important way to promote meaning from group activities. It refers to asking questions—*processing questions*—that are designed to encourage group members to reflect, analyze, and discuss their experience in a particular activity (Kees & Jacobs, 1990; Luckner & Nadler, 1997; Smead, 1995). They scaffold the meaning-making process. Activities can be "processed" in a variety of ways, but Smead (1995) suggests that the leader engage members in processing discussions that include these four components:

1. ***Intrapersonal learning:*** Invite members to examine their experiences in the activity.
2. ***Interpersonal learning:*** Ask members to consider what happened interpersonally between members of the group during the activity.
3. ***New thoughts or learning:*** Ask questions about what was learned as a result of engagement in the activity.
4. ***Application:*** Engage members to think and discuss how they will use the new information gleaned from the activity in their lives both inside and outside of the group.

These meaning-making discussions can be structured within the larger group, in smaller subgroups, in dyads, or privately in journal or other reflective writing activities. Additionally, an outsider witness or process observer, as will be discussed below, can be used to bring attention to process dynamics that occurred during the activity.

The decision on the use of activities in a particular group, as mentioned, is based on a number of variables. But if using an activity, the leader should be familiar with the activity before it is used (Geroski & Kraus, 2010). That is, the leader should read the books, play the games, and preview all DVDs or videos in advance of using them in a group. Additionally, while it can be fun to plan and use activities in groups, it is critical that leaders do not attempt to use facilitate activities that are beyond their experience and ability level (Geroski & Kraus, 2010).

LEADER EXECUTIVE FUNCTION DUTIES

According to the American Group Psychotherapy Association (2007), "The group therapist's primary function in that role is to monitor and safeguard the rational, work-oriented boundaries of the group, ensuring that members experience it as a safe, predictable and reliable container with an internal space for psychological work to occur" (p. 37). Lieberman et al. (1973) coined the term *executive function*, in reference to the administrative aspects of running a group, such as those mentioned above. It begins with good preparation and also includes establishing and maintaining the parameters of the group through enactment of rules and limits, managing time and pacing, interceding when the group moves away from content goals, and providing appropriate structure so that members are able to take risks and feel safe (American Group Psychotherapy Association, 2007; Bernard et al., 2008; DeLucia-Waack, 2006). This executive function role of leaders is used in varying ways across all group types, so as to assure that individual and group needs and goals are met and to manage an appropriate balance between group process and content. Here we will talk about this in a bit more detail.

BALANCING INDIVIDUAL AND GROUP NEEDS AND GOALS

Part of what makes facilitating groups complex for leaders is their role in keeping sight of the needs of the group as well as the individual needs of each group member. People join groups for a variety of reasons and there is no simple formula to explain why some individuals are attracted to one group over another (Beebe & Masterson, 2006). But, we do know that all members come to groups with certain expectations, and those expectations translate to what group leaders refer to as **individual goals**. **Group goals**, on the other hand, reflect a more general expectation that is shared by all members or defined by the task or purpose of the group (Beebe & Masterson, 2006). Group goals are the outcome expectations regarding the general purpose of the group. As part of executive function responsibilities cross various group types, then, the group leader assumes responsibility for insuring that individual member goals are appropriately aligned with the group intent, that there are opportunities in the group for individual goals to be met, and for assuring that the group goals are in focus. This is to say that it is the leader's responsibility to assure that

that the group is focused on its purpose. The example below is borrowed from Geroski (2017) to illustrate this point:

> Mr. Rivera signed up for a parenting class because he was struggling with how to help his young son grieve—his wife, the boy's mother, had recently died of cancer. The group leader intended to use a set curriculum to teach basic parenting skills in this particular group. When the leader learned of Mr. Rivera's specific needs that focused more on how to help his grieving son rather than general parenting information, he immediately determined that the group would not be a good fit, and referred Mr. Rivera to another group that was more appropriate for his needs. Mr. Heinzer, on the other hand, was a single parent struggling with basic parenting skills and was referred to the class because he hoped to learn better techniques for raising his children. This parenting group, then, appeared to be a good match for Mr. Heinzer. (pp. 283–284)

The hopes that Mr. Heinzer was bringing into the group in the example above—his individual goals—appeared to be aligned with the group intent and goals. However, Mr. Heinzer's specific needs for parenting his particular child would not be the central focus of the group—the group was about parenting, but not about Mr. Heinzer's daughter. So, it would be a shared responsibility between Mr. Heinzer and the group leader to assure that his individual goals would be met in the group. We can easily imagine that Mr. Heinzer will raise questions in the group that relate specifically to the challenges he has at home. But, as Beebe and Masterson (2006) point out, group leaders must remain focused on the group goals rather than putting too much attention on any individual member's individual goals. While leaders also promote the transfer of learning from group to one's life outside, individual group members really must bear the responsibility of taking what they learn in a group into their lives outside.

DUAL FOCUSING ON CONTENT AND PROCESS

Recall that the *content* is the topic, focus or purpose of the group. It is what the group is about. Attending to the content in a group, then, refers to being sure that the group is on task—that the group is focused on its intended goals. *Group process* refers to the group dynamics—the interactions among group members and between members and the group leader. Group process interventions are those that draw attention to the ways in which individuals are interacting with each other in the group (Carroll & Wiggins, 1997).

Hulse-Killacky, Kraus, and Schumacher (1999) asserted that "process facilitates content, and process needs to be balanced with content or a group will fail to attain its objectives" (p. 114). This is true, they suggested, across group types. The point they make is that attending to interpersonal group process dynamics is critical for group content goals to be met. The example below is intended to illustrate the ways in which group process dynamics can hinder progress toward group goals.

A work group was established at a school to plan a midyear fund-raiser. The principal of the school appointed three teachers to the group, and the remaining three members were parents who volunteered. Within this group, and unbeknownst to the principal, there was an unsettled conflict between one of the parents and one of the teachers in the group. In fact, during the prior administration, this parent had succeeded, after a series of vocal and angry meetings, in his request to have his son removed from that teacher's classroom. The ripple effect of this conflict was felt within the school community for the remainder of the year—some speculated that it was a large part of why the former principal resigned from his position. We can imagine, then, that if the conflict between these two group members was not resolved, it could seriously impede group functioning. Of course, this is not a forgone conclusion, and it is possible that careful leader intervention—both within and outside of the group—could be used to manage this potential challenge effectively.

In the moment decisions on whether to focus on group process dynamics versus content in a group are difficult. These decisions are based on a number of variables, including who is in the group, the extent to which the group process dynamics impede group functioning, and the group type (Geroski & Kraus, 2002). In therapy and counseling groups, leaders tend to focus on group process by engaging members to actively interact with each other. In these groups, this focus on group process is typically used to facilitate content, especially if the group goals are about developing interpersonal or social skills (Geroski & Kraus, 2002). However, task and psychoeducational group leaders typically emphasize content goals, so group tasks are often prioritized over interpersonal processes (Geroski & Kraus, 2010; Gladding, 2003). In a work group focused on investigating access to service in a mental health agency, for example, this content is the focus and the major task of the group. The group leader may not need to spend a great deal of time on having all of the group members get to know each other at great depth, especially when they may already know each other. Nor will she ask them to reveal their personal and interpersonal challenges, unless this revealing is necessary for accomplishing the group task. Instead, the work group leader is likely to use her executive function skills to direct the group to stay focused on the task at hand. If in this group, however, the participants do not know each other and they have no idea of each other's skills and strengths, they may have difficulties conversing with each other, the level of safety within the group may prohibit the level of risk taking needed for creative and innovative thinking, some may feel unengaged and stop coming to the group, and this lack of unknowing and cohesion may impede task completion. So, even in task or work groups, leaders need to appropriately attention to process dynamics.

INFORMED CONSENT AND CONFIDENTIALITY

In Chapter 1, we talked about the process by which a client becomes aware of and agrees to the services offered—this is called *informed consent*. As mentioned, guidelines regarding informed consent for clinical work are outlined by virtually all of the mental health organizations and emphasize that this is both a legal and an ethical duty that occurs prior to initiating services (Trachsel, Grosse Holtforth, Biller-Andorno, & Appelbaum, 2015). Informed consent is also applicable to group work. However, the processes of obtaining informed consent obviously differ across groups and group types. Regardless of group type—even when participation is mandatory, and even in work-assigned task groups—group members should be provided with information about the content of the group.

Confidentiality is somewhat more complex in group work because group leaders can never insure complete confidentiality to group members. This is because they cannot control what individual group members say and do outside of the group. Because of this, the *Ethical Standards for School Counselors* (American School Counselor Association, 2016), *ACA Code of Ethics and Standards of Practice* (American Counseling Association, 2014), and the *ASGW Best Practice Guidelines* (Thomas & Pender, 2008) assert that group leaders be perfectly clear and developmentally sensitive about this—explicitly discussing the risks related to confidentiality associated with personal self-disclosure. Members need to know that what they say in a group can slip out of the group at any time. While group leaders, then, especially in counseling and therapy groups, should inform all potential group members that they cannot fully protect their confidentiality (American Group Psychotherapy Association, 2007; Bernard et al., 2008), they should also help group members think about the boundaries they want to construct for the amount of personal sharing they will do in the group. In fact, helping individual group members maintain these boundaries might be a personal goal for some members. The bottom line is that it is the responsibility of the group leader to oversee group member safety. It is an executive function task of the group leader to insure that the level and content of personal sharing in the group is appropriate (Geroski & Kraus, 2010).

RECORD KEEPING

A final executive function duty of group leadership we will discuss here is documentation. While it is helpful to keep notes regarding the proceedings across group types, doing so is critical for psychotherapy and counseling group work (Knauss, 2006). Clinical records are legal documentation of what has happened in the group. They track important data; guide clinical decision making and document goal attainment; and clinical records are used for third-party reimbursement (American Group Psychotherapy Association, 2007; Bernard et al., 2008; Knauss, 2006; Wilson, Rapin, & Haley-Banez, 2000). Knauss (2006) recommends that clinicians conducting therapy groups maintain individual records corresponding to group members rather than an integrated record for the whole group. This is done in order to protect individual member confidentiality. If records are accessed by a third party, for example, information about all of the group members would be exposed.

GROUP FACILITATION SKILLS

Across group types, group leaders typically use the basic welcoming, listening, and fundamental responding skills discussed in Chapters 6 and 7. They also use the more advanced skills of feedback, immediacy, and confrontation discussed in Chapter 8. Because of the complex interpersonal dynamics that exist in groups, group leaders use additional "tools" or skills to navigate group process so that content goals can be met. The skills listed alphabetically below and also summarized later in Table 11.2, are staples of good group leadership practice across all group types.

BLOCKING

Leaders use *blocking* to stop inappropriate comments or to deflect potentially inappropriate interactions among group members (Gladding, 2003). It is a metaphoric "stepping in between or standing in the way" (Geroski & Kraus, 2010, p. 173). For example, a leader might use his hand to signal a stop sign, or interrupt by saying something like "let me stop you for a minute." Blocking is used when member behavior is not conducive to achieving individual and group goals, when the contribution of a group member is off topic or somewhat unfocused, and it is also used to protect an individual group member or group process dynamics. Blocking is a highly nuanced skill, and it must be used with utmost care and respect. Blocking is frequently used in combination with other skills such as reframing or shifting the focus below.

CUTTING OFF

Like blocking, *cutting off* is also used to regulate what is said in the group (Gladding, 2003), when a member monopolizes or takes up too much "space" (Geroski & Kraus, 2010), or when the behavior of a member is interfering with group functioning. Also like blocking, cutting off is a highly nuanced skill requiring the leader to be very aware of the stage of the group and group dynamics. If members perceive that the leader is unfair to a group member or if the leader uses the blocking or cutting off skills inappropriately, the climate of the group will be affected. When members believe that a member is being treated unfairly or disrespectfully, they may become fearful that this will happen to them as well.

When cutting off, it is usually best to be clear and straightforward, using verbal communication. For example, a leader might nudge forward in her seat, looking directly at one of the members who is speaking and say something like "Excuse me, Sophie. I am sorry to interrupt but we seem to be a little off task and I wanted to stop you here since we have a limited amount of time left today." This can be followed by refocusing onto the appropriate topic: "Sophie, we were talking about the change in application guidelines. Can you start us off on that?"

DRAWING OUT

Sometimes group leaders need to intervene to encourage less verbal members to participate more fully. They do this by creating openings and invitations (Geroski & Kraus, 2010)—this is what is meant by *drawing out*. One way to draw out a quieter or nonparticipatory member is to invite them to help with a particular task. For example, the leader could ask one person in the group to hand out a work sheet, collect something, or to start a response round. For example, "Cyrus, can you start us off by selecting which mindfulness activity we will use today?"

Waiting patiently and holding a silence in the group can also be used to draw out a quiet member. In fast moving discussions, space is not always available for reluctant or quieter members, so the leader may need to actively hold that space and invite the quiet member to join. In one such group, the leader attempted to draw out Aja by saying, "Okay, so let's just take a pause here to give everyone a chance to collect their thoughts. We will start up in a minute or two with Aja's comments about what happened."

Leaders can also use rounds. A round is a leader-prompted response set where everyone is invited to respond in a predetermined orderly way. "Let's take a minute to rate our anxiety here. We'll start with Jean Luc and move around the group in this way (pointing to the right). Jean Luc, can you tell us the number that describes your level of anxiety in this moment?" When using rounds, it is usually a good idea to start the round with a group member who will respond in a predictable and desired way so as to set the correct response set desired by the leader (Geroski & Kraus, 2010). In this example, the leader selected Jean Luc to be the one starting the round because she had a good sense that he understood how to scale emotions and would be comfortable initiating such an activity. The "popcorn" version of a round is when no order for response is identified and members are invited to share their response to the prompt in whatever order they decide.

LEVELING

In some groups, particular members appear to have more power than others. For example, group members may defer to one member for group decision making, follow that one member's lead in tone and level of sharing, or appear reluctant to participate too much when a particular member is present. *Leveling* is a leader intervention of drawing out some members and shifting the focus from others. It is used to equalize power within a group, often during the norming and storming stages of group development (Gladding, 2003). For example, "Ravi, let's have you wait a minute before responding. Julian, you go first." The point of leveling is to modify group process dynamics so that all of the members have an opportunity to share and benefit from the group.

LIMITS

It is the responsibility of the group leaders to create a group climate that assures that all participants are safe in the group (Geroski & Kraus, 2010). Safety here, of course, refers to emotional safety. Leaders are responsible for structuring the development of appropriate and respectful group norms and rules, and enforcing those rules as needed. Leaders may need to enforce group rules when they perceive a threat to the functioning of the group or safety of any individual group member. For example, leaders should intervene in response to sarcasm, teasing, and breaches in confidentiality, as these behaviors are likely to create anxiety and interfere with productive group process dynamics.

One way of enforcing limits is to begin by restating the rule. For example, "let's remember the rule that we do not speak for others in the group." Sometimes adding an explanation is helpful. "We want to be sure that everyone has the opportunity to express their own opinion, even when that is difficult to do." Then offering a directive may be required. For example, "Zelia, please let us give Merka an opportunity to speak for herself. Okay? Thank you." And then, after a minute, "Merka, would you like to add something now or at a later time?"

Since group leaders have the ultimate responsibility for assuring that group goals are being addressed, they may sometimes need to step in to set and enforce limits related to staying on task. This can be accomplished by offering a process observation and then redirecting members back to the intended task of the group. For example, the leader of the test-taking strategies group intervened when the conversation digressed by saying "It looks like we've lost our focus in here. Can we please come back to testing skill number 5?" Or, in a counseling group, members began to express frustration about a student who was not in the group. The leader intervened by saying, "I know that we all like to have an opportunity to vent, but when we started this group, one of the rules we identified was to not speak about others who are not in the group. We can talk about what we can do when we have concerns about someone in general, but the rule we came up with early on was that we don't talk about people who are not in the group."

LINKING

Linking is the process of calling attention to shared ideas, concepts, and other commonalities between group members. It is an intervention that is used to enhance meaning making and facilitate interpersonal connections among group members. Linking happens in groups in a variety of ways. For example, the leader can point out that two members are thinking in similar ways: "it sounds like you and Johnny had the same idea, Abigail." The leader can also use linking to invite individuals to respond to an idea that has been stated in the group (Toseland & Rivas, 2005). For example, "Some people were talking about feeling lonely and isolated when they begin this medical treatment protocol. Bea, can you talk a little about your experiences when you first got the diagnosis?" Another way that linking happens is when the leader asks one member to speak directly to another (Geroski & Kraus, 2010). "Pedro, it sounds like you are upset about something that happened in here. I am not sure what happened and who you are upset with. Can you speak directly to the person who you are upset with, so we can all be clear about what happened?"

PROCESS OBSERVATIONS

Process observation is a group technique that entails having someone in the role of observing group process dynamics (Zieman, Romano, Blanco, & Linnell, 1981). This technique was first used in therapy groups by Kurt Lewin in the late 1940s to help group leaders analyze and talk about group dynamics after group therapy sessions (Kislev, 2015). Yalom also believed that having process observers in therapy groups enabled group leaders to better understand their groups (Yalom, Brown, & Bloch, 1975). Process observers typically sit quietly in a group, often taking notes, and they usually do not otherwise participate in the group. They typically share their notes or observations with the leader and/or group members after the group has ended. In some cases, the process observer may take a more active role in the group (Bieschke, Matthews, & Wade, 1996) by sharing an observation during the group session.

The practice of using process observers in therapy groups may lower group member anxiety levels, enhance cognitive processing or meaning making, and provide an opportunity for group members to receive feedback (Yalom et al., 1975). Zieman et al. (1981) added that process observations are useful for stimulating group member thinking between group sessions, providing direction or focus in subsequent group meetings, helping structure continuity across group meetings, and in some cases these comments can be the framework for constructing behavior contracts among group members.

The use of process observers is not limited to therapy groups. Hulse-Killacky, Killacky, and Donigian (2000) for example, promote the use of process observers in task groups in order to help members reflect on the work of the group, focus attention on group member interaction, and to help ascertain the extent to which the task is being addressed in the group. Fazio-Griffith and Curry (2008) suggest that school counselors could also serve in the role of process observers in school classrooms, helping teachers better understand their classroom dynamics and thus improving the learning environment. Similarly, process observers are sometimes used to teach group facilitation skills in counselor training programs (Bieschke et al., 1996). Regardless of group type, Kislev (2015) warns, however, that an observer in a group constitutes an expression of power as a silent member recording group processes may be perceived as someone who is "policing" the group. So, process observers may not be appropriate for all group settings and when used, group members should understand the purpose of or role of the process observer, so as to promote transparency as much as possible.

REDIRECTING OR SHIFTING THE FOCUS

Because there are many voices in a group, leaders sometimes take on the role of managing group "air time" and assuring that the group is on task. *Redirecting* a speaker or a conversation or *shifting the focus* from one member or idea to another are skills used for these purposes (Gladding, 2003). "Wonderful, now let's see what the men in the group think about that point. Mathias can you add something?" or "Cori, I think that the group decided that they didn't want to focus on that today. Can you help us by offering one temper-taming tip that you learned from someone in the group?" As with cutting off and blocking, redirecting and shifting the focus are skills that require careful attention to communicating clearly and with respect. If group members feel that someone in the group is being singled out unfairly or attacked, it will have a detrimental effect on group climate.

REFRAMING

Reframing is the skill of offering an "alternative lens" or explanation about something that has happened in the group or related to the topic under discussion (Geroski & Kraus, 2010; Toseland & Rivas, 2005). It is used to prompt thoughtfulness, stimulate conversation, and facilitate meaning making. Reframing may be used to move a group through complex dynamics, when members seem to be misunderstanding each other, and in response to aggressive or potentially aggressive statements made in the group.

For example, in a therapy group Caroline seemed defensive when Dagna said, "Why am I the one who is doing all the heavy lifting in here?" Caroline apparently thought that this comment was a personal attack and a criticism. Thinking that the "heavy lifting" comment was speaking more about feeling vulnerable, the group leader reframed the comment so that Caroline and the others might understand it better. "You have taken many risks in this group, Dagna," the counselor said. "This is in line with some of the goals you had set for yourself. It sounds like you are feeling a little vulnerable—as we often do when we take risks like these. Can you tell us what you need from us in the group to help you feel safe in here?"

Table 11.2: Summary of Group Leadership Skills

SKILL	DESCRIPTION
Blocking	Blocking is a way of stopping or deflecting inappropriate comments or interactions between members.
Cutting off	Cutting off is a way of stopping one member from speaking—it is a form of setting limits in the group.
Drawing out	Drawing out is used to encourage members to participate more fully in the group.
Group process observations	A process observer is someone who sits silently in the group recording group process dynamics for the purpose of sharing these observations with group members and the group leader.

SKILL	DESCRIPTION
Leveling	Leveling is an intervention designed to equalize power among members in the group. Leaders do this by drawing out one member and blocking or shifting the focus from another.
Limits	Setting limits is sometimes necessary to refocus the group on agreed-upon norms or rules and to enforce safety in the group.
Linking	The purpose of linking is to foster connection between members or between ideas or concepts.
Redirecting or shifting the focus	Redirecting and shifting the focus are interventions designed to change the topic or speaker.
Reframing	Reframing is used to stimulate meaning making by offering an alternative explanation or interpretation about something said or done in the group.

CHAPTER SUMMARY

Group work has the potential to be a powerful and effective venue for addressing a variety of therapeutic, educational, and work tasks. This is largely because it offers group members an opportunity to learn from each other, practice new behaviors, and collaborate on projects and shared goals. The success of a group, however, is inextricably tied to how it is planned and managed by the group leader. Group leaders—across all group types—must have a solid understanding of group development, the therapeutic factors that create the kind of group cohesion that allows members to fully engage, and group process dynamics. The group principles, group practices, and group leader skills identified in this chapter, in addition to the basic skills identified in the preceding chapters, are applicable to a variety of group types. All group leaders, and particularly those who will be facilitating counseling and psychotherapy groups, should acquire group work training and engage in supervision before navigating groups on their own.

REFLECTION QUESTIONS

1. What interventions might a group leader use when strong cliques or subgroups appear to be inhibiting cohesion and group functioning? Might these interventions be different in different types of groups (psychotherapy, counseling, psychoeducation, task)?

2. What is a group leader's responsibility in regard to confidentiality in counseling, therapy, and psychoeducational groups?
3. Think about a class in which you are currently enrolled. What group dynamics do you notice? How does the professor navigate those dynamics?

CHAPTER

Helping People in Crisis

Chapter Outline

INTRODUCTION

Helping people who are in crisis requires all of the skills we have discussed in this text. However, crisis counseling differs from other types of counseling practices as it focuses on the client's immediate needs at a specific point in time and in response to a particular situation. The goal is always safety and stabilization. Even clinicians who do not work primarily in the area of crisis response are likely to encounter people who are in crisis. So, all clinicians need at least a basic understanding of crisis response. This is the intent of this chapter—to offer a basic foundation from which to intervene in these situations.

We begin with an overview of what we mean by a crisis, in its broadest sense, and we will review what are considered to be normal or typical reactions to crises. We end with a review of crisis intervention strategies that can be used when working in response to natural or human made disasters as well as in situations of harm to self or others. You will notice that our discussion in this chapter tends to use the term *victim* more than *client*. Crises and disasters are equal opportunity offenders—they strike in situations where people have not invited them and are not prepared to deal with them. So, in this sense, people who experience crises truly are victims of these situations. The use of this term here, however, is not intended to connote a positioning of helplessness. Also, there likely will be situations when a clinician is compelled to intervene in response to a crisis that does not involve someone who is on their caseload, which is another reason for the term *victim* rather than *client*.

TYPES OF CRISES

In clinical mental health circles, *crisis* refers to a situation in which a critical event has occurred with significant impact in one's life. It is when someone has experienced a severe acute stressor or trauma, resulting in a temporary sense of disequilibrium and a breakdown in normal coping mechanisms (Cavaiola & Colford, 2006; Collins & Collins, 2005). A *situational* crisis, also sometimes called an *accidental-situational* crisis (Kulic, 2005), is triggered by an unexpected precipitating event that is beyond the control of the individual and is typically experienced as extremely scary, hurtful, or disruptive (Cavaiola & Colford, 2006; Collins & Collins, 2005). The effects of these experiences may be transient or they may last a lifetime. Situational crises that are the result of natural causes are typically referred to as *disasters*. In this category are things such as major and damaging storms, floods, or other dangerous natural events such as forest fires or earthquakes. Situational crises may also result from a human action or human-based events. This includes being the victim of violence or, for example, experiencing an automobile accident. Also difficult and unexpected personal events such as the end of a relationship, the loss of a job, or the death of a loved one are considered to be situational crises. Just to clarify—the term *disaster* is often used to describe crises that are a result of something that has happened in the natural environment, whereas *crisis* often refers to situational events that are human-made. But these two terms are often used interchangeably.

A second category of crisis we will discuss here is a *psychiatric crisis*. A psychiatric crisis, too, often begins with a precipitating event—although the

Photo 12.1

trigger in these situations is not always visible to others—resulting in a temporary departure from one's normal level of functioning (Cavaiola & Colford, 2006; Collins & Collins, 2005). They are more likely to be experienced by individuals who have a dispositional vulnerability—a chronic stressor or persistent medical or mental health issues—that is then triggered by a current stressor (Ellis, 2011; Rudd, Joiner, & Rajab, 2001). A psychiatric crisis typically presents as emotional or mental dysregulation, some individuals in this state may experience hallucinations or delusions, and this type of crisis may result in suicidal or homicidal ideation. According to Sands, Elsom, Marangu, Keppich-Arnold, and Henderson (2013), severe disturbances in cognition, extreme agitation or manic behavior, suicidal gestures or talk, irritability, paranoia, and aggressive behaviors may signal that a psychiatric crisis is leading to violence—harm to self or others.

When a person shows signs of an acute psychiatric crisis episode, first responders may include mental health, medical, and law enforcement personnel (Ellis, 2011) and crisis stabilization through hospitalization or short term residential treatment is often required (Balkin & Roland, 2007; Gould et al., 2006). People who experience chronic or persistent mental health challenges, serious medical issues, and sometimes those who grapple with substance abuse, tend to be vulnerable to psychiatric crises (Ellis, 2011). It is important to point out, however, that not everyone who experiences a psychiatric crisis has a history of mental illness or substance misuse and vice versa—not everyone who grapples with these conditions is in crisis.

A *developmental* or *maturational-developmental* crisis refers to the sense of confusion that one feels while transitioning through various phases of life or it may be used to describe a situation when a person seems to remain in or regress toward a particular or earlier stage of development (Cavaiola & Colford, 2006; Collins & Collins, 2005; Kulic, 2005). For example, we often hear about a "mid-life crisis" where an older person's behavior is described as "adolescent." In fact, many describe the period of adolescence itself as a period of "crisis." As these examples suggest, developmental crises do not typically initiate from a situational event and they are not crises in the same sense as a situational or psychiatric crisis as discussed above.

The concept of an *existential* crisis, too, has some currency in mental health practitioner circles. An existential crisis refers to a state of mind where one is engaged in a profound process of questioning—the questioning about one's existence or some foundational principles about life; it is a seeking of meaning or purpose in life. Yalom (1980) proposed that an existential crisis "flows from the individual's confrontation with the givens of existence" (p. 8), resulting primarily in concerns related to death, freedom, isolation, and meaninglessness. An existential crisis may be triggered by a situational event, but it typically results in a process of self- and life-questioning rather than a crisis state of disequilibrium. Developmental, maturational-developmental, and existential crises are important topics for clinicians, but they are not typically addressed through the crisis counseling interventions, so they are not the focus of our discussion in this chapter.

Regardless of how it is triggered, any time a situation leaves someone in a compromised state psychologically or emotionally, the response is typically called a *trauma response*. As discussed earlier in Chapter 4, trauma response and complex trauma are the effects of traumatic events or conditions in which one is exposed to chronic stress or other adverse events over a period of time, and especially during childhood. Whether they come on suddenly or result from repeated experiences over time, traumatic events can have long-lasting effects on those who are affected (Cavaiola & Colford, 2006;

Collins & Collins, 2005). Also, as discussed in Chapter 5, trauma can even affect helpers and bystanders—something that is referred to as *vicarious traumatization*. Consider, for example, the impact that witnessing a death might have on a bystander, or listening to a story of assault recounted in a therapy session. So, repeated experiences of trauma can lead to complex trauma; witnessing the trauma experience of others may result in vicarious traumatization.

THE EXPERIENCE OF CRISIS

As discussed in Chapter 4, a series of neural firings initiate the body's response to a stressful event by creating a state of arousal (e.g., increased heart rate, deactivation of nonessential systems, and activation of threat-relevant memories). These firings activate stress hormones, which, in turn, increase blood flow to the large muscles of the body (arms and legs), preparing them to react—the flight, fight, or freeze response (Cavaiola & Colford, 2006). When the triggering event has passed and the brain has assessed that there is no longer any danger, a complex series of neurons and hormones then enable the body to return to homeostasis (Courtois & Ford, 2013; Westphal & Bonanno, 2004).

An outsider—such as a therapist or first responder—is often alerted to the triggering of a crisis response by a number of visible behaviors. These we discuss here but they are also summarized in Table 12.1. First, during a traumatic event, and sometimes often long afterward, victims may feel anxious, upset, and disorganized (Cavaiola & Colford, 2006; Collins & Collins, 2005). They sometimes become immobilized—this state of freeze resulting from a situational crisis is usually called being "in shock." Others become agitated; they may lash out or be unable to calm themselves. They often have difficulties regulating their emotions—they become over- or underregulated—and people in a crisis state frequently have difficulties performing normal everyday tasks. Victims of crisis may feel vulnerable and consumed with worry or fear. Indeed, in many cases, people who have experienced crisis truly are vulnerable—they have experienced loss, struggle to manage themselves, and they often are impressionable to the ideas and suggestions of others. People in crisis are often isolated or they perceive themselves to be isolated, their usual coping systems are compromised, and they typically have difficulties making decisions. Added to all of this, depending on the event that triggered the crisis, they may be filled with self-blame and guilt (Cavaiola & Colford, 2006).

Table 12.1: Common Reactions to Situational Crises

Cognitive difficulties	• Confusion • Difficulties with concentration • Thought disorganization • Difficulties making decisions
Motor behaviors	• Sleep disturbances • Changes in eating patterns • Immobility or excessive motor activity
Affective states	• Emotion dysregulation (over or underregulation) • Anxiety, fear, anger • Feeling out of control • Feeling vulnerable, helpless, or hopeless

Based on:
Cavaiola, A. A., & Colford, J. E. (2006). *A practical guide to crisis intervention.* Boston, MA: Houghton Mifflin.
Collins, B. G., & Collins, T. M. (2005). *Crisis and trauma: Developmental-ecological intervention.* Boston, MA: Houghton Mifflin.

The stress response pattern for psychiatric crises is similar to that of situational crises as outlined above. However, people who experience underlying psychiatric conditions or who live in conditions of chronic stress are particularly vulnerable to triggering situational events as their ability to regulate in response to a trigger is already limited to start with. That is, people who live in chronic stress often already have elevated baseline levels of stress-related hormones, abnormal rhythms of hormonal release, dendrite apathy, and inhibited neural growth (Siegel, 2012). When they experience an acute stressor, they may easily become disinterested in previously enjoyable activities or become emotionally dysregulated—they may experience anxiety, depression, and general irritability. Some behavioral manifestations of dysregulation include "temper tantrums" or anger outbursts.

The return to normal after an experience of trauma or crisis occurs at different rates for everyone. It is a function of multiple variables, including the nature of the traumatic event itself, one's baseline functioning and, as mentioned, whether the victim already lives with chronic stress or has had early experiences of trauma.

HARM TO SELF OR OTHERS

Any of these trauma responses, whether they are the result of situational, psychiatric, and sometimes even developmental or existential crises, may result in intentions to harm. This harm may be directed inward or projected on to someone else. Here we will briefly review information related to the risk of perpetrating harm on self or others.

PREDICTING HARM

According to Byrnes (2002), the impulse to perpetrate harm against others typically begins with a trigger, leading to increased escalation, and finally to the perpetration of aggression (Byrnes, 2002). The same is true for those who self-harm (Laux, 2002; Rudd et al., 2001). For example, an individual may have an ongoing chronic condition that becomes triggered by an acute situation, such as a loss of a job or the end of relationship. This triggers an acute state of suicidal ideation. Access to a means for acting on this impulse is what makes this situation lethal. In some cases, we may be able to anticipate or prevent such harm if we are able to recognize risk factors and triggers.

Examining data related to harm to self and others offers insight into who may be at significant risk of perpetrating harm to self or others. However, as you review this information, keep in mind that risk factors are a little like odds in gambling. They give you a sense of a potential or a likelihood that something may occur, but they do not offer anything conclusive. It is important to understand that it is typically a convergence of multiple factors, rather than the experience of any one of these risk factors, that creates a fertile ground for actually committing harm to self or to others. The information discussed here is also summarized in tables 12.1 and 12.2.

TERMS

Suicide attempt refers to a deliberate action that is carried out with the intent of causing death. While this may seem to be straightforward, nuances here are important. There are a number of terms that are used in reference to nonfatal suicide attempts—suicide attempts that do not lead to death. For example, *parasuicide* is often used interchangeably with *attempted suicide*, referencing suicide attempts that are nonfatal (Crowell et al.,

2005). In contrast, *deliberate self-harm* refers to "the deliberate, direct destruction or alteration of body tissue without conscious suicidal intent, but resulting in injury severe enough for tissue damage to occur" (Gratz, 2001, p. 253). So, while deliberate self-harm is intentional, it is generally understood to refer to non-life-threatening behaviors that are conducted *without* the conscious intent to commit suicide (Gratz, 2001; Hawton & James, 2005; Laye-Gindhu & Schonert-Reichl, 2005). The intent is to harm oneself, but not to suicide. Research suggests that girls who use deliberate self-harm most commonly engage in cutting, whereas boys are more likely to hit, bite, or punch themselves (Laye-Gindhu & Schonert-Reichl, 2005). More dangerous behaviors are also sometimes used as deliberate self-harm. For example, attempted hanging and self-poisoning make up about 90% of deliberate self-harm cases that require medical attention (Hawton & James, 2005).

Different from suicide or parasuicidal behavior, deliberate self-harm is considered by many to reflect maladaptive coping mechanisms, a poor attempt to regulate overwhelming emotions, or an effort to decrease tension (Gratz, 2001). Research suggests that individuals engage in deliberate self-harm in an attempt to reduce symptoms of depression, anxiety, loneliness, and anger, and to manage stress. It may be a reflection of self-hatred, a way of coping with a feeling of alienation, used as a distraction to one's problems, or it may be an antidote to dissociation and depersonalization (Laye-Gindhu & Schonert-Reichl, 2005). The motivation of deliberate nonsuicidal self-harm seems to have to do with sending a signal of distress and having a desire to escape a troubling situation (Hawton & James, 2005). While people of all ages may engage in deliberate self-harm, adolescents and young adults are at the highest risk (Fliege, Lee, Grimm, & Klapp, 2009). Research also suggests an association between deliberate self-harm and other health-risk behaviors such as smoking, tattooing, reckless or dangerous thrill seeking behaviors, and also with suicide ideation (Laye-Gindhu & Schonert-Reichl, 2005). In fact, Laye-Gindhu and Schonert-Reichl, (2005) found that 89% of the participants in their study who had suicide ideation had also engaged in nonsuicidal self-harm behaviors in the past. So this is a good reminder that anyone who is engaging in self-harm behaviors should be screened for suicide risk as well as other risky or health-compromising behaviors.

SUICIDE RISK FACTORS

Hoyert and Xu (2012) noted that in 2011, suicide was the 10th leading cause of death in the United States, and it was the 2nd leading cause of death among children ages 15–24. Adults between the ages of 45 and 65 and those over 85 years are particularly vulnerable to suicidal ideation as well (American Foundation for Suicide Prevention, n.d.). While women are more likely to attempt suicide, men more often complete suicide because their attempts typically include more lethal actions (Laux, 2002). We also know that in the United States, Whites have the highest suicide rates, followed closely by American Indians and Alaska Natives (American Foundation for Suicide Prevention, n.d.). Youth who identify as gay, lesbian, bisexual, and transgender are also particularly vulnerable to suicide (Centers for Disease Control and Prevention, 2011; Grossman & D'Augelli, 2007). This risk factor is related their experiences of coming out (in a generally hostile climate), rather than anything inherent to their gender or sexual orientation itself (Laux, 2002; LeFevre, 2014). Research also indicates that over 8,000 veterans die each year by completed suicide—this is an alarming rate of approximation of 22 suicides a day (Castro & Kintzle, 2014; National Institute of Mental Health, 2014). This is at least in part due to combat and deployment experiences that leave many vets with long-term challenges related to post-traumatic stress reactions.

People who experience mental health difficulties such as depression, schizophrenia, and posttraumatic stress disorder are also in a higher risk category for suicide (LeFevre, 2014). Risk related to these issues may be due, in part, to neurochemical abnormalities involving the serotonin neurons (Stockmeier, 2006). The most significant suicide risk factor, however, is a previous suicide attempt—about 20% to 25% of those who die by suicide have made precious suicide attempts (American Foundation for Suicide Prevention, n.d.; LeFevre, 2014; Owens, Horrocks, & House, 2002). Related to this, patients who have been recently discharged from a psychiatric or emergency hospitalization for services related to a suicide attempt are at a particularly high risk of a second suicide attempt (LeFevre, 2014). Finally, people who have a family member who has committed suicide are also at risk (American Foundation for Suicide Prevention, n.d.; LeFevre, 2014), as are those who are isolated or who have little social support (Brems, 2000).

The experience of a sudden loss or critical incident can also trigger suicidal ideation. Experiencing a chronic medical condition (American Foundation for Suicide Prevention, n.d.; Brems, 2000; LeFevre, 2014), being victim of violence or bullying (Varia, 2013), changes in employment or income status, and the loss of a loved one (LeFevre, 2014) have all be identified as potential suicide triggers for some people. People who live with chronic stress and those who experience trauma are at risk for suicide. They also are at risk for developing some type of psychiatric disorder—something that can largely be explained by a stress response system that is hyper-activated or damaged at a neurobiological level (Griffiths & Hunter, 2014). Finally, there are a number of personal behaviors that are also associated with suicide risk such as having limited coping strategies and being highly self-critical or having perfectionistic tendencies (Brems, 2000). People with impulsive or reckless behavior and substance misuse are also at high risk (American Foundation for Suicide Prevention, n.d.; Brems, 2000).

Again, these risk factors speak to suicide vulnerability; they alone do not indicate suicide ideation. Even though harm to self is often premeditated, triggers and precipitating events are not always visible to outsiders nor even to those of us who are trained to look for them. People with suicidal intentions do not always articulate or demonstrate those intentions. And even if we were to notice, it is not always possible stop someone who is determined to inflict self-harm or suicide. And, of course, some self-harm behaviors are not premeditated at all—for some, self-harm is an impulsive act. Because of these complexities, clinicians should never make harm assessment and intervention decisions alone. Keeping people safe must be a shared responsibility.

Table 12.2: Suicide Risk Factors

STRESSORS/TRIGGERS
• **Chronic or prolonged stress:** This may include experiences of bullying, harassment, discrimination, unemployment, or homelessness • **Sudden loss:** The death of a loved one, separation, loss of employment. • **Medical condition:** This generally refers to a chronic, debilitating, progressive, or painful medical condition, such as cancer, HIV, lupus, traumatic brain injury, chronic pain, insomnia, or the adverse effects of medications.
HISTORY
• **Previous suicide attempts.** • **Exposure to suicide:** Witnessing others commit suicide or being exposed to graphic accounts of suicide.

- **Mental health disorder:** The most common mental health problems that co-occur with suicide ideation include major depression and other mood disorders, substance use disorders, schizophrenia, and personality disorders.
- **Personal history of abuse** (physical, sexual, emotional).

ACCESS

Individuals who have

- **Access to lethal means** for committing suicide, particularly firearms and drugs.
- **Access to/use of alcohol and/or substances.**

OTHER RISK FACTORS

- **Gender:** Greater risk for males.
- **Sexual orientation:** Greater risk for LGB and questioning.
- **Transgender gender identity.**
- **Social isolation and limited support.**
- **Cognitive impairment:** Irrational thoughts, cognitive rigidity (an inability to understand others' perspectives/unable to consider new ideas), limited problem-solving abilities.
- **Emotion dysregulation:** This may include emotional dysphoria (profound unease or dissatisfaction), helplessness, hopelessness, guilt, anxiety/panic, or anhedonia (inability to experience pleasure).
- **Substance use/misuse.**
- **Impulse control difficulties.**

MOST IMPORTANT RISK FACTOR

- **Suicide ideation** (actively thinking about suicide).

Based on:

American Foundation for Suicide Prevention. (n.d.). *Understanding suicide: Facts and figures.* Retrieved from https://www.afsp.org/understanding-suicide/facts-and-figures

Laux, J. M. (2002). A primer on suicidology: Implications for counselors. *Journal of Counseling & Development, 80,* 380–383. https://doi.org/10.1002/j.1556-6678.2002.tb00203.x

LeFevre, M. L. (2014). Screening for suicide risk in adolescents, adults, and older adults in primary care: U.S. preventive services task force recommendation statement. *Annals of Internal Medicine, 160*(10), 719–726. https://doi.org/10.7326/M14-0589

Rudd, M. D., Joiner, T., & Rajab, M. H. (2001). *Treating suicide behavior.* New York, NY: Guilford.

SUICIDE WARNING SIGNS

When we talk about suicide warning signs, we are talking about those small and sometimes barely discernable indicators that a person is feeling suicidal. The general rule of thumb is that the more warning signs that are present, the greater the risk for suicide (American Foundation for Suicide Prevention, n.d.). However, someone who is suicidal may display different warning signs in different places, so the magnitude of risk may not be obvious to any one person. For this reason, it is important to attend to any single warning sign when we are with someone who has one or multiple predisposing risk factors and has experienced a recent triggering event. In the next section, we will discuss how to conduct a suicide assessment to determine suicide ideation more thoroughly. But first, we outline some of the more common warning signs.

The most obvious suicide warning sign is **suicide talk** (American Foundation for Suicide Prevention, n.d.). This is when a person actually says that he is considering suicide. For example, he may say, "I want to kill myself." An articulation of suicide intent is often less straightforward than this, of course. Sometimes, for example, it comes as a statement about not being around for much longer, being a burden to others, feeling trapped, being unable to escape pain, feeling revengeful, or feeling that one has no reason to live. Any suicide talk, even in the absence of risk factors, should be taken seriously and warrants further assessment.

A second warning sign is **unusual or different behavior.** When a client who is at risk of suicide and/or has experienced a triggering event, displays new, different, or extreme behavior, this may be an indication of suicide intent (American Foundation for Suicide Prevention, n.d.). Examples may include use of alcohol or substances, reckless behavior, withdrawal or social isolation, restlessness, insomnia or excessive sleep, saying good-bye or appearing to make amends with people, giving away prized possessions, and a preoccupation with death. Occasionally, a client may write a suicide note or **seek out means**—collecting pills or weapons, for example. While all unusual behavior should be examined, when these behaviors are demonstrated in combination with risk factors and/or a triggering event, suicide ideation may be serious and requires a more thorough suicide assessment.

Finally, the **mental status** of a client may constitute a warning sign, particularly in combination with other warning signs and risk factors. Feelings of hopelessness, helplessness, depression, and despair are strong predictors of suicide (Brems, 2000). A combination of depression and distorted thinking or inaccurate perceptions about oneself or others may be an indication of escalation moving to suicide crisis (Brems, 2000). For example, when a person is severely clinically depressed and perceives that others are alienating or avoiding him despite evidence to the contrary, this may be a signal of an unstable mental status and possibly an indication of suicide ideation.

Table 12.3: Suicide Warning Signs

Verbal	Expressions of • Hopelessness—not having a reason to live • Being a burden to others • Feeling trapped • Desire to no longer feel pain • Not being around much longer/no future • Feeling revengeful
Behavior change	• Any new, different, extreme behaviors • Excessive use of alcohol or substances • Reckless or risky behavior • Withdrawal • Restlessness, insomnia, sleeping excessively • Behaving in ways that suggest that one is saying good-bye (e.g., making amends or giving away prized possessions)
Mental status	• Expressed or apparent feelings of hopelessness, helplessness, depression, and despair • Disoriented • Distorted thinking • Preoccupation with death

This list is compiled from:

American Foundation for Suicide Prevention. (n.d.). *Understanding suicide: Facts and figures.* Retrieved from https://www.afsp.org/understanding-suicide/facts-and-figures

Brems, C. (2000). *Dealing with challenges in psychotherapy and counseling.* Belmont, CA: Brooks/Cole.

HARM TO OTHERS RISK FACTORS

For the purpose of our discussion, *harm to others* refers to aggressive, injurious, or hostile behavior that is destructive to others (Siever, 2008). **Premeditated aggression** is planned and intentional behavior that is not typically associated with frustration or in response to a particular threat or trigger (Siever, 2008). It is also not typically related directly to autonomic arousal (stress response). In fact, this type of aggression is sometimes actually socially sanctioned—a war, for example. **Impulsive aggression** is different—this is an exaggerated response—an autonomic arousal response—to a perceived threat or stress (Siever, 2008). Here we will limit our discussion in this chapter to impulsive aggression as an adequate discussion regarding premeditated aggression would go well beyond the scope of this text. However, all clinicians are recommended to learn more about working with people who display all types of aggression.

The definition of *violent crime* that is used in most statistics includes murder and nonnegligent manslaughter (willful murder without premeditation), rape, robbery, and aggravated assault (Federal Bureau of Investigation [FBI], n.d.). FBI arrest data for the year 2012 confirm the trend that nearly three quarters of all people arrested in the United States for committing a crime were men (FBI, n.d.). Most of these, it turns out, are White—70% in 2012, while that same year, 28% of arrests were of Black men, and the remaining 3% were of other races. Males, too, are the most frequent perpetrators of sexual violence, with a high percentage of sexual assaults committed by individuals who are known to their victims (National Institute of Justice, 2010). Morgan (2017) reports that in the 4-year period from 2012 to 2015, approximately half of all violent victimization (reported and nonreported) was intraracial, meaning that both victims and offenders were of the same race. During this time period White on White violent crime was 4 times higher than Black on White violent crime. Data indicate that between 2004 and 2013, adolescents between the ages of 12 and 17 committed more than one fifth of all nonfatal violent victimizations (Bureau of Justice Statistics, 2016). Data also reveal that most juveniles under the age of 18 who are arrested are charged with property crime. However, Black juveniles in this age bracket are more likely than their White counterparts to be arrested for a violent crime (Office of Juvenile Justice and Delinquency Prevention (2017).

Perpetrators of harm to others tend to have difficulties regulating anger, and they often have a low tolerance for frustration, impulsivity, poor problem solving abilities, difficulties reading social cues, and they typically resist complying with behavioral expectations that are set by others (Cavaiola & Colford, 2006; Dubin & Jagarlamudi, 2010; Kaplan, 2008; Siever, 2008). Miczek et al. (2007) and Siever (2008) help us understand the neurobiology of these types of aggression. They propose that violent behavior may result from brain structure impairments that impact moral cognition perceptions and emotional expression. Siever (2008) suggests that some people have a neurobiological imbalance in the inhibiting function or "brakes" (p. 430) in the frontal cortex, which is normally responsible for reading social cues and coordinating behavioral responses. This imbalance affects the limbic system, particularly the amygdala, which is triggered into a hyper-mode "drive" (p. 431) of emotional reactivity or aggression. This hyper-mode also leads to reduced levels of serotonin and gamaminergic (GABA) activity, which is problematic because these hormones are associated with regulating and suppressing aggressive behaviors.

A number of social and neurobiological risk variables are associated with such aggression. These include a history of trauma or childhood experiences of living in harsh home or social environments (Blake & Hamrin, 2007), a prior history of violence, a lack of social support (Pereira, Fleischhacker, & Allen, 2007), antisocial or borderline personality tendencies, and substance misuse (Siever, 2008). While any one or some combination of these variables are typically associated with aggressive behavior, the most reliable predictor of aggression toward others is a past history of violent behavior (Cavaiola & Colford, 2006) or patterns of anti-social behavior and high levels of aggression (Sprague & Walker, 2000). This is to say that people who have been violent in the past may very well become violent again in the future.

Not everyone in these risk categories becomes violent, of course. But unfortunately there is no fool-proof system of predicting when someone will intentionally harm others (Sprague & Walker, 2000). This is because lashing out on others is usually also based on situational variables that occur in an interpersonal context. That is—violence is typically triggered in the heat of the moment. So, it is the combination of risk factors, specific triggers, and an unmediated escalation of aggression, which will be discussed shortly, that result in the perpetration of violence (Byrnes, 2002; Pereira et al., 2007).

Table 12.4: Risk Factors Associated With Aggression

HISTORY
Individuals who have had these experiences in the past may be at greater risk of aggression: • **Past aggression:** A history of perpetrating violence toward others is one of the most reliable risk factors for aggression toward others. • **Family functioning:** A home environment (present or in the past) experience of violence, social isolation, harsh or inconsistent parenting, instability, emotional rejection, or living with someone who has a serious psychiatric illness. • **Instability:** A history of inconsistent or unstable schooling or employment. • **Rejection:** Experiences of peer rejection or poor peer relationships during adolescence.

(Continued)

Table 12.4 (*Continued*)

OTHER RISK FACTORS
These characteristics are associated with aggression statistics: • **Gender:** Males are more likely than females to perpetrate violence. Disadvantaged inter-city males are the highest risk group for perpetrating violence. • **Age:** Individuals between ages 15 and 30 are more likely to commit violence than those in other age groups. • **Thoughts:** Holding beliefs that aggression is justified, condoning or encouraging others to be aggressive or violent, when an individual displays a lack of empathy or inability to engage in perspective taking, and in some cases of cognitive impairments (low intelligence, limited cognitive complexity). • **Emotions:** Hostility, anger, irritability, fear, and frustration, • **Behaviors:** Low frustration tolerance, temper outbursts, poor impulse control, recklessness, cruelty to animals, frequent engagement in fights, truancy, oppositional behaviors, and poor interpersonal skills. • **Weapons:** Individuals who have a fascination with or access to weapons. • **Stress:** Individuals who are experiencing acute or prolonged stress. • **Substance use:** The ingestion of some substances or withdrawal from substance misuse disorders. • **Mental health disorders:** When there are symptoms of conduct disorder, antisocial personality disorder, intermittent explosive disorder, and paranoid schizophrenia.
MOST IMPORTANT RISK FACTORS
• **Aggression or homicide ideation** (i.e., an expressed feeling of aggression toward someone) **and** the existence of an **identified victim** (i.e., someone has been named as a potential target of these aggressive tendencies).

This list is compiled from:

Brems, C. (2000). *Dealing with challenges in psychotherapy and counseling.* Belmont, CA: Brooks/Cole.

Cavaiola, A. A., & Colford, J. E. (2006). *A practical guide to crisis intervention.* Boston: Houghton Mifflin.

HARM TO OTHERS WARNING SIGNS

The first part of coming up with a reliably accurate way of predicting violence is to pay careful attention to the risk factors mentioned above. Despite these factors, impulsive violence is typically activated by a trigger, and these triggers can happen in response to almost anything: one's friends, one's family, strangers on the street. They can be specific events or disappointments that have happened in the course of one's day—anything. Two key ingredients that affect whether a trigger becomes an aggressive impulse are (a) perceptions or meaning making and (b) self-regulation abilities. In terms of perceptions, recall from our discussion in Chapter 4 that the ways in which individuals make sense of the events in their lives—their cognitive appraisals—affect how they will respond to those events. A triggering event becomes significant based on how it is interpreted. For most of us, everyday triggers lead to a state of arousal that is manageable—we may become angry but then we are able to return to homeostasis. Or we become sad, but soon recalibrate. But, when a subjective perception of a trigger is matched with a compromised ability to self-regulate, we may see a problem. When someone is stressed beyond their ability to cope, and particularly for those in the social or neurobiological risk categories mentioned, controlling one's autonomic arousal can be difficult, and aggression may be the result (Byrnes, 2002). Having said this, it is important to remember that aggression rarely occurs suddenly and unexpectedly, even when triggered by a precipitating event; it typically escalates over time (sometimes a short amount of time). The most effective way to manage aggression, then, as we will discuss shortly, is to prevent it from escalating (Dubin & Jagarlamudi, 2010). For this reason, attending to aggression warning signs is critical. These are discussed here and summarized in Table 12.5.

Aggression often starts as **agitation** made visible by an **increased level of motor activity** or restlessness (Cavaiola & Colford, 2006; Fauteux, 2010; Sands et al., 2013). For example, you might see someone pacing, punching her fist into her hand, or rapidly tapping an object or a foot. Agitation may also manifest as **verbally abusive or combative statements** (Dubin & Jagarlamudi, 2010; Sands et al., 2013). This includes intimidation or threats to others. During this stage of escalation, the person appears hardened, rigid, or **inflexible** (Byrnes, 2002). For example, the person may be convinced that someone purposely wronged her, and won't back off of this perception, even in the face of contradictory evidence. Similarly, the person who is agitated may be **hypersensitive to criticism** or may take a **victim position**—a perception that she is the victim of slights or threats from others (James & Gilliland, 2001).

Dubin and Jagarlamudi (2010) point out that aggression sometimes happens when a person feels trapped, helpless, or humiliated. In response, the person may appear **defensive** (Cavaiola & Colford, 2006) or attempt to establish a **position of power**, engage in debates, or become **argumentative** (Byrnes, 2002). This is often accompanied by **mistrust of others** (Byrnes, 2002). For example, Kyoko was sure that her friend was being critical of her. While pounding her fist into her own hand, Kyoko shouted, "You don't know what you're talking about. I saw it with my own eyes. I know what you were thinking. You are lying. I could punch you out." These types of behaviors suggest a high level of agitation, an increase in loss of control, and are probably warning signs of potential aggression (Cavaiola & Colford, 2006; Sands et al., 2013).

Other factors that may signal potential risk or warning about violence toward others may include social withdrawal, isolation, or peer rejection or victimization (Dwyer, Osher, & Warger, 1998). These authors also recommend being alert in schools to students with uncontrolled anger; who demonstrate patterns of impulsivity and/or aggression; who have a history of discipline problems—particularly involving violence; who display an intolerance of difference; and to those who appear to lack interest in school or who demonstrate poor academic performance. School personnel should also be alert when they see violent themes in students' writing or pictures; or when they become aware of gang affiliation, substance misuse, or access to firearms; and expressed threats of violence to others. All of these factors, of course, must be understood in context. Again the reminder is not to misinterpret or rush to judgment about anyone based on an isolated incident, but to be alert to potential signs of violence.

Table 12.5: Aggression Warning Signs

An increase of these behaviors may indicate potential aggression:

- Agitation, increased motor activity, restlessness
- Verbal abuse, combative statements, argumentativeness, issuing ultimatums to others
- Inflexibility
- Hypersensitivity to criticism
- Statements positioning the oneself as victim and/or the other as enemy
- Defensiveness
- Mistrust
- Violent themes in writing
- Masked threats and other attempts to establish a position of power
- Existence of risk factors, such as anger management problems, aggressive behavior toward others, intolerance of difference, social isolation, rejection by peers, gang affiliation, substance misuse, and poor school performance

This list is compiled from:

Brems, C. (2000). *Dealing with challenges in psychotherapy and counseling.* Belmont, CA: Brooks/Cole.

Cavaiola, A. A., & Colford, J. E. (2006). *A practical guide to crisis intervention.* Boston, MA: Houghton Mifflin.

Dubin, W. R., & Jagarlamudi, K. (2010, July). Safety in the evaluation of potentially violent patients. *Psychiatric Times*, 15–17.

Fauteux, K. (2010). De-escalating angry and violent clients. *American Journal of Psychotherapy, 64*(2), 195–213.

CRISIS RESPONSE

Counseling response to crisis is typically referred to as *psychological first aid.* This first line of response for when clients are in crisis has sole focus on proving safety and support (Flannery, Juliano, Cronin, & Walker, 2006; Wong, Schreiber, & Gurwitch, 2008). Psychological first aid is used across crisis situations, including disaster response, in situations of harm to self or others, and is the first line triage response for call-center crisis response work as well. Also sometimes called *supportive crisis counseling*, the aim is stabilization. It is a brief model of intervention.

Very generally, psychological first aid or crisis counseling typically entails assessing the situation, determining the appropriate response/course of action, and formulating a plan for returning to normalcy or long-term coping (for more on models of crisis response, see American Counseling Association, n.d.a.; Cavaiola & Colford, 2006; Collins & Collins, 2005; James & Gilliland, 2001; National Center for School Crisis and Bereavement, n.d.a; n.d.b; n.b.c; Roberts & Ottens, 2005). What psychological first aid looks like on the ground level is establishing rapport; inviting the client to "tell his story" about what happened; listening, acknowledging, and demonstrating empathy; providing encouragement, reassurance and support; and later, assisting the client in connecting to resources or accessing information and options, as needed (Sands et al., 2013). Before moving into more specific details about these components of crisis response, it is important to offer the reminder that all clinicians should receive specific training in crisis response, particularly conducting a harm assessment, and they should work under the supervision of an experienced clinician before working alone in situations of crisis response.

INITIAL CONTACT

Crisis response begins with the very first contact you have with the victim, so it is important to attend to the details of that first encounter. When a person is victim to a situational crisis, he is probably feeling shaken and disoriented. So, it is a good idea to initiate contact with a simple introduction and brief explanation about why you are there (Cavaiola & Colford, 2006). For example, "Hi, I am Anne. You have been in an accident and I am here to get you help. I will sit with you until the ambulance arrives." You may want to ask the victim her name, try to maintain a sense of calm, and offer empathy and warmth. For example, "It makes sense that you are upset and jittery. This was a scaring thing that just happened."

ASSURE SAFETY

Once you have approached the victim and established initial contact, the next step is to determine the victim's needs and how to move toward stabilization. This begins, of course, with assessing the situation and minimizing, as much as possible, the physical and psychological danger that is posed by the event (James & Gilliland, 2001; Wong et al., 2008). Usually, this entails not leaving the person alone and getting additional appropriate help as needed (Schreiber & Gurwitch, 2011; Schreiber, Gurwitch, & Wong,2006; Wong et al., 2008). To these ends, it may be helpful to let the victim know when the immediate danger has passed, to accompanying the victim to a safe location, or provide a screen or barrier from unwanted others, including the press. For example, "The firefighters are asking that everyone move over here across the street, so that we are out of the way and we can make sure everyone is accounted for. Can I walk with you over there?" Or, "the press is starting to arrive. Would you like me to tell them to give you some privacy?" Sometimes, first responders will need to take control of the situation, recognizing that the victim or client may not be in a position make or carry out decisions on her own.

Another way of promoting psychological safety is by providing information and addressing some of the victim's worries. For example, "You were in a pretty serious accident. You are in the hospital now and you are safe. The doctors are monitoring you, and they are attending to others who were in the accident. Your family has been called. I am here with you and will stay with you until your family arrives. Please let me know if there are any questions you have." Or, "I know that you are worried about your dog. They have found a number of pets and they will be holding them in a safe location until their owners can be found. When they give us permission, we can go over there to see if your dog is there. Okay?" Keep in mind, however, that in some situations it may not be appropriate for you to disclose some information to a victim. For example, talking to one victim about specifics and details regarding another victim is a breach of confidentiality, especially in situations where the relationships between victims is not clear. Also, it is important to realize that as a first responder who does not have a relationship with a victim, you may *not* be the best person to convey bad news to a victim who is already extremely vulnerable or alone without any personal supports. Finally, it is important to remember that in larger crisis response efforts, communication is typically coordinated at a centralized level, so you may not be "authorized" to provide information even if you have it. What is important and always appropriate is to assure the victim that you will try to find answers to his questions as quickly as possible and, of course, it is appropriate for you to advocate for the victim so that his needs for information are appropriately addressed.

Finally, Cavaiola and Colford (2006) point out that since the experience of crisis often leaves victims with no or limited control, it is often helpful to invite the victim to be in control of those things that she can and should control. This means, then, to have the victim participate in simple decision making, if possible and when appropriate. For example, asking "would you like some water?" or "would you like to use my phone?" are simple questions that invite a small amount of agency. The caveat here is a big one, however: people who have experienced a crisis are often confused and may feel overwhelmed by even simple decisions. So, navigate the agency versus overwhelming line carefully. Also, during or just after a crisis, the extent to which a victim is actually free to make decisions may be limited—they may not, for example, be able to return immediately to a crime scene, they may not be able to go into a hospital room to see a loved one, and it may not be medically safe for them to stand up. So, be sure that the decision options you offer are safe, appropriate, and viable. The bottom line for first responders here is to always work within the limitations of your experience and level of training, and work

Photo 12.2
Copyright © 2013 Depositphotos/AntonioGuillemF.

in collaboration with others. Remember that crisis response often requires a team of responders all with different areas of training and expertise (Ellis, 2011).

LISTEN

In the *Listen, Protect, Connect* model of psychological first aid (Schreiber & Gurwitch, 2011; Schreiber et al., 2006; Wong et al., 2008) the recommendation is to initiate crisis response by listening. This is particularly helpful because the experience of crisis often leaves victims with a lack of control, as mentioned. When you step back and listen, you are inviting the victim to dictate the terms of the conversation. This kind of listening is not passive, however. You will want to listen carefully to what the victim says, acknowledge her experience of what has happened, and also listen for signs of significant distress, including harm ideation. While it can be difficult to conduct an initial assessment without asking many questions, you want to be careful not to bombard the victim with too many questions. Instead, offer space for her to express whatever she needs to express, as much as possible. For example, you can say, "I'm here if you want to talk about what happened. Otherwise, we can sit quietly and wait if you want. It's really up to you."

As much as possible, first responders should also endeavor to provide encouragement, reassurance and support. This should include attending to cultural nuances that may make it difficult for the victim to receive services or recover from the traumatic event that has occurred (Substance Abuse and Mental Health Services Administration [SAMHSA], 2005). For example, if it is more culturally appropriate for the victim to be comforted by a religious leader, member of his particular cultural group, or even someone of a different gender, it is important to make these things happen as soon as possible.

NEEDS ASSESSMENT

In many crisis situations, the mental health clinician is tasked with gathering information and determining the mental status of the victim. This often begins with a simple question about what happened—to get a sense of how the victim comprehends or is making sense of the critical incident. For example, "Michael, I can see that you are very upset. Can you tell me what happened?" You also may conduct a cursory assessment of the victim's

Photo 12.3

physical condition if you are the first on the scene and there is no medical personnel yet available. "Are you hurt?" "Where did you fall?" "Do you need medical assistance?"

You can then move into the other components of the mental status exam, as discussed in Chapter 9. This typically entails assessing mood, with attention to symptoms of major depressive disorder including agitation, insomnia, anhedonia (inability to experience pleasure), and difficulties in concentration (Cavaiola & Colford, 2006). Factors such as a victim's appearance, speech, affect, cognitive processes, and general behavior are also parts of the mental status exam (Brannon, 2016). Clearly, emotionality is expected during crisis. But you will want to determine if the victim appears to have difficulties with regulation beyond what you might expect, and also assess if they appear to be a danger to self or others. Observation of the victim's behavior may help in this assessment. For example, is he agitated? Withdrawn? Reckless? Confused? Does she appear to be injured? Stable? Does her behavior suggest the existence of irrational thoughts, hallucinations, paranoia, confusion, incoherent ideas, memory blanks? Have you noticed substance use or misuse? It is important not to pressure the victim to answer questions that she does not want or is not able to answer, however. The point here is solely to determine what kind of help is needed and to provide immediate safety and support.

Finally, it can sometimes be helpful to ask or attend to the comments and observations of others. For example, it may be another victim who alerts you to the fact that someone has just retrieved a gun for retaliation, or that the person you are attending to has been drinking alcohol all morning since the crisis occurred. Be reminded, of course, that your duty is to protect the confidentiality of the people you are working with, so you must be careful not to compromise victim safety and integrity by offering information to others that is not yours to give. However, this does not preclude you from gathering collateral information to ascertain a more complete picture of the situation or the mental status of a victim.

The overall message here is to listen, watch, and not make rash decisions. Crisis situations are not going to look "normal." Expect unusual behavior in unusual situations; your job is to determine how unusual something may be before it is unsafe or inappropriate, and when more assistance is needed. When your assessment indicates a possible situation of harm to self or others, it is critical to engage in a harm assessment, which is described below.

HARM ASSESSMENT

Accurate harm assessment requires being able to consider the complex and nuanced mix of triggers and risk factors, looking for warning signs, and asking the right questions. The point is to determine the extent to which a person displays signs of imminent risk of harm to self or others that includes intent and access to potentially lethal means. Here we review the key components of harm assessment that are used in situations of potential harm to self or others.

1. **Intent.** Intent, of course, refers to the extent to which a person displays harm ideation. That is, does the person appear to be thinking about hurting himself or someone else?

   Questions to ask:
   - Are you suicidal? Are you thinking about killing yourself?
   - Are you thinking about hurting someone? Killing someone?

A few points are important here: First, as mentioned in Chapter 3, clinicians *must* break confidentiality in situations of threat of harm to self or others—so as to provide protection. Clinicians should be particularly concerned when there is an **identified potential target or victim** of harm (in cases of intent to harm others). As discussed in Chapter 3, clinicians also have a duty to warn known potential third-party victims of violence—this is a legal mandate in many states (Sommers-Flanagan & Sommers-Flanagan, 2007). In situations where there is a clear and imminent danger to identifiable others, clinicians should work with law enforcement personnel. Second, harm intentions are not always easy to see, and they may be expressed in subtle ways. For example, vague expressions of not being around or that someone might get himself killed may be a masked expression of harm intent. So, working under close supervision or in consultation with others while conducting a harm assessment is crucial. Third, because harm conversations are so very difficult, they will understandably make many clinicians a little anxious. Some clinicians worry about offending clients, others worry that they will miss important cues, and many of us are worried about our ability to actually de-escalate or dissuade harm intentions. This anxiety, however, can interfere with a good harm assessment, causing us to miss important information or have difficulties being fully present and empathic. Comprehensive training in harm assessment is one good way for clinicians to feel more confident in this process. Finally, clients in crisis often feel isolated, alone, and trapped, so all harm assessments must be conducted with unabated empathy and caring.

2. **Plan.** Another component of a harm assessment is to try to determine the depth of the client's harm intentions. Very generally, the more extensive or detailed the plan around self-harm, the higher the risk that the person will attempt suicide. Asking about suicide plans, then, offers insight into the extent to which the client has thought about self-harm. In cases of potential harm to others, the existence of plans may also signal a high level of intent.

   Questions to ask:
   - "What are your thoughts about how you would kill yourself?" Followed by more questions, based on the client's responses.

- "You said that you wanted to kill him. Did you have some ideas formulated on how you might do that?" Followed by additional questions, depending on the client's response.

3. **Means.** Another important detail in determining the extent of one's threat of harm is to determine what method the client has thought about for perpetrating harm. This is important because some methods are more lethal than others. For example, firearms are extremely dangerous; suicide by holding one's breath should be taken seriously, but it is not likely to have a lethal outcome.

   Questions to ask:
   - "You have been thinking about suicide. What are some of the ways you have thought about killing yourself?"
   - "You mentioned wanting to swallow some pills to end it all. What kind of pills are you thinking about?"
   - "When you say you want to kill him, what would you want to do?"

4. **Access.** Having access to means—actually being able to use the method as planned—makes intent potentially lethal. For example, wanting to shoot someone is less worrisome when we know that the person does not have a gun and does not know anyone who has a gun. Here again, this does not mean that the intent to harm is not serious, but perhaps less lethal if there is no access to the means.

   Questions to ask:
   - "You say you would swallow some Ativan. Do you have Ativan?"
   - "You said you would shoot him. Do you have a gun?"

   Both of these questions, like all of those before them, require some follow up. For example, if the person does not have a gun, does someone in his house have one? Does he know someone who has one?

5. **Hope or future aspirations.** When a person is feeling depressed, understanding that he will feel better one day is an important protection against suicide. When one has no hope that his current

pain will go away or when one believes that his current situation will not change, he may see suicide as a good option. When the client speaks about future plans or aspirations, this suggests that he can visualize himself in a better place. In a similar vein, asking about existing support systems—people in the client's life who he believes can offer some help—also provides a window of insight into how one potentially thinks about his situation in the future. If the person believes that others are concerned about him, this may help mediate any suicidal or homicidal ideation.

Questions to ask:

- "So, can you talk about what you think it will be like between the two of you when you are no longer fighting?"
- "You mentioned that you had hoped to go to college next year. Can you tell me about those plans?"
- "Is there anyone you can think of who would be able to stop you from committing suicide?"

6. **Review of existing risk factors and warning signs.** As mentioned earlier, a number of risk factors are associated with suicide but having previous suicide attempts is one of the most critical. So, asking about previous suicide attempts is important. Asking about other risk factors and assessing the presence of warning signs is also important, of course. This is especially true in situations of harm to others. As mentioned earlier, for example, agitation, mild aggression, and impulsivity may be warning signs suggesting a potential for harm. When these are paired with an expressed intent and a plan with access to means, the potential for harm is high.

Questions to ask:

- "Have you ever attempted suicide before?"
- "Do you know someone who has committed suicide?"
- "Have you tried to hurt her or anyone else in the past?"

Do not leave a suicidal client alone—if necessary, escort him to emergency services and remove all dangerous objects. You should also never be in a position of working alone when intervening in situations involving harm to self or others. Always seek consultation or supervision.

CONNECTION TO RESOURCES

Reestablishing routines and reconnecting with loved ones after a crisis promotes a sense of predictability and stability (Wong et al., 2008). Yet, a common reaction to crisis or a traumatic experience is to withdraw or isolate oneself from others. So, victims often need help reconnecting with their support systems and routines (Schreiber & Gurwitch, 2011; Schreiber et al., 2006; Wong et al., 2008). While many people are best supported by people in their existing circle of friends or family, others may not have a support system available to them during or immediately after a crisis. So a clinician or first responder may be the support until other systems of support become available.

The kinds of support that victims of crisis need will vary. Some many need an ear, while others may need help making decisions. If you are not able to provide a particular service, you can help arrange for what is needed. Of course, you should never offer to provide services for which you have not been trained, you should be very cautious about offering services that have not been asked for, and it is always a good idea to seek consultation before making any recommendations regarding services or service providers that you are not familiar with. But, an individual who is in danger of harming himself must be evaluated and monitored until he is safe, even if he hasn't specifically asked for this type of assistance. Also, remember that in situations of potential harm to others, law enforcement personnel should be alerted and in many states, mental health clinicians have a legal duty to warn any potential target of aggression when a credible threat has been made.

When the initial crisis has passed, the next stage of crisis response is to help the client plan to get back to normal functioning. What is needed in this phase will, of course, depend on the needs of the victim or client and the particulars of the situation. Some will need continued assistance—finding housing, follow up medical care, or navigating the legal system, for example. In these cases, you can offer a warm handover to the next support personnel—this can ease the transition for the victim or client. Some victims, of course, will need nothing.

RESPONDING TO AGGRESSION

When frustration or aggression impulses are beyond an individual's ability to cope, the risk of harm is elevated. As mentioned, impulsive aggression often initially presents as agitation, irrationality, and an inability to make sound decisions or regulate oneself. If you are able to intervene before the person has escalated beyond control, you may be able to avert harm. In Byrnes's (2002) words, "the more we allow an aggressor to escalate, the less opportunity we will have to diffuse him" (p. 13). Responding to aggression, then, begins with helping the person become calm. Then the focus turns to trying to resolve the situation that created the problem or crisis. These suggestions, based on the work of Cavaiola and Colford (2006), can be used to deescalate a person who is at risk of harm to others, but they also are relevant in situations of potential self-harm:

1. **Connect with the individual.** Invite the person to talk. Listen carefully, validate their experience. Do not dispute their version of events, even if you disagree. Avoid making accusations or reprimands and do not diminish the person's experience. In short, do not debate, argue, or criticize.

2. **Respect and empathy.** Remember that it never feels good to be in an out-of-control state. So always be respectful and empathic. Validate the person's reality and frustrations. For example, "Wow, you look upset, Yassah. What happened?" "How did you feel when she said that?" "I can see how that felt bad." It is important to allow others to express their grievances and frustrations without being judged. Remember that inviting conversation and helping someone feel less alone can calm a tense situation.

3. **Gather information.** As you listen, conduct a harm assessment. Does the person have intentions to harm self or others? Are there specific plans? Means? Access to means? Is there an identifiable target or potential victim of harm?

4. **Avoid confrontation.** When a person is unable to self-regulate, it is important that you do not further escalate the situation by arguing with them. This does not mean that you have to accept everything that the person has said, especially if it is inaccurate or irrational. But, it is not productive to argue with someone who is not thinking clearly. It is always best to listen and be respectful and empathic. You can show empathy by saying, "I can see why you were angry

at him if you thought he was saying that to you." Or, "given what happened in the past, it's easy to see why you felt ridiculed." Find opportunities for the person to "save face." Never shame a person for what he feels or how he has behaved.

5. **Remain calm.** Always use a calm and rational voice. So as to avoid the perception of being accusatory, it is also a good idea to avoid staring directly at the person who is upset. Additionally, it can be helpful to talk slowly and to stop and breathe with intentionality, as these methods of self-regulation may serve to co-regulate the other person as well.

6. **Avoid a threatening stance**. You want to be sure that your presence does not create an additional trigger for someone who is already a bit out of control. So, in a tense situation, do not tower over someone who is agitated, and avoid assuming any stance that could be perceived as threatening. Be sure to "telegraph" your movements—let the person know what you are doing before doing it. For example, "I am going to move this chair over so we can sit down. Okay?" or "I am going to move this bat out of the room now so it doesn't get in our way of talking and calming down." You want to communicate that you are in control but not that you are seeking to control the other person.

7. **Be safe**. It is important that you do not put yourself in danger. When intervening with someone who is out of control or potentially dangerous, be sure to alert others to your situation, remove any throwable objects, and position yourself in a place that is easily accessible to an exit—do not allow yourself to be cornered by someone who is out of control. Again, if your own safety is threatened (either directly or by implication), you should leave the situation and/or call for help immediately. **It is not appropriate to put yourself in harm's way.**

8. **Restraint.** If you are still not able to deescalate the situation or if you see that there is an increase in emotionality, irrationality, and aggression, physical restraint may be required. You should never provide physical restraint unless you have received training in appropriate restraint procedures—something that is probably a good idea for

all clinicians, and particularly those working with individuals who are prone to aggression. If you find yourself in a situation that you think requires restraint, get help immediately. Do not work alone.

9. **Duty to warn.** Remember that if you have information that an individual is intending to harm another person, you have a professional duty to warn the potential victim. In these situations, you should always work in connection with emergency responders, law enforcement officials, and supervisors.

10. **Connect to resources.** Keep in mind that when people are chronically out of control, they often have disrupted relationships with others. This may mean that they are isolated and have few support systems in place. So, after the crisis has been averted and the person is stable and calm, it is appropriate to help the person try to establish connections with others. While social connections are important, clients may also need help from professionals to learn how to regulate their emotions and form meaningful relationships with others.

11. **Making amends and saving face.** Remember that when a person is in a dysregulated state, they are not able to think rationally. For this reason, it is never a good idea to *require* someone to apologize or make amends with others. In fact, doing so may very well ignite another round of agitation and potential aggression. But when stability has been established, you can have a private conversation with the individual to debrief the situation and to help them think about the damage that may have occurred. At this time, there may be some interest in making amends and reestablishing relationships that may have been damaged during the harm episode. The bottom line is, however, that we cannot force people to feel authentically apologetic and we also cannot force a victim to offer forgiveness to his perpetrator. What we can do, however, is help people think through the consequences of their actions and, in some cases, to come up with the language that may help them express remorse or ask for forgiveness.

Finally, one point needs to be reiterated here. When intervening in situations of aggression, your immediate attention should be on safety—your own safety, the safety of the potential victim or victims, and the safety of the individual who is out of control. You should never work alone in these situations—call for assistance (Brems, 2000). Interventions with individuals who are aggressive should always be handled by a professional who has been trained in crisis response.

Table 12.6: Responding to Crises and Threats of Harm

CRISIS RESPONSE	
Initial contact and listening	Introductions and explanations, as needed.
	Listen to the person's story, feelings, and perceptions of events/others.
	Express empathy and respect, and validate the person's perceptions and experiences.
	Provide encouragement, reassurance, and support, as appropriate.
Assure safety	Determine needs for stabilization.
	Get help, as appropriate.
	Do not leave the person unattended.
	Protect the victim from unwanted media and other attention.
	Address initial worries and offer choices as appropriate.
Needs and harm assessment	Initiate a needs assessment and an assessment risk of harm (self or others) when risk factors and warning signs are present.
Connection to resources	Connect the individual to emergency or mental health services.
	Connect the person to family and other support systems after the crisis has passed or when the victim is stable.

HARM ASSESSMENT	AGGRESSION RESPONSE
Assess the following: • Intent • Plan • Means • Access • Hope/future aspirations • Risk factors/warning signs	• Connect • Show respect and empathy • Gather information • Avoid confrontation • Remain calm • Avoid a threatening stance • Be safe—protect yourself, consult with colleagues, and never work alone • Use restraint (if trained) • Exercise duty to warn • Connect to resources • Make amends/save face

CHAPTER SUMMARY

Crisis response is a challenging line of work—whether intervening in response to a natural or human-made disaster or to a crisis of harm to self or others. The important things to remember are to assure safety, pay attention to risk factors and warning signs, and in the case potential of harm, intervene early to protect. The goal is to enable the victim to stabilize and return to normal functioning as much as possible. If you are part of a larger crisis response intervention, be sure to work only within the role assigned to you, within your area of expertise, and do not offer services that put you in danger. It is always important to work with others whenever possible. All mental health professionals should acquire additional training in crisis response and responding to harm to self or others.

REFLECTION QUESTIONS

1. What behaviors might we see from someone who has experienced a disaster or trauma? How long might you expect to see these behaviors, and how do you know if they are problematic or normal?

2. According to the statistics, what populations are particularly vulnerable to suicide? What factors make these people particularly vulnerable?

3. What should you do when someone is showing signs of agitation and expressing thoughts of wanting to harm someone?

REFERENCES

Academic Mindfulness Interest Group. (2006). Mindfulness-based psychotherapies: A review of conceptual foundations, empirical evidence and practical considerations. *Australian and New Zealand Journal of Psychiatry, 40*(4), 285–294. https://doi.org/10.1080/j.1440-1614.2006.01794.x

Adrian, M., Zeman, J., & Veits, G. (2011). Methodological implications of the affect revolution: A 35-year review of emotion regulation assessment in children. *Journal of Experimental Child Psychology, 110*(2), 171–197. https://doi.org/10.1016/j.jecp.2011.03.009

Ainsworth, M. S. (1979). Infant–mother attachment. *American Psychologist, 34*(10), 932–937. http://doi.org/10.1037/0003-066X.34.10.932

Ainsworth, M. D. S., Blehar, M. C., Waters, E., & Wall, S. (1978). *Patterns of attachment*. Hillsdale, NJ: Erlbaum.

Alvarez, A. R. (2003). Pitfalls, pratfalls, shortfalls and windfalls: Reflections on forming and being formed by groups. *Social Work With Groups, 25*(1–2), 93–105. https://doi.org/10.1300/J009v25n01_13

American Counseling Association. (n.d.a). Fact sheet #10: 1:1 Crisis counseling. Retrieved from https://www.counseling.org/knowledge-center/trauma-disaster

American Counseling Association. (n.d.b). Vicarious trauma [Fact sheet]. Retrieved from http://www.counseling.org/docs/trauma-disaster/fact-sheet-9---vicarious-trauma.pdf

American Counseling Association. (2014). *ACA code of ethics*. Alexandria, VA: Author. Retrieved from http://www.counseling.org/docs/ethics/2014-aca-code-of-ethics.pdf

American Foundation for Suicide Prevention. (n.d.). Facts and figures. Retrieved from https://www.afsp.org/understanding-suicide/facts-and-figures

American Group Psychotherapy Association. (2007). *Practice guidelines for group psychotherapy*. New York, NY: American Group Psychotherapy Association. Retrieved from http://www.agpa.org/home/practice-resources/practice-guidelines-for-group-psychotherapy

American Mental Health Counselors Association. (n.d.). Facts about clinical mental health counselors. Retrieved from https://amhca.site-ym.com/?page=facts

American Psychiatric Association. (n.d.). What is psychiatry? Retrieved from https://www.psychiatry.org/patients-families/what-is-psychiatry

American Psychiatric Association. (2010). *The principles of medical ethics*. Arlington, VA: Author.

American Psychiatric Association. (2013). *Diagnostic and statistical manual of mental disorders* (5th ed.). Washington, DC: Author. https://doi.org/10.1176/appi.books.9780890425596.680172

American Psychiatric Nurses Association. (n.d.). Psychiatric mental health nurses. Retrieved from https://www.apna.org/i4a/pages/index.cfm?pageid=3292

American Psychological Association. (n.d.). Science of psychology. Retrieved from http://www.apa.org/action/science/index.aspx

American Psychological Association. (2005). *Report of the 2005 Presidential Task Force on evidence-based practice*. Washington, DC: Author. Retrieved from https://www.apa.org/practice/resources/evidence/evidence-based-report.pdf

American Psychological Association. (2008). *Resilience in African American children and adolescents: A vision for optimal development*. Washington, DC: Author. Retrieved from http://www.apa.org/pi/families/resources/resiliencerpt.pdf

American Psychological Association. (2017). Ethical principles of psychologists and code of conduct. Retrieved from http://www.apa.org/ethics/code/index.aspx

American School Counselor Association. (n.d.). What does a school counselor do? Retrieved from https://www.schoolcounselor.org/press/what-does-a-school-counselor-do

American School Counselor Association. (2016). *ASCA ethical standards for school counselors*. Retrieved from https://www.schoolcounselor.org/asca/media/asca/Ethics/EthicalStandards2016.pdf

Andersen, M. L., & Collins, P. H. (2004). *Race, class, and gender: An anthology* (5th ed.). Belmont, CA: Wadsworth/Thompson Learning.

Anderson, T., Lunnen, K. M., & Ogles, B. M. (2010). Putting models and techniques in context. In B. L. Duncan, B. E. Wampold, & M. A. Hubble (Eds.), *The heart and soul of change* (2nd ed., pp. 143–166). Washington, DC: American Psychological Association.

Annan, K. (1997, June 22). *If information and knowledge are central to democracy, they are conditions for development*. World Bank Conference on Global Knowledge, Toronto, Canada. Retrieved from http://www.un.org/press/en/1997/19970623.sgsm6268.html

Arredondo, P., Toporek, R., Brown, S. P., Jones, J., Locke, D. C., Sanchez, J., & Stadler, H. (1996). Operationalization of the multicultural counseling competencies. *Journal of Multicultural Counseling and Development, 24*(1), 42–78. doi:10.1002/j.2161-1912.1996.tb00288.x

Association for Specialists in Group Work. (2000). *Professional standards for the training of group workers*. Retrieved from https://static1.squarespace.com/static/55cea634e4b083e448c3dd50/t/55d3f615e4b0d900e228c831/1439954453323/ASGW_training_standards.pdf

Balkin, R. S., & Roland, C. B. (2007). Reconceptualizing stabilization for counseling adolescents in brief psychiatric hospitalization: A new model. *Journal of Counseling & Development, 85*(1), 64–72. https://doi.org/10.1002/j.1556-6678.2007.tb00445.x

Bandura, A. (1977). *Social learning theory*. Englewood Cliffs, NJ: Prentice Hall.

Bardeen, J. R., Fergus, T. A., & Orcutt, H. K. (2013). Testing a hierarchical model of distress tolerance. *Journal of Psychopathology and Behavioral Assessment, 35*(4), 495–505. https://doi.org/10.1007/s10862-013-9359-0

Barnett, J. E., Baker, K. E., Elman, N. S., & Schoener, G.R. (2007). In pursuit of wellness: The self-care imperative. *Professional Psychology: Research and Practice, 38*(6), 603–612. https://doi.org/10.1037/0735-7028.38.6.603

Barnett, J. E., & Cooper, N. (2009). Creating a culture of self-care. *Clinical Psychology: Science and Practice, 16*(1), 16–20. https://doi.org/10.1111/j.1468-2850.2009.01138.x

Barnett, J. E., & Johnson, W. B. (2015). *Ethics desk reference for counselors* (2nd ed.). Alexandria, VA: American Counseling Association.

Baron-Cohen, S. (2011). *Zero degrees of empathy: A new theory of human cruelty.* London, England: Penguin UK.

Beahrs, J. O., & Gutheil, T. G. (2001). Informed consent in psychotherapy. *American Journal of Psychiatry, 158*, 4–10. https://doi.org/10.1176/appi.ajp.158.1.4

Beauchamp, T. L., & Childress, J. F. (1979). *Principles of biomedical ethics*. New York, NY: Oxford University Press.

Beauchamp, T. L., & Childress, J. F. (2013). *Principles of biomedical ethics* (7th ed.). New York, NY: Oxford University Press.

Beck, M. J., Rausch, M. A., & Wood, S. M. (2014). Developing the fearless school counselor ally and advocate for LGBTQIQ youth: Strategies for preparation programs. *Journal of LGBT Issues in Counseling, 8*(4), 361–375. https://doi.org/10.1080/15538605.2014.960126

Beebe, S. A., & Masterson, J. T. (2006). *Communicating in small groups* (8th ed.). Boston, MA: Pearson.

Beer, J. S., & Lombardo, M. V. (2007). Insights into emotion regulation from neuropsychology. In J. J. Gross (Ed.), *Handbook of emotion regulation* (pp. 69–86). New York, NY: Guilford Press.

Bell, A. C., & D'Zurilla, T. J. (2009). Problem-solving therapy for depression: A meta-analysis. *Clinical Psychology Review, 29*(4), 348–353. https://doi.org/10.1016/j.cpr.2009.02.003

Bell, M. P., McLaughlin, M. E., & Sequeira, J. M. (2002). Discrimination, harassment, and the glass ceiling: Women executives as change agents. *Journal of Business Ethics, 37*(1), 65–76. https://doi.org/10.1023/A:1014730102063

Bemak, F., & Chung, R. C. Y. (2005). Advocacy as a critical role for urban school counselors: Working toward equity and social justice. *Professional School Counseling, 8*(3), 196–202. Retrieved from http://www.jstor.org/stable/42732459

Bemak, F., & Chung, R. C. Y. (2008). New professional roles and advocacy strategies for school counselors: A multicultural/social justice perspective to move beyond the nice counselor syndrome. *Journal of Counseling & Development, 86*(3), 372–381. https://doi.org/10.1002/j.1556-6678.2008.tb00522.x

Ben-Ari, A. T. (2002). Dimensions and predictions of professional involvement in self-help groups: A view from within. *Health & Social Work, 27*(2), 95–103. https://doi.org/10.1093/hsw/27.2.95

Benish, S. G., Imel, Z. E., & Wampold, B. E. (2008). The relative efficacy of bona fide psychotherapies for treating post-traumatic stress disorder: A meta-analysis of direct comparisons. *Clinical Psychology Review, 28*(5), 746–758. https://doi.org/10.1016/j.cpr.2007.10.005

Berg, I. K., & de Shazer, S. (1993). Making numbers talk: Language in therapy. In S. Friedman (Ed.), *The new language of change: Constructive collaboration in psychotherapy* (pp. 5–24). New York, NY: Guilford Press.

Berman-Rossi, T. (1993). The tasks and skills of social worker across stages of group development. *Social Work With Groups, 16*(1–2), 69–81. https://doi.org/10.1300/J009v16n01_07

Bernard, H., Burlingame, G., Flores, P., Greene, L., Joyce, A., Kobos, J. C., ... Feirman, D. (2008). Clinical practice guidelines for group psychotherapy. *International Journal of Group Psychotherapy, 58*(4), 455–542. https://doi.org/10.1521/ijgp.2008.58.4.455

Bernard, J. M. (1979). Supervision training: A discrimination model. *Counselor Education and Supervision, 19*(1), 60–68. https://doi.org/10.1002/j.1556-6978.1979.tb00906.x

Bernard, J. M., & Goodyear, R. K. (1998). *Fundamentals of clinical supervision* (2nd ed.). Boston, MA: Allyn & Bacon.

Berthoz, S., & Hill, E. L. (2005). The validity of using self-reports to assess emotion regulation abilities in adults with autism spectrum disorder. *European Psychiatry, 20*(3), 291–298. https://doi.org/10.1016/j.eurpsy.2004.06.013

Bertrand, B., & Mullainthan, S. (2004). Are Emily and Greg more employable than Lakisha and Jamal?: A field experiment on labor market discrimination. *American Economic Review, 94*(4), 991–1013. https://doi.org/10.1257/0002828042002561

Beutler, L. E., Alomohamed, S., Moleiro, C., & Romanelli, R. K. (2002). Systemic treatment selection and prescriptive therapy. In F. W. Kaslow (Ed.), *Comprehensive handbook of psychotherapy: Integrative/eclectic, Vol. 4.* (pp. 255–271). New York, NY: Wiley.

Bieschke, K. J., Matthews, C., & Wade, J. (1996). Training group counselors: The process observer method. *Journal for Specialists in Group Work, 21*(3), 181–186. http://dx.doi.org/10.1080/01933929608412250

Birnbaum, M. L., & Cicchetti, A. (2005). A model for working with the group life cycle in each group session across the life span of the group. *Groupwork, 15*(3), 23–43. https://doi.org/10.1921/0951824X.15.3.23

Blake, C., & Hamrin, V. (2007). Current approaches to the assessment and management of anger and aggression in youth: A review. *Journal of Child and Adolescent Psychiatric Nursing, 20*(4), 209–221. https://doi.org/10.1111/j.1744-6171.2007.00102.x

Blaustein, M. E., & Kinniburgh, K. M. (2010). *Treating traumatic stress in children and adolescents.* New York, NY: Guilford Press.

Bohart, A. C., & Tallman, K. (2010). Clients: The neglected common factor in psychotherapy. In B. L. Duncan, B. E. Wampold, & M. A. Hubble (Eds.), *The heart and soul of change* (2nd ed., pp. 83–112). Washington, DC: American Psychological Association.

Borrell-Carrió, F., & Epstein, R. M. (2004). Preventing errors in clinical practice: A call for self-awareness. *Annals of Family Medicine, 2*(4), 310–316. https://doi.org/10.1370/afm.80

Bowlby, J. (1969). *Attachment and loss, Vol. I: Attachment.* New York, NY: Basic Books.

Bowlby, J. (1988). *A secure base.* New York, NY: Basic Books.

Boysen, G. A. (2010). Integrating implicit bias into counselor education. *Counselor Education and Supervision, 49*(4), 210–227. https://doi.org/10.1002/j.1556-6978.2010.tb00099.x

Brammer, L. M., & MacDonald, G. (2003). *The helping relationship: Process and skills* (8th ed.). Boston, MA: Pearson.

Brannon, G. E. (2016). History and mental status examination. Medscape. Retrieved from http://emedicine.medscape.com/article/293402-overview

Bratter, T. E. (2011). Compassionate confrontation psychotherapy: An effective and humanistic alternative to biological psychiatry for adolescents in crisis. *Ethical Human Psychology and Psychiatry, 13*(2), 115–133. https://doi.org/10.1891/1559-4343.13.2.115

Breggin, P. R. (2008). Practical applications: 22 guidelines for counseling and psychotherapy. *Ethical Human Psychology and Psychiatry, 10*(1), 43–57. https://doi.org/10.1891/1559-4343.10.1.43

Breitborde, N. J., Woods, S. W., & Srihari, V. H. (2009). Multifamily psychoeducation for first-episode psychosis: A cost-effectiveness analysis. *Psychiatric Services, 60*(11), 1477–1483. https://doi.org/10.1176/ps.2009.60.11.1477

Brems, C. (2000). *Dealing with challenges in psychotherapy and counseling*. Belmont, CA: Brooks/Cole.

Brodsky, K. L., & Ostacher, M. J. (2015). Substance-related disorders and addictive disorders. In L. W. Roberts & A. K. Louie (Eds.), *Study guide to DSM-5* (pp. 349–379). Arlington, VA: American Psychiatric Association.

Brown, B. (2010, June). *Brené Brown: The power of vulnerability* [TED talk]. Retrieved from http://www.ted.com/talks/brene_brown_on_vulnerability

Brown, B. (2013, December 10). *Brené Brown on empathy* [Video file]. Retrieved from https://www.youtube.com/watch?v=1Evwgu369Jw

Brown, K. W., & Ryan, R. M. (2003). The benefits of being present: Mindfulness and its role in psychological well-being. *Journal of Personality and Social Psychology, 84*(4), 822–848. https://doi.org/10.1037/0022-3514.84.4.822

Brown, L. J., & Astell, A. J. (2012). Assessing mood in older adults: A conceptual review of methods and approaches. *International Psychogeriatrics, 24*(8), 1197–1206. https://doi.org/10.1017/S1041610212000075

Brown, S., Brack, G., & Mullis, F. (2008). Traumatic symptoms in sexually abused children: Implications for school counselors. *Professional School Counseling, 11*(6), 368–379. https://doi.org/10.5330/PSC.n.2010-11.368

Bruner, J. (1990). *Acts of meaning*. Cambridge, MA: Harvard University Press.

Bureau of Justice Statistics. (2016). *Co-offending among adolescents in violent victimizations, 2004–13*. NCJ 249756. Retrieved from https://www.bjs.gov/content/pub/pdf/caavv0413_sum.pdf

Bureau of Labor Statistics. (2015). Rehabilitation counselors. In *Occupational outlook handbook. Retrieved from* https://www.bls.gov/ooh/community-and-social-service/rehabilitation-counselors.htm

Burkard, A. W., Knox, S., Groen, M., Perez, M., & Hess, S. A. (2006). European American therapist self-disclosure in cross-cultural counseling. *Journal of Counseling Psychology, 53*(1), 15–25. https://doi.org/10.1037/0022-0167.53.1.15

Burnham, J. J., & Jackson, C. M. (2000). School counselor roles: Discrepancies between actual practice and existing models. *Professional School Counseling, 4*(1), 41–49.

Butler, E. A., Lee, T. L., & Gross, J. J. (2007). Emotion regulation and culture: Are the social consequences of emotion suppression culture-specific? *Emotion, 7*(1), 30–48. https://doi.org/10.1037/1528-3542.7.1.30

Byrnes, J. D. (2002). *Before conflict: Preventing aggressive behavior*. Lanham, MD: Scarecrow Press.

Cabral, R. R., & Smith, T. B. (2011). Racial/ethnic matching of clients and therapists in mental health services: A meta-analytic review of preferences, perceptions, and outcomes. *Journal of Counseling Psychology, 58*(4), 537–554. https://doi.org/10.1037/a0025266

Cameron, S., & turtle-song, i. (2002). Learning to write case notes using the SOAP format. *Journal of Counseling & Development, 80*(3), 286–292. https://doi.org/10.1002/j.1556-6678.2002.tb00193.x

Caper, R. (2001). The goals of clinical psychoanalysis: Notes on interpretation and psychological development. *Psychoanalytic Quarterly, 70*(1), 99–116. https://doi.org/10.1002/j.2167-4086.2001.tb00591.x

Cardemil, E. V., & Battle, C. L. (2003). Guess who's coming to therapy? Getting comfortable with conversations about race and ethnicity in psychotherapy. *Professional Psychology: Research and Practice, 34*(3), 278–286. https://doi.org/10.1037/0735-7028.34.3.278

Carroll, M. R., & Wiggins, J. D. (1997). *Elements of group counseling: Back to the basics*. Denver: Love.

Carter, O., Pannekoek, L., Fursland A., Allen, K. L., Lampard, A. M., & Byrne, S. M. (2012). Increased wait-list time predicts dropout from outpatient enhanced cognitive behaviour therapy (CBT-E) for eating disorders. *Behaviour Research and Therapy, 50*(1), 487–492. https://doi.org/10.1016/j.brat.2012.03.003

Casey, B. J., Jones, R. M., & Hare, T. A. (2008). The adolescent brain. *Annals of the New York Academy of Sciences, 1124*, 111–126. https://doi.org/10.1196/annals.1440.010

Castro, C. A., & Kintzle, S. (2014). Suicides in the military: The post-modern combat veteran and the Hemingway effect. *Current Psychiatry Reports, 16*(8), 1–9. https://doi.org/10.1007/s11920-014-0460-1

Cavaiola, A. A., & Colford, J. E. (2006). *A practical guide to crisis intervention*. Boston, MA: Houghton Mifflin.

Centers for Disease Control and Prevention. (2011). *Sexual identity, age of sexual contacts, and health-risk behaviors among students in grades 9-12: Youth risk behavior surveillance*. Atlanta, GA: US Department of Health and Human Services.

Chambless, D. L., & Ollendick, T. H. (2001). Empirically supported psychological interventions: Controversies and evidence. *Annual Review of Psychology, 52*, 685–716. https://doi.org/10.1146/annurev.psych.52.1.685

Charlemagne-Odle, S., Harmon, G., & Maltby, M. (2014). Clinical psychologists' experiences of personal significant distress. *Psychology and Psychotherapy: Theory, Research and Practice, 87*(2), 237–252. https://doi.org/10.1111/j.2044-8341.2012.02070.x

Chatoor, I., & Kurpnick, J. (2001). The role of non-specific factors in treatment outcome of psychotherapy studies. *European Child & Adolescent Psychiatry, 10*(S1), S19. https://doi.org/10.1007/s007870170004

Chen, M., & Rybak, C. J. (2004). *Group leadership skills*. Belmont, CA: Brooks/Cole.

Chu, B. C. (2007). Considering culture one client at a time: Maximizing the cultural exchange. *Pragmatic Case Studies in Psychotherapy, 3*(3), 34–43. https://doi.org/10.14713/pcsp.v3i3.905

Claiborn, C. D., Goodyear, R. K., & Horner, P. A. (2001). Feedback. *Psychotherapy, 38*(4), 401–408. https://doi.org/10.1037/0033-3204.38.4.401

Claus, R. E., & Kindleberger, L. R. (2002). Engaging substance abusers after centralized assessment: Predictors of treatment entry and dropout. *Journal of Psychoactive Drugs, 34*(1), 25–31. https://doi.org/10.1080/02791072.2002.10399933

Coan, J. A. (2008). Toward a neuroscience of attachment. In J. Cassidy & P. R. Shaver (Eds.), *Handbook of attachment* (2nd ed., pp. 3–54). New York, NY: Guilford Press.

Cohen, A. M., & Smith, R. D. (1976). *The critical incident in growth groups: Theory and technique*. La Jolla, CA: University Associates.

Cohen, J. A., Mannarino, A. P., Kliethermes, M., & Murray, L. A. (2012). Trauma-focused CBT for youth with complex trauma. *Child Abuse & Neglect, 36*(6), 528–541. https://doi.org/10.1016/j.chiabu.2012.03.007

Collins, B. G., & Collins, T. M. (2005). *Crisis and trauma: Developmental-ecological intervention*. Boston, MA: Houghton Mifflin.

Collins, F. S. (2004). What we do and don't know about 'race', 'ethnicity', genetics and health at the dawn of the genome era. *Nature Genetics, 36*(11s), S13–S15. https://doi.org/10.1038/ng1436

Collins, S., & Arthur, N. (2010a). Culture-infused counselling: A fresh look at a classic framework of multicultural counselling competencies. *Counselling Psychology Quarterly, 23*(2), 203–216. https://doi.org/10.1080/09515071003798204

Collins, S., & Arthur, N. (2010b). Culture-infused counselling: A model for developing multicultural competence. *Counselling Psychology Quarterly, 23*(2), 217–233. https://doi.org/10.1080/09515071003798212

Connors, J. V., & Caple, R. B. (2005). A review of group systems theory. *Journal for Specialists in Group Work, 30*(2), 93–110. https://doi.org/10.1080/01933920590925940

Cook, A., Spinazzola, J., Ford, J., Lanktree, C., Blaustein, M., Cloitre, M., … Van der Kolk, B. (2005). Complex trauma in children and adolescents. *Psychiatric Annals, 35*(5), 390–398. https://doi.org/10.3928/00485713-20050501-05

Copeland, B. (n.d.). Quotery. Retrieved from http://www.quotery.com/quotes/the-trouble-with-not-having-a-goal-is-that-you

Corey, G., Corey, M. S., & Callanan, P. (2003). *Issues and ethics in the helping professions* (6th ed.). Pacific Grove, CA: Brooks/Cole.

Corey, M. S., & Corey, G. (2006). *Process and practice groups* (7th ed.). Belmont, CA: Thompson Brooks/Cole.

Courtois, C. A., & Ford, J. D. (2013). *Treatment of complex trauma: A sequenced, relationship-based approach*. New York, NY: Guilford Press.

Coverdale, J. H., Louie, A. K., & Roberts, L. W. (2015). Arriving at a diagnosis. In L. W. Roberts & A. K. Louie (Eds.), *Study guide to DSM-5* (pp. 19–31). Arlington, VA: American Psychiatric Association.

Cozolino, L. (2010). *The neuroscience of psychotherapy* (2nd ed.). New York, NY: Norton.

Cozolino, L. (2014). *The neuroscience of human relationships* (2nd ed.). New York, NY: Norton.

Creed, T. A., Reisweber, J., & Beck, A. T. (2011). *Cognitive therapy for adolescents in school settings*. New York, NY: Guilford Press.

Crews, F. T., & Boettiger, C. A. (2009). Impulsivity, frontal lobes and risk for addiction. *Pharmacology Biochemistry and Behavior, 93*(3), 237–247. doi:10.1016/j.pbb.2009.04.018

Crowell, S. E., Beauchaine, T. P., McCauley, E., Smith, C. J., Stevens, A. L., & Sylvers, P. (2005). Psychological, autonomic, and serotonergic correlates of parasuicide among adolescent girls. *Development and Psychopathology, 17*(4), 1105–1127. https://doi.org/10.1017/S0954579405050522

Daniel, M., & Gurczynski, J. (2010). Mental status examination. In D. L. Segal & M. Hersen (Eds.), *Diagnostic interviewing* (pp. 61–88). New York, NY: Springer.

Davies, B., & Harré, R. (1999). Positioning: The discursive production of selves. *Journal for the Theory of Social Behaviour, 20*(1), 43–63. https://doi.org/10.1111/j.1468-5914.1990.tb00174.x

Davis, T., & Ritchie, M. (2003). Confidentiality and the school counselor: A challenge for the 1990s. In T. P. Remley, M. A. Hermann, & W. C. Huey (Eds.), *Ethical & legal issues in school counseling* (pp. 197–207). Alexandria, VA: American School Counselor Association.

Davis, T. E. (2015). *Exploring school counseling* (2nd ed.). Stanford, CT: Cengage.

Day, S. X. (2007). *Groups in practice*. Boston, MA: Houghton Mifflin.

Day-Vines, N. L., Wood, S. M., Grothaus, T., Craigen, L., Holman, A., Dotson-Blake, K., & Douglass, M. J. (2007). Broaching the subjects of race, ethnicity, and culture during the counseling process. *Journal of Counseling & Development, 85*(4), 401–409. https://doi.org/10.1002/j.1556-6678.2007.tb00608.x

Dechawatanapaisal, D., & Siengthai, S. (2006). The impact of cognitive dissonance on learning work behavior. *Journal of Workplace Learning, 18*(1), 42–54. https://doi.org/10.1108/13665620610641300

De Jong, P., & Berg, I. K. (2008). *Interviewing for solutions* (3rd ed.). Pacific Grove, CA: Brooks/Cole.

DeLucia-Waack, J. L. (2006). *Leading psychoeducational groups for children and adolescents*. Thousand Oaks, CA: Sage.

de Shazer, S. (1985). *Keys to solution in brief therapy*. New York, NY: Norton.

de Shazer, S., & Dolan, Y. (2012). *More than miracles: The state of the art of solution-focused brief therapy*. Abingdon, UK: Routledge.

Diller, J. V. (2007). *Cultural diversity* (3rd ed.). Belmont, CA: Thompson Brooks/Cole.

DiMeo, M. A., Moore, G. K., & Lichtenstein, C. (2012). Relationship of evidence-based practice and treatments: A survey of community mental health providers. *Journal of Community Psychology, 40*(3), 341–357. https://doi.org/10.1002/jcop.20516

Doidge, N. (2007). *The brain that changes itself: Stories of personal triumph from the frontiers of brain science*. New York, NY: Penguin Books.

Dollarhide, C. T., & Saginak, K. A. (2012). *Comprehensive school counseling programs: K–12 delivery systems in action* (2nd ed.). Upper Saddle River, NJ: Pearson Education.

Donati, M., & Watts, M. (2005). Personal development in counselor training: Towards a clarification of inter-related concepts. *British Journal of Guidance & Counselling, 33*(4), 475–484. https://doi.org/10.1080/03069880500327553

Drewery, W. (2005). Why we should watch what we say: Position calls, everyday speech and the production of relational subjectivity. *Theory & Psychology, 15*(3), 305–324. https://doi.org/10.1177/0959354305053217

Drewery, W., & Winslade, J. (1997). The theoretical story of narrative therapy. In G. Monk, J. Winslade, K. Crocket, & D. Epston (Eds.), *Narrative therapy in practice: The archaeology of hope* (pp. 32–52). San Francisco, CA: Jossey-Bass.

Dubin, W. R., & Jagarlamudi, K. (2010, July). Safety in the evaluation of potentially violent patients. *Psychiatric Times*, 15–17.

Duncan, L. E. (2003). Black male college students' attitudes toward seeking psychological help. *Journal of Black Psychology, 29*(1), 68–86. https://doi:.org/10.1177/0095798402239229

Dwyer, K., Osher, D., & Warger, C. (1998). *Early warning, timely response: A guide to safe schools*. Washington, DC: US Department of Education.

Earle, W. J. (2014). DSM-5. *Philosophical Forum, 45*(2), 179–196. https://doi.org/10.1111/phil.12034

Eberth, J., & Sedlmeier, P. (2012). The effects of mindfulness meditation: A meta-analysis. *Mindfulness, 3*(3), 174–189. https://doi.org/10.1007/s12671-012-0101-x

Egan, G. (2010). *The skilled helper* (9th ed.). Pacific Grove, CA: Brooks/Cole.

Ehlers, A., Bisson, J., Clark, D. M., Creamer, M., Pilling, S., Richards, D., ... Yule, W. (2010). Do all psychological treatments really work the same in posttraumatic stress disorder? *Clinical Psychology Review, 30*(2), 269–276. https://doi.org/10.1016/j.cpr.2009.12.001

Eid, M., & Diener, E. (2001). Norms for experiencing emotions in different cultures: Inter- and intranational differences. *Journal of Personality and Social Psychology, 81*(5), 869–885. https://doi.org/10.1037//0022-3514.81.5.869

Eisenberg, N., Hofer, C., & Vaughan, J. (2007). Effortful control and its socioemotional consequences. In J. J. Gross (Ed.), *Handbook of emotion regulation* (pp. 287–306). New York, NY: Guilford Press.

Eliot, J. A. (2013). Hope-lore and the compassionate clinician. *Journal of Pain and Symptom Management, 45*(3), 628–634. https://doi.org/10.1016/j.jpainsymman.2012.10.233

Ellis, H. A. (2011). The crisis intervention team—a revolutionary tool for law enforcement: The psychiatric-mental health nursing perspective. *Journal of Psychosocial Nursing and Mental Health Services, 49*(11), 37–43. https://doi.org/10.3928/02793695-20111004-01

Epley, N., Keysar, B., Van Boven, L., & Gilovich, T. (2004). Perspective taking as egocentric anchoring and adjustment. *Journal of Personality and Social Psychology, 87*(3), 327–339. https://doi.org/10.1037/0022-3514.87.3.327

Epley, N., Morewedge, C. K., & Keysar, B. (2004). Perspective taking in children and adults: Equivalent egocentrism but differential correction. *Journal of Experimental Social Psychology, 40*(6), 760–768. https://doi.org/10.1016/j.jesp.2004.02.002

Evidence-based practice in psychology. (2006). *American Psychologist, 61*(4), 271–285. https://doi.org/10.1037/0003-066X.61.4.271

Fahy, A. (2007). The unbearable fatigue of compassion: Notes from a substance abuse counselor who dreams of working at Starbuck's. *Clinical Social Work Journal, 35*(3), 199–205. https://doi.org/10.1007/s10615-007-0094-4

Family Education Rights and Privacy Act, 20 U.S.C. § 1232g; 34 CFR Part 99 (1974).

Fauteux, K. (2010). De-escalating angry and violent clients. *American Journal of Psychotherapy, 64*(2), 195–213.

Fazio-Griffith, L., & Curry, J. R. (2008). Professional school counselors as process observers in the classroom: Collaboration with classroom teachers. *Journal of School Counseling, 6*(20), 1–15.

Federal Bureau of Investigation. (n.d.). Crime in the U.S. Retrieved from http://www.fbi.gov/about-us/cjis/ucr/crime-in-the-u.s/2012/crime-in-the-u.s.-2012/violent-crime/violent-crime

Festinger, L. (1957). *A theory of cognitive dissonance*. Stanford, CA: Stanford University Press.

Fields, A. J. (2010). Multicultural research and practice: Theoretical issues and maximizing cultural exchange. *Professional Psychology: Research and Practice, 41*(3), 196–201. https://doi.org/10.1037/a0017938

Fink, I. K., Boersma, K., MacDonald, S., & Linton, S. J. (2012). Understanding catastrophizing from a misdirected problem-solving perspective. *British Journal of Health Psychology, 17*(2), 408–419. https://doi.org/10.1111/j.2044-8287.2011.02044.x

Flannery, R. B., Juliano, J., Cronin, S., & Walker, A. P. (2006). Characteristics of assaultive psychiatric patients: Fifteen-year analysis of the Assaulted Staff Action Program (ASAP). *Psychiatric Quarterly, 77*(3), 239–249. https://doi.org/10.1007/s11126-006-9011-1

Fliege, H., Lee, J. R., Grimm, A., & Klapp, B. F. (2009). Risk factors and correlates of deliberate self-harm behavior: A systematic review. *Journal of Psychosomatic Research, 66*(6), 477–493. https://doi.org/10.1016/j.jpsychores.2008.10.013

Floyd, R. G., Phaneuf, R. L., & Wilczynski, S. M. (2005). Measurement properties of indirect assessment methods for functional behavioral assessment: A review of research. *School Psychology Review, 34*(1), 58–73.

Folstein, M. F., Folstein, S. E., & McHugh, P. R. (1975). "Mini-mental state": A practical method for grading the cognitive state of patients for the clinician. *Journal of Psychiatric Research, 12*(3), 189–198. https://doi.org/10.1016/0022-3956(75)90026-6

Forester-Miller, H., & Davis, T. E. (1995). *A practitioner's guide to ethical decision making*. American Counseling Association.

Foucault, M. (1972). *The order of things: An archaeology of the human sciences*. New York, NY: Pantheon Books.

Frances, A. J., & Widiger, T. (2012). Psychiatric diagnosis: Lessons from the DSM-IV past and cautions for the DSM-5 future. *Annual Review of Clinical Psychology, 8*, 109–130. https://doi.org/10.1146/annurev-clinpsy-032511-143102

Frankel, R. M. (2009). Empathy research: A complex challenge. *Patient Education and Counseling, 75*(1), 1–2. https://doi.org/10.1016/j.pec.2009.02.008

Frankl, V. E. (1963). *Man's search for meaning*. New York, NY: Simon & Schuster.

Freedman, J., & Combs, G. (1996). *Narrative therapy: The social construction of preferred realities*. New York, NY: Norton.

Freeman, J., Epston, D., & Lobovits, D. (1997). *Playful approaches to serious problems: Narrative therapy with children and their families*. New York, NY: Norton.

Fried, D. (2002). Corrective emotional experience. *Encyclopedia of Psychotherapy, 1*, 551–555. Retrieved from https://s3.amazonaws.com/academia.edu.documents/32736575/Encyclopedia_of_Psychotherapy.pdf?AWSAccessKeyId=AKIAIWOWYYGZ2Y53UL3A&Expires=1511213578&Signature=KU9ix95HX8nSnpC08yN9AcxThjk%3D&response-content-disposition=inline%3B%20filename%3DEncyclopedia_of_Psychotherapy.pdf#page=535

Friedberg, R. D, & McClure, J. (2009). *Cognitive therapy techniques for children and adolescents: Tools for enhancing practice*. New York, NY: Guilford Press.

Funk, M., Minoletti, A., Drew, N., Taylor, J., & Saraceno, B. (2006). Advocacy for mental health: Roles for consumer and family organizations and governments. *Health Promotion International, 21*(1), 70–75. https://doi.org/10.1093/heapro/dai031

Furukawa, T. A. (2010). Assessment of mood: Guides for clinicians. *Journal of Psychosomatic Research, 68*(6), 581–589. https://doi.org/10.1016/j.jpsychores.2009.05.003

Gallagher, K. C. (2005). Brain research and early childhood development: A primer for developmentally appropriate practice. *YC: Young Children, 60*(4), 12–21.

Gallese, V., & Goldman, A. (1998). Mirror neurons and the simulation theory of mind-reading. *Trends in Cognitive Sciences, 2*(12), 493–501. https://doi.org/10.1016/S1364-6613(98)01262-5

Galotti, K. M., Ciner, E., Altenbaumer, H. E., Geerts, H. J., Rupp, A., & Woulfe, J. (2006). Decision-making styles in a real-life decision: Choosing a college major. *Personality and Individual Differences, 41*(4), 629–639. https://doi.org/10.1016/j.paid.2006.03.003

Gaston, L. (1990). The concept of the alliance and its role in psychotherapy: Theoretical and empirical considerations. *Psychotherapy, 27*(2), 143–153. https://doi.org/10.1037/0033-3204.27.2.143

Geller, J. D. (2003). Self-disclosure in psychoanalytic–existential therapy. *Journal of Clinical Psychology, 59*(5), 541–554. https://doi.org/10.1002/jclp.10158

Geroski, A. M. (2017). *Skills for helping relationship professionals*. Thousand Oaks, CA: Sage.

Geroski, A. M., & Kraus, K. L. (2002). Process and content in school psychoeducational groups: Either, both or none? *Journal for Specialists in Group Work, 27*(2), 233–245. https://doi.org/10.1080/742848694

Geroski, A. M., & Kraus, K. L. (2010). *Groups in schools: Preparing, leading, and responding*. Boston, MA: Pearson.

Gert, B. (2012). The definition of morality. In E. N. Zalta (Ed.), *The Stanford Encyclopedia of Philosophy* (Fall 2012 Edition). Retrieved from http://plato.stanford.edu/archives/fall2012/entries/morality-definition

Gladding, S. T. (2003). *Group work: A counseling specialty* (4th ed.). Upper Saddle River, NJ: Prentice Hall.

Glodich, A., Allen, J. G., & Arnold, L. (2001). Protocol for a trauma-based psychoeducational group intervention to decrease risk-taking, reenactment, and further violence exposure: Application to the public high school setting. *Journal of Child and Adolescent Group Therapy, 11*(2–3), 87–107. https://doi.org/10.1023/A:1014745915141

Glosoff, H. L., & Pate, R. H. Jr. (2002). Privacy and confidentiality in school counseling. *Professional School Counseling, 6*(1), 20–27. Retrieved from http://www.jstor.org/stable/42732386

Goldfried, M. R., Burckell, L. A., & Eubanks-Carter, C. (2003). Therapist self-disclosure in cognitive-behavior therapy. *Journal of Clinical Psychology, 59*(5), 555–568. https://doi.org/10.1002/jclp.10159

Goldin, P. R., & Gross, J. J. (2010). Effects of mindfulness-based stress reduction (MBSR) on emotion regulation in social anxiety disorder. *Emotion, 10*(1), 83–91. https://doi.org/10.1037/a0018441

Gould, M., Theodore, K., Pilling, S., Bebbington, P., Hinton, M., & Johnson, S. (2006). Initial treatment phase in early psychosis: Can intensive home treatment prevent admission? *Psychiatrist, 30*(7), 243–246. https://doi.org/10.1192/pb.30.7.243

Gratz, K. L. (2001). Measurement of deliberate self-harm: Preliminary data on the Deliberate Self-Harm Inventory. *Journal of Psychopathology and Behavioral Assessment, 23*(4), 253–263. https://doi.org/10.1023/A:1012779403943

Greene, L. R. (2007). The theory & practice of group psychotherapy (5th ed.). *International Journal of Group Psychotherapy, 57*(4), 550–554. Retrieved from https://search-proquest-com.ezproxy.uvm.edu/docview/194772295?accountid=14679

Greenough, W. T., Black, J. E., & Wallace, C. S. (1987). Experience and brain development. *Child Development, 58*(3), 539–559. https://doi.org/10.2307/1130197

Gresham, F. M., Watson, T. S., & Skinner, C. H. (2001). Functional behavioral assessment: Principles, procedures, and future directions. *School Psychology Review, 30*(2), 156–172.

Griffiths, B. B., & Hunter, R. G. (2014). Neuroepigenetics of stress. *Neuroscience, 275*, 420–435. https://doi.org/10.1016/j.neuroscience.2014.06.041

Grills, A. E., & Ollendick, T. H. (2002). Issues in parent-child agreement: The case of structured diagnostic interviews. *Clinical Child and Family Psychology Review, 5*(1), 57–83. https://doi.org/10.1023/A:1014573708569

Gross, J. J. (1998). The emerging field of emotional regulation: An integrative review. *Review of General Psychology, 2*(3), 271–299. https://doi.org/10.1037/1089-2680.2.3.271

Gross, J. J. (2008). Emotion regulation. In M. Lewis, J. M. Haviland-Jones, & L. F. Barrett (Eds.), *Handbook of emotions* (3rd ed., pp. 497–512). New York, NY: Guilford Press.

Gross, J. J., & Thompson, R. A. (2007). Emotion regulation: Conceptual foundations. In J. J. Gross (Ed.), *Handbook of emotion regulation* (pp. 3–24). New York, NY: Guilford Press.

Grossman, A. H., & D'Augelli, A. R. (2007). Transgender youth and life-threatening behaviors. *Suicide and Life-Threatening Behaviors, 37*(5), 527–537. https://doi.org/10.1521/suli.2007.37.5.527

Hagedorn, W. B., & Hirshhorn, M. A. (2009). When talking won't work: Implementing experiential group activities with addicted clients. *Journal for Specialists in Group Work, 34*(1), 43–67. https://doi.org/10.1080/01933920802600832

Hahn, R. A., & Stroup, D. F. (1994). Race and ethnicity in public health surveillance: Criteria for the scientific use of social categories. *Public Health Reports, 109*(1), 7–15.

Hall, K. R. (2006). Solving problems together: A psychoeducational group model for victims of bullies. *Journal for Specialists in Group Work, 31*(3), 201–217. https://doi.org/10.1080/01933920600777790

Halstead, R. W., Wagner, L. D., Vivero, M., & Ferkol, W. (2002). Counselors' conceptualizations of caring in the counseling relationship. *Counseling and Values, 47*(1), 34–47. https://doi.org/10.1002/j.2161-007X.2002.tb00222.x

Hamilton, N. A., Karoly, P., Gallagher, M., Stevens, N., Karlson, C., & McCurdy, D. (2009). The assessment of emotion regulation in cognitive context: The emotion amplification and reduction scales. *Cognitive Therapy and Research, 33*(3), 255–263. https://doi.org/10.1007/s10608-007-9163-9

Hardy, K. V. (2013). Healing the hidden wounds of racial trauma. *Reclaiming Children and Youth, 22*(1), 24–28.
Hardy, K. V. (2017, September 22). *Towards a psychology of the oppressed: Treating the invisible wounds of sociocultural trauma*. Presented at Northeastern Family Institute, Essex, Vermont.
Hardy, K. V., & Laszloffy, T. A. (2005). *Teens who hurt: Clinical interventions to break the cycle of adolescent violence*. New York, NY: Guilford Press.
Hardy, K. V., & Qureshi, M. E. (2012). Devaluation, loss, and rage: A postscript to urban African American youth with substance abuse. *Alcoholism Treatment Quarterly, 30*(3), 326–342. https://doi.org/10.1080/07347324.2012.690699
Harré, R., & Moghaddam, F. (2003). Introduction: The self and others in traditional psychology and in positioning theory. In R. Harré & F. Moghaddam (Eds.), *The self and others: Positioning individuals and groups in personal, political, and cultural contexts* (pp. 1–11). Westport, CT: Praeger.
Harré, R., & Van Langenhove, L. (1991). Varieties of positioning. *Journal for the Theory of Social Behaviour, 21*(4), 393–407. https://doi.org/10.1111/j.1468-5914.1991.tb00203.x
Harris, T. E., & Sherblom, J. C. (2005). *Small group and team communication* (3rd ed.). Boston, MA: Pearson.
Hawton, K., & James, A. (2005). Suicide and deliberate self harm in young people. *BMJ: British Medical Journal, 330*(7496), 891–894. https://doi.org/10.1136/bmj.330.7496.891
Hayes, J. A., Owen, J., & Bieschke, K. J. (2015). Therapist differences in symptom change with racial/ethnic minority clients. *Psychotherapy, 52*(3), 308–314. https://doi.org/10.1037/a0037957
Hazler, R. J., & Barwick, N. (2001). *The therapeutic environment: Core conditions for facilitating therapy*. Philadelphia, PA: Open University Press.
Heagle, A. I., & Rehfeldt, R. A. (2006). Teaching perspective-taking skills to typically developing children through derived relational responding. *Journal of Early and Intensive Behavior Intervention, 3*(1), 1–34. https://doi.org/10.1037/h0100321
Health Insurance Portability and Accountability Act of 1996, Pub. L. No. 104-191, § 264, 110 Stat. 1936 (1996).
Hedtke, L., & Winslade, J. (2016). *Remembering lives: Conversations with the dying and the bereaved*. New York, NY: Routledge.
Heffernan, V. (2015, April 14). The muddled meaning of mindfulness. *New York Times Magazine*. Retrieved from https://www.nytimes.com/2015/04/19/magazine/the-muddied-meaning-of-mindfulness.html
Helfat, C. E., Harris, D., & Wolfson, P. J. (2006). The pipeline to the top: Women and men in the top executive ranks of US corporations. *Academy of Management Perspectives, 20*(4), 42–64. https://doi.org/10.5465/AMP.2006.23270306
Henkelman, J. J., & Everall, R. D. (2001). Informed consent with children: Ethical and practical implications. *Canadian Journal of Counselling and Psychotherapy/Revue canadienne de counseling et de psychothérapie, 35*(2), 109–121. Retrieved from http://cjc-rcc.ucalgary.ca/cjc/index.php/rcc/article/view/182
Hersoug, A. G. (2004). Assessment of therapists' and patients' personality: Relationship to therapeutic technique and outcome in brief dynamic psychotherapy. *Journal of Personality Assessment, 83*(3), 191–200. https://doi.org/10.1207/s15327752jpa8303_03

Hogan-Garcia, M. (1999). *The four skills of cultural diversity competence: A process for understanding and practice*. Belmont, CA: Brooks/Cole.

Hook, J. N., Farrell, J. E., Davis, D. E., DeBlaere, C., Van Tongeren, D. R., & Utsey, S. O. (2016). Cultural humility and racial microaggressions in counseling. *Journal of Counseling Psychology, 63*(3), 269–277. https://doi.org/10.1037/cou0000114

Hoyert, D. L., & Xu, J. (2012). Deaths: Preliminary data for 2011. *National Vital Statistics Reports, 61*(6), 1–34. Retrieved from Centers for Disease Control and Prevention website: http://www.cdc.gov/nchs/data/nvsr/nvsr61/nvsr61_06.pdf

Hubble, M. A., Duncan, B. L., Miller, S. D., & Wampold, B. E. (2010). Introduction. In B. L. Duncan, B. E. Wampold, & M. A. Hubble (Eds.), *The heart and soul of change* (2nd ed., pp. 23–46). Washington, DC: American Psychological Association.

Hulse-Killacky, D., Killacky, J., & Donigian, J. (2000). *Making task groups work in your world.* Upper Saddle River, NJ: Merrill/Prentice Hall.

Hulse-Killacky, D., Kraus, K. L., & Schumacher, R. A. (1999). Visual conceptualizations of meetings: A group work design. *Journal for Specialists in Group Work, 24*(1), 113–124. https://doi.org/10.1080/01933929908411423

Hulse-Killacky, D., Orr, J. J., & Paradise, L. V. (2006) The corrective feedback instrument—Revised. *Journal for Specialists in Group Work, 31*(3), 263–281. https://doi.org/10.1080/01933920600777758

Hutchinson, D. (2012). *The essential counselor* (2nd ed.). Los Angeles, CA: Sage.

Ilies, R., & Judge, T. A. (2005). Goal regulation across time: The effects of feedback and affect. *Journal of Applied Psychology, 90*(3), 453–467. https://doi.org/10.1037/0021-9010.90.3.453

International School Psychology Association. (2011). *Code of ethics*. Retrieved from http://www.ispaweb.org/wp-content/uploads/2013/01/The_ISPA_Code_of_Ethics_2011.pdf

Isaacs, M. L. (2003). The duty to warn and protect: Tarasoff and the elementary school teacher. In T. P. Remley, M. A. Hermann, & W. C. Huey (Eds.), *Ethical & legal issues in school counseling* (pp. 111–129). Alexandria, VA: American School Counselors Association.

Ivey, A. E., Ivey, M. B., & Zalaquett, C. P. (2010). *Intentional interviewing and counseling* (7th ed.). Belmont, CA: Brooks/Cole.

Jacobs, E. E., Masson, R. L., & Harvill, R. L. (2005). *Group counseling: Strategies and skills* (5th ed.). Pacific Grove, CA: Brooks/Cole.

James, R. K., & Gilliland, B. E. (2001). *Crisis intervention strategies* (4th ed.). Belmont, CA: Wadsworth/Thompson.

Johansson, P., Høglend, P., Ulberg, R., Amlo, S., Marble, A., Bøgwald, K. P., … Heyerdahl, O. (2010). The mediating role of insight for long-term improvements in psychodynamic therapy. *Journal of Consulting and Clinical Psychology, 78*(3), 438–448. https://doi.org/10.1037/a0019245

Johnson, D. W., & Johnson, F. P. (2006). *Joining together: Group theory and group skills* (9th ed.). Boston, MA: Pearson.

Johnson, M. H. (2005). Sensitive periods in functional brain development: Problems and prospects. *Developmental Psychobiology, 46*(3), 287–292. https://doi.org/10.1002/dev.20057

Kabat-Zinn, J. (1994). *Wherever you go, there you are: Mindfulness meditation in everyday life*. New York, NY: Hyperion Books.

Kaplan, A. (2008). Violent attacks by patients: Prevention and self-protection. *Psychiatric Times, 25*(7), 1, 6–8.
Kayler, H., & Sherman, J. (2009). At-risk ninth-grade students: A psychoeducational group approach to increase study skills and grade point averages. *Professional School Counseling, 12*(6), 434–439. https://doi.org/10.5330/PSC.n.2010-12.434
Kees, N. L., & Jacobs, E. (1990). Conducting more effective groups: How to select and process group exercises. *Journal for Specialists in Group Work, 15*(1), 21–29. https://doi.org/10.1080/01933929008411908
Keng, S. L., Smoski, M. J., & Robins, C. J. (2011). Effects of mindfulness on psychological health: A review of empirical studies. *Clinical Psychology Review, 31*(6), 1041–1056. https://doi.org/10.1016/j.cpr.2011.04.006
Kerwin, M. E., Kirby, K. C., Speziali, D., Duggan, M., Mellitz, C., Versek, B., & McNamara, A. (2015). What can parents do? A review of state laws regarding decision making for adolescent drug abuse and mental health treatment. *Journal of Child & Adolescent Substance Abuse, 24*(3), 166–176. https://doi.org/10.1080/1067828X.2013.777380
Keysar, B., Lin, S., & Barr, D. J. (2003). Limits on theory of mind use in adults. *Cognition, 89*(1), 25–41. https://doi.org/10.1016/S0010-0277(03)00064-7
Keyton, J. (1993). Group termination: Completing the study of group development. *Small Group Research, 24*(1), 84–100. https://doi.org/10.1177/1046496493241006
Killian, K. D. (2008). Helping till it hurts? A multimethod study of compassion fatigue, burnout, and self-care in clinicians working with trauma survivors. *Traumatology, 14*(2), 32–44. https://doi.org/10.1177/1534765608319083
Kindsvatter, A., & Geroski, A. (2014). The impact of early life stress on the neurodevelopment of the stress response system. *Journal of Counseling & Development, 92*(4), 472–480. https://doi.org/10.1002/j.1556-6676.2014.00173.x
Kislev, E. (2015). The use of participant-observers in group therapy: A critical exploration in light of Foucauldian theory. *Group, 39*(1), 9–24. Retrieved from http://www.jstor.org/stable/10.13186/group.39.1.0009
Kitchener, K. S. (1984). Intuition, critical evaluation and ethical principles: The foundation for ethical decisions in counseling psychology. *Counseling Psychologist, 12*(3), 43–55. https://doi.org/10.1177/0011000084123005
Kitchener, K. S., & Anderson, S. K. (2011). *Foundations of ethical practice, research, and teaching in psychology and counseling*. New York, NY: Routledge.
Kivlighan, D. M. Jr., & Goldfine, D. C. (1991). Endorsement of therapeutic factors as a function of stage of group development and participant interpersonal attitudes. *Journal of Counseling Psychology, 38*(2), 150–158. https://doi.org/10.1037/0022-0167.38.2.150
Kivlighan, D. M. Jr., & Luiza, J. W. (2005) Examining the credibility gap and the mum effect: Rex Stockton's contributions to research on feedback in counseling groups. *Journal for Specialists in Group Work, 30*(3), 253–269. https://doi.org/10.1080/01933920591003131
Knauss, L. K. (2006). Ethical issues in recordkeeping in group psychotherapy. *International Journal of Group Psychotherapy, 56*(4), 415–430. https://doi.org/10.1521/ijgp.2006.56.4.415
Knudsen, E. I. (2004). Sensitive periods in the development of the brain and behavior. *Journal of Cognitive Neuroscience, 16*(8), 1412–1425. https://doi.org/10.1162/0898929042304796

Kolostoumpis, D., Bergiannaki, J. D., Peppou, L. E., Louki, E., Fousketaki, S., Patelakis, A., & Economou, M. P. (2015). Effectiveness of relatives' psychoeducation on family outcomes in bipolar disorder. *International Journal of Mental Health, 44*(4), 290–302. https://doi.org/10.1080/00207411.2015.1076292

Kottler, J. A. (1991). *The compleat therapist*. San Francisco, CA: Jossey-Bass.

Kottman, T. (2002). *Partners in play: An Adlerian approach to play therapy* (2nd ed.). Alexandria, VA: American Counseling Association.

Kraus, K., & Hulse-Killacky, D. (1996). Balancing process and content in groups: A metaphor. *Journal for Specialists in Group Work, 21*(2), 90–93. https://doi.org/10.1080/01933929608412236

Kubiak, S. P. (2005). Trauma and cumulative adversity in women of a disadvantaged social location. *American Journal of Orthopsychiatry, 75*(4), 451–465. https://doi.org/10.1037/0002-9432.75.4.451

Kulic, K. R. (2005). The crisis intervention semi-structured interview. *Brief Treatment and Crisis Intervention, 5*(2), 143–157. https://doi.org/10.1093/brief-treatment/mhi010

Kuntze, J., Van der Molen, H. T., & Born, M. P. (2009). Increase in counselling communication skills after basic and advanced microskills training. *British Journal of Educational Psychology, 79*(1), 175–188. https://doi.org/10.1348/000709908X313758

Kurland, R. (2006). Debunking the "blood theory" of social work with groups: Group workers are made and not born. *Social Work With Groups, 30*(1), 11–24. https://doi.org/10.1300/J009v30n01_03

Kuyken, W., Watkins, E., Holden, E., White, K., Taylor, R. S., Byford, S., … Dalgleish, T. (2010). How does mindfulness-based cognitive therapy work? *Behaviour Research and Therapy, 48*(11), 1105–1112. https://doi.org/10.1016/j.brat.2010.08.003

Lambert, M. J. (2013). The efficacy and effectiveness of psychotherapy. In M. J. Lambert (Ed.), *Bergin and Garfield's handbook of psychotherapy and behavior change* (6th ed., pp. 169–207). New York, NY: Wiley.

Lamm, C., Batson, C. D., & Decety, J. (2007). The neural substrate of human empathy: Effects of perspective-taking and cognitive appraisal. *Journal of Cognitive Neuroscience, 19*(1), 42–58. https://doi.org/10.1162/jocn.2007.19.1.42

Larsen, D. J., & Stege, R. (2010). Hope-focused practices during early psychotherapy sessions: Part II: Explicit approaches. *Journal of Psychotherapy Integration, 20*(3), 293–311. https://doi.org/10.1037/a0020821

Laux, J. M. (2002). A primer on suicidology: Implications for counselors. *Journal of Counseling & Development, 80*(3), 380–383. https://doi.org/10.1002/j.1556-6678.2002.tb00203.x

Lavender, J. M., Tull, M. T., DiLillo, D., Messman-Moore, T., & Gratz, K. L. (2017). Development and validation of a state-based measure of emotion dysregulation: The State Difficulties in Emotion Regulation Scale (S-DERS). *Assessment, 24*(2), 197–209. https://doi.org/10.1177/1073191115601218

Laye-Gindhu, A., & Schonert-Reichl, K. A. (2005). Nonsuicidal self-harm among community adolescents: Understanding the "whats" and "whys" of self-harm. *Journal of Youth and Adolescence, 34*(5), 447–457. https://doi.org/10.1007/s10964-005-7262-z

Leahy, R. L. (2017). *Cognitive therapy techniques: A practitioner's guide* (2nd ed.). New York, NY: Guilford Press.

Ledoux, K. (2015). Understanding compassion fatigue: Understanding compassion. *Journal of Advanced Nursing, 71*(9), 2041–2050. https://doi.org/10.1111/jan.12686

Lee, C. C., & Rodgers, R. A. (2009). Counselor advocacy: Affecting systemic change in the public arena. *Journal of Counseling & Development, 87*(3), 284–287. https://doi.org/10.1002/j.1556-6678.2009.tb00108.x

LeFevre, M. L. (2014). Screening for suicide risk in adolescents, adults, and older adults in primary care: U.S. preventive services task force recommendation statement. *Annals of Internal Medicine, 160*(10), 719–726. https://doi.org/10.7326/M14-0589

Leffert, M. (2010). *Contemporary psychoanalytic foundations: Postmodernism, complexity, and neuroscience*. New York, NY: Routledge.

Levitt, H. M., Minami, T., Greenspan, S. B., Puckett, J. A., Henretty, J. R., Reich, C. M., & Berman, J. S. (2016). How therapist self-disclosure relates to alliance and outcomes: A naturalistic study. *Counselling Psychology Quarterly, 29*(1), 7–28. https://doi.org/10.1080/09515070.2015.1090396

Lewis, J. A., Arnold, M. S., House, R., & Toporek, R. L. (2002). ACA advocacy competencies. Retrieved from http://www.counseling.org

Lewis, J. A., Lewis, M. D., Daniels, J. A., & D'Andrea, M. J. (1998). *Community counseling: Empowerment strategies for a diverse society* (2nd ed.). Pacific Grove, CA: Brooks/Cole.

Lewis-Fernández, R., Aggarwal, N. K., Bäärnhielm, S., Rohlof, H., Kirmayer, L. J., Weiss, M. G., ... Lu, F. (2014). Culture and psychiatric evaluation: Operationalizing cultural formulation for DSM-5. *Psychiatry: Interpersonal and Biological Processes, 77*(2), 130–154. https://doi.org/10.1521/psyc.2014.77.2.130

Lieberman, M. A., Yalom, I. D., & Miles, M. B. (1973). *Encounter groups: First facts*. New York, NY: Basic Books.

Linehan, M. M. (1993). *Cognitive-behavioral treatment of borderline personality disorder*. New York, NY: Guilford Press.

Linehan, M. M. (2015). *DBT® skills training manual* (2nd ed.). New York, NY: Guilford Press.

Linehan, M. M., Armstrong, H. E., Suarez, A., Allmon, D., & Heard, H. L. (1991). Cognitive-behavioral treatment of chronically parasuicidal borderline patients. *Archives of General Psychiatry, 48*(12), 1060–1064. https://doi.org/10.1001/archpsyc.1991.01810360024003

Linehan, M. M., Heard, H. L., & Armstrong, H. E. (1993). Naturalistic follow-up of a behavioral treatment for chronically parasuicidal borderline patients. *Archives of General Psychiatry, 50*(12), 971–974. https://doi.org/10.1001/archpsyc.1993.01820240055007

List of psychotherapies. (n.d.). In *Wikipedia*. Retrieved from https://en.wikipedia.org/wiki/List_of_psychotherapies

Loganbill, C., Hardy, E., & Delworth, U. (1982). Supervision: A conceptual model. *Counseling Psychologist, 10*(1), 3–42. https://doi.org/10.1177/0011000082101002

Luckner, J. L., & Nadler, R. S. (1997). *Processing the experience: Strategies to enhance and generalize learning*. Dubuque, IA: Kendall/Hunt.

Lupien, S. J., McEwen, B. S., Gunnar, M. R., & Heim, C. (2009). Effects of stress throughout the lifespan on the brain, behaviour and cognition. *Nature Reviews Neuroscience, 10*(6), 434–445. https://doi.org/10.1038/nrn2639

Lyman, D. R., Braude, L., George, P., Dougherty, R. H., Daniels, A. S., Ghose, S. S., & Delphin-Rittmon, M. E. (2014). Consumer and family psychoeducation: Assessing the evidence. *Psychiatric Services, 65*(4), 416–428. https://doi.org/10.1176/appi.ps.201300266

Ma, S. H., & Teasdale, J. D. (2004). Mindfulness-based cognitive therapy for depression: Replication and exploration of differential relapse prevention effects. *Journal of Consulting and Clinical Psychology, 72*(1), 31–40. https://doi.org/10.1037/0022-006X.72.1.31

Macleod, E., Woolford, J., Hobbs, L., Gross, J., Hayne, H., & Patterson, T. (2017). Interviews with children about their mental health problems: The congruence and validity of information that children report. *Clinical Child Psychology and Psychiatry, 22*(2), 229–244. https://doi.org/10.1177/1359104516653642

Macnair-Semands, R. R., & Lese, K. P. (2000). Interpersonal problems and the perception of therapeutic factors in group therapy. *Small Group Research, 31*(2), 158–174. https://doi.org/10.1177/104649640003100202

Madigan, S. P. (1992). The application of Michel Foucault's philosophy in the problem externalizing discourse of Michael White. *Journal of Family Therapy, 14*(3), 265–279. https://doi.org/10.1046/j..1992.00458.x

Malouff, J. M., Thorsteinsson, E. B., & Schutte, N. S. (2007). The efficacy of problem solving therapy in reducing mental and physical health problems: A meta-analysis. *Clinical Psychology Review, 27*(1), 46–57. https://doi.org/10.1016/j.cpr.2005.12.005

Mancia, M. (2006). Implicit memory and early unrepressed unconscious: Their role in the therapeutic process (how the neurosciences can contribute to psychoanalysis). *International Journal of Psychoanalysis, 87*(1), 83–103. https://doi.org/10.1516/d43p-8upn-x576-a8v0

Marin, M. F., Lord, C., Andrews, J., Juster, R. P., Sindi, S., Arsenault-Lapierre, G., … Lupien, S. J. (2011). Chronic stress, cognitive functioning and mental health. *Neurobiology of Learning and Memory, 96*(4), 583–595. https://doi.org/10.1016/j.nlm.2011.02.016

Maslow, A. H. (1967). Synanon and Eupsychia. *Journal of Humanistic Psychology, 7*(1), 28–35. https://doi.org/10.1177/002216786700700104

Masten, A. S., Herbers, J. E., Desjardins, C. D., Cutuli, J. J., McCormick, C. M., Sapienza, J. K., … Zelazo, P. D. (2012). Executive function skills and school success in young children experiencing homelessness. *Educational Researcher, 41*(9), 375–384. https://doi.org/10.3102/0013189X12459883

Masten, C. L., Eisenberger, N. I., Pfeifer, J. H., Colich, N. L., & Dapretto, M. (2013). Associations among pubertal development, empathic ability, and neural responses while witnessing peer rejection in adolescence. *Child Development, 84*(4), 1338–1354. https://doi.org/10.1111/cdev.12056

Masterwork Productions (Producer). (2002). *Narrative therapy with a young boy* [Motion picture]. Retrieved from http://masterswork.com/david-epston-individual/david-epston-dvd-narrative-therapy-with-a-young-boy

Mays, V. M., Ponce, N. A., Washington, D. L., & Cochran, S. D. (2003). Classification of race and ethnicity: Implications for public health. *Annual Review of Public Health, 24*(1), 83–110. https://doi.org/10.1146/annurev.publhealth.24.100901.140927

McKenzie, W., & Monk, G. (1997). Learning and teaching narrative ideas. In G. Monk, J. Winslade, K. Crocket, & D. Epston (Eds.), *Narrative therapy in practice: The archaeology of hope* (pp. 82–117). San Francisco, CA: Jossey-Bass.

Merriman, J. (2015). Enhancing counselor supervision through compassion fatigue education. *Journal of Counseling & Development, 93*(3), 370–378. https://doi.org/10.1002/jcad.12035

Mertin, P. (2014). What do we know about the correlates and underlying causes of auditory hallucinations in nonpsychotic children and adolescents, and what are the implications for diagnosis and treatment? *Pragmatic Case Studies in Psychotherapy, 10*(4), 287–296. https://doi.org/10.14713/pcsp.v10i4.1876

Miczek, K. A., de Almeida, R. M., Kravitz, E. A., Rissman, E. F., de Boer, S. F., & Raine, A. (2007). Neurobiology of escalated aggression and violence. *Journal of Neuroscience, 27*(44), 11803–11806. https://doi.org/10.1523/JNEUROSCI.3500-07.2007

Miller, A. L., Rathus, J. H., Linehan, M. M., Wetzler, S., & Leigh, E. (1997). Dialectical Behavior Therapy adapted for suicidal adolescents. *Journal of Practical Psychiatry and Behavioral Health, 3*, 78–86. https://doi.org/10.1097/00131746-199703000-00002

Miller, W. R., & Rollnick, S. (2013). *Motivational interviewing*. New York, NY: Guilford Press.

Mind. (n.d.). In *Merriam-Webster* online. Retrieved from https://www.merriam-webster.com/dictionary/mind

Monk, G., Winslade, J., Crocket, K., & Epston, D. (1997). *Narrative therapy in practice: The archaeology of hope*. San Francisco, CA: Jossey-Bass/Wiley.

Monk, G., Winslade, J., & Sinclair, S. (2008). *New horizons in multicultural counseling*. Thousand Oaks, CA: Sage.

Morgan, A. (2000). *What is narrative therapy? An easy-to-read introduction*. Adelaide, South Australia: Dulwich Centre.

Morgan, R. E. (2017). Race and Hispanic origin of victims and offenders, 2012–15. Bureau of Justice Statistics (NCJ250747). Retrieved from https://www.bjs.gov/index.cfm?ty=pbdetail&iid=6106

Morran, D. K., Stockton, R., Cline, R. J., & Teed, C. (1998). Facilitating feedback exchange in groups: Leader interventions. *Journal for Specialists in Group Work, 23*(3), 257–268. https://doi.org/10.1080/01933929808411399

Mosak, H. H., & Maniacci, M. (2008). Adlerian psychotherapy. In R. J. Corsini & D. Wedding (Eds.), *Current psychotherapies* (9th ed., pp. 67–112). Belmont, CA: Brooks/Cole.

Moulding, R., Aardema, F., & O'Connor, K. P. (2014). Repugnant obsessions: A review of the phenomenology, theoretical models, and treatment of sexual and aggressive obsessional themes in OCD. *Journal of Obsessive-Compulsive and Related Disorders, 3*(2), 161–168. https://doi.org/10.1016/j.jocrd.2013.11.006

National Association of School Psychologists. (2010). *Principles for professional ethics*. Retrieved from https://www.nasponline.org/standards-and-certification/professional-ethics

National Association of Social Workers. (n.d.a). *School social work*. Retrieved from https://www.socialworkers.org/Practice/School-Social-Work

National Association of Social Workers. (n.d.b). *Social work history*. Retrieved from https://www.socialworkers.org/News/Facts/Social-Work-History
National Association of Social Workers. (2008). Code of ethics of the National Association of Social Workers. Retrieved from https://www.socialworkers.org/About/Ethics/Code-of-Ethics
National Center for School Crisis and Bereavement. (n.d.a). Guidelines for responding to a death by suicide. Retrieved from https://www.schoolcrisiscenter.org/resources/guide-responding-suicide
National Center for School Crisis and Bereavement. (n.d.b). Guidelines for responding to a death of a student or school staff. Retrieved from https://www.schoolcrisiscenter.org/resources/guide-responding-death
National Center for School Crisis and Bereavement. (n.d.c). Natural disasters. Retrieved from http://www.nctsn.org/trauma-types/natural-disasters
National Institute of Justice. (2010). Victims and perpetrators. Retrieved from http://www.nij.gov/topics/crime/rape-sexual-violence/Pages/victims-perpetrators.aspx
National Institute of Mental Health. (n.d.). Psychotherapies. Retrieved from http://www.nimh.nih.gov/health/topics/psychotherapies/index.shtml
National Institute of Mental Health. (2014). Suicide in the military: Army-NIH funded study points to risk and protective factor. Retrieved from http://www.nimh.nih.gov/news/science-news/2014/suicide-in-the-military-army-nih-funded-study-points-to-risk-and-protective-factors.shtml
Neighbors, H. W., Trierweiler, S. J., Ford, B. C., & Muroff, J. R. (2003). Racial differences in DSM diagnosis using a semi-structured instrument: The importance of clinical judgment in the diagnosis of African Americans. *Journal of Health and Social Behavior, 44*(3), 237–256. https://doi.org/10.2307/1519777
Nelson, D. L., & Burke, R. J. (2000). Women executives: Health, stress, and success. *Academy of Management Perspectives, 14*(2), 107–121. https://doi.org/10.5465/AME.2000.3819310
Neumann, M., Bensing, J., Mercer, S., Ernstmann, N., Ommen, O., & Pfaff, H. (2009). Analyzing the "nature" and "specific effectiveness" of clinical empathy: A theoretical overview and contribution towards a theory-based research agenda. *Patient Education and Counseling, 74*(3), 339–346. https://doi.org/10.1016/j.pec.2008.11.013
Nevo, I., & Slonim-Nevo, V. (2011). The myth of evidence-based practice: Towards evidence-informed practice. *British Journal of Social Work, 41*(6), 1176–1197. https://doi.org/10.1093/bjsw/bcq149
Nezu, A. M. (2004). Problem solving and behavior therapy revisited. *Behavior Therapy, 35*(1), 1–33. https://doi.org/10.1016/S0005-7894(04)80002-9
Noddings, N. (2002). *Starting at home: Caring and social policy*. Berkeley: University of California Press.
Norcross, J. C. (2010). The therapeutic relationship. In B. L. Duncan, B. E. Wampold, & M. A. Hubble (Eds.), *The heart and soul of change* (2nd ed., pp. 113–142). Washington, DC: American Psychological Association.
Norcross, J. C., Krebs, P. M., & Prochaska, J. O. (2010). Stages of change. *Journal of Clinical Psychology: In Session, 67*(2), 143–154. https://doi.org/10.1002/jclp.20758

Nuckolls, T., & Baker, C. (2003, Nov. 9). Watch these straight people answer a question gay people have been asked for years. Upworthy. Retrieved from http://www.upworthy.com/watch-these-straight-people-answer-a-question-gay-people-have-been-asked-for-years-6

O'Brien, W. H., & Carhart, V. (2011). Functional analysis in behavioral medicine. *European Journal of Psychological Assessment, 27*(1), 4–16. https://doi.org/10.1027/1015-5759/a000052

Office of Juvenile Justice and Deliquency Prevention. (2017). Statistical briefing book. Retrieved from https://www.ojjdp.gov/ojstatbb/crime/qa05104.asp?qaDate=2015

Overholser, J. C. (2013). Guided discovery: Problem-solving therapy integrated within the Socratic method. *Journal of Contemporary Psychotherapy, 43*(2), 73–82. https://doi.org/10.1007/s10879-012-9229-1

Owen, J., Quirk, K., Hilsenroth, M. J., & Rodolfa, E. (2012). Working through: In-session processes that promote between-session thoughts and activities. *Journal of Counseling Psychology, 59*(1), 161–167. https://doi.org/10.1037/a0023616

Owens, D., Horrocks, J., & House, A. (2002). Fatal and non-fatal repetition of self-harm. *British Journal of Psychiatry, 181*(3), 193–199. https://doi.org/10.1192/bjp.181.3.193

Øyum, L. (2007). Dilemmas of confrontation: Challenging the participants while keeping the process going. *Systemic Practice and Action Research, 20*(1), 41–52. https://doi.org/10.1007/s11213-006-9048-y

Pearlin, L. I. (1989). The sociological study of stress. *Journal of Health and Social Behavior, 30*(3), 241–256. https://doi.org/10.2307/2136956

Pereira, S., Fleischhacker, W., & Allen, M. (2007). Management of behavioural emergencies. *Journal of Psychiatric Intensive Care, 2*(2), 71–83. https://doi.org/10.1017/S1742646407000325

Perry, B. D., & Szalavitz, M. (2006). *The boy who was raised as a dog*. New York, NY: Basic Books.

Pieterse, A. L., Lee, M., Ritmeester, A., & Collins, N. M. (2013). Towards a model of self-awareness development for counselling and psychotherapy training. *Counselling Psychology Quarterly, 26*(2), 190–207. https://doi.org/10.1080/09515070.2013.793451

Polcin, D. L. (2003). Rethinking confrontation in alcohol and drug treatment: Consideration of the clinical context. *Substance Use & Misuse, 38*(2), 165–184. https://doi.org/10.1081/JA-120017243

Pope-Davis, D. B., & Liu, W. M. (1998). The social construction of race: Implications for counselling psychology. *Counselling Psychology Quarterly, 11*(2), 151–161. https://doi.org/10.1080/09515079808254051

Portman, T. A. A., & Portman, G. L. (2002). Empowering Students for Social Justice (ES^2J): A structured group approach. *Journal for Specialists in Group Work, 27*(1), 16–31. https://doi.org/10.1177/0193392202027001003

Prochaska, J. O., & DiClemente, C. C. (1982). Transtheoretical therapy: Toward a more integrative model of change. *Psychotherapy: Theory, Research & Practice, 19*(3), 276–288. https://doi.org/10.1037/h0088437

Prochaska, J. O., & DiClemente, C. C. (1986). Toward a comprehensive model of change. In W. E. Miller & N. Heather (Eds.), *Treating addictive behaviors: Processes of change* (pp. 3–27). New York, NY: Plenum Press.

Prochaska, J. O., Johnson, S., & Lee, P. (2009). The transtheoretical model of behavior change. In S. A. Shumaker, J. K. Ockene, & K. A. Riekert (Eds.), *The handbook of health behavior change* (3rd ed., pp. 59–83). New York, NY: Springer.

Prochaska, J. O., & Norcross, J. C. (2007). *Systems of psychotherapy: A transtheoretical analysis* (6th ed.). Belmont, CA: Thompson Brooks/Cole.

Prochaska, J. O., Norcross, J. C., & DiClemente, C. C. (1994). *Changing for good.* New York, NY: HarperCollins.

Psychopathology Committee of the Group for the Advancement of Psychiatry. (2001). Reexamination of therapist self-disclosure. *Psychiatric Services, 52*(11), 1489–1493. https://doi.org/10.1176/appi.ps.52.11.1489

Quiñones, T. J., Woodward, E. N., & Pantalone, D. W. (2017). Sexual minority reflections on their psychotherapy experiences. *Psychotherapy Research, 27*(2), 189–200. https://doi.org/10.1080/10503307.2015.1090035

Raghubir, P., & Valenzuela, A. (2010). Male-female dynamics in groups: A field study of the weakest link. *Small Group Research, 41*(1), 41–70. https://doi.org/10.1177/1046496409352509

Rathus, J. H., & Miller, A. L. (2015). *DBT® skills manual for adolescents*. New York, NY: Guilford Press.

Ratts, M. J., Singh, A. A., Nassar-McMillan, S., Butler, S. K., McCullough, J. R., & Hipolito-Delgado, C. (2015). *Multicultural and social justice counseling competencies*. Alexandria, VA: Association for Multicultural Counseling and Development. Retrieved from https://www.counseling.org/docs/default-source/competencies/multicultural-and-social-justice-counseling-competencies.pdf

Roberts, A. R., & Ottens, A. J. (2005). The seven-stage crisis intervention model: A road map to goal attainment, problem solving, and crisis resolution. *Brief Treatment and Crisis Intervention, 5*(4), 329–339. https://doi.org/10.1093/brief-treatment/mhi030

Roberts, J. (2005). Transparency and self-disclosure in family therapy: Dangers and possibilities. *Family Process, 44*(1), 45–63. https://doi.org/10.1111/j.1545-5300.2005.00041.x

Roccas, S., & Brewer, M. B. (2002). Social identity complexity. *Personality and Social Psychology Review, 6*(2), 88–106. https://doi.org/10.1207/S15327957PSPR0602_01

Rogers, C. R. (1951). *Client-centered therapy: Its current practice, implications, and theory*. Boston, MA: Houghton Mifflin.

Rogers, C. R. (1961). *On becoming a person*. Boston, MA: Houghton Mifflin.

Rogers, C. R. (1975). Empathic: An unappreciated way of being. *Counseling Psychologist, 5*(2), 2–10. https://doi.org/10.1177/001100007500500202

Rosenbloom, S. T., Denny, J. C., Xu, H., Lorenzi, N., Stead, W. W., & Johnson, K. B. (2011). Data from clinical notes: A perspective on the tension between structure and flexible documentation. *Journal of the American Medical Informatics Association, 18*(2), 181–186. https://doi.org/10.1136/jamia.2010.007237

Roth, M. (2011, June 7). Recession has taken a toll on black families. *Pittsburgh Post-Gazette*. Retrieved from http://www.post-gazette.com/stories/local/neighborhoods-city/recession-has-taken-hidden-toll-on-black-families-300882

Roy-Byrne, P. (2015). Translating research to practice: Too much research, not enough practice? *Depression and Anxiety, 32*(11), 785–786. https://doi.org/10.1002/da.22443

Rudd, M. D., Joiner, T., & Rajab, M. H. (2001). *Treating suicide behavior*. New York, NY: Guilford Press.

Russell, S., & Carey, M. (2002). Re-membering: Responding to commonly asked questions. *International Journal of Narrative Therapy & Community Work, 3*, 23–31. Retrieved from http://search.informit.com.au/documentSummary;dn=661551679355288;res=IELHEA

Rzeszutek, M., & Partyka, M. (2015). Temperament traits, social support, and secondary traumatic stress disorder symptoms in a sample of trauma therapists. *Professional Psychology: Research and Practice, 46*(4), 213–220. http://dx.doi.org/10.1037/pro0000024

Salzer, M. S., Rappaport, J., & Segre, L. (2001). Mental health professionals' support of self-help groups. *Journal of Community & Applied Social Psychology, 11*(1), 1–10. https://doi.org/10.1002/casp.606

Sands, N., Elsom, S., Marangu, E., Keppich-Arnold, S., & Henderson, K. (2013). Mental health telephone triage: Managing psychiatric crises and emergencies. *Perspectives in Psychiatric Care, 49*(1), 65–72. https://doi.org/10.1111/j.1744-6163.2012.00346.x

Scaturo, D. J. (2002). Fundamental dilemmas in contemporary psychodynamic and insight-oriented psychotherapy. *Journal of Contemporary Psychotherapy, 32*(2–3), 145–165. https://doi.org/10.1023/A:1020540909172

Schermer, V. L. (2011). Interpreting psychoanalytic interpretation: A fourfold perspective. *Psychoanalytic Review, 98*(6), 817–842. https://doi.org/10.1521/prev.2011.98.6.817

Schreiber, M., & Gurwitch, R. (2011). *Listen, protect and connect: Family to family, neighbor to neighbor*. Irvine: University of California School of Medicine. Retrieved from http://www.ready.gov/sites/default/files/documents/files/LPC_Booklet.pdf

Schreiber, M., Gurwitch, R., & Wong, M. (2006). *Listen, protect, connect—model & teach: Psychological First Aid (PFA) for students and teachers*. US Department of Homeland Security. Retrieved from https://www.ready.gov/sites/default/files/documents/files/PFA_SchoolCrisis.pdf

Schwarz, R. (2002). *The skilled facilitator: A comprehensive resource for consultants, facilitators, managers, trainers, and coaches* (2nd ed.). New York, NY: Wiley.

Serrano Burneo, D. C., Bowden, S. C., & Simpson, L. C. (2016). Incremental validity of the Minnesota Multiphasic Personality Inventory, Second Edition (MMPI-2) relative to the Beck Depression Inventory-Second Edition (BDI-II) in the detection of depressive symptoms. *Australian Psychologist, 51*(5), 389–399. https://doi.org/10.1111/ap.12231

Shearin, E. N., & Linehan, M. M. (1994). Dialectical behavior therapy for borderline personality disorder: Theoretical and empirical foundations. *Acta Psychiatrica Scandinavica, 89*(s379), 61–68. https://doi.org/10.1111/j.1600-0447.1994.tb05820.x

Shin, R. Q., Smith, L. C., Welch, J. C., & Ezeofor, I. (2016). Is Allison more likely than Lakisha to receive a callback from counseling professionals? A racism audit study. *Counseling Psychologist, 44*(8), 1187–1211. https://doi.org/10.1177/0011000016668814

Shlonsky, A., & Stern, S. B. (2007). Reflections on the teaching of evidence-based practice. *Research on Social Work Practice, 17*(5), 603–611. https://doi.org/10.1177/1049731507301527

Siegel, D. J. (2001). Toward an interpersonal neurobiology of the developing mind: Attachment relationships, "mindsight," and neural integration. *Infant Mental Health Journal, 22*(1–2), 67–94. https://doi.org/10.1002/1097-0355(200101/04)22:1<67::AID-IMHJ3>3.0.CO;2-G

Siegel, D. J. (2012). *The developing mind* (2nd ed.). New York, NY: Guilford Press.

Siegel, R. D. (2010). *The mindfulness solution: Everyday practices for everyday problems*. New York, NY: Guilford Press.

Siever, L. J. (2008). Neurobiology of aggression and violence. *American Journal of Psychiatry, 165*(4), 429–442. https://doi.org/10.1176/appi.ajp.2008.07111774

Sklare, G. B. (2014). *Brief counseling that works: A solution-focused therapy approach for school counselors and other mental health professionals*. Thousand Oaks, CA: Corwin Press.

Skovholt, T. M. (2001). *The resilient practitioner: Burnout prevention and self-care strategies for counselors, therapists, teachers, and health professionals*. Boston, MA: Allyn & Bacon.

Skovholt, T. M. (2005). The cycle of caring: A model of expertise in the helping professions. *Journal of Mental Health Counseling, 27*(1), 82–93. https://doi.org/10.17744/mehc.27.1.mj5rcvy6c713tafw

Smead, R. (1995). *Skills and techniques for group work with children and adolescents*. Champaign, IL: Research Press.

Smith, C. D., & King, P. E. (2004). Student feedback sensitivity and the efficacy of feedback interventions in public speaking performance improvement. *Communication Education, 53*(3), 203–216. https://doi.org/10.1080/0363452042000265152

Smith, L. C., Geroski, A. M., & Tyler, K. B. (2014). Abandoning colorblind practice in school counseling. *Journal of School Counseling, 12*(16). Retrieved from http://jsc.montana.edu/articles/v12n16.pdf

Smith, P. L., & Moss, S. B. (2009). Psychologist impairment: What is it, how can it be prevented, and what can be done to address it? *Clinical Psychology: Science and Practice, 16*(1), 1–15. https://doi.org/10.1111/j.1468-2850.2009.01137.x

Sommers-Flanagan, J., & Sommers-Flanagan, R. (2004). *Counseling and psychotherapy theories in context and practice*. Hoboken, NJ: Wiley.

Sommers-Flanagan, R., & Sommers-Flanagan, J. (2007). *Becoming an ethical helping professional: Cultural and philosophical foundations*. Hoboken, NJ: Wiley.

Southam-Gerow, M. A., & Kendall, P. C. (2002). Emotion regulation and understanding: Implications for child psychopathology and therapy. *Clinical Psychology Review, 22*(2), 189–222. https://doi.org/10.1016/S0272-7358(01)00087-3

Sprague, J., & Walker, H. (2000). Early identification and intervention for youth with antisocial and violent behavior. *Exceptional Children, 66*(3), 367–379. https://doi.org/10.1177/001440290006600307

Spunt, R. P., & Lieberman, M. D. (2012). An integrative model of the neural systems supporting the comprehension of observed emotional behavior. *Neuroimage, 59*(3), 3050–3059. https://doi.org/10.1016/j.neuroimage.2011.10.005

Stasiewicz, P. R., Bradizza, C. M., Schlauch, R. C., Coffey, S. F., Gulliver, S. B., Gudleski, G. D., & Bole, C. W. (2013). Affect Regulation Training (ART) for alcohol use disorders: Development of a novel intervention for negative affect drinkers. *Journal of Substance Abuse Treatment, 45*(5), 433–443. https://doi.org/10.1016/j.jsat.2013.05.012

Stegge, H., & Terwogt, M. M. (2007). Awareness and regulation of emotion in typical and atypical development. In J. J. Gross (Ed.), *Handbook of emotion regulation* (pp. 269–286). New York, NY: Guilford Press.

Stockmeier, C. A. (2006). Neurobiology of serotonin in depression and suicide. *Annals of the New York Academy of Sciences, 836*(1), 220–232. https://doi.org/10.1111/j.1749-6632.1997.tb52362.x

Stone, J., & Cooper, J. (2001). A self-standards model of cognitive dissonance. *Journal of Experimental Social Psychology, 37*(3), 228–243. https://doi.org/10.1006/jesp.2000.1446

Strong, T., & Zeman, D. (2010). Dialogic consideration of confrontation as a counseling activity: An examination of Allen Ivey's use of confronting as a microskill. *Journal of Counseling & Development, 88*(3), 332–339. https://doi.org/10.1002/j.1556-6678.2010.tb00030.x

Substance Abuse and Mental Health Services Administration. (2005). *Psychological first aid for first responders: Managing intense emotions*. Retrieved from http://store.samhsa.gov/shin/content//NMH05-0210/NMH05-0210.pdf

Sue, D., & Sue, D. M. (2008). *Foundations of counseling and psychotherapy: Evidence-based practices for a diverse society*. Hoboken, NJ: Wiley.

Sue, D. W. (2010). Microaggressions, marginality, and oppression: An introduction. In D. W. Sue (Ed.), *Microaggressions and marginality: Manifestations, dynamics, and impact* (pp. 3–22). Hoboken, NJ: Wiley.

Sue, D. W., Arredondo, P., & McDavis, R. J. (1992). Multicultural counseling competencies and standards: A call to the profession. *Journal of Counseling & Development, 70*(4), 477–486. https://doi.org/10.1002/j.1556-6676.1992.tb01642.x

Sue, D. W., Capodilupo, C. M., Torino, G. C., Bucceri, J. M., Holder, A. M. B., Nadal, K. L., & Esquilin, M. (2007). Racial microaggressions in everyday life: Implications for clinical practice. *American Psychologist, 62*(4), 271–286. https://doi.org/10.1037/0003-066X.62.4.271

Sue, D. W., & Sue, D. (2003). *Counseling the culturally diverse: Theory and practice* (4th ed.). New York, NY: Wiley.

Swartz, S. (2006). The third voice: Writing case-notes. *Feminism & Psychology, 16*(4), 427–444. https://doi.org/10.1177/0959353506068750

Teasdale, J. D., Segal, Z., & Williams, J. M. G. (1995). How does cognitive therapy prevent depressive relapse and why should attentional control (mindfulness) training help? *Behaviour Research and Therapy, 33*(1), 25–39. https://doi.org/10.1016/0005-7967(94)E0011-7

Teasdale, J. D., Segal, Z. V., Williams, J. M. G., Ridgeway, V. A., Soulsby, J. M., & Lau, M. A. (2000). Prevention of relapse/recurrence in major depression by mindfulness-based cognitive therapy. *Journal of Consulting and Clinical Psychology, 68*(4), 615–623. https://doi.org/10.1037//0022-006X.68.4.615

Teng, E. L., & Chui, H. C. (1987). The Modified Mini-Mental State (3MS) examination. *Journal of Clinical Psychiatry, 48*(8), 314–318.

Theory. (n.d.). In *Dictionary.com*. Retrieved from http://www.dictionary.com/browse/theory

Thomas, C. R., & Pastusek, A. (2012). Boundary crossings and violations: Time for child psychiatry to catch up. *Journal of the American Academy of Child & Adolescent Psychiatry, 51*(9), 858–860. https://doi.org/10.1016/j.jaac.2012.06.011

Thomas, R. V., & Pender, D. A. (2008). Association for Specialists in Group Work: Best practice guidelines 2007 revisions. *Journal for Specialists in Group Work, 33*(2), 111–117. https://doi.org/10.1080/01933920801971184

Thompson, R. A. (2008). Early attachment and later development. In J. Cassidy & P. R. Shaver (Eds.), *Handbook of attachment: Theory, research, and clinical applications* (2nd ed., pp. 348–365). New York, NY: Guilford Press.

Tombaugh, T. N. (2005). Test-retest reliable coefficients and 5-year change scores for the MMSE and 3MS. *Archives of Clinical Neuropsychology, 20*(4), 485–503. https://doi.org/10.1016/j.acn.2004.11.004

Tomlinson-Clarke, S. (2013). Multicultural counseling competencies: Extending multicultural training paradigms toward globalization. *Ideas and Research You Can Use: VISTAS 2013*. Retrieved from https://www.counseling.org/docs/default-source/vistas/multicultural-counseling-competencies.pdf

Top, E. D., & Karaçam, Z. (2016). Effectiveness of structured education in reduction of postpartum depression scores: A quasi-experimental study. *Archives of Psychiatric Nursing, 30*(3), 356–362. https://doi.org/10.1016/j.apnu.2015.12.009

Toporek, R. L., Lewis, J. A., & Crethar, H. C. (2009). Promoting systemic change through the ACA advocacy competencies. *Journal of Counseling & Development, 87*(3), 260–268. https://doi.org/10.1002/j.1556-6678.2009.tb00105.x

Toseland, R. W., & Rivas, R. F. (2005). *An introduction to group work practice* (5th ed.). Boston, MA: Pearson.

Trachsel, M., Grosse Holtforth, M., Biller-Andorno, N., & Appelbaum, P. S. (2015). Informed consent for psychotherapy: Still not routine. *Lancet Psychiatry, 2*(9), 775–777. https://doi.org/10.1016/S2215-0366(15)00318-1

Trippany, R. L., White Kress, V. E., & Wilcoxon, S. A. (2004). Preventing vicarious trauma: What counselors should know when working with trauma survivors. *Journal of Counseling & Development, 82*(1), 31–37. https://doi.org/10.1002/j.1556-6678.2004.tb00283.x

Tschacher, W., Haken, H., & Kyselo, M. (2015). Alliance: A common factor of psychotherapy modeled by structural theory. *Frontiers in Psychology, 6*, 1–11. https://doi.org/10.3389/fpsyg.2015.00421

Tuckman, B. W. (1965). Developmental sequence in small groups. *Psychological Bulletin, 63*(6), 384–399. https://doi.org/10.1037/h0022100

Tuckman, B. W., & Jensen, M. A. C. (1977). Stages of small-group development revisited. *Group & Organization Management, 2*(4), 419–427. https://doi.org/10.1177/105960117700200404

Urofsky, R. I., Engels, D. W., & Engebretson, K. (2008). Kitchener's principle ethics: Implications for counseling practice and research. *Counseling and Values, 53*(1), 67–78. https://doi.org/10.1002/j.2161-007X.2009.tb00114.x

Van Ausdale, D., & Feagin, J. R. (2001). *The first R: How children learn race and racism*. Lanham, MD: Rowman & Littlefield.

Van Langenhove, L., & Harré, R. (1994). Cultural stereotypes and positioning theory. *Journal for the Theory of Social Behaviour, 24*(4), 359–372. https://doi.org/10.1111/j.1468-5914.1994.tb00260.x

Varia, S. (2013). *Bullying and suicide*. Waltham, MA: Education Development Center. Retrieved from http://www.suicidepreventioncolorado.org/resources/Documents/bullying_and_suicide_-_smita_varia.pdf

Vescio, T. K., Sechrist, G. B., & Paolucci, M. P. (2003). Perspective taking and prejudice reduction: The mediational role of empathy arousal and situational attributions. *European Journal of Social Psychology, 33*(4), 455–472. https://doi.org/10.1002/ejsp.163

Vetere, A., & Dowling, E. (2016). Narrative concepts and therapeutic challenges. In A. Vetere & E. Dowling (Eds.), *Narrative therapies with children and their families: A practitioner's guide to concepts and approaches* (2nd ed., pp. 3–23). New York, NY: Taylor & Francis.

Waguespack, A., Vaccaro, T., & Continere, L. (2006). Functional behavioral assessment and intervention with emotional/behaviorally disordered students: In pursuit of state of the art. *International Journal of Behavioral Consultation and Therapy, 2*(4), 463–474. https://doi.org/10.1037/h0101000

Walsh, D. (2004). *Why do they act that way?* New York, NY: Free Press.

Waltman, S. H., Frankel, S. A., & Williston, M. A. (2016). Improving clinician self-awareness and increasing accurate representation of clinical competencies. *Practice Innovations, 1*(3), 178–188. https://doi.org/10.1037/pri0000026

Wampold, B. E. (2010). The research evidence for common factors models: A historically situated perspective. In B. L. Duncan, S. D. Miller, B. E. Wampold, & M. A. Hubble (Eds.), *The heart and soul of change: Delivering what works in therapy* (2nd ed., pp. 49–82). Washington, DC: American Psychological Association.

Wampold, B. E., Imel, Z. E., Laska, K. M., Benish, S., Miller, S. D., Flückiger, C., … Budge, S. (2010). Determining what works in the treatment of PTSD. *Clinical Psychology Review, 30*(8), 923–933. https://doi.org/10.1016/j.cpr.2010.06.005

Waters, M. C. (2004). Optional ethnicities: For Whites only? In M. L. Anderson & P. H. Collins (Eds.), *Race, class, and gender: An anthology* (5th ed., pp. 418–427). Belmont, CA: Wadsworth/Thompson Learning.

Weinfield, N. S., Sroufe, L. A., Egeland, B., & Carlson, E. (2008). Individual differences in infant-caregiver attachment. In J. Cassidy & P. R. Shaver (Eds.), *Handbook of attachment: Theory, research, and clinical applications* (2nd ed., pp. 78–101). New York, NY: Guilford Press.

Weingarten, K. (2003). *Common shock: Witnessing violence every day: How we are harmed, how we can heal.* New York, NY: Dutton/Penguin Books.

Weinrach, S. G., & Thomas, K. R. (2002). A critical analysis of the multicultural counseling competencies: Implications for the practice of mental health counseling. *Journal of Mental Health Counseling, 24*(1), 20–35.

Welfel, E. R., Danzinger, P. R., & Santoro, S. (2000). Mandated reporting of abuse/maltreatment of older adults: A primer for counselors. *Journal of Counseling & Development, 78*(3), 284–292. https://doi.org/10.1002/j.1556-6676.2000.tb01909.x

Westphal, M., & Bonanno, G. A. (2004). Emotion self-regulation. In M. Beauregard (Ed.), *Consciousness, emotional self-regulation, and the brain* (pp. 1–34). Philadelphia, PA: John Benjamins North America.

Wheeler, A. M., & Bertram, B. (2012). *The counselor and the law: A guide to legal and ethical practice* (6th ed.). Alexandria, VA: American Counseling Association.

Wheeler, C. D., & D'Andrea, L. M. (2004). Teaching counseling students to understand and use immediacy. *Journal of Humanistic Counseling, Education and Development, 43*(2), 117–128. https://doi.org/10.1002/j.2164-490X.2004.tb00012.x

White, M. (2005). Workshop notes. Dulwich Centre. Retrieved from http://www.dulwichcentre.com.au/articles-about-narrative-therapy.html

White, M., & Epston, D. (1990). *Narrative means to therapeutic ends*. Adelaide, South Australia: Dulwich Centre.

Wilson, F. R., Rapin, L. S., & Haley-Banez, L. (2000). Association for specialists in group work professional standards for the training of group workers. *Journal for Specialists in Group Work, 25*(4), 327–342. https://doi.org/10.1080/01933920008411677

Winker, M. A. (2004). Measuring race and ethnicity: Why and how? *JAMA, 292*(13), 1612–1614. https://doi.org/10.1001/jama.292.13.1612

Winslade, J. M. (2005). Utilising discursive positioning in counselling. *British Journal of Guidance & Counseling, 33*(3), 351–364. https://doi.org/10.1080/03069880500179541

Winslade, J., Crocket, K., & Monk, G. (1997). The therapeutic relationship. In G. Monk, J. Winslade, K. Crocket, & D. Epston (Eds.), *Narrative therapy in practice: The archaeology of hope* (pp. 53–81). San Francisco, CA: Jossey-Bass.

Winslade, J., & Geroski, A. (2008). A social constructionist view of development. In K. L. Kraus (Ed.), *Lenses: Applying lifespan development theories in counseling* (pp. 7–51). Boston, MA: Lahaska/Houghton Mifflin.

Wiseman, T. (1996). A concept analysis of empathy. *Journal of Advanced Nursing, 23*(6), 1162–1167. https://doi.org/10.1046/j.1365-2648.1996.12213.x

Wong, M., Schreiber, M., & Gurwitch, R. (2008). Psychological first aid (PFA) for students and teachers: Listen, protect, connect–model & teach. *Helpful Hints for School Emergency Management (US Department of Education-Readiness and Emergency Management for Schools Technical Assistance Center), 3*(3), 1–11. Retrieved from https://rems.ed.gov/docs/HH_Vol3Issue3.pdf

Wynn, R., & Bergvik, S. (2010). Studying empathy as an interactional three-part sequence. *Patient Education and Counseling, 80*(1), 150. https://doi.org/10.1016/j.pec.2009.05.007

Yalom, I. D. (1980). *Existential psychotherapy*. New York, NY: Basic Books.

Yalom, I. D. (1995). *The theory and practice of group psychotherapy* (4th ed.). New York, NY: Basic Books.

Yalom, I., Brown, S., & Bloch, S. (1975). The written summary as a group psychotherapy technique. *Archives of General Psychiatry, 32*(5), 605–613. https://doi.org/10.1001/archpsyc.1975.01760230071006

Yalom, I. D., & Leszcz, M. (2005). *The theory and practice of group psychotherapy* (5th ed.). New York, NY: Basic Books.

Yalom, V. J., & Yalom, I. (1990). Brief interactive group psychotherapy. *Psychiatric Annals, 20*(7), 362–367. https://doi.org/10.3928/0048-5713-19900701-06

Yontef, G., & Jacobs, L. (2008). Gestalt therapy. In R. J. Corsini & D. Wedding (Eds.), *Current psychotherapies* (9th ed., pp. 328–367). Belmont, CA: Brooks/Cole.

Young, M. E. (2013). *Learning the art of helping: Building blocks and techniques* (5th ed.). Boston, MA: Pearson.

Zeanah, C. H., Gunnar, M. R., McCall, R. B., Kreppner, J. M., & Fox, N. A. (2011). Sensitive periods. *Monographs of the Society for Research in Child Development, 76*(4), 147–162. https://doi.org/10.1111/j.1540-5834.2011.00631.x

Zieman, G. L., Romano, P. A., Blanco, K., & Linnell, T. (1981). The process-observer in group therapy. *Group, 5*(4), 37–47. https://doi.org/10.1007/BF01456612

INDEX

A

B

C

H

I

J

K

L

M

N

O

P

Q

R

CPSIA information can be obtained
at www.ICGtesting.com
Printed in the USA
LVHW050604011222
734287LV00001B/12